Blackstone's

Senior Investigating Officers' Handbook

Fourth Edition

Tony Cook

Consultant Editor

Andy Tattersall

OXFORD
UNIVERSITY PRESS

OXFORD
UNIVERSITY PRESS

Great Clarendon Street, Oxford, OX2 6DP,
United Kingdom

Oxford University Press is a department of the University of Oxford.
It furthers the University's objective of excellence in research, scholarship,
and education by publishing worldwide. Oxford is a registered trade mark of
Oxford University Press in the UK and in certain other countries

© Oxford University Press 2016

The moral rights of the authors have been asserted

First Edition published in 2008
Fourth Edition published in 2016

Published in the United States of America by Oxford University Press
198 Madison Avenue, New York, NY 10016, United States of America

British Library Cataloguing in Publication Data
Data available

ISBN 978–0–19–874747–5

Contents

Contents

Foreword to the Fourth Edition

This handbook is primarily aimed at explaining essential SIO investigative tasks, responsibilities, processes and procedures and condensing as much useful information as possible into one practical and convenient volume. The challenge was to make accurate and readily accessible reference material available to all those who do, will or may have to undertake the SIO role whatever their level of experience, grade or rank.

The contents focus upon what SIOs need to know and do by providing simple guidance and explanatory material. A relatively straightforward and concise design has, as before, been quite deliberate, together with a widespread use of simplified bulleted lists, checklists and key points.

There may not always be sufficient time or opportunity to locate and research textbooks, access APP guidance, manuals, course notes, handouts, DVDs, websites, etc for that much-needed information. A trusted colleague or adviser might not be within easy range either; and for some, advice and guidance may not be accessible at all. When under pressure to make a decision in a complicated investigation, or at times when the brain is slow getting into gear, or when searching for that important strategy, tactic or idea, this is the go-to handy resource. Hence, the original idea behind an intentionally convenient handbook, which has proved remarkably popular and I'm glad to say attracted sufficient popularity to justify writing a fourth edition.

This edition features a brand-new chapter on child sexual exploitation. It is in response to the changing landscape and intense national and international focus on these vile crimes. Unfortunately the publisher's word-count restrictions have meant appendices that featured in previous editions have had to make way for the additional chapter.

Finally, it is sincerely hoped the book proves to be a valuable source of advice and inspiration, particularly to those who are in the highly privileged position of performing the SIO investigative role. You are the ones who will always have my utmost admiration, respect and sincerest best wishes. I salute you for your enthusiasm, courage and fortitude in performing what is a very challenging role and making the world a safer place in which to live. Good hunting to you all.

Tony Cook

Acknowledgements

This fourth edition would not have been possible without the foundations of the first three, therefore those acknowledged previously deserve continued appreciation. I now wish to express my appreciation to colleagues and friends from whom advice has been taken to produce various contents of this book. Organisations as well as individuals have provided practical assistance and access to information, in particular the College of Policing, International Homicide Investigators Association (IHIA), and National Police Chiefs Council (NPCC) Homicide Working Group.

To Oxford University Press, whose staff have once again been extremely patient and forgiving. They granted me numerous extended deadlines while trying to complete the book and juggle the demands of a time-consuming and demanding full-time role within the National Crime Agency.

Finally, my immense gratitude must goes to particular trusted and reliable individuals and subject matter experts whom I have called upon to contribute their wisdom, knowledge, expertise, support and advice. In alphabetical order they are as follows:

Debora Beaufort-Moore (author of Blackstone's *Crime Scene Management and Evidence Recovery*)

Colin Hope (Police Inspector and National Search Adviser NCA)

Mike Hyde (National Digital Media Adviser NCA)

Sian Lewis Williams QPM (National Family Liaison Adviser NCA)

Dr Matthew Long (Senior Manager/SIO, NCA CEOP Command)

Dave Marshall QPM (retired DCI from MPS and author of Blackstone's *Effective Investigation of Child Homicide and Suspicious Deaths*)

Dr Richard Mee (Senior Geographic Profiler NCA)

John Mooney (retired Detective Superintendent and National HOLMES Adviser)

Lee Rainbow (Senior Behavioural Investigative Adviser, Head of Profession, NCA)

Gary Shaw MBE (National Investigative Interviewing Adviser NCA)

Dr Kevin Smith (Witness Intermediary Adviser NCA)

Chris Walker (Detective Chief Inspector, West Yorkshire Police)

Dr Michelle Wright (Senior Lecturer in Psychology at Manchester Metropolitan University)

Glossary of Terms, Abbreviations and Acronyms

3xPs Principle	Positive, Positive, Positive
4G	fourth generation (phones)
5WH	Who?, What?, Where?, When?, Why? and How?
A	Action
A&E	Accident and emergency
ABC	Assume nothing, Believe nothing, Challenge/check everything
ABE	Achieving Best Evidence
ACPO	Association of Chief Police Officers
AFI	Accredited Financial Investigator
AKA	also known as
AM	Action Manager
ANPR	Automatic Number Plate Recognition
AO	Authorising Officer (RIPA)
APP	Authorised Professional Practice
AQVF	alibi questionnaire verification form
ARV	armed response vehicle
ASAP	as soon as possible
AYR	Are You Ready?
BASE	Barnardos Against Sexual Exploitation
BCU	Basic Command Unit
BF	UK Border Force
BIA	Behavioural Investigative Advisor
BST	British Standard Time
BTP	British Transport Police
BWV	body-worn video cameras
CAID	Child Abuse Image Database
CAIU	Child Abuse Investigation Unit
CAM	child abuse material
CAP	common approach path
CAST	Centre for Applied Science and Technology
CASWEB	casualty bureau weblink
CATCHEM	Centralised Analytical Team Collating Homicide Expertise and Management
CAU	Crime Analysis Unit
CBA	Crime Business Area
CCRC	Criminal Cases Review Commission

CCTV	closed circuit television
CD	communications data
CDI	Communications Data Investigator
CDOP	Child Death Overview Panel
CEOP	Child Exploitation and Online Protection Centre
CHIS	covert human intelligence source
CI	critical incident
CIA	Community Impact Assessment
CICA	Criminal Injuries Compensation Authority
CICS	Criminal Injuries Compensation Scheme
CII	Covert Internet Investigator
CIM	critical incident management
CISO	Crime Investigative Support Officer (NCA)
CJA	Coroners and Justice Act 2009
CJS	Criminal Justice System
CLO	Communications Liaison Officer
COD	cause of death
CoP	Codes of Practice
COS	Crime Operational Support (NCA)
CPA	crime pattern analysis
CPD	continued professional development
CPIA	Criminal Procedure and Investigations Act 1996
CPR	Child Practice Review
CPS	Crown Prosecution Service
CRA	child rescue alert
CSC	Crime Scene Coordinator
CSE	child sexual exploitation
CSI	Crime Scene Investigator
CSM	Crime Scene Manager
CSO	child sex offender
CSP	Community Safety Partnership
CSR	current situation report
CTAIL	NSPCC Child Trafficking Advice and Information Line
CT scan	Computed Tomography scan
DC	Detective Constable
DCI	Detective Chief Inspector
DCSF	Department for Children, Schools and Families
DHR	Domestic Homicide Review
DI	Detective Inspector
DIDP	Detective Inspectors Development Programme
DMI	Digital Media Investigator
DNA	deoxyribonucleic acid
DO	Disclosure Officer
DOA	dead on arrival

DPP	Director of Public Prosecutions
DR	Document Reader
DS	Detective Sergeant
DSA	directed surveillance authorities
DSIO	Deputy Senior Investigating Officer
DSU	Dedicated Source Unit
DSupt	Detective Superintendent
DV	domestic violence
DVCV	Domestic Violence, Crime and Victims Act 2004
DVCVA	Domestic Violence Crime and Victim's (Amendment) Act 2012
DVDD	Drowned Victim Detection Dogs
DVI	disaster victim identification
DVLA	Driver & Vehicle Licensing Agency
EA	Equality Act 2010
EAD	Expert Advisors' Database
ECHR	European Convention for the Protection of Human Rights
EEK	early evidence kit
ENQS	make enquiries
EO	Exhibits Officer
EU	European Union
FCP	forward command post
FCP	Forensic Clinical Psychologist
fDNA	Familial DNA
FI	Financial Investigator
FIB/U	Force Intelligence Bureau/Unit
FIIP	Fighting International Internet Paedophilia Project
FLA	Family Liaison Advisor
FLC	Family Liaison Coordinator
FLO	Family Liaison Officer(s)
FME	Force Medical Examiner
FMG	Forensic Management Group
FOD	fact of death
FOI	Freedom of Information Act 2000
FPO	File Preparation Officer
FPSG	Forensic Pathology Specialist Group
FSS	Forensic Science Service
FTO	Foreign Travel Order
GP	General practitioner
GPRS	General Packet Radio Service
GPS	Global Positioning System
GSB	Gold, Silver, Bronze
H-2-H	house-to-house (enquiries)
H-2-HC	House-to-House Co-ordinator

HMC	Her Majesty's Coroner
HMIC	Her Majesty's Inspectorate of Constabulary
HMRC	Her Majesty's Revenue and Customs
HOLMES	Home Office Large Major Enquiry System
HORFP	Home Office Registered Forensic Pathologist
HOSDB	Home Office Scientific Development Branch
HP	high priority
HR	human resource
HRA	Human Rights Act 1998
HSE	Health and Safety Executive
HTA	Human Tissue Act 2004
HTC	Human Trafficking Centre
HUMINT	human intelligence
HVM	high volume messaging
HWG	Homicide Working Group
I	Indexer
IAG	independent advisory group
ICIDP	Initial Crime Investigators Development Programme
ICR	internet connection records
ICSE	International Child Sexual Exploitation
IDENT1	UK central national database for holding, searching and comparing biometric information (fingerprints, palm prints and crime scene marks)
IED	improvised explosive device
IIMARCH	information, intention, method, administration, risk assessment, communications, human rights
IMSC	Initial Management of Serious Crime Course
INI	Impact Nominal Index
IO	Investigating Officer
IIOC	indecent images of children
IP	internet protocol
IPCC	Independent Police Complaints Commission
IPLDP	Initial Police Learning and Development Programme
ISA	Information Sharing Agreement
ISP	internet service provider
ISP	identify, secure, protect
ISVA	Independent Sexual Violence Advisers
IT	information technology
IVC	initial visual check
JDLR	just doesn't look right
JP	Justice of the Peace
KDL	Key Decision Log
KIRAT	Kent Internet Risk Assessment Tool
LCN	low copy number

LCU	Logistics Coordination Unit
LEA	law enforcement agency
LKP	last known position
LOE	lines of enquiry
LP	low priority
LSCB	Local Safeguarding Children Board
M	message form
MACP	Military Aid to Civil Power
MAPPA	Multi-Agency Public Protection Arrangements
MBWA	management by walkabout
MHR	Mental Health Review
MI	major incident
MIM	Murder Investigation Manual
MIR	Major Incident Room
MIRSAP	Major Incident Room Standardised Administrative Procedures
MIRWeb	major incident room weblink
Misper	missing person
MIT	Major Investigation Team
MLAT	Mutual Legal Assistance Treaty
MLO	Media Liaison Officer
MLOE	main lines of enquiry
MLSC	Management Linked Serious Crime
MO	modus operandi
MOD	manner of death
MODP	Ministry of Defence Police
MOU	Memorandum of Understanding
MP	medium priority
MPB	Missing Persons Bureau (NCA)
MPS	Metropolitan Police Service
MRI scan	Magnetic Resonance Imaging scan
mtDNA	mitochondrial DNA
N	Nominal
NABIS	National Ballistics Intelligence Service
NCA	National Crime Agency
NCPE	National Centre for Policing Excellence
NCTT	National Community Tension Team
NDM	National Decision Model
NDNAD	National DNA Database
NFLMS	National Firearms Licensing Management System
NGO	non-governmental organisation
NHS	National Health Service
NID	National Injuries Database (NCA)
NIIS	National Investigative Interviewing Strategy
NIM	National Intelligence Model

NMAT	National Mutual Aid Telephony
NOK	next of kin
NOS	National Occupational Standards
NPCC	National Police Chiefs' Council
NPIA	National Policing Improvement Agency
NPT	neighbourhood policing team
NRPSI	National Register of Public Service Interpreters
NSA	National Search Adviser (NCA)
NSIOA	National SIO Adviser
NSPCC	National Society for the Prevention of Cruelty to Children
NSTCG	National Strategic Tasking and Coordinating group
NWG	National Working Group for Sexually Exploited Children and Young People
OBT	obtain
OCG	organised crime gang
OCGM	Organised Crime Group Mapping
OCSE	online child sexual exploitation
OCU	Operational Command Unit
OIC	Officer In Charge
OIOC	Officer in Overall Command
OOH	out of hours
OM	Office Manager
OP(s)	Operation(s)
OSCB	Oxfordshire Safeguarding Children Board
OSINT	open source intelligence
P2P	peer-to-peer (sharing of IIOC)
PACE	Police and Criminal Evidence Act 1984
PAS	Prison Advisers Section
PAT	Problem Analysis Triangle
PCA	Protection of Children Act 1978
PCC	Press Complaints Commission
PCCs	Police and Crime Commissioners
PCSO	Police Community Support Officer
PDF	personal descriptive form
PEACE	P—Preparation and planning
	E—Engage and explain
	A—Account clarification and challenge
	C—Closure
	E—Evaluation
PII	public interest immunity
PIO	Prison Intelligence Officer
PIP	Professionalising Investigation Programme
PLE	pronouncing life extinct
PLS	place last seen

PM	post-mortem
PMA	positive mental attitude
PNC	Police National Computer
PND	Police National Database
PNLD	Police National Legal Database
POCA	Proceeds of Crime Act 2002
PoFA	Protection of Freedoms Act 2012
POI	person of interest
POL	proof of life
POLKA	Police Online Knowledge Area
PolSA	Police Search Adviser
PolSC	PolSA Coordinator
PoT	position of trust
PPE	personal protective equipment
PPP	(persons with) prominent public profiles
PPU	Public Protection Unit
PSNI	Police Service of Northern Ireland
PST	Police Search Team
PTB	person to blame
R	receiver
RA	Regional Adviser (NCA)
RADI	Rotation, Acceleration, Deceleration, Impact
RARA	Remove, Avoid, Reduce, Accept
RAT	Routine Activity Theory
RI	re-interview
RIPA	Regulation of Investigatory Powers Act 2000
ROCU	Regional Organised Crime Units
RoSHO	Risk of Sexual Harm Order
RRAA	Race Relations Amendment Act 2000
RSO	registered sex offender
RVP	rendezvous point
SA	situational awareness
SAD CHALETS	Survey, Assess, Disseminate, Casualties, Hazards, Access, Location, Emergency services, Type of incident, Safety
SAFCOM	situation, aim, factors, choices, option, monitoring
SAG	Specialist Advisory Group
SAM	scent article method (police dogs)
SAR	Suspicious Activity Report
SCAS	Serious Crime Analysis Section (NCA)
SCD	Serious Crime Division
SCG	Strategic Coordination Group
SCR	Serious Case Review
SCT	standards, competencies and training
SEOC	sexual exploitation of children

SGII	self-generated indecent imagery
SHPO	Sexual Harm Prevention Order
SIDS	sudden infant death syndrome
SigWIT	significant witness
SIM	Senior Identification Manager
SIO	Senior Investigating Officer
SIODP	Senior Investigating Officer Development Programme
SIRENE	Supplementary Information Request at National Entry (Bureau)
SIS	Schengen Information System
SISII	Schengen Information System II (2nd generation pan-European database)
SMARTER	(Actions/tasks) Specific, Meaningful, Achievable, Realistic, Time-Specific, Ethical, Recorded
SMT	Senior Management Team
SOA	Sexual Offences Act 2003
SOC	Specialist Operations Centre (NCA)
SOCA	Serious Organised Crime Agency
SOCMINT	social media intelligence
SOCO	Scenes of Crime Officer
SOCPA	Serious Organised Crime and Police Act 2005
SOE	sequence of events
SOLO	Sexual Offence Liaison Officers
SOP	Standard Operating Procedure
SOPO	Sexual Offences Prevention Order
SOS	Specialist Operational Support (NCA)
SPoC	single point of contact
SPR	Strategic Policing Requirement
SRO	Sexual Risk Order
STI	sexually transmitted infection
SUDC	sudden unexpected death in children
SUDI	sudden unexpected death in infancy
SUDICA	sudden unexpected death in infants, children and adolescents
SWOT	strengths, weaknesses, opportunities and threats
TACT	Terrorism Act 2000
TB	tuberculosis
TCSO	transnational child sex offender
TFST	take further statement
TI	trace/interview (or trace/investigate)
TIE	trace/interview/eliminate (or trace/investigate/evaluate)
TLO	Telecommunications Liaison Officer
TOD	time of death
TOR	terms of reference
TRIAD	triad of injuries

TST	take statement
TTL	threats to life
UF	unidentified female
UKBA	United Kingdom Border Agency
UM	unidentified male
UU	unidentified unknown
UV	unidentified vehicle
VCO	Victim Care Officer
VCS	Victim Contact Scheme
ViSOR	Violent and Sex Offender Register
VODS	vehicle online descriptive search
VOIP	voice over internet protocol
VOWI	voice over wi-fi
VPS	Victim Personal Statement
VPT	Vulnerable Persons Team
WCU	Witness Care Unit
WOFD	warrant of further detention
W/T	'Working Together' report 2015
YJCE	Youth Justice and Criminal Evidence Act 1999
YOT	Youth Offending Team

Medical Glossary: Useful Medical Terminology

Abrasion An injury caused by blunt force rubbing off the epidermis, which is the most superficial layer of the skin. In everyday language, an abrasion would be called a graze.

Acute Appearing rapidly (eg acute inflammation), but not necessarily severe as in common usage (contrast with chronic).

Aetiology Cause of a disease.

Agonal Terminal event, immediately prior to death.

Allele A viable DNA coding that occupies a given *locus* or position on a chromosome.

Allele frequency A measure of the relative frequency of an allele showing the genetic diversity of a population or the richness of its gene pool.

Amnesia Loss of memory.

Anaemia Abnormally low blood haemoglobin concentration.

Angina Spasmodic pain.

Ante-mortem Before death.

Anterior The front.

Anoxia Lack of oxygen.

Ascites Abnormal accumulation of fluid in the peritoneal cavity.

Asphyxia Consequence of suffocation or mechanically impaired respiration.

Atheroma Furring up of the arteries by fatty deposits.

Atherosclerosis Atheroma causing hardening of the arteries.

Atrophy Pathological or physiological cellular or organ shrinkage.

Autoeroticism Arousal and satisfaction of sexual emotion within or by oneself through fantasy and/or genital stimulation (and partial asphyxiation).

Autopsy Synonymous with necropsy or post-mortem examination (autopsy = 'to see for oneself' rather than relying on signs and symptoms).

Bacteraemia Presence of bacteria in the blood.

Biopsy The process of removing tissue for diagnosis, or a piece of tissue removed during life for diagnostic purposes.

Bruises An injury caused by blood leaking out of damaged blood vessels beneath the skin. Fresh bruises are usually red, blue, purple or black, depending on their depth beneath the skin. Though they may enlarge or become more prominent at a variable rate after infliction, this does not help to age a bruise. Later, the bruise may turn brown, yellow, green or orange due to release of pigments from the breakdown of red blood cells. The earliest change is said to be yellow discolouration, which does not usually occur until approximately 18 hours after the bruising began. However, such changes are quite variable, and may be subjected to observer variation. The rate of healing in a bruise is very variable, but it is not unusual for a bruise to be visible several weeks after it was inflicted. Consequently, it is not possible to be accurate about the ageing of bruises.

Cancer A general term, in the public domain, implying any malignant tumour.

Carbon monoxide A colourless, odourless, very toxic gas, formed by burning carbon or organic fuels.

Carcinoma A malignant tumour.

Cardio Denoting relationship to the heart.

Cardiovascular Pertaining to the heart and blood vessels.

Carotid Arteries of the neck.

Cellulitis Diffuse acute inflammation of the skin caused by bacterial infection.

Cerebral Pertaining to the cerebrum which is the main portion of the brain occupying the upper part of the cranium.

Cervical Pertaining to the neck, or cervix—neck of womb.

Chronic Persisting for a long time (eg chronic inflammation) (contrast with acute).

Cirrhosis (liver) Irreversible architectural disturbance characterised by nodules of liver cells with intervening scarring, a consequence of many forms of chronic liver injury, especially alcohol abuse.

Clot (blood) Coagulated blood outside the cardiovascular system (contrast with thrombus).

Coagulate Become clotted.

Comatose Unconscious and unresponsive to stimuli (note that a comatose person is not dead).

Comminuted (fracture) Bone broken into fragments at fracture site.

Complications Events secondary to the primary disorder (eg complicated fracture involves adjacent nerves and/or vessels; cerebral haemorrhage is a complication of hypertension).

Congenital Condition attributable to events prior to birth, not necessarily genetic or inherited.

Congestion Engorgement with blood.

Consolidation Solidification of lung tissue, usually by an inflammatory exudation; a feature of pneumonia.

Contusion Bruise that results from rupture of the blood vessels.

COP Codes of Practice.

Coronary Pertaining to the heart.

Cranium The skull or brainpan.

Cyanosis Blueness of the skin, often due to cardiac malformation resulting in insufficient oxygenation to the blood.

Degeneration Disorder characterised by loss of structural and functional integrity of an organ or tissue.

Diffuse Affecting the tissue in a continuous or widespread distribution.

Disease Abnormal state causing or capable of causing ill health.

Dorsal Pertaining to the back.

Duodenum First portion of the small intestine.

Ecchymoses Any bruise or haemorrhagic spot, larger than petechiae, on the skin (may be spontaneous in the elderly, usually due more to vascular fragility than to coagulation defects).

Ectopic Tissue or substance in or from an inappropriate site (but not by metastasis).

Effusion Abnormal collection of fluid in a body cavity (eg pleura, peritoneum, synovial joint).

Embolus Fluid (eg gas, fat) or solid (eg thrombus) mass mobile within a blood vessel and capable of blocking its lumen.

Emphysema Characterised by the formation of abnormal thin-walled gas-filled cavities; pulmonary emphysema—in lungs; 'surgical' emphysema—in connective tissues.

Erosion Loss of superficial layer (not full thickness) of a surface (eg gastric erosion).

Erythema Abnormal redness of skin due to increased blood flow.

Fibrillation Fluttering of the heart not controlled by motor nerves.

Focal Localised abnormality (contrast with diffuse).

Gangrene Bulk necrosis of tissues; 'dry' gangrene—sterile; 'wet' gangrene—with bacterial putrefaction.

Haematoma Local swelling filled with effused blood, generally the result of a haemorrhage or internal bleeding.

Haemorrhage Heavy bleeding.

Histology The study of the form of structures seen under the microscope. Also called microscopic anatomy, as opposed to gross anatomy, which involves structures that can be observed with the naked eye.

Hyoid bone Small U-shaped bone at base of tongue.

Hypertension High blood pressure.

Hypostasis The settling of blood in the lower half of an organ or the body as a result of decreased blood flow, or poor or stagnant circulation in a dependent part of the body or an organ.

Hypoxia Reduction in available oxygen.

Iatrogenic Caused by medical intervention (eg adverse effect of a prescribed drug).

Idiopathic Unknown cause; synonymous with primary, essential and cryptogenic.

Incision A wound inflicted by an instrument with a sharp cutting edge.

Infarction Death of tissue (an infarct) due to insufficient blood supply.

Intestine The membranous tube that extends from the stomach to the anus.

Intra Prefix meaning within.

Ischaemia An inadequate supply of blood to an organ or part of it.

Lacerations An injury caused by blunt force splitting and/or tearing the full thickness of the skin.

Lesion Any abnormality associated with injury or disease.

Lividity Post-mortem discoloration due to the gravitation of blood.

Malformation Congenital structural abnormality of the body.

Malignant Condition characterised by relatively high risk of morbidity and mortality (eg malignant hypertension—high blood pressure leading to severe tissue damage; malignant neoplasm—invasive neoplasm with risk of metastasis) (contrast with benign—relatively harmless).

Membrane A thin layer of tissue which covers a surface or divides a space or organ.

Meninges Thin membranous covering of the brain.

Mitochondrial DNA Mitochondrial DNA is inherited from the mother and offers reduced discriminating factors.

Myocardium The heart muscle.

Parallel intradermal bruising A specific pattern of injury caused when a linear object strikes the body, leaving parallel tracks of bruising in the skin either side of the impacting surface.

Petechial haemorrhages Minute (pin-like) haemorrhages that occur at points beneath the skin. Classic signs of asphyxia usually found in skin and eyes, the conjunctivae, sclera, face, lips, and behind the ears—due to raised venous pressure.

Phalanx Any bone of a finger or toe.

Posterior The rear, behind.

Post-mortem After death.

Prognosis Probable length of survival of injury or disease.

Pulmonary Pertaining to the lungs.

Putrefaction Decomposition of soft tissues by bacteria and enzymes.

Rancid Having a musty, rank taste or smell.

Rigor mortis A rigidity or stiffening of the muscular tissue and joints of the body after death.

Sclerosis Induration or hardening.

Septic Infected.

Septicaemia Chronic blood disease characterised by blood poisoning.

Sharp force injury Sharp force injuries are traditionally divided into incised wounds and stab wounds. In an incised wound, the length of the wound on the skin surface is longer than the depth of the wound, which implies that the wound was inflicted with a slashing or cutting motion. Incised wounds may be made by a variety of weapons, including broken glass and sharp plastic, as well as the more obvious bladed weapons.

In a stab wound, the length of the wound on the skin surface is shorter than the depth of the wound, which implies that the wound was inflicted with a stabbing or thrusting motion.

Shock State of cardiovascular collapse characterised by low blood pressure (eg due to severe haemorrhage).

Signs Observable manifestations of disease (eg swelling, fever, abnormal heart sounds).

Steatosis Fatty change, especially in the liver.

Stroke Sudden or severe attack, with rupture of the blood vessel.

Suppuration Formation of pus; a feature of acute inflammation.

Tamponade (cardiac) Compression of the heart, and therefore restriction of its movement, by excess pericardial fluid (eg haemorrhage, effusion).

Thorax Chest.

Thrombo Denoting relationship to a clot.

Thrombophlebitis Venous inflammation associated with a thrombus.

Thrombus Solid mass of coagulated blood within cardiovascular system.

Toxaemia Presence of a toxin in the blood.

Toxicologist An expert in the knowledge and detection of poisons.

Toxin Substance having harmful effects, usually of bacterial origin by common usage.

Trachea The windpipe.

Trauma Wound or injury.

Vascular Pertaining to or full of blood vessels.

Vein A vessel which conveys the blood to or towards the heart.

Venereal Transmitted by sexual intercourse or intimate foreplay.

Ventricle One of the two lower cavities of the heart.

Viraemia Presence of a virus in the blood.

Vulva The external genital organs in the woman.

Note: Bruising, abrasion and laceration may all occur in the same injury. Both abrasions and lacerations heal initially by formation of a scab over the injury. The scab is made from blood and tissue fluid which forms an early protective layer, then new skin grows over the damaged area. The new growth of skin may heap up as the healing progresses, forming scar tissue. Both abrasions and lacerations can form scar tissue, but in general the more severe the injury, the more likely it is to scar. Therefore since lacerations are by definition deeper than abrasions, they tend to scar more and take longer to heal. Early scar tissue is red and shiny. It becomes silvery within a week or so, then gradually shrinks, becoming firm and white within a few weeks to months. The rate of scar tissue formation and resolution is very variable—some scars may be invisible within weeks, while others may persist for years.

Role of the SIO

1.1 **Introduction**

Fictional portrayals of lead or senior detectives traditionally depict them as shrewd and calculating individuals, able to solve cases and outwit criminals almost single-handedly. In reality this does not reflect the true complexities facing the leader of a serious and complex crime investigation, especially as the emphasis has swung from a 'search for the proof' to a 'search for the truth'.[1] This has led to highly consistent success rates in the UK, with the national average annual detection rate for serious crimes such as homicide remaining at or above the 85 per cent mark.[2]

In the UK police, a Senior Investigating Officer (SIO) is usually in command of a dedicated team of specialist trained and accredited officers, including staff and experts from a Major/Serious Crime Unit/Division. More often they have at their disposal experienced and trained professional staff. Metaphorically speaking, the SIO role can be compared to that of a musical conductor who similarly has to unify performers, set the tempo, give clear instructions, listen critically and shape the product of their ensemble.

A contemporary SIO, however, no longer has the luxury of being able to solely focus upon and prepare for solving and dealing with homicides. The role has evolved, with a gradual move towards responsibility for investigating a much wider selection of serious and complex criminality, such as organised crime, child sexual exploitation (CSE), modern slavery and suspicious missing persons, especially those involving vulnerable people such as children and young persons. The criminal exploitation of the internet and digital communication technology by offenders across the globe has changed the way in which serious offences are now committed and in turn added to skills and knowledge of the modern-day SIO that are required.

Leading complex crime investigations places extremely high personal and professional expectations and demands upon an individual, and the role is undoubtedly one of the most challenging in law enforcement. SIOs can be held to account by judicial processes, politicians, Police and Crime Commissioners, intrusive internal and external review mechanisms, the media and, not least of all, victims, their families, friends and communities. They are also answerable to bodies such as the Independent Police Complaints Commission (IPCC), the Criminal Cases Review Commission (CCRC), the Coroner, Serious Case and Domestic Homicide Review panels and their own organisation and team. When things go wrong, they become the most obvious 'PTB' (person to blame); and when they go right, plenty of praise and recognition is rightly heaped upon them. SIOs are wholly responsible for the performance of their team and their own actions and decisions during an investigation and well beyond, particularly

---

[1] P Taylor and R Chaplain (eds), *Crimes Detected in England and Wales 2010/11*, Home Office Statistical Bulletin 11/11, London, Home Office.

[2] Also cited in A Sanders and R Young, 'From Suspect to Trial', in M Maguire, R Morgan and R Reiner (eds), *The Oxford Handbook of Criminology*, 5th edn (Oxford University Press, 2012), 953–89.

when there are 'cold case' teams examining unsolved cases. High expectations are placed upon those who occupy the position, especially from victims who place an enormous amount of moral obligation, hope and trust in the SIO.

The UK Government and College of Policing are justifiably proud of how the Professionalising Investigative Process (PIP) has led to significant advancements in SIO skills and training. Cumulative learning derived from studies of investigative success and failure, together with established structures, national occupational standards and continuous professional development and training have been introduced for those entrusted with the task of managing investigations into serious crime. Guidance on roles, responsibilities, good practice and procedures have been produced alongside a mechanism for implementation and delivery through the process of national accreditation. This is now what drives, delivers and maintains the SIO skills framework with a combination of ongoing professional training and expertise.

Being an SIO is not the easiest of career moves, nor is it for the faint-hearted. It is, however, by far the most satisfying and rewarding role in law enforcement. This first chapter seeks to outline some of the requirements, skills and attributes for the role, together with some useful pointers and topics for consideration.

> Not everyone who is in police service has the temperament, personality, perseverance or skills to be an effective Homicide Squad Commander. The supervision and management of an investigative unit, specifically as a Homicide Squad Commander, requires a drastically different approach than the strict patrol-oriented paramilitary model, which does not allow for any input from the subordinates or variations at the point of execution.[3]

1.2 **Challenges for the SIO**

There can be nothing more important for a civilised society than ensuring the safety and security of its citizens. When details of incidents such as those involving horrific acts of cruelty and offending such as the murder or sexual exploitation of young children and vulnerable people emerge, the focus of attention is on the investigation and the hope and expectation of achieving justice for victims, their families and outraged communities. This responsibility has to be balanced against the constant political pressure to reduce costs and find huge financial savings, and yet continue to achieve the lowest UK crime rates for decades.

There is nowadays a much wider range and variety of cases and investigations an SIO has to take charge of. Some were never originally included as part of the PIP3 accreditation process and others traditionally were never considered to be police matters. The following list indicates those an SIO may encounter:

---

[3] V J Geberth, 'Homicide Unit and its Commander' (2011) 59(11) *Practical Homicide Investigation, Law & Order Magazine*.

- Serious and organised crime[4]
- Linked series serious crimes
- Suspicious and unexplained deaths
- Crimes in action (eg kidnap, abduction, extortion, serial/mass/spree killings)
- Suspicious and high-risk missing person enquiries and 'no body' murders
- Honour killings
- Increased suicide rates (ie amongst sex offenders)
- Serious case and Domestic Homicide Reviews
- Gang-related criminality such as CSE, firearms and drugs
- Violence and public protection
- SUDC/SUDI deaths (sudden unexpected deaths of children and infants)
- Child sexual abuse and serious sexual offences, eg CSE
- Human (including children) commercial trafficking and modern-day slavery, servitude and forced labour
- Cybercrime
- Economic crime, financial investigations, proceeds of crime and identity theft
- Article 2 deaths and corporate manslaughter
- Prison-related deaths and those in healthcare settings
- Threats from extremism and terrorism
- Mass fatality atrocities, accidents and civil emergencies
- Historic (cold) cases and those involving public figures and celebrities
- Foreign and transnational offenders.

Crimes that aren't quickly or easily solved usually pose more of a challenge, particularly if the case is high profile. A long-running undetected case, such as homicide, soon attracts attention, internally and externally. Borrowed, temporary or shared resources under collaborative agreements may be recalled or redeployed despite the fact that there could be numerous important outstanding lines of enquiry. This is when an SIO can benefit most from having good support and advice to provide reassurance they are getting the best out of their resources and that the enquiry is still heading in the right direction.

1.2.1 **Consequences of unsolved crimes**

The performance and capabilities of an SIO are significant when considering the consequences of unresolved crimes such as homicide and serious sexual offences. Apart from reputational risk (personal/organisational) and financial cost implications, unresolved cases hinder the healing process for victims, families and

---

[4] Serious crime as defined in s 93(4) of the Police Act 1997 is: (a) conduct which involves the use of violence, results in financial gain or is conducted by a large number of persons in pursuit of a common purpose; or (b) an offence for which a person who has attained the age of 21 years and has no previous convictions could reasonably be expected to be sentenced to imprisonment for a term of three years or more.

local communities and allow offenders to commit further crimes and create further victims.

Increased fear and loss of public trust and confidence can lead to reluctance of people coming forward to report crimes and assist investigations. This fear is heightened in communities that are blighted by fear (caused, for example, by organised crime gangs and drugs, guns and 'turf-war' type criminality). In such cases unsolved cases become a self-fulfilling prophecy due to lack of confidence in law enforcement and the judicial system.

Each case begins with a level of solvability and probability of success. Most murder cases, for example, are relatively straightforward, with the majority (up to 70 per cent) being 'self-solvers' rather than 'whodunits'.[5] Others can be more difficult or seemingly impossible (such as those where there are no witnesses, no intelligence nor forensic evidence and no suspects) and are a greater test for the SIO.

1.2.2 **High-profile cases**

Some cases attain high-profile status, and if not solved may frequently reappear in the public spotlight, even though relatively old or historical. This occurs for a variety of reasons, such as public and media interest, scrutiny, complexity or simple high-profile notoriety. Some UK and European examples are the Stephen Lawrence case (1993); Moors murderers (Ian Brady and Myra Hindley, 1965); Yorkshire Ripper (Peter Sutcliffe, 1981); Hillsborough football stadium disaster (1989); Madeleine McCann, missing child investigation in Portugal (2007); and the Claudia Lawrence missing person/murder enquiry in York (2009). There are lots of others that for one reason or another have blighted communities. Such cases are the supreme test of any law enforcement agency (and SIO), as decisions made and outcomes are frequently reviewed, queried and re-analysed.

This means the performance of the SIO and the effectiveness of the criminal justice system have a long-lasting effect on the general public, either positively or negatively, and this cannot be understated.

1.2.3 **Joint and linked series crimes**

Linked series homicides and other serious offences pose specific challenges, particularly in relation to a joint command and control structure of what are separate but linked investigations. For example, information sharing, communication flows and shared intelligence management functions between forces, regions or agencies (that might have different powers or jurisdictions) will require a sophisticated approach, plus linking up data and managing joint investigative strategies such as family liaison and TIE (trace/interview/eliminate) enquiries.

---

[5] M Innes, 'The Process Structures of Police Homicide Investigations' (2002) 42 *British Journal of Criminology* 669–88.

In determining whether to link offences, an early consideration is the accurate evaluation of the interrelation between offences and offenders. Similarities between victims, crime scenes and modus operandi need careful examination, together with the linking up of data and good communication flows.

SIOs are advised to seek help and support from the National Crime Agency (NCA) Specialist Operations (telephone: 0845 000 5463) as soon as they suspect a link between crimes. A number of their services, such as comparative case analysis and behavioural investigative advice, can help guide judgements on the identification of commonalities and linkage.

KEY POINT

If there are multiple victims and offences, it is certain to be deemed a serious and complex criminal investigation. It is also likely to be designated a critical incident or 'crime in action', for which most chief officers would appoint a senior and experienced SIO to take the lead with support from an accredited PIP 4 SIO and NCA National SIO Adviser plus supporting team.

1.3 **SIO Role and Key Skills**

The *Murder Investigation Manual* or 'MIM' states:

An SIO is the lead investigator in cases of homicide, stranger rape, kidnap or other investigations. This requires the SIO to:

- Perform the role of officer in charge of an investigation as described in the Code of Practice under Part II of the Criminal Procedure and Investigations Act 1996.
- Develop and implement the investigative strategy.
- Develop the information management and decision-making systems for the investigation.
- Manage the resources allocated to the investigation.
- Be accountable to chief officers for the conduct of the investigation.

The role of the SIO in a homicide investigation is potentially one of the most complex and challenging positions within the police service. It combines two elements—the role of investigator and the role of manager, each of which must be performed to the highest standards.[6]

The Criminal Procedure and Investigations Act 1996 (CPIA) sets out duties for the SIO (and all investigators involved in the case), not simply in relation to disclosure, but also in respect of the investigation itself. Section 23 refers to the treatment and retention of material and information generated during such an

---

[6] ACPO, *Murder Investigation Manual* (NCPE, 2006), 25–6.

investigation, and subs 23(1)(a) contains a requirement for the police to carry out an investigation.[7] It states:

> that where a criminal investigation is conducted all reasonable steps are taken for the purposes of the investigation and, in particular all reasonable lines of enquiry are pursued.

Part II of the CPIA Code of Practice defines the 'officer in charge of an investigation' and what their role is within the Act:

> The *officer in charge of an investigation* is the officer responsible for directing a criminal investigation. S/he is also responsible for ensuring that proper procedures are in place for recording information, and retaining records of information and other material, in the investigation.

1.3.1 Key skill areas

According to a police research paper,[8] the SIO role requires a combination of three different categories of skills. These come under the following headings:

(1) Investigative ability
(2) Professional knowledge
(3) Management skills.

These can be expanded upon in the following way:

Investigative ability

- Investigative competence (eg formulating lines of enquiry, hypotheses building, problem solving and decision making)
- Ability to appraise, analyse, retain and recall salient facts and information (including interpreting and assimilating information, challenging assumptions, checking for accuracy and relevance)
- Adaptability and flexibility
- Strategic and tactical awareness (eg understanding the bigger picture)
- Innovation and creativity
- High standard of communication skills (verbal and written, such as recording decisions in a policy file and laying out investigative strategies)
- Keen powers of observation
- Sharp mental agility and self-belief
- Ability to remain calm, cope under pressure and multi-task

---

[7] A disclosure policy should be included in the SIO's policy file *stating* that, for example, all used material will be served on the defence; all unused material connected to the investigation will be treated as 'unused material' and only included on the MG6C form if considered relevant to the case.

[8] N Smith and C Flanagan, 'The Effective Detective: Identifying the Skills of an Effective SIO' (2000), Home Office Police Research Series, Paper 122.

- Nerve, strength of character, composure and confidence
- Time management skills
- Ability to prioritise and remain resilient when managing competing demands, including coping with multiple simultaneous complex responsibilities

Professional knowledge

- Legal frameworks, powers and procedures, case law, rules of evidence, definitions (eg the terms 'reasonable suspicion' and 'reasonable grounds to believe'), Codes of Practice (eg Code of Practice for Victims of Crime, 2015—see Chapter 11.2).
- 'Well read' by continuously developing and improving/expanding knowledge, using numerous sources such as Home Office circulars and statistics, internal and national policies and reviews, legal databases eg Police National Legal Database (PNLD), police journals, conferences and seminars, National Police Library at College of Policing and the intranet/internet.
- Knowledge of national guidelines, best practice guidance, and learning points (eg via POLKA[9] communities and College of Policing Authorised Professional Practice[10]), strategic debrief reports, National Police Chiefs' Council (NPCC) position statements, IPCC and Her Majesty's Inspectorate of Constabulary (HMIC) recommendations and nationally disseminated good practice.
- Knowledge of forensic procedures and techniques, eg DNA17 and familial DNA (fDNA), investigative and technological advances, crime scene search tactics and examination, body recovery and pathology principles, procedures relating to exhibit recovery and processing, specialisms, experts and national assets (eg NCA) that might be available.
- Understanding of terminology, eg in the medico-legal world when communicating with professionals, pathologists, doctors and scientists, and understanding their language and interpreting findings; or understanding frequently used organisational acronyms.
- Operational knowledge, such as Major Incident Room (MIR) procedures and HOLMES, eg TIE actions, Achieving Best Evidence (ABE) guidelines, covert and overt proactive tactics, investigative strategies, digital and social media opportunities, how to conduct CSE investigations, and knowledge of cybercrime.
- Awareness of wider community, safeguarding issues and national strategic threat levels (ie the 'bigger picture').

Leadership and management skills

(Covered in Chapter 2)

---

[9] POLKA is the Police Online Knowledge Area provided by the College of Policing. One of their communities is aimed at supporting SIOs entitled 'Major Crime Investigation' (see <https://polka.pnn.police.uk/communities/home>).

[10] Authorised Professional Practice (APP), <http://www.app.college.police.uk/>.

KEY POINTS

- 'Creative thinking' involves looking at problems from different perspectives and questioning assumptions to produce innovative ideas.
- Bright ideas often come at odd times (off duty or out of working hours, eg middle of the night) and are sometimes triggered by unrelated activities or events. It is useful to have at the ready a means of recording them to aid memory.
- SIOs always remain students and must continuously invest in their own skills and knowledge, seizing every opportunity to (re)train and develop. Training others, mentoring, coaching, providing inputs to courses and attending training events and seminars will improve personal learning and development.

1.3.2 **MIRSAP requirements**

The Major Incident Room Standardised Administrative Procedures, or MIRSAP manual[11] outlines the roles and responsibilities of the SIO relating to the functions of the Major Incident Room (MIR). These are standardised to ensure that in linked or series cases there are similar practices across forces.

Checklist—MIRSAP SIO requirements

- Responsibility for investigation of the crime.

- Ensuring an incident room with appropriate resources is created.

- Regular assessment of work levels to maintain appropriate staffing.

- Setting timescales for review and progress of actions and documents.

- Logging all decisions in a policy file against signature.

- Reading and making decisions on filing of documents.

- Determining and communicating current lines of enquiry.

- Setting parameters, eg TIEs, SOE (sequence of events), scene(s), house-to-house (H-2-H), witness statements and personal descriptive forms (PDF), unidentified nominal and vehicle policies.

1.4 **Professionalising Investigation Programme (PIP)**

PIP is aimed at ensuring investigators and SIOs remain competent to practise by the registration of their skills and competency at both national and local levels, which is built on and maintained through continued professional development (CPD). PIP

---

[11] ACPO, *MIRSAP Manual* (NCPE, 2005), 18–20.

has been in place for a number of years and continued through the transition from the NPIA to the College of Policing and development of Approved Professional Practice (APP), together with the introduction of Police and Crime Commissioners (PCCs) and the Strategic Policing Requirement (SPR). The national policing crime business area (CBA) portfolio for standards, competencies and training (SCT) identifies the levels required to investigate the range of criminal offences dealt with by the police service. It implements the original objectives of PIP to establish a professional approach to the development and maintenance of the skills required by investigators at all levels.

The various PIP levels are:

- Priority and volume crime investigations—PIP level 1.
- Serious and complex investigations—PIP level 2.
- Major investigations—PIP level 3.
- Strategic management of highly complex investigations—PIP level 4.

There are plenty of useful training programmes that can be incorporated into an SIO's PIP training and CPD. Much will depend on the individual and what skills or knowledge gaps are identified.

KEY POINT

The College of Policing defines CPD as a range of learning activities through which policing professionals maintain or enhance their capacity to practise legally, safely, ethically and effectively. They recommend that full-time staff should undertake a minimum of 35 hours of CPD activity per year.

1.5 **Preparing for the Role**

Calls or requests for Senior Investigating Officers often come at unusual times or during unsociable hours, particularly when 'on call'. These are moments when they need to be well prepared and ready to hit the ground running. An acronym to remember is AYR:

A Are
Y You
R Ready?

SIOs may have to remain on duty for a considerable time, particularly in the early stages of an enquiry. Working long hours without sufficient rest and food, together with pressure and time constraints, do not help when having to make critical decisions. Therefore an SIO has to be well prepared and ready for the challenge that lies ahead and able to manage themselves effectively in order to successfully perform the role. Having some basic kit and accessories in a 'grab bag/case' or similar to hand is a good place to start.

Checklist—SIO's basic tool kit

- Reliable and accurate watch/timepiece.
- 'Casebook' or work/note/day book (and spare) with reliable writing implements to record information, sketches, notes, details and decisions (or digital equivalent).
- Fresh policy file (and spare).
- Official identification (for self) and personal business cards.
- Weatherproof clipboard (or similar) to rest on with sufficient writing/drawing paper.
- Useful forms/documents (eg paper management system, list of actions raised, blank actions, officer debriefing sheets, major incident (MI) write-up sheets, message and H-2-H forms, aides-memoires and checklists).
- Communication devices (eg mobile phone plus charger, radio, tablet, laptop).
- Useful contact numbers (eg supervisory staff, Crime Scene Investigator (CSI), Pathologist, Family Liaison Officer (FLO) and radio channels).
- Foul weather gear (eg waterproof/warm protective clothing and suitable footwear, hat/gloves).
- Personal protection equipment (PPE).
- Standby refreshments (food and drink).
- Maps (eg digital mapping or satellite navigation system).
- Flashlight and batteries.
- Crime-scene barrier tape, scene logbooks, exhibit bags/labels, permanent markers for use on tamper-proof bags.
- Digital camera (with charged batteries plus memory card).
- Forensic suit/mask/gloves/overshoes.
- Suitable transportation (eg vehicle filled with fuel and window notice to identify to whom it belongs).
- Money/loose change/credit/debit cards for emergencies.
- Personal comfort and welfare necessities and supplies (eg spectacles, medicines).

- Addresses of, directions to and access codes for buildings and details of parking facilities.

- Overnight bag plus details for booking short-notice overnight accommodation.

- Blackstone's *The SIOs' Handbook*.

KEY POINTS

- Practical clothing or dress worn for cold or wet outdoor scenes may be unsuitable for more formal duties later on, eg when conducting briefings, meeting victims' relatives or during media interviews. It is wise to have a suitable change of clothing available.
- Some SIOs may have to cover and travel across large geographical areas and prior planning for suitable overnight accommodation may be required to avoid fatigue and make a quick turnaround. Good transport and parking facilities, hot food, and secure and discreet facilities (to make/receive phone calls) are essential for being suitably refreshed and ready to return the next day.

1.6 **Recognising Diversity**

Part of the role involves ensuring investigations take full account of any matters appertaining to race, gender, ethnic origin, religion, culture, age, disability, sexual orientation, nationality or place of abode. There is no place for personal prejudices, discriminatory behaviour or stereotyping of any sort and it is particularly important that assumptions are not influenced by any prejudice or bias. Full account must be taken of vulnerable persons, whether that vulnerability is the result of learning difficulties, trauma or any other circumstances.

Communication breakdowns can occur if there are perceptions of alienation, distrust or negativity that can result in a loss of confidence in the investigation. This ultimately leads to a loss of public assistance and non-receptiveness. The SIO must remain cognisant of this potential and manage the requirement in a Community Impact Assessment document (CIA) and policy file. There must be a clear strategy on how to communicate with hard-to-reach and minority groups in order to maintain confidence and build and sustain relationships. Community focus and the benefits of equality and diversity in operational delivery are major components of most policing strategies and of importance to community and race relations.[12]

The Equality Act 2010 (EA) consolidated discrimination legislation and contained new measures to strengthen protection against discrimination, stipulat-

---

[12] See ACPO, *Equality, Diversity and Human Rights Strategy for the Police Service* (Home Office, January 2010).

ing protected characteristics in relation to age, disability, gender reassignment, race, religion or belief, sex and sexual orientation. The SIO in their leadership role must remain committed to managing diversity and ensure it is demonstrably part of an enquiry team's culture and philosophy. Positive action must be taken against any inappropriate and illegal language or behaviour at all times, with adequate mechanisms to monitor compliance with the legislation.

1.7 **Ethical Standards and Integrity**

An SIO retains the ultimate responsibility for ensuring a criminal investigation is conducted to the highest degree of moral and ethical standards. Lack of professional behaviour and standards adversely affect reputations as well as leading to potential miscarriages of justice. Public trust and confidence depends on honesty, transparency and integrity. Statutory regulations such as the Human Rights Act 1998 (HRA) and the Police and Criminal Evidence Act 1984 (PACE) and bodies such as the Independent Police Complaints Commission (IPCC) provide the public with ways of challenging inappropriate investigative activities and actions, and the CPIA puts a legal requirement on ensuring evidence is captured that points away as well as towards any possible suspect.

A concept known as 'tunnel vision' or 'closed mind syndrome' must be avoided at all costs. This occurs when there is a determined focus on a theory or an individual (or individuals) at the exclusion of other possibilities. Narrow-minded approaches do not bode well for the integrity of investigations and attract criticism. The effects can also produce miscarriages of justice, corruption, incompetence, and expensive court and human costs. The concept of the 'investigative mindset' helps significantly avoid this (see Chapter 3).

External leaks of information can pose a problem on major and sensitive enquiries, particularly when there is extensive public and media interest. This must be prevented or investigated if it happens, as it can lead to serious complications much later. Close monitoring must be applied with strong standard setting, guidance and direction from the SIO and their management team for all those who are necessarily exposed to, perceived 'at risk' with, or in receipt or possession of information that must be treated with the strictest confidentiality. This has become more of a problem since the increase in usage of digital media devices such as smartphones that have powerful cameras and fast, easy access to social media sites and the internet (see also Chapter 10).

Misguided concepts based upon notions of 'noble cause corruption' must never be allowed. There cannot be any cutting of corners and it is ultimately the SIO who is held accountable in a court of law or public inquiry. While creativity and innovation among entrepreneurial investigators is to be encouraged, deception of any kind that breaches the law must not. This is different from finding legal and practical solutions to problems that is a core skill of all crime investigators.

The framework offered by the law (eg PACE, HRA, Regulation of Investigatory Powers Act 2000 (RIPA), CPIA 1996, EA and Freedom of Information Act 2000 (FOI)) create rigid boundaries for ethical practice. Compliance with the legislation provides SIOs and their investigators with a degree of protection from ill-founded allegations of dishonesty, unfairness or discrimination. This is illustrated in what is known as the 'integrity paradigm':

INTEGRITY PARADIGM

Right method Right result	Right method Wrong result
Wrong method Right result	Wrong method Wrong result

During serious crime investigations, investigators are usually under much closer supervision through regular briefings and a highly controlled administrative system (ie HOLMES). All activity is tasked, allocated, monitored, reviewed and supervised with a far greater degree of scrutiny. This should produce a robust and almost inquisitorial system. These integrated administrative controls are in place to ensure compliance with legislation, correct guidelines and procedures.

1.7.1 Code of Ethics

In 2014 the College of Policing issued a 'Code of Ethics'[13] as a code of practice under s 39A of the Police Act 1996 (as amended by s 124 of the Anti-Social Behaviour, Crime and Policing Act 2014). It outlines principles and standards of professional behaviour for police in England and Wales. These principles are intended to inform every decision and action across the police service and apply to everyone in the profession of policing. They also add: 'those with leadership roles have additional expectations placed upon them to lead by example'.

The Code of Ethics promotes the use of the National Decision Model (NDM) to embed its principles at the centre of decision making (see Chapter 3).

The code outlines ten standards of professional behaviour under the following headings:

1. Honesty and integrity
2. Authority, respect and courtesy
3. Equality and diversity
4. Use of force

---

[13] College of Policing, 'Code of Ethics: Principles and Standards of Professional Behaviour for the Policing Profession of England and Wales' (April 2014),

5. Orders and instructions
6. Duties and responsibilities
7. Confidentiality
8. Fitness for work
9. Conduct
10. Challenging and reporting improper behaviour

References

ACPO, *Equality, Diversity and Human Rights Strategy for the Police Service* (Home Office, January 2010)

ACPO, *Murder Investigation Manual* (NCPE, 2006)

ACPO, *MIRSAP Manual* (NCPE, 2005)

College of Policing, 'Code of Ethics: Principles and Standards of Professional Behaviour for the Policing Profession of England and Wales' (April 2014) <http://www.college.police.uk/what-we-do/Ethics/Documents/Code_of_Ethics.pdf>

Home Office, *Multi-Agency Statutory Guidance for the Conduct of Domestic Homicide Reviews* (Home Office, 2013)

Maslow, A H, 'A Theory of Human Motivation' (1943) *Psychological Review* 55, 370–97

Pascale, R, *Managing on the Edge* (Penguin Books, 1990)

Rogers, C, *Leadership Skills in Policing* (Oxford University Press, 2008)

Smith, N and Flanagan, C, 'The Effective Detective: Identifying the Skills of an Effective SIO' (2000), Home Office Police Research Series, Paper 122

Leadership and Management

2.1 **Introduction**

Supervision and management of a serious crime investigation are quite unique in comparison to other senior law enforcement management roles. Apart from the extensive investigative skills and knowledge required, an SIO is expected to actively participate in and manage an investigation in addition to managing their staff. This does not usually include performing tasks such as interviewing witnesses and suspects, searching crime scenes or collecting exhibits. Active participation does not mean micro-management either, but it does involve maintaining an extensive knowledge and keen overview of all aspects of the investigation in addition to directing, controlling and managing the resources that perform the more 'hands on' functions.

Regardless of how absorbing an interesting and challenging case is, an SIO retains overall responsibility and primacy for professional people management. Staff in their enquiry team, temporary or otherwise, are entitled to be supervised and led properly by an effective role model. SIOs carry a duty of care for the staff under their control, not only for performance and welfare, but also standard setting, policy implementation, motivation, learning, professional development and conflict resolution.

The style chosen can fluctuate. For example, in dynamic operational law enforcement environments, high-risk situations require more directive command and control to ensure correct procedures are followed and the National Decision Model (NDM) is applied. In other less critical situations, a different style of leadership and management may be appropriate that is more engaging and consultative. The key is to adopt a leadership style suitable for the occasion.

A subtle difference between managers and leaders is that managers maximise *output* and *outcomes* from their teams through various administrative processes and implementation, such as organising, planning, coordinating, directing and controlling; whereas leaders lead, engage, inspire and motivate their teams. It is useful to understand the difference between the two, and these topics are discussed in this chapter.

KEY POINT

Managers do things right ... while leaders do the right thing.[1]

2.2 **Leadership and Management Styles**

Leadership and management styles vary and what works for one does not always work for another. Some believe good leaders give off a certain 'presence', 'gravitas'

---

[1] P Drucker cited in R Pascale, *Managing on the Edge* (Penguin Books, 1990), 65.

or 'authority'; while others believe it is more about being charismatic and popular. It depends on what is suitable and appropriate for an individual and the circumstances. Gaining open and honest '360 degree' feedback may help determine what works best.

In time-critical and urgent situations, such as crimes in action like kidnaps, suspects at large and high-risk ongoing incidents, leadership and decision making will need to be more authoritative, dynamic and direct. Such situations demand prompt and decisive leadership in order to manage investigations and staff effectively to protect the public, prevent offending and pursue offenders. That is why the police service, for example, has a disciplined, military-style rank structure. Usually in other less urgent times a well-managed and self-sufficient team can function on a less direct but more inclusive and democratic approach.

There are a number of different styles of leadership. One theorist named Kurt Lewin suggests there are three:[2]

1. **Autocratic.** Direct orders and directives made through one-way communication with little or no involvement from subordinates. Advantages include speed of response by enabling a quick decision-making process through greater control and immediate direction. Drawbacks are that staff may become frustrated by the autocratic manner of decision making which allows for little or no involvement from those who have good or better ideas.

2. **Democratic.** Involvement of subordinates in the decision-making process through consultation. Advantages are that staff become more involved and can contribute towards strengthening the outcome of a decision and will feel more motivated. Drawbacks are that this style can become too slow and cumbersome, which means it becomes difficult to make time-critical decisions, or an SIO cannot get to make the decision they prefer. It also allows those who are risk-averse to avoid making tough decisions.

3. **Laissez-faire.** Involves minimal involvement in decision making by the leader or manager by allowing subordinates to decide for themselves. This may be feasible when staff are fully competent to make their own decisions. Advantages are similar to the democratic style, with motivational levels being high as power and control is devolved, which may enrich team and individual roles and jobs. Drawbacks are that this leadership style may mean that subordinates have little or no leadership, direction or coordination, and that their work is largely unstructured and inconsistent.

SIOs are free to choose which style suits them best or the situation and circumstances. Sometimes an autocratic style is entirely justifiable and necessary (eg in urgent operational or time-critical situations), and at others a more democratic style, or even a hybrid, is more appropriate, ie somewhere in between ('auto/democrat').

---

[2] K Lewin, *Resolving Social Conflicts* (Souvenir Press, 1973).

Great leaders have the ability to adapt, adopt and improve their style and call upon a wide spectrum of behaviours and personal qualities. When required they are able to put the 'extra' into 'ordinary'. Personal style may depend, however, on character and personal preference for the situation as opposed to keeping to one preferred style. An SIO must decide which style to select, remembering that effective leadership needs to be moving, fluid and dynamic.

There is no standard set of qualities that make the perfect leader, yet 'influencing' and 'inspiring' seem well suited. Confidence in decision-making and problem-solving is central to leadership (dealt with in Chapter 3) because it enables tasks to be properly communicated and completed. Leaders often have to do the tough right thing even though it may be unpopular, rather than take the easy or soft option.

KEY POINTS

- Leadership involves influencing (and inspiring[3]).
- Where there are leaders, there are followers.
- Leaders are able to make tough decisions and take decisive action when required.
- Leaders are visible and respected by their team.
- Leaders are people who have a clear idea of what they want to achieve, how and why.[4]

Good leaders remain calm and considered and can control their emotions under pressure. Panic or freezing are totally unacceptable. At some incidents and crime scenes there may be pandemonium, with the initial response being somewhat disorganised through chaos and requiring a good leader to take control. In such a case the attending SIO must not allow themselves to become paralysed but remain cool, calm, composed and in control. Displaying confidence, inner calm and self-assurance in high-pressure situations (being unflappable) are key attributes and reassures those around that an effective leader is in charge.

Checklist—Good leadership traits

- Staff are encouraged to contribute and speak freely and frankly, not just to comply and conform out of loyalty or fear.
- Leaders demonstrate they are knowledgeable and up to date on information, facts, actions, events, activities, key names and details.
- Consistent decision making avoids confusion, with no moody or changing attitudes and behaviour. Staff need to know where they stand.
- Good self-control and professional ethical and moral standards; being wholly dependable, not displaying inappropriate behaviour or abusing levels of authority.

---

[3] Words added by the author.
[4] Taken from C Rogers, *Leadership Skills in Policing* (Oxford University Press, 2008).

- Relaying a belief in others that the role is taken very seriously and that decisions can and will be made when and where necessary.
- Doing the tough right thing even though it may be unpopular.
- Commitment—putting in as much if not more effort than the team.

KEY POINT

How an SIO presents is important. This involves good appearance, behaviour, style, confidence, impressive verbal and bodily communication skills, posture, voice tonality and projection with steady pace and volume, clear, open gestures and facial expressions—ie looking, sounding and acting the part.

2.3 **Team-Building**

Management and leadership involves building a team into an efficient and cohesive unit. The modern approach to serious crime investigation recognises there is no place for the lone entrepreneur. The role is to be the leader of a team, to provide investigative focus, to coordinate and motivate and be accountable for every aspect of the enquiry whilst managing a whole host of resources.

Professor John Adair (internationally renowned in the field of management and leadership development) describes how team-building consists of three complementary and overlapping requirements:

1. Task
2. Team
3. Individual.

What he says is tasks that need completing create frustration and low morale if those who have them to complete are prevented from doing so or are unable to do so. Team maintenance needs are equally important, as group cohesiveness is essential under the 'united we stand, divided we fall' principle. Individual needs are also key and include psychological and physical needs such as reward and recognition, a sense of doing something worthwhile, job satisfaction and status. The three overlapping elements are represented in this diagram:

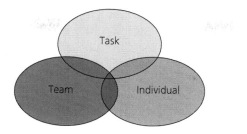

The overlapping circles indicate how all three elements are mutually inter-dependent. In theory, if team maintenance fails, performance of tasks becomes impaired and individual satisfaction reduced. If individual needs are not met, the team will lack cohesiveness and performance of tasks will be affected. Effective managers tend to try and satisfy all three elements. In other words, too much emphasis on one can be detrimental to the other two.[5]

2.4 **Supervision and Support**

The ability to supervise indirectly can be a great asset, provided swift interven-tion is made when things aren't going well. This sends out the right message regarding (non-) acceptable professional standards. Being able to pick up, read and interpret signals is important—eg quickly noticing and acting when morale is dipping or complacency and lethargy are creeping in. This includes managing and dealing with tensions and inappropriate behaviour when they arise.

The SIO must know or find out what, if any, problems their team are facing and must never assume they know 'what it is like' for their staff. Teams respect a leader who is visible and willing to leave their comfort zone, talk to them and find out for themselves what working environments are like first hand (often referred to as 'management by walkabout' or through the acronym 'MBWA').

2.5 **Maximising Potential**

It is advisable to have a rich mix and spread of skills and attributes amongst team members. Some, for example, may have a relaxed, easy communication style, readily adaptable to fit most circumstances, and like to be seen and heard. They are most likely to be extrovert personalities. Quieter, more introverted types may just get on with allocated tasks in a less obvious fashion and prefer to be left alone. Some thought must go into understanding individuals and how best to get the most out of them. A skilful manager analyses the strengths and weak-nesses of their team and allocates tasks according to attributes. For example, trying to encourage and support potential witnesses to give evidence or informa-tion may be more suited to some than others. Watching hours and hours of

---

[5] J Adair, *The Best of Adair on Leadership and Management* (Thorogood, 2008).

CCTV footage or ferreting about gathering intelligence, although arguably core detective skills, may be better suited to particular types of individual.

SIOs should also be aware of their own strengths and weaknesses too in order to build a team around them. This helps identify gaps where an SIO's needs are greatest. Taking responsibility for self-development, setting high personal standards and 'leading by example' involve accepting liability when things go wrong or when others cannot handle situations. Giving credit, praise and recognition for any effort, struggle and determination is enormously beneficial to building team spirit.

A good level of command and control should not seek to stifle an investigator's natural desire to use their skills, flair and experience. SIOs should empower their staff to apply their skills and experience within their investigative strategies and the framework of action management imposed by an MIR. This will allow the team to realise their full potential and not only maintain a high standard of morale, but also perform at the highest level.

2.6 **Motivation and Positive Psychology**

Motivated individuals are generally more productive due to their sheer enthusiasm, commitment and energy. These attributes rub off onto others and very little can be achieved without them; whereas negative attitudes can be 'enthusiasm drainers'. Negative and pessimistic traits are unhelpful, self-fulfilling and become culturally the norm. Optimistic, positive mental attitudes (PMA), however, allow tasks to be approached with greater vigour, energy and vitality, focusing on what can be achieved and not what cannot. Those who constantly raise problems to solutions, play the 'devil's advocate' and destruct rather than construct need to be challenged with balancing their negative views with positive ones.

SIOs should regularly remind themselves and their staff to remember the 3P principle, which can be summed up in three very important words:

POSITIVE
POSITIVE
POSITIVE

KEY POINT

Negative attitudes are energy drainers. They suck the life out of people until everyone gets down to that low level of thinking. SIOs *must not allow this to happen* as it impacts on morale, levels of motivation, performance and overall job satisfaction.

2.7 **Managing Oneself**

Management in the context of the role has to include an element of being able to manage oneself in order to cope with the demands. There are both physical and mental demands placed on an SIO, particularly in the early stages of a fast-moving enquiry when it is often necessary to be on duty long before others arrive and long after they leave. It is essential, no matter how experienced or professional the individual is, to be able to cope under pressure, manage fatigue, heavy workloads and juggle the demands of a work/personal life balance.

Stress has psychological and physiological elements that are quite normal human reactions. Some people cope with them better than others and some even perform better when their adrenalin is flowing and under pressure. Managing stress is a personal thing, the consequences of which surface in many different forms, eg loss of patience, being argumentative, showing anger or unusual and inappropriate behaviour. These symptoms must be recognised in order to manage the causes.

KEY POINT

Stress and pressure can actually raise performance, which is why world records are not broken during training sessions.

An SIO's office/desk may resemble a doctor's surgery with people queuing up waiting to speak urgently on a one-to-one basis. An 'open-door policy' is fine, but sometimes it needs closing in order to get on with some work, read and study important material, to focus clearly or hold meetings in private. There must be some control over who makes personal or unplanned demands of an SIO's time and that other supervisors down the chain of command are not being circumvented.

Having a reliable and trustworthy deputy increases resilience, and having a trusty assistant (aka 'staff officer') who can also monitor the SIO's welfare, is highly recommended. The SIO cannot and should not try to do everything themselves, and the delegation of key tasks relieves workloads. Deputies can be tasked with arranging and managing searches and team tasks, conducting cascade briefings, and managing administrative tasks, provided whoever has delegated responsibilities reports back at regular intervals. This can be at stipulated times, such as during formal or informal briefings.

Time management is absolutely critical to avoid becoming overburdened and remaining effective. An SIO must be ruthlessly efficient at getting the most out of their available and valuable time. Some matters and certain individuals (including senior/chief officers) can conspire to commandeer valuable time if allowed to do so and the SIO must sometimes be firm and polite, pointing out that some matters are more pressing and urgent. Investigative strategic meetings need careful management to ensure pre-prepared agendas and allocated times are rigidly adhered to. Planning and managing the day's priorities is extremely important, while appreciating there can be changes at a moment's notice. Being unable to complete all necessary and urgent tasks can unnecessarily raise stress levels and become counterproductive.

> **KEY POINT**
>
> Nominating a personal assistant or 'staff officer' who is trusted and reliable is a good way of relieving workloads and to control access, answer calls, take notes, write policy entries at dictation, etc. Other roles in the police service have this function routinely embedded within their command structure (eg firearms and public order commanders) and SIOs should be afforded the same benefit.

Mentally 'switching off' can help relieve stress, unwind and facilitate a fresh approach. It can be tempting to concentrate on very little else other than a stimulating and challenging enquiry, yet creating time to focus on something completely unrelated and pursuing other interests and tasks at a suitable point can be hugely beneficial in reducing mental anxiety and stress. It also helps refresh the mind and clear the head, ready to refocus after interrupting levels of intensity. Being able to press the 'off button' every now and again is an effective coping mechanism.

Personal health management is fundamentally important, with a need to match energy and stamina levels with workloads. It is unprofessional and unhealthy to go without proper rest, food and nourishment as energy and adrenalin levels will eventually crash, which is when it becomes far more difficult to focus and function correctly. Everyone has physiological and psychological needs and SIOs are no different.

Remaining on duty for hours on end with a short turnaround time, no matter how keen and committed, is something that could be highlighted by a review team or external enquiry as being detrimental to decision making. The same rule applies to staff on the enquiry team, including specialists such as CSIs, who sometimes have to spend long periods at difficult crime scene locations. An SIO does not want added victims from, say, road traffic collisions involving staff travelling home after long shifts suffering from fatigue and tiredness.

An SIO need not and should not be alone in managing complex enquiries. They should take every opportunity to surround themselves by trusted and reliable peers and colleagues who can help in making tough decisions and offering supportive and useful advice. Having someone available to 'bounce' ideas off and chat through complex theories and areas of an investigation, bringing experience from a wider field of experience, is extremely reassuring. The role of a PIP 4 (SIO/Gold Strategic and Tactical Advisor) has been introduced to perform this function in large-scale enquiries. The NCA also has experienced accredited PIP 4 National SIO Advisers (NSIOAs) who can offer their UK-wide experience, knowledge and specialist services to act as a critical friend or provide reassurance and advice at any stage during an enquiry.

Checklist—SIO welfare

- SIOs must manage themselves as well as their teams.
- Trusted individuals can perform role of 'staff officer'.
- Delegated responsibility (where appropriate) relieves pressure.
- Handovers to deputies will facilitate necessary time off and rest periods.
- Nominate a driver if needs be or arrange nearby overnight accommodation.
- Don't get too emotionally involved in a case as it limits objectivity.
- Good peer support networks are essential.
- Don't be afraid to ask for advice (eg from NCA National PIP 4 SIO Advisers).

References

Adair, J, *The Best of Adair on Leadership and Management* (Thorogood, 2008)

Adhami, E and Browne, D P, 'Major Crime Enquiries: Improving Expert Support for Detectives' Police Research Group Special Interest Series, Paper 9 (Home Office, 1996)

Adam, E C, 'Fighter Cockpits of the Future' (1993) Proceedings of 12th IEEE/AIAA Digital Avionics Systems Conference (DASC), 318–23

Innes, M, 'The Process Structures of Police Homicide Investigations' (2002) 42 *British Journal of Criminology*, 669–88

Kelley, H, 'The Warm-cold Variable in First Impressions of Persons' (1950) 18 *Journal of Personality*, 431–9

Moray, N, *Robotics, Control and Society* (CRC Press, 2005)

Peters, S, *The Chimp Paradox* (Vermillon, 2012)

Investigative Decision Making

3.1 **Introduction**

The ability to make exceptional decisions and sound judgements and to solve difficult problems is a core skill and attribute for an SIO. This should be combined with a solid understanding of the processes that underpin them. These are inextricably linked to the core roles and responsibilities of a lead investigator because decision making was identified as a key skill requirement of SIOs by Smith and Flanagan (2000) as stated in Chapter 1.

There is often no right or wrong approach to decision making. Much will depend on the individual and case circumstances, for clarity and most decisions involve an element of risk; good problem solving helps manage that risk. Having an appreciation of and becoming acquainted with the different types of processes (some being academically acclaimed) enables an SIO to become more confident and effective in their decision-making and problem-solving skills.

Making quick and bold decisions is often necessary when time is critical and the stakes are high (eg during the 'golden hour' period). When a decision has to be made, it should be made rather than showing signs of weakness or poor leadership. However, more routine situations generally provide a little more time to pause and methodically think things through. During a complex investigation there will be many opportunities when more time, care and effort can and should be taken when applying some of the techniques covered in this chapter.

This chapter is aimed at providing guidance to help create a deeper understanding of the processes, concepts and methods available for effective decision making and problem solving. Learning, applying and improving these skills will help develop a more grounded capacity for not only making consistent decisions and understanding the processes, but also in producing clearer audit trails to explain how they were arrived at. This will protect an SIO and their organisation from criticism and provide the means to explain why and how a decision was made. What counts is not only what is decided and recorded in a key decision log (policy file), but also transparency on the process applied. SIOs must anticipate their decisions being challenged and heavily scrutinised, not just on how they turned out but also on how they were made.

3.2 **'Fast' and 'Slow' Decision Making**

Daniel Kahneman's popular book *Thinking, Fast and Slow* describes two different systems of decision thinking:

1. 'operates automatically and quickly with little or no effort and no sense of voluntary control'
2. 'allocates attention to the effortful mental activities that demand it, including complex computations. The operations of system 2 are often associated with the subjective experience of agency, choice and concentration...only the slower system 2 can construct thoughts in an orderly series of steps. When

system 1 runs into difficulty, it calls upon system 2 to support more detailed and specific processing that may solve the problem of the moment. System 1 has biases, however, systematic errors that it is prone to make in specified circumstances and can sometimes try and answer easier questions than the one it is asked, and has little understanding of logic and statistics.'[1]

3.2.1 **Fast-time decision making**

Fast-time decisions have a place in most investigations at some point and, as stated earlier, if a decision is time critical and needed rapidly, then a decision should be made without hesitation. The risks of making a decision versus not making one may have to be determined quickly and these are facts that may need to be explained in a policy file entry.

A principle known as *paralysis by analysis* must be avoided as it can lead to no decision ever being made at all and perhaps golden hour tasks (eg arresting escaping suspects) being adversely affected. Sometimes there isn't the luxury of discretional time; the pace and requirements of the circumstances dictate that time is critical and limited. In 'crimes in action', for example, where lives of individuals and the safety of the public are at stake, the mindset required is one of being far more proactive and not overly hesitant in deciding tactics and making snap decisions. Live time operations such as large-scale suspect hunts are occasions when decision making has to be much more dynamic and move with changing circumstances (see also Chapter 12 on suspect management). Effective situational awareness will help recognise occasions when such rules apply.

Fast-time decisions can sometimes be influenced by intuitive beliefs and previous experiences, which are often reliable. This is how most people perform feats of intuitive expertise every day, and an approach that can prove very useful in the initial stages of an investigation when there is very little information or time available. Initial responders, for example, may have to rely upon this method when important and time-critical decisions are required.

Good training, knowledge and experience enable bold and confident decision making in *time-critical* situations rather than deliberate reasoning or analysis. This allows the association of current circumstances with past examples in order to help select appropriate and effective options:

> In certain types of investigations such as those where there is a lack of information available, detectives will rely more heavily upon their experience and knowledge, thereby engaging in more intuitive decision making processes... the ability to draw inferences and make decisions from basic information during the crucial 'golden hour' is an extremely important skill for detectives to develop.[2]

Intuition relies heavily upon an ability to deal with information swiftly and efficiently and to call upon personal knowledge and previous experience. Usually

---

[1] D Kahneman, *Thinking Fast and Slow* (Penguin, 2012).
[2] M Wright, *Detective Intuition: The Role of Homicide Schemas* (University of Liverpool, 2008).

it is a reliable tool and should not be ignored given the right circumstances. Previous experience, however, can sometimes introduce bias and prejudice or the wrong interpretation.

Jumping to the wrong conclusions and instantly believing what is seen can occur, as illustrated in the famous Muller-Lyer illusion. These horizontal lines are in fact identical in length:

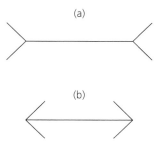

3.2.2 Selective attention

There is a psychological concept termed 'selective attention' which may happen in fast-time decision making. It refers to a mental process whereby a single feature or message is selected and focused upon to the detriment of other information that is available simultaneously. This has been academically proven and referred to in many scientific tests and theories (one of the most famous being 'The invisible gorilla'[3]) and is a method relied upon by illusionists and magicians. It is a dilemma worth considering when making or reviewing early assessments of decisions made on an 'interpretation' of what was thought to have been presented, eg at crime scenes and incidents. As a general rule, the more astute investigators consider the 'bigger' or 'wider' picture and *all* available information upon which to base their thoughts, conclusions and decisions (which is when good observation skills come in useful—see list in Chapter 1.3.1).

3.2.3 Heuristics and biases

The theory of 'heuristics' refers to the use of experience-based knowledge (or 'working rules') for problem solving, particularly in fast-time and initial-response situations. This occurs when previous knowledge or experience is used to compare scenarios and draw similar conclusions from perceived commonalities (ie 'it looks like something I've dealt with or seen before, so that is what it must be'). Unfortunately this method is never completely reliable. It can be unduly influenced by personal bias, such as perceptions of people, situations, locations or stereotypes; or affected by lack of information or incorrect recall of the knowledge or

---

[3] Selective attention is defined in <http://www.dictionary.reference.com> and 'The invisible gorilla' test can be retrieved from a number of internet sources such as <http://www.theinvisiblegorilla.com/gorilla_experiment.html>.

experience being relied upon. An obvious example of a heuristic bias is in a sexual assault investigation, where an officer who has previously dealt with a false allegation assigns a greater probability to the next allegation he/she deals with as being fabricated.

Such failings can adversely affect other important lines of enquiry if, for example, a preferred hypothesis based on intuition is chosen at the expense of others. In turn this may lead to decisions, evidence gathering and selection of material supportive of the preferred choice rather than exploring multiple hypotheses. This is known as 'verification' or 'confirmation bias'.

KEY POINTS

1. Avoid selective attention, be observant and look at the bigger picture.
2. 'Instinct can be either your best friend or your worst enemy. This is the "gut instinct" paradox and therefore needs to be managed carefully and kept under control. The problem is that instinctiveness will probably come first before rational thought processes kick in. The skill is in getting them to work together. Your instinct is offering up a suggestion not a command and you have a choice to accept or reject it' (cited in S Peters, 'The Chimp Paradox' (Vermillon, 2012).

The contribution of a Behavioural Investigative Adviser can be highly useful for both recognising any potential reasoning error and objectively assessing hypotheses. They are able to make reference to empirical research findings and bulk data sets to provide an appropriate safeguard against any bias and selective information usage. They can also help generate hypotheses that are supported or refuted with reference to psychological theory, relevant research findings and experiential knowledge, ie an objective viewpoint. They can also assist in building an hypothesis tree (see Figure 3.1).

3.2.4 Slow-time decision making

Some SIOs are renowned for switching to a slower, more deliberate and controlled form of operating and thinking. This allows them to replace chaos with structure and order by slowing things down and creating an element of what is often described as 'slow time'. The technique provides a distinct advantage when making tough decisions, as it allows further information to be gathered and an opportunity to work through things more methodically and consider a greater number of alternatives. Taking a step back facilitates greater situational awareness to observe the bigger picture and avoid selective attention (mentioned earlier). High-pressure situations should not be allowed to cloud judgement when it is more advantageous to remain cool, calm and detached. Rushing around can also create an impression of being under stress and in panic mode.

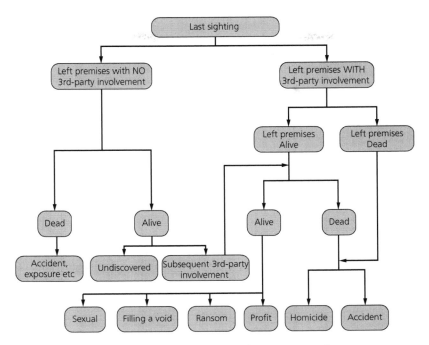

Figure 3.1 Hypothesis tree (in a suspicious missing person case)

3.2.5 **Situational awareness**

Situational awareness typically refers to being aware of what is going on all around. It is a term often mentioned in law enforcement circles (and other professions such as the military and aviation industry, eg pilots and air traffic controllers). The concept is linked to perceptions of time and environmental information (temporal and spatial elements) that are critical and influential in complex and dynamic circumstances. Situational awareness (SA) involves being aware of what is happening in and around the vicinity of an incident in order to understand what information, location, events and actions are helpful to decision making. Having a good sense of situational awareness provides an innate feel for situations, people and events and helps prevent errors in decision making. This is particularly important when there is a high level of information flow and decisions rely upon the recognition of SA factors.

There are a number of definitions available for SA, including the following:

- 'The perception of elements in the environment within a volume of time and space, the comprehension of their meaning, and the projection of their status in the near future.'[4]

---

[4] M R Ensley, 'Toward a Theory of Situation Awareness in Dynamic Systems' (1995) 37(1) *Human Factors*, 32–64.

- 'Knowing what is going on so you can work out what to do.'[5]
- 'Accessibility of a comprehensive and coherent situation representation which is continuously being updated in accordance with the results of recurrent situation assessments.'[6]
- 'Keeping track of what is going on around you in a complex, dynamic environment.'[7]

SA indicates how decision making and problem solving are more than one dimensional and must take into account what is happening in 3D dynamic environments, which is of enormous value to serious crime investigation. Key decisions often have to take into account information and 'situational' factors within complex circumstances that might have to be quickly assimilated, interpreted and incorporated into effective decisions. Being dynamically aware of events that are occurring, surroundings and available information is the preferred state to adopt when making key decisions.

KEY POINTS

- Some circumstances require fast-time critical decision making when previous experience and intuition can be a useful resource.
- Heuristics and biases can be kept in check by later reviewing with a slower, more systematic, methodical and controlled approach.
- Avoid selective attention and don't be too hasty in jumping to conclusions.
- Be observant and remain sceptical about first impressions.
- Adopt a methodical and logical decision-making approach and utilise good situational awareness by looking at everything that is going on.
- Taking a step back and slowing things down enables a clearer look at all the facts and wider circumstances.

3.3 **Investigative Mindset**

Following on from the theme of previous sections is a concept termed an 'investigative mindset'.[8] This is the theory of keeping an open mind and remaining receptive to alternative suggestions, looking for other explanations and not becoming too focused on one or two theories or hypotheses. The appliance of

---

[5] E C Adam, 'Fighter Cockpits of the Future' (1993) Proceedings of 12th IEEE/AIAA Digital Avionics Systems Conference (DASC), 318–23.

[6] N B Sarter and D D Woods, 'Situation Awareness: A Critical but Ill-defined Phenomenon' (1991) 1 *International Journal of Aviation Psychology*, 45–57.

[7] N Moray, *Robotics, Control and Society* (CRC Press, 2005), 4.

[8] ACPO, *Practice Advice on Core Investigative Doctrine*, 2nd edn (NPIA, 2012).

an investigative mindset is aimed at having a more logical and methodical approach to decision making and has become a very important doctrine that should always be championed by SIOs.

3.4 'ABC' Rule

Decision making also relies upon good information which must be carefully scrutinised, reviewed and assessed. It involves remaining sceptical and testing the accuracy, reliability and relevance of material relied upon. This rule is known as the 'ABC' principle.[9]

> A—Assume nothing
> B—Believe nothing
> C—Challenge/check everything

Nothing should be taken for granted nor accepted at 'face value'. It is a mistake to assume things are what they seem. SIOs must try to seek corroboration and recheck, review and confirm facts, information and material. Applying scepticism is the best approach before placing too much reliance on information. Good SIOs are confident and wise enough to remain sceptical and challenge or check everything by good probing.

3.5 **Problem Solving**

Decision making involves an element of problem solving. Detective work requires a sequential and logical approach and there are some useful techniques aimed at simplifying the process. The aim is to incorporate a methodical collection and analysis of information and alternative solutions into a process that will help generate well-informed decisions. Good problem-solving skills are an important part of decision making and will produce different options, leading to a more informed, rational choice and decision.

There are different varieties of problem-solving models, though most contain a similar structure. One recommended contains a simple step-by-step process[10] and involves choosing a course of action or decision only after collecting sufficient information, then analysing the pros and cons of alternative solutions before making a choice.

A useful problem-solving model is shown in Figure 3.2.

---

[9] Cited in ACPO, *Practice Advice on Core Investigative Doctrine*, 2nd edn (NPIA, 2012), 88.
[10] Also cited in J Adair, *The Best of Adair on Leadership and Management* (Thorogood, 2008).

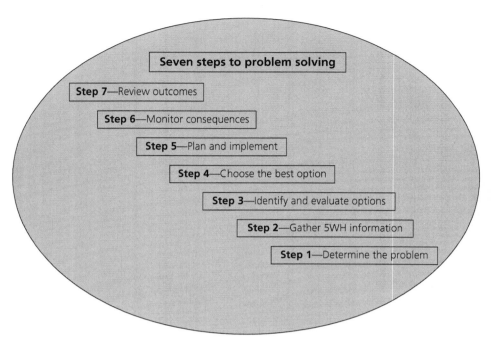

Figure 3.2 Seven steps to problem solving

3.5.1 **Evaluating options and alternatives (SWOT analysis)**

The 'investigative mindset' rule applies when considering alternative solutions and options for making key decisions. The more alternatives considered, the greater the chance of not missing the best option or solution. The decision may be to choose various options for different tactical stages and timescales of an investigation, eg in the short, medium or long term. Alternative options can also be graded as part of a contingency, eg plan A or plan B (if plan A fails).

One method of analysing the pros and cons or advantages and disadvantages of options is to examine their strengths, weaknesses, opportunities and threats (SWOT analysis). For example, looking at what threats there are (such as time, resources and cost implications) against what opportunities the option can provide.

3.5.2 **'Do nothing', 'defer' or 'monitor' options**

Sometimes a decision has to consider whether any action is necessary. It may be, for example, that cost outweighs gain. Therefore there may be an option to 'do nothing' (ie take no further action), 'defer' (put off until later) or 'monitor' (eg wait and see). In an arrest decision example, it may be that a suspect is detained in prison or critically ill in hospital. This may provide an option to 'defer' an arrest until such time it becomes feasible—a decision that can be monitored and remain under review.

KEY POINT

Any decision to 'do nothing' or 'defer' must be justifiable. Not making a decision is a decision itself which should be made for the right reasons, fully recorded and communicated clearly where necessary to supervisors, colleagues and, in some cases, to victims and their families.

3.5.3 **National Decision Model**

The College of Policing via APP (Authorised Professional Practice)[11] decrees the National Decision Model (NDM) is suitable for all decisions and should be used by everyone in policing. They state:

It can be applied:

- to spontaneous incidents or planned operations
- by an individual or team of people
- to both operational and non-operational situations

and to

structure a rationale of what a decision maker did during an incident and why and by managers and others to review decisions and actions and promote learning.

Understanding the NDM will help SIOs develop an appreciation of the professional judgement expected when making effective decisions. The NDM has six key elements which, together with the Code of Ethics at the centre, are illustrated in Figure 3.3.

3.6 **Gathering Information—The '5WH' Method**

Problem solving and decision making rely upon accurate information and material upon which to base a decision. The gathering of relevant information is therefore a crucial factor in making good decisions. A decision is only a decision if there are choices and asking the right questions is the best way of getting the right answers. The more accurate and comprehensive the information, the greater the chance of making the correct decision. More information provides a greater number of options and alternatives leading to 'informed decision making'.

---

[11] See <https://www.app.college.police.uk/app-content/national-decision-model/>.

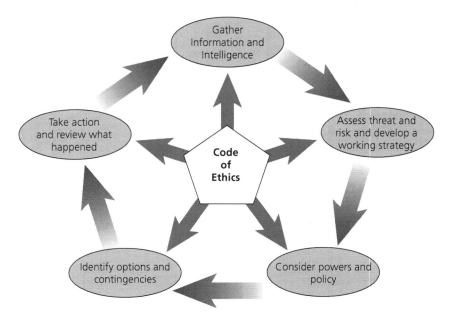

Figure 3.3 The National Decision Model

Central Pentagon: Code of Ethics (see Chapter 1.9.1)

Stage 1: INFORMATION: Gather Information and Intelligence
During this stage the decision maker defines the situation (ie defines what is happening or has happened) and clarifies matters relating to any initial information and intelligence.

- What is happening?
- What do I know so far?
- What do I not know?
- What further information (or intelligence) do I want/need?

Stage 2: ASSESSMENT: Assess Threat and Risk and Develop a Working Strategy
This stage involves assessing the situation, including any specific threat, the risk of harm and the potential for benefits.

- Do I need to take action immediately?
- Do I need to seek more information?
- What could go wrong? (And what could go well?)
- What is causing the situation?
- How probable is the risk of harm?
- How serious would it be?
- Is that level of risk acceptable?
- Is this a situation for the police alone to deal with?
- Am I the appropriate person to deal with this?
- What am I trying to achieve?
- Will my action resolve the situation?

Stage 3: POWERS AND POLICY: Consider Policy and Powers

This stage involves considering what powers, policies and legislation might be applicable in this particular situation.

- What police powers might be required?
- Is there any national guidance covering this type of situation?
- Do any local organisational policies or guidelines apply?
- What legislation might apply?
- Is there any research evidence?

As long as there is a good rationale for doing so, it may be reasonable to act outside policy.

Stage 4: OPTIONS: Identify Options and Contingencies

This stage involves considering the different ways to make a particular decision (or resolve a situation) with the least risk of harm.

Decision maker should consider:

- options that are open
- immediacy of the threat
- limits of information to hand
- amount of time available
- available resources and support
- own knowledge, experience and skills
- impact of potential action on the situation and the public.

Contingencies

- What will I do if things do not happen as I anticipate?

Stage 5: ACTION and REVIEW: Take Action and Review What Happened

This stage requires decision makers to make and implement appropriate decisions. It also requires decision makers, once an incident is over, to review what happened.

Action

Respond:

- Implement the option you have selected;
- Does anyone else need to know what you have decided?

Record:

- If you think it appropriate, record what you did and why.

Monitor:

- What happened as a result of your decision?
- Was it what you wanted or expected to happen?

If the incident is continuing, go through the NDM again as necessary.

Review

If the incident is over, review your decisions, using the NDM.

- What lessons can you take from how things turned out?
- What might you do differently next time?

Also known as the 6Ws or the 5W & H, the 5WH method is a highly effective tool for gathering information. It helps stimulate thought processes, generate information and structure pertinent questions. It also helps meet the requirements of step 2 of the problem-solving model (as outlined earlier). The 5WH method stands for six strong, leading interrogative pronouns and critical questions (which can be used in any particular order):

---

6 critical questions

Who	Who is the victim?
What	What happened?
Where	Where did it happen?
When	When did it happen?
Why	Why did it happen?
How	How did it happen?

The primary 'Wh' prompts supplementary questions to produce a quick, simple, easy–to-apply method that can be adapted to fit most circumstances. The following table provides an example:

Primary question	Supplementary questions
Who is the victim?	How many victims are there?
	What are their details, name, age, address, etc?
	Why was the victim targeted?
	How was the victim(s) selected?
	What type of victim was targeted (ie characteristics?)
	Were they a repeat victim?
	What risks are there of repeat victimisation?
	What 'victimology' information is available?
	Who and where are their family, relatives and close friends?
	Where is the victim?
	What has the victim said happened?
	How is the victim's welfare being managed?
	What injuries have been inflicted?
	What did the victim do after the offence?
	Who else has the victim spoken to since the offence?
	What protection measures are required?
Where did the crime take place?	What has been done to preserve and protect the crime scene(s)?
	Who is at the scene?
	Who has control of the scene?
	What has been done to avoid cross-contamination?

	What is known about the location?
	Why was the location chosen?
	Was it a repeat location?
	What does geographic spread suggest?
	How was the location chosen?
	How did offenders get to/from the crime scene?
	What type of property has been targeted?
	What is the link between the location, victim and offender?
	What/who else is in the locality that could be linked?
	What are the situational/economic/environmental factors?
	How many crime scenes are there?
	Have they been sequentially numbered?
	What has been done at/with the crime scene(s)?
What searches have taken place?	What type of searches and where?
	Who by and how?
	How long did they take?
	What equipment or resources were used?
	What has been found? Where is/are it/they now?
	What records of searches have been made?
	What H-2-H enquiries have been conducted?
	What CCTV has been recovered or is available?
When did the offence take place?	What is significant about the time and date?
	Why has the crime been committed at this time?
	Was this a core operating time?
	How have the time and date been confirmed?
	What else was taking place at the same time?
	What peak times, days, seasons or cyclical links are there?
	What are the frequency and intervals between offences?
	Has there been an increase in these types of offences?
When was the crime discovered?	Who discovered it, and how?
	Why was the crime discovered?
	Who was it reported to and by and how?
	What actions did the person reporting the crime take?
How was the crime reported?	When was the crime reported?
	Where was the crime reported?
	Why was the crime reported?
	What was said (exact words) by the person reporting the crime?
	What has been done with the person reporting?

(continued)

39

Primary question	Supplementary questions
What exactly happened?	What crime has been committed/not committed?
	What is currently known?
	What information gaps are there?
	What are the likely hypotheses?
	What category of crime has taken place?
	Who is known to carry out this type of crime?
	What has been done to verify information?
	What other incident(s) may be linked to the crime?
	How many other similar crimes have there been?
	What risks are there further offences might occur?
	What information has been given out?
What was the modus operandi?	Was any weapon, tool or implement used?
	Was any trace or forensic evidence left behind?
	What transport might have been required/used?
	What is unique about the crime?
	What are the associated traits and methods?
	What knowledge/skills were required by the offender?
	Have specific methods been used to evade capture?
Who are the witnesses?	Where are they now?
	What has been done with them?
	What is their reliability, credibility or vulnerability?
	What current intelligence is available?
	Why and how did they witness the crime?
	What is the relationship between victim, offender and witness?
	Who are the witnesses' associates?
	What is their status (significant, vulnerable or intimidated)?
	Who else have they spoken to about the crime?
	What is their relationship to the location?
Who is (are) the offender(s)?	What has been done to trace/arrest the offender(s)?
	What is known about the offender(s)?
	How many offenders were involved?
	What can the offender's behaviour tell us?

	What is the profile of the offender(s)?
	What is the description of the offender(s)?
	How were/can the offenders be identified?
	Who are the key suspects?
	What intelligence is suggesting possible offenders?
	Who has previously carried out this type of offence?
	Who has recently been released from prison?
	Where is the offender(s) now?
What are the main lines of enquiry?	What fast-track actions are required?
	What is the outcome of any enquiries completed?
	Who has conducted them?
	Where and how have the results been recorded?
	What are the supporting investigative strategies?
	What are the likely solvability factors?
Why was the crime committed?	What was the motive?
	How was it committed—spontaneous or pre-planned?
	Was there any involvement of alcohol/drugs?
	Was it due to jealousy, revenge, financial gain?
	Was it part of a series?
	Was it sexually or racially motivated?
	Was it gang- or OCG-related?
What specialist resources are required?	What are they?
	What and whose authority is required?
	Where can they be obtained from?
	How can they be obtained?
	How much will they cost?
	Who will brief and manage them?
	What is required of them?
	Where and whom should they report to?
What forensic and fingerprint evidence is there?	Who is the lead CSI/CSM and where are they now?
	What type of forensic examination is required?
	What type of evidence is it?
	How has it been preserved?
	What arrangements have been made to examine it?
	Who has been asked to examine it?
What exhibits are there?	What exhibits have been recovered?
	What has been done with the exhibits?
	Where are they stored?
	How have they been labelled and packaged?
	Who is in charge of all the exhibits?
	What needs to be fast-tracked?

Table 3.1 Primary and supplementary 5WH questions

This information can then be developed into a useful table/matrix, which will help identify any gaps by setting out all the relevant details in a logical sequence and is much easier to visually display and understand. The table can be populated as the enquiry progresses and used as a source of reference for the basis of applying the problem-solving model and any associated decision making. The matrix can be cross-referenced to decisions as and when they are made and can serve to illustrate just what was known or not known at the time any particular decision was made—a very important point for justifying why a particular course of action was taken (or not taken).

The matrix can be populated by adding three extra columns to cover what is known, unknown and possible sources of where it can be found (see Table 3.2). This is not just for an SIO and analyst to complete and should be a shared responsibility amongst the entire team during a continuing process of raising and answering the questions and filling the gaps, particularly during meetings and (de)briefings.

The matrix is useful for identifying gaps in what is known about the offence and making decisions on determining main lines of enquiry; it also assists the SIO to prioritise. Once created, the matrix should be treated as a 'living document' that is to be amended or extended as the enquiry progresses. A trained analyst can assist in helping to analyse, identify and fill gaps using standard analytical techniques. This process will generate key information and significantly aid decision making during the investigation.

KEY POINT

Source material should remain under dynamic review with frequent checks to confirm validity, accuracy and relevance. Investigative decision-making processes, strategies and main lines of enquiry that rely upon this process should be constantly scrutinised and evaluated to determine:

(1) accuracy of information relied upon;
(2) conflicting or contradicting material;
(3) emerging patterns or consistencies;
(4) relevance of material, eg if it supports a particular hypothesis;
(5) whether there is sufficient material or evidence on which to raise the status of any subject in the enquiry;
(6) whether any evidence would be admissible in judicial proceedings;
(7) whether it is 'relevant' under CPIA requirements.

The 5WH method can also be useful when being briefed or updated about an incident or circumstances. Questions can be posed using the headings in order to establish sufficient detail about what may already be known. The method can be used to ensure clear and concise information is acquired in a structured and sequential format rather than at random and disjointed. Any additional detail can be captured at the end by adding a further question as to what else is known that has not been covered.

5WH	KNOWN	UNKNOWN	SOURCE
Who was killed?	31-year-old lone white female (victim named). Single and has child from previous relationship. Well known/liked in local area. Resides with parents. Possibly had/having affairs with married men. Had two smartphones. Worked local convenience store.	Detailed victimology. Any previous attacks? Was she intended victim? Other attacks likely? Details of previous relationships.	Family/friends, colleagues, local community, intelligence, profile and lifestyle analysis, house/work search. Crime recording. Insurance claims checks. Comparative case analysis (SCAS database) and crime pattern analysis. Full intelligence checks. Risk analysis for further victims. Social media checks.
Who is/are the suspect(s)?	Victim in stormy relationship with boyfriend—possible suspect? Recent dispute at place of work by 2 unknown males.	Having any other affairs? Full details of incident and of persons involved.	Identify and declare suspect(s) and TIE categories. Victimology. Subject profile(s). T/I work colleagues. Comms. data analysis. Intelligence assessment.
Who witnessed?	Male walking dog found body at 06.30.	Identify potential significant witnesses.	Media appeals and H-2-H enqs. Priority TI actions.
What happened?	Battered and strangled. Found in woods near to home address. Semi-naked, trousers pulled down around ankles. Contents of handbag emptied onto ground. Bra wrapped around neck in form of ligature.	Anything stolen? Defensive marks on body? Does manner of death give indication as to age, sex, physical capability of offender? Weapon—present/missing? Brought to scene by the offender, victim, or improvised?	Conduct inventory of personal belongings. Re-examine body for further marks/bruises. Check clothing for damage, rips, and tears. Consult NCA National Injuries Database. Check origin of ligature.

(continued)

5WH	KNOWN	UNKNOWN	SOURCE
What occurred prior to murder?	Victim in public house with friends. Then spent time alone with her boyfriend. Walked home alone, having left boyfriend's flat after argument.	Sequence of events for movements of victim. Est. if any forensic evidence in boyfriend's flat. Did victim have any significant arguments or activities in hours before last known sighting?	Crime scene—examination of flat. Comms. data analysis. TIE all persons in vicinity of scene and at public house (time parameters?). Search for CCTV in area. Check boyfriend's account.
		After leaving boyfriend's flat did victim meet anyone by prior arrangement or by chance?	Analysis of witness statements. H-2-H enquiries.
What other significant events took place?	Raised voices heard—couple possibly arguing at approx. 01.15 hrs.	If linked to murder incident.	HP action—TI/TST witness(es). Consider media appeal and conduct H-2-H enqs in vicinity. Check if any other non-linked incidents.
When did it happen?	Bet. 12.30 am and 06.30 Sat. (date).	More precise time of death.	Witnesses, 'back record conversion' of alcohol/blood levels, pathologist, entomologist. Gastroenterology (stomach contents exam), CCTV, assessment of physical evidence in conjunction with other events—eg weather—victim's clothing on ground and clothing wet after the rain. Is ground under clothing wet—yes/no? What time did rain start/end?
Where did it happen?	(named location)	Where attack occurred or deposition site? Risk analysis for further attacks. How did victim/offender get to location? Prior knowledge required?	Full scene interpretation. Forensic analysis of body plus palynological survey. Crime pattern analysis. Social and demographic information. NCA geographic profiling. Local intelligence re regular users/visitors.

Why did it happen?		Motive. Victim knew offender? Stranger/sexual attack? Robbery/theft? Anger/jealousy?	Check mobile calls and texts from/to victim. Forensic and pathological interpretation of scene. Use of offender profiler. Interpretation of injuries. BIA scene assessment.
Cause and manner of death.	Post-mortem cause of death—asphyxiation.	Re-examine to see bruising/marks visible? Full medical history of victim and antecedents. Toxicology results for alcohol levels and drug traces.	Forensic pathologist. Victim's GP and hospital records. Forensic Service provider results. Second post-mortem, National Injuries Database interpretation.
How was location chosen?		On or near victim's route home? Scene interpretation. Has victim or offender visited previously? Linked to suspect or TIE?	Victimology. CPA data analysis. Subject profile analysis. Possible media reconstruction. High-profile enquiries in location. Check of precursor incidents.
How offender got to/from scene?		Is there easy escape route? Offender on foot? Or vehicle used? Local transport? Bus/taxi?	Scene examination. Enqs with local taxis and bus companies. CCTV trawl and speed cameras. Intelligence checks on suspect/TIEs. Stolen vehicles check.

Table 3.2 Table for identifying information gaps

3.7 The 'What' Question

A primary 5WH question is usually 'What happened?'. It is important to retain an investigative mindset and not become overly influenced by initial contact and evaluation details (which might already have their own interpretation) or scene assessment, initial accounts, information and statements.

An objective of the initial response and assessment is to accurately determine what happened and ascertain the precise nature and type of incident. Initial responders (including Investigating Officer (IO)/SIOs) MUST exercise extreme caution, remain sceptical and keep an open mind by making good use of the investigative mindset and obtaining as much information from the scene and any witnesses as possible (with the 5WH model). Care should be taken to question and clarify any facts presented (applying ABC principle), and record and note everything.

3.7.1 Applying hypotheses

An hypothesis, according to the *Oxford Dictionary of English,*[12] is defined as 'a supposition or proposed explanation made on the basis of limited evidence as a starting point for further investigation'. In simple terms, it means 'playing the percentages' to come up with plausible explanations or theories about what happened which can be graded and eliminated one by one until the most likely remains.

When posing 5WH questions (eg what happened?), the process of generating and building hypotheses is a useful technique. It is a means of populating step 3 of the problem-solving model (ie developing suggestions and options). Investigators generally like to speculate, and well-developed hypotheses are particularly useful when there isn't much information to go on, though a good hypothesis should make full use of all available information and material.[13]

KEY POINT

Developing and applying hypotheses is a technique that establishes an explanation, theory or inference. E Adhami and D P Browne in 'Major Crime Enquiries: Improving Expert Support for Detectives', Police Research Group Special Interest Series, Paper 9 (Home Office, 1996) referred to these inferential processes as a series of 'if–then' rules (involving a sentence that begins 'If...' closely followed by 'then...').

Information relied upon for any hypothesis must be subject to the ABC rule. As an investigation ebbs and flows, more information becomes available and

---

[12] *Oxford English Dictionary*, 3rd edn revised (OUP, 2009).
[13] See also the hypothesis tree shown in Figure 3.1.

developing facts emerge: therefore *hypotheses should always remain provisional*. This means they can be changed at any time and can and should remain under regular and dynamic review. Wherever possible it is worthwhile making a record of the information that was available at the precise time at which the hypothesis/hypotheses was/were made, which, as previously stated, is an important part in any recording process linked to decision making.

3.7.2 **Rule of Occam's Razor**

William of Occam (also spelt Ockham) was a 14th-century medieval logician, philosopher and Franciscan friar. Ockham was the village in the English county of Surrey where he was born. The rule of Occam's Razor (sometimes expressed in Latin as *lex parsimoniae*, meaning the law of parsimony, economy or succinctness) is a principle recommending that, from among competing hypotheses, the theory that makes the fewest complex assumptions is usually the right one. In other words, when there are multiple competing theories, the simplest explanation is usually right.

Often crime investigations are characterised by missing or ambiguous information, and decision making can become quite complex, which in turn encourages complicated theories and hypotheses. SIOs can become easily drawn into developing *overly* complex theories and hypotheses causing errors in decision making and judgement. Remembering the principle of Occam's Razor helps to minimise this risk.

Checklist—Hypotheses generation

- Hypotheses are useful when there is limited information.
- Apply an investigative mindset—don't become overly reliant on intuition ('keeping an open mind').
- Always consider whether there could be other/alternative hypotheses.
- Ensure a thorough check of relevance and reliability of any material relied upon (wrong information = wrong conclusion).
- Identify what information gaps are linked to any hypothesis generated.
- Hypotheses should always remain provisional and remain under review.
- Use colleagues and specialists (eg analyst or a Behavioural Investigative Adviser) to discuss and formulate ideas and hypotheses.
- Rule of Occam's Razor = the simplest explanation is probably right.
- Ensure team awareness of SIO's hypotheses.

3.8 **The 'Where' Question**

The location where an offender commits a crime (ie crime scene) and surrounding geography, community and environment can reveal information and offer up clues about them and their relationship to the victim. Geographical profiling is a recognised method of using techniques which focus on the likely spatial behaviour of offenders within the context of locations and the relationships between various crime sites. It also helps in determining the most probable location of an offender's anchor point (eg their place of residence or other base, such as their place of work). It is a proven method and forms part of the guidelines in the *Murder Investigation Manual* (MIM)[14] (advice on geographic profiling can be obtained from the NCA on 0845 000 5463). There follows some helpful academic theories to consider in terms of the 'where' question and the significance of geography and typical human behaviour.

3.8.1 **Routine Activity Theory**

The Routine Activity Theory (RAT) developed by Lawrence Cohen and Marcus Felson[15] is based on the premise that offenders tend to commit crimes in areas they are familiar with (ie in their normal routine), and in which they have had the opportunity to do so without someone or something being able to prevent them.

Examining the spatial and geographic characteristics of the surrounding crime scene environment, eg local neighbourhood, usually provides a good 'feel' for the crime under investigation. This is one reason why personally visiting and assessing a crime scene is so important. It is recommended, however, that any visit (which may be further or supplementary to the initial one) is done at the same time and day on which the offence occurred. This makes it more realistic and informative. For example, entering a crime scene that would have been dark at the relevant time should be done under the same conditions to gain an appreciation of what an offender, victim or witness would have experienced.

3.8.2 **Rational Choice Theory**

Rational Choice Theory states that most offenders make a conscious decision to commit a crime by weighing up the pros and cons of what the rewards are against the chances of being caught. It means that a decision to commit a crime is a rational and predictable one.[16] This is relevant because it relates to the geographic differences in opportunities for committing crime, ie some locations providing

---

[14] ACPO, *Murder Investigation Manual* (NCPE, 2006).

[15] L E Cohen and M Felson, 'Social Change and Crime Rate Trends: A Routine Activity Approach' (1979) 44 *American Sociological Review*, 588–608.

[16] See D Cornish and R Clarke, *Understanding Crime Displacement—An Application of Rational Choice Theory*, cited in ACPO, *Practice Advice on Analysis* (NPIA, 2008), 12.

better opportunities than others, and this may be the reason why a particular location and victim have been chosen over others.

3.8.3 Least Effort Principle

The Least Effort Principle was set out by George Zipf (1949), and claims that most human beings seek to minimise the effort required to achieve their goals. This simply means that offenders choose offence locations which are closer to them. This, however, can be affected by barriers: physical (natural and built environment) and mental (individual's subjective perception, Rossmo, 1999). Routes taken are usually those perceived as the most direct. This principle can be important in understanding the choice of crime location and offender's pre- and post-offence movement and is helpful in identifying the location of an unknown offender's anchor point.

3.8.4 Distance Decay

Most offender journeys (criminal and non-criminal) are short and close to an anchor point. As distance from an anchor point or awareness space increases, according to this principle their activity decreases. The aforementioned 'Least Effort Principle' can also be a key determinant, together with the Routine Activity Theory (Brantingham and Brantingham, 1981).

3.8.5 Problem Analysis Triangle

A further theoretical dimension to the importance of geographic information at crime scenes is the Problem Analysis Triangle (PAT) aka 'Coincidental Elements of a Crime'. This refers to the theory that for a crime to occur, an offender and suitable target must come together in a specific location without an effective deterrent.[17] This association can be considered when making decisions as to who an offender might be in the context of their links to the victim and location.

Figure 3.4 Problem Analysis Triangle

---

[17] Cited in ACPO, *Practice Advice on Analysis* (NPIA, 2008).

> **KEY POINT**
>
> The SIO/DSIO should never underestimate the value of visiting a crime scene, no matter how much time has elapsed since the incident took place, to gain a better perspective of the location, social environment, and local community (and situational awareness, mentioned earlier).

3.9 The 'When' Question

The timing (temporal) aspect of an offence is also significant. It not only links into important parameters for sightings and movements of potential suspects, elimination procedures and alibis, viewing times for passive data and CCTV, but also informs how and when reactive and proactive investigative tactics should occur (eg observations for an offender returning to commit further crime) and ensuring resources are deployed at the most effective times and locations.

The time when a crime is committed may in itself be highly significant. An offender may have calculated the best time to commit their crime, based on the risk or most beneficial time to achieve their objective or avoid capture. The time of the offence may also have been chosen deliberately because it is of significance or personal to the offender, eg it coincides with a particular anniversary or event that is meaningful or personal to the offender or victim.

In some cases producing a 'timeline' is a useful technique for piecing together movements, activities or events. This helps identify sequential gaps in time or highlight moments and timings that can overlap and become significant to the investigation. Analysts can be tasked with producing charts on computer software to act as a visual aid for the investigation team and for court purposes.

An accurate time and date must be established for when an event, eg the primary offence under investigation, occurred. When recording times and dates from victims, witnesses and CCTV, they must be carefully checked and reviewed for accuracy. Corroboration should be sought using an accurate time source (eg via the BT speaking clock '123' service) and dates reliably confirmed. Prosecutions can fail when defendants are able to prove they were somewhere else when the offence is alleged or believed to have been committed.

Prompts can prove useful for those unable to recall times and dates. Popular and reliable times of events can be used, such as TV programmes, sporting or national fixtures or (inter)national events of note. These may have to be evidentially verified if timing becomes an issue later in judicial proceedings.

SIOs must also ensure their own record of times and dates are accurate. For example, the time and date a decision was made, or when they arrived at a crime scene, or when they were informed of something. The possession and use of an accurate timepiece and calendar are important accessories to have readily available (see also Chapter 1.5).

3.10 **The 'Why' Question**

Establishing what cause, reason or motive induced an offender to commit a crime is a line of enquiry, as it may indicate who the offender(s) is(are). It may also assist in linking incidents and matching modus operandi.

It needs to be borne in mind, however, that if a motive is wrongly diagnosed and publicly stated, it may in some cases unfairly demonise a victim and/or the community with which they are associated. Examples include wrongly identifying the motive as hate crime or as a result of criminal revenge, or associating a victim with a particular activity (eg sex worker) or crime or gang. This could alienate the investigation team from important sources of information they need and discourage the public from assisting.

Checklist—Types of motives

- Gain (financial or otherwise).

- Revenge.

- Personal cause.

- Jealousy.

- Criminal enterprise.

- Gang-related (eg drugs, territory or power).

- Hate crime (racism, homophobia or other prejudice).

- Anger or loss of control (rejection, argument, drug- or alcohol-induced).

- Crime concealment or witness elimination purposes.

- Sexual or violence gratification.

- Power, control.

- Thrill and excitement.

- Mental illness/personality disorders (eg psychopath, narcissism, paranoid, schizoid).

- Political/religious/ritualistic causes.

- Terrorism-related.

- Cover-up or in the process of another crime (eg arson, burglary).

- Noble cause (eg mercy killing).

Motives can link into contributory causes of crime, such as drugs and alcohol. There is considerable evidence to suggest that violent offenders have often taken/consumed either prior to committing a violent act and this may feature as a line of defence. It is possible for victims to have taken them too, which may provide an indication as to what sort of activity they were involved in prior to a crime being committed. This can be useful for building up an accurate picture on which to base a motive and understand the personality and habits of a victim or the profile of an offender. Violent offences such as a serious assault may also involve an element of victim precipitation, whereby the victim is the first to initiate violence towards the offender.

3.11 **Management of Risk**

Decision making usually involves an element of risk, particularly if there is uncertainty about the likelihood and impact of outcomes which cannot be predicted or guaranteed. Operational decision making requires risk management,[18] ie recognising and taking sensible steps and reasonable precautions to avoid harm from either taking or not taking a course of action. In the seven steps model (Figure 3.2) and the NDM this would be relevant when weighing up the pros and cons (benefits and harms) of each option. Risk/threat management is included in one of the stages of the NDM (see Figure 3.3).

Decision making needs to include the consideration of risk management to ensure that the public and staff are fully protected (particularly where child victims are concerned—see Chapter 16.11). This does not mean bureaucratic 'back covering' nor the creation of a total 'risk-free' or 'risk-averse' working environment. It does mean, however, the identification, assessment and sensible management of risks and threats in order to minimise, monitor and control the probability and impact of unwanted events AND to maximise potential benefits.

3.11.1 **Risk identification**

This is the first step in the proactive risk management process. It is probably the most important part of the process and depends entirely on the decision activity

---

[18] APP on the COP website cites ten risk principles, see <http://www.app.college.police.uk/risk>.

and subject matter. It is important to recognise the entire process depends upon accurate identification of the inherent risks and the process needs to remain dynamic and under constant review/monitoring to ensure the correct risk(s) have been identified. The usefulness of the next two stages depends on the accurate defining of the risk or threat.

Assistance in identifying risks can come from a variety of sources, eg:

- accurate and comprehensive information (5WH-type material)
- organisational learning and policy
- reviews (internal and external)
- public enquiries and case studies (eg IPCC findings)
- empirical knowledge and experience
- historical information and documented knowledge
- consultation with and advice from experts and specialists
- team members, staff, colleagues and peers.

Some examples:

- Identifying safety risks in deploying family liaison officers to a hostile family/ community or where the suspect is believed to be residing.
- When deciding which area to search for a vulnerable missing person, when, how and the method and geographic parameters with a risk of looking in the wrong place or using a technique that doesn't find the person when looking in the right place.
- When deciding to delay an arrest for a known suspect with possible risks to the safety of the public and other potential victims.
- When investigating CSE or abuse cases and there is risk to the welfare of a child or further child victims.

3.11.2 **Risk assessment**

Risk assessments are generally rated as being low, medium or high, and may be either:

1. **Generic**—produced for a variety of activities, eg executing a search warrant. Identifying significant hazards that may be encountered and introducing suitable control measures aimed at reducing them, but they must be regularly reviewed.
2. **Specific**—a systematic and detailed examination of a particular activity.
3. **Dynamic**—some hazards and control measures may have to be identified and introduced spontaneously.

3.11.3 **Risk assessment scoring matrix**

The matrix in Table 3.3 shows how the top column (impact) can be multiplied by the left-hand column (probability) to produce a risk assessment score factor.

The risk assessment scoring matrix measures probability against impact. This uses the principle that the greatest risk is caused when the probability and impact scores are high. Risks that are both low in impact and low in probability are not usually worthy of great concern.

For example, if it is 'highly probable' (5) that when going to arrest a suspect there will be strong resistance and violence used to resist and if this occurs the impact will be very serious (4), the assessment score can be calculated as 20 (ie 5 × 4). This score can be reduced by introducing effective control measures, such as using a team of specially trained officers to conduct the arrest who carry protective equipment, and staging the operation in the early hours of the morning. The score can then be recalculated because it is now unlikely (2) the arrest will be resisted, which produces a more acceptable score of 8 (ie 2 × 4).

IMPACT ➡ PROBABILITY ⬇	CATASTROPHIC (5)	VERY SERIOUS (4)	SERIOUS (3)	MODERATE (2)	MINIMAL (1)
HIGHLY PROBABLE(5)	High (25)	High (20)	High (15)	Moderate (10)	Low (5)
PROBABLE(4)	High (20)	High (16)	High (12)	Moderate (8)	Low (4)
POSSIBLE (3)	High (15)	High (12)	Moderate (9)	Moderate (6)	Low (3)
UNLIKELY (2)	Moderate (10)	Moderate (8)	Moderate (6)	Low (4)	Low (2)
VERY UNLIKELY (1)	Low (5)	Low (4)	Low (3)	Low (2)	Negligible (1)

Table 3.3 Risk assessment scoring matrix

3.11.4 **Risk management**

Once a risk has been identified, a control strategy should be introduced. Generally speaking there are four options that can be adopted in relation to risks, represented by the acronym RARA:

R—Remove
A—Avoid
R—Reduce
A—Accept

Changing tactics to achieve the same objectives will afford a means of removing, avoiding or reducing risks. Alternatively, the risks can be deemed to be so negligible that they can be accepted.

Organisational risk factors must be taken into account when deciding how to manage risk such as the availability of finance and resources, competing demands, legal requirements, internal policies and processes, and influence/directives from more senior management. Other influences can be time constraints or external factors such as official reviews or public expectations, other agency involvement or the high levels of likely threat or harm.

A carefully scripted record of risk management decisions and their rationale is always advisable for whenever they have to be explained or defended. This is one reason why an SIO should maintain a record of their decisions in a policy file, a topic that is covered in Chapter 4.

KEY POINTS

- Effective identification, assessment and management of risk is an important part of all decision making.
- Risk management is about making benefits more likely than harms.
- Risk decisions are judged on how they were made/managed rather than just the outcome, and they should be properly recorded.
- More effort should go into managing risks that could cause the most harm.
- Risks are usually dynamic in a law enforcement environment and require dynamic monitoring and review.
- Risk assessments will identify control measures that involve a combination of all three types of risk, ie generic, specific and dynamic.
- Control measures are designed to lower and counter any element of risk.
- Assessments depend on thorough research and intelligence. It is important to keep an audit trail of all enquiries made and material used, and highly advisable to obtain hard copies of any intelligence reference material relied upon. This is preferable to reliance upon verbal briefings and information that can sometimes become misinterpreted or lack specific detail.
- Any lessons learnt (good or bad) can assist in any future similar risk management and decision making.

References

Alison, L and Rainbow, L (eds), *Professionalising Offender Profiling: Forensic and Investigative Psychology in Practice* (Routledge, 2011)

Asch, S, 'Forming Impressions on Personality' (1946) 41 *Journal of Abnormal and Social Psychology*, 258–90

Ask, K and Granhag, P, 'Hot Cognition in Investigative Judgements: The Differential Influence of Anger and Sadness' (2007) 31 *Law and Human Behavior*, 537–51

Ask, K and Granhag, P, 'Motivational Sources of Confirmation Bias in Criminal Investigations: The Need for Cognitive Closure' (2005) 2 *Journal of Investigative Psychology and Offender Profiling*, 43–63

Bar-Hillel, M, 'The Base Rate Fallacy in Probability Judgements' (1980) 44 *Acta Psychologica*, 211–33

Bernoulli, D, 'Specimen theoriae novae de mensura sortis [exposition of a new theory of the measurement of risk]' (1738) 5 *Commentari Academiae Scientrum Imperialis Petropolitanae*, 175–92

Brantingham, P and Brantingham, P, *Environmental Criminology* (1981)

Chabris, C, and Simons, D, 'The Invisible Gorilla' (1999) available at <http://theinvisiblegorilla.com/gorilla_experiment.html> (May 2015)

Chapman, L J, 'Illusory Correlation in Observational Report' (1967) 5 *Journal of Verbal Learning and Verbal Behavior*, 151–5

Cohen, L E and Felson, M, 'Social Change and Crime Rate Trends: A Routine Activity Approach' (1979) 44 *American Sociological Review*, 588–608

College of Policing, *Authorised Professional Practice* <http://www.app.college.police.uk/risk>,<https://www.app.college.police.uk/app-content/national-decision-model/>

Cornish, D and Clarke, R, *Understanding Crime Displacement—an application of Rational Choice Theory* (cited in ACPO, *Practice Advice on Analysis* (NPIA, 2008)), 12

Davies, M, 'Belief Persistence after Evidential Discrediting: The Impact of Generated versus Proved Explanations on the Likelihood of Discredited Outcomes' (1997) 33 *Journal of Experimental Social Psychology*, 561–78

Endsley, M R, 'Situational Awareness Global Assessment Technique (SAGAT)' Proceedings of the National Aerospace and Electronics Conference (NAECON) (IEEE, 1988), 789–95

Endsley, M R, 'Toward a Theory of Situation Awareness in Dynamic Systems' (1995) 37(1) *Human Factors*

Evans, J, *Bias in Human Reasoning: Causes and Consequences* (Erlbaum, 1989)

Gilovich, T, Vallone, R and Tversky, A, 'The Hot Hand in Basketball: On the Misperception of Random Sequences' (1985) 17 *Cognitive Psychology*, 295–314

Jacowitz, K and Kahneman, D, 'Measures of Anchoring in Estimation Tasks' (1995) 21 *Personality and Social Psychology Bulletin*, 1161–7

Kahneman, D, *Thinking, Fast and Slow* (Penguin, 2012)

Kahneman, D and Tversky, A, 'On the Psychology of Prediction' (1973) 80 *Psychological Review*, 237–51

Katz, S and Mazur, M A, *Understanding the Rape Victim: Synthesis of Research Findings* (John Wiley, 1979)

Keren, G and Tiegen, K, 'Yet Another Look at the Heuristics and Biases Approach', in D Koehler and N Harvey (eds), *Blackwell Handbook of Judgement and Decision Making* (Blackwell Publishing, 2004)

Klein, G A, Orasanu, J, Calderwood, R and Zsambok, C E (eds), *Decision Making in Action: Models and Methods* (Ablex, 1993)

Koriat, A, Lichtenstein, S and Fischoff, B, 'Reasons for Confidence' (1980) 6 *Journal of Experimental Psychology: Human Learning and Memory*, 107–18

Marshall, B and Alison, L, 'Stereotyping, Congruence and Presentation Order: Inter-pretative Biases in Utilising Offender Profiles' (in press) *Psychology, Crime and Law*

Moray, N, 'Where are the Snows of Yesteryear?', in D A Vincenzi, M Mouloua and P A Hancock (eds), *Human Performance, Situational Awareness and Automation: Current Research and Trends* (LEA, 2004), 1–31

Nickerson, R, 'Confirmation Bias: A Ubiquitous Phenomenon in Many Guises' (1998) 2 *Review of General Psychology*, 175–220

Nisbett, R, Borgida, E, Crandall, R and Reed, H, 'Popular Induction: Information is not Necessarily Informative', in D Kahneman, P Slovic and A Tversky (eds), *Judgement under Uncertainty: Heuristics and Biases* (Cambridge University Press, 1976)

Ormerod, T C, Barrett, E C and Taylor, P J, *Investigative sense-making in criminal contexts*. Proceedings of the seventh international NDM conference, Amster-dam, The Netherlands, ed J M C Schraagen (June 2005)

Oxford English Dictionary, 2nd edn revised (Oxford University Press, 2005)

Payne, J, Bettman, J and Luce, M, 'Behavioral Decision Research: An Overview', in M Birnbaum (ed), *Measurement, Judgment and Decision Making* (Academic Press, 1998)

Petty, R and Cacioppo, J, *Communication and Persuasion: Central and Peripheral Routes to Attitude Change* (Springer-Verlag, 1986)

Rossmo, D K, *Geographic Profiling* (1999)

Ross, L and Anderson, C, 'Shortcomings in the Attribution Process: On the Origins and Maintenance of Erroneous Social Assessments', in A Tversky, D Kahneman and P Slovic (eds), *Judgement under Uncertainty: Heuristics and Biases* (Cambridge University Press, 1982)

Ross, L, Lepper, M and Hubbard, M, 'Perseverance in Self-perception and Social Perception: Biased Attributional Process in the Debriefing Paradigm' (1975) 32 *Journal of Personality and Social Psychology*, 880–92

Sarter, N B and Woods, D D, 'Situation Awareness: A Critical but Ill-defined Phe-nomenon' (1991) 1 *International Journal of Aviation Psychology*, 45–57

Schwartz, N, Strack, F, Hilton, D and Naderer, G, 'Base Rates, Representativeness and the Logic of Conversation: The Contextual Relevance of "Irrelevant" Infor-mation' (1991) 9 *Social Cognition*, 67–84

Synder, M and Swann, W, 'Hypothesis-testing Processes in Social Interaction' (1978) 36 *Journal of Personality and Social Psychology*, 1202–12

Tversky, A and Kahneman, D, 'Judgement under Uncertainty: Heuristics and Biases' (1974) 185 *Science*, 1124–31

Tversky, A and Kahneman, D, 'Judgements of and by Representativeness', in D Kahneman, P Slovic and A Tversky (eds), *Judgement under Uncertainty: Heuristics and Biases* (Cambridge University Press, 1982)

Watson, P, 'On the Failure to Eliminate Hypotheses in a Conceptual Task' (1960) 12 *Quarterly Journal of Experimental Psychology*, 129–40

Zipf, G, *Human Behaviour and the Principle of Least Effort* (1949)

4

Policy Files and Key Decision Logs

4.1 **Introduction**

Policy files (or Key Decision Logs, 'KDLs' as they are sometimes known) are a vital element of an SIO's decision-making process. They are a record of key decisions and the rationale as to why they were made, or in some cases not made, at a particular time in an investigation.

Decision logs are an important decision support tool and can help explain ideas and considerations during decision making. They are used in most if not all major incidents and serious crime investigations where strategic and tactical decision making is deemed critical. In most forces there are standard formats and procedures for their completion contained within internal standard operating procedures..

Policy files and the decisions recorded within them can be scrutinised in many settings, such as in court, during public enquiries, internal reviews and Independent Police Complaints Commission (IPCC) investigations. The logs serve as an important audit trail and safety net for both decision maker and their organisation. They are the official and definitive record to be relied upon when having to recall and account for important decisions made.

Some believe the professionalism of a major investigation can be measured not only against the quality of the decisions made but also by the way in which they have been recorded. Decisions contained within KDLs that are properly recorded and auditable are a sure means of ensuring there are adequate methods of accountability in complex investigations and operational scenarios. How decisions are judged when they come under close scrutiny might depend on the meticulousness of entries made in policy files. It is not uncommon for an SIO to be called to account, eg at court, to explain a policy decision, at which time their policy file becomes a hugely important asset.

Long after an investigation has ended, a KDL can assist in the review of the quality of the management of an investigation by facilitating an understanding of investigative decisions. Recording the rationale behind decisions when they were made helps to explain why they were made, under what circumstances, who by and how. This is extremely useful when explaining to third parties much later about particular individual decisions. It can also show if and why decisions were amended or the course of an investigation was changed in the light of developing information and events.

The process of recording key decisions in a policy log assists the decision maker to carefully think through the potential risks, benefits, threat and harms involved and how important they are likely to be. This chapter is aimed at demystifying the topic of policy files or key decision logs, the completion of which is a key skill and one that must be learnt, developed and mastered.

4.2 **Key Decision Logs**

A key decision log (KDL) is an up-to-date record of the *key decisions* that affect the course of an investigation and the *reasons* or *rationale* behind them. A KDL is not a diary of the actions taken, nor is it meant to substitute for an investigation day/notebook, which are maintained separately.

KEY POINTS

- It is equally important to record decisions and reasons for *not* doing something as for doing something and to record any changes or retractions of previous decisions.
- The richer the decision log, the smoother the transition when a new SIO takes over.

4.2.1 **When to record a decision**

Only one KDL needs to be completed for each investigation to ensure a coordinated investigation strategy and cohesive overall management control. The KDL is not intended to capture each and every decision made during an investigation, but most certainly the key ones. Key decisions are those made that materially affect the course of the investigation. Routine investigative decisions and ones that merely reflect the implementation of the investigation procedure, for example, need not always be recorded. According to Sir Ronnie Flanagan (Review of Policing—Interim Report (2007), p 8), 'a distinction must be made between necessary and unnecessary bureaucracy and there must be greater discretion allowed for the exercise of professional judgement in making this decision'.

As a general rule, the importance and seriousness of the decision and circumstances are factors to consider, together with the extent of risk and likelihood of harm occurring. It must be remembered that recording a decision has enormous benefits and ultimately serves as a record to protect the decision maker and their organisation. These records can demonstrate long after a decision was made that various factors and options were rigorously considered, placing the SIO in a much stronger position to defend their actions if and when necessary. A written or electronic record is much more beneficial than relying upon memory or rough notes. Some cases come under scrutiny many years later and sometimes long after the original SIO has left the investigation and/or retired from the organisation.

4.3 **Three Key Elements**

There are three important elements to all policy file decisions and entries. These are:

1. Decision.
2. Reasoning and rationale behind the decision.
3. Information and resources that were known and available at the time the decision was made.

Point 3 is often neglected or omitted, yet it is all-important that decisions are put into context and combined with essential detail regarding what was *known* at the precise time they were made.

In support of this point, the IPCC stated the following:[1]

> Police officers and staff are accountable for the decisions and actions they take and are expected to provide a rationale for those decisions when questioned...we recognize that police operational decisions involve taking risks and in assessing decision-making we will focus on whether the decision was reasonable and proportionate in all circumstances (including the information and intelligence available and the operational policing context) as they existed at the time...in considering the decisions and actions of individual officers we recognize that police operational decisions often need to take into account competing objectives, timescales and limited resources.

4.4 **Policy Files Explained**

A policy file or 'decision log' is normally a bound book, A4 in size (and/or typed directly onto a case management system such as HOLMES) that is serial numbered on the front, internally paginated and labelled with details of the investigation, incident, victim or operation it refers to. It also includes details of the SIO and their deputy and the date the enquiry commenced and concluded. Each and every entry is sequentially numbered for ease of reference. More often, bound books are individually designed and produced specifically for the purpose with self-carbonating pages, instructions and prompts sometimes included within the first or final pages.

Each and every one of the SIO's **key** policies and decisions should be comprehensively recorded in the file in a legible and durable format, usually as one decision per page. This is done contemporaneously or as soon as practicable afterwards. Entries can be made at the SIO's dictation if a nominated entry/log maker, staff officer or designated assistant is working alongside them. All entries should be timed and dated (ie both when the decision was made and when the entry was made, if different), and signed by the person making the entry and the person making the decision (if not the SIO, the SIO should countersign to say they agree to the decision and have noted the entry).

In practical terms, the SIO usually begins recording decisions as initial note taking in a 'day' or 'notebook' during the busy first few hours of an enquiry. These can later be transferred into an official policy file at a more convenient time.

---

[1] IPCC, 'Learning the Lessons, Risk in Police Decision Making and Accountability in Operational Policing' (2011) Bulletin 14 available at <http://www.learningthelessons.org.uk/>.

It should be stressed there should be no undue delay in making or transferring decision entries into the correct file format. Every effort must be made to avoid an unwieldy backlog of decision details that will inevitably require transferring into a policy book, especially if there is to be a handover and smooth transition from one SIO to another (who needs to be aware of key decisions already made).

KEY POINTS

1. Large numbers of important policy decisions are usually made in the early stages of an investigation, which is why it is advisable to nominate someone else to record them at dictation so they are accurate and contemporaneous.
2. Countersigning policy entries made by others on behalf of the SIO shows good control and is a necessary quality assurance measure.

The systematic recording of the SIO's policies is one of the most important aspects of management for any complex investigation. This is an important skill to learn. Policy files need to be skilfully and methodically maintained to serve as an accurate record and audit trail of the rationale behind each and every decision made and to outline the overall management strategy and tactics for a serious crime investigation. An SIO does not have to work in isolation in deciding and recording policy. Consultation can be had with the enquiry management team or other experts, with details of that consultation recorded in the policy file. At the conclusion of an enquiry, the policy file must be retained and stored with the case papers, even if it has been typed and formally registered as a 'document' onto a system such as HOLMES.

KEY POINTS

1. Policy files help others (eg handover, review or cold case teams) understand the construction of decisions and key components of an investigation. They also serve as a permanent point of reference to rely upon in any subsequent court proceedings, public hearings, IPCC enquiries, inquests, etc.
2. Decisions recorded in the policy file should identify the decision maker. If someone other than the SIO makes a policy decision, the entry should be countersigned to confirm the SIO agrees and it is made on their behalf, showing they are in full control of the decision-making process.
3. A policy file is maintained on a regular basis throughout the life of the investigation, including up to the trial and beyond if an appeal or case review is likely.
4. Policy files are usually typed onto a system such as HOLMES and registered (eg Document 1, or D1). Care must be taken to ensure they are accurately recorded by proofreading and checking against original entries.

4.5 **Timing of Policy File Entries**

It is advisable to carry a blank KDL ready for immediate use. As the SIO is the person in charge of the investigation and usually makes all the key decisions, they should keep it in their possession or with the person nominated to make entries at dictation.

Entries can usually be recorded at an appropriate and practical time, bearing in mind the longer the gap between a decision and the time an entry is made may render it harder to remember the precise reason what the decision was and why. In reactive investigations it is reasonable for there to be a tolerable distance between the time a decision is made and the time a policy file entry is made. It may appear unauthentic and impractical for entries to be consistently written contemporaneously unless done so at dictation.

However, in fast-moving proactive-style investigations (such as suspect hunts and 'crimes in action') there **will** be an operational requirement to record all decisions and reasons contemporaneously. The dynamic nature of these incidents and operations will mean there is too much occurring in fast time to have the luxury of being able to play catch up, so all decisions need to be recorded as they happen. Ideally there will be either a computerised proactive action management system that records and links in with key decisions and/or there will be a speed typist/writer to record them as they are made sequentially.

If a policy file is not being entered (typed or scanned) onto a case management system such as HOLMES, then a hard (wet) copy should always be maintained.

KEY POINT

The precise time and date a key decision is made is of vital significance and must be correct and accurate, showing when it was made in context of the sequence of events. This is why it is necessary to have instant access to a reliable timepiece (and calendar) to ensure the time/date a decision is made is recorded correctly.

4.6 **Content of Policy File Entries**

The content of a policy file is a matter for the SIO's discretion. As a general rule the SIO, or a nominated person, systematically and timely records all key policy decisions. It is difficult to be too prescriptive about guidance on the construction of good policy file entries, other than to comment on the requirement to ensure that all decisions are recorded accurately and with sufficient explanatory reasons and rationale.

The structure of a policy file is outlined in the MIRSAP manual,[2] which states that policy file entries should be written in a decision/reason divided format

---

[2] ACPO, *MIRSAP Manual* (NCPE, 2005), 66–7 and 245.

with only one entry per page to run alongside a log of events. However, depending on preference, another option is to use a single policy file that combines a log of events and all decisions in a free-text narrative 'storybook' style.

This makes progress of the enquiry easier to follow and decisions remain in chronological order, flowing alongside events as they occur in sequence; it is also much simpler to complete. More importantly, decisions can be made alongside developments as and when they happen, which helps indicate information that was available at the time a decision was made. A typical combined page may look something like the example in Figure 4.1.

The content of a policy file generally includes all the key decisions affecting the management of the investigation. The entries might contain topics that can be divided into broad headings, for example:

Figure 4.1 Sample Policy File Entry

Consec no time/date	Log entry	Cross-ref
47. 13.20 hrs (date)	Decision: At 10.00 a.m. on (date) a forensic strategy meeting was held in the SIO's office at the incident room to discuss the current progress of examinations that have been submitted and results that are still awaited. The agenda and minutes of the meeting, including all details of those present, have been fully minuted and submitted into the incident room for registering as a 'document'. Reason: The SIO wished to review the progress of ongoing forensic examinations. Officer making entry: DCI M. Long Officer Making Decision: DCI Matt Long (SIO)	D.72 refers
48. 14.35 hrs (date)	Decision: A search warrant shall be obtained for the address of 53, Kings Road, Pimlico, and executed. An operational briefing order has been prepared (D.75). Reason: An intelligence log (D.74) rated B24 relates to evidential items of blood stained clothing belonging to the suspect N.7 Johnson believed to be living at the address. Research indicates this is the home of Johnson's half-brother Stephen Smith born 21/05/75. Officer making entry: DC Ian James (Loggist) Officer making decision (if different): D/C/I Matt Long (SIO)	Intelligence Log D.74 refers Operational order for search D.75

Investigation management

- Strategic considerations eg Gold Commander or PIP4 roles and primacy if other forces or agencies involved (eg Fire Service, Health and Safety Executive, LCSB).[3]
- Community and victim family impact/concern assessment and management.
- Appointment of SIO/DSIO.
- Appointment of key roles such as Crime Scene Manager (CSM), FLO, H-2-H coordinator, analysts, researchers, intelligence cells, Media Liaison Officers.
- Role of any designated/linked Silver Commanders (including terms of reference).
- Details of incident/enquiry room location and case management system.
- Management structure and enquiry teams.
- Increase/reduction/refusal for increase in staff numbers and budget allowance.
- Identification of key posts in MIR (eg Receiver, Disclosure Officer, indexers).
- Appointment of typing services—documents (eg recorded interviews) to be typed and arrangements.
- Details of any parallel investigation such as a Serious Case Review, Domestic Homicide Review or IPCC referral.

Finance and administration

- Appointment of finance/administration officer.
- Resources required, obtained, refused or withdrawn (eg. collaborative agreements, covert assets, part-time agency staff, specialists).
- Arrangements for payment and monitoring of staff overtime.
- Use of vehicles, mileage allowances, pool or hire cars.
- Booking on and off arrangements for staff, tours of duty, leave and public-holiday working arrangements.
- Management of welfare issues/health and safety.
- Management (eg timing) of briefings/debriefings and management meetings.
- Additional equipment required.

Enquiry management

- Identification, definition and parameters of any scene(s) and policy for security and eventual release.
- Decisions relating to witness statements (ie when required), personal description forms (PDFs), TIE categories and investigation criteria, alibi times and verification.
- Prioritisation of actions and returns policy.
- House to house (H-2-H) and CCTV trawl parameters.

---

[3] Gold Commanders, PIP 4s and other agency senior managers will also probably complete their own policy files/key decision logs.

- Deployment of mobile incident caravan.
- Criteria for intelligence research on nominals, eg TIEs.
- Witness evidence, witness identification and categories, eg vulnerable witnesses, interview strategies.
- Suspect identification, unsolicited comments, arrest and interview strategy.
- HOLMES indexing policy.
- Liaison arrangements with Crown Prosecution Service (CPS).
- Action management policy (eg how many per team, timescales for submission).

Lines of enquiry

- Outline of all main lines of enquiry (MLOE), indicating those with high priority.
- Current hypotheses details.
- Suspect hunt strategies/crimes in action management details.
- Variations on discontinued lines of enquiry (with reasons).
- Details of any declared suspects.
- Investigative strategies (eg witnesses, suspects, intelligence, passive data, communications data, H-2-H, TIEs, digital forensic).
- Important strategic or tactical decisions affecting the enquiry.
- Important events or changes to the direction of the investigation.
- Details of any linked incidents under consideration.
- Use of specialists/experts/NCA.

KEY POINT

When appropriate, decision log entries should incorporate an important feature of the NDM, ie assessment of threat and risk. (This subject is covered in more detail in Chapter 3.11.)

The precise wording of every policy decision is very important. Care should be taken to record entries so they convey with certainty the intended meaning and are clear and understandable. Details and facts need to be correct, including the spelling of names and places, to show the SIO has a keen eye for detail and is meticulous.

A policy file should enable anyone who is not directly involved in the investigation to be able to understand in clear language the decisions and thought processes of the decision maker. This will assist when having to explain or defend against any challenges made of decisions during judicial processes, reviews or reinvestigations.

4.6.1 **Cross-referencing**

Policy file entries may need cross-referencing against any 'stand-alone documents' that are in existence, eg if there is a separate arrest strategy, or CCTV recovery and viewing strategy, or forensic strategy, which may be lengthy separate entities/policy documents in their own right. It may be preferable to make reference to their existence (and which version is referred to) rather than try to cram all the details into a single entry (as most pre-printed policy books only allow for single-page entries). The policies themselves can be completed in a format similar to a usual policy file entry, with the decision and accompanying reasons included, signed and dated by the SIO, then registered and loaded onto HOLMES. The recording of such a cross-referencing process provides reassurance that any 'stand-alone' strategy document has been commented upon and noted in the main policy file.

If there are multiple entries focusing on the same topic or subject area, it may also be useful to cross-reference between them for consistency and ease of reference. Some policy books allow the subject matter to be categorised using headings in a grid format or index which is printed at the rear of the book. This is to assist others not familiar with the policy log to locate decisions within the book when and where necessary, eg during reviews or when the course of the investigation changes or decisions made earlier are changed. It can also be used to group topics under headings to locate all the decisions that may, for example, relate to media, victims, witnesses, CCTV, forensic, etc.

4.7 **'Sensitive' Policy Files**

As a general rule all members of an enquiry team need to be made aware of the SIO's key decisions and be allowed unfettered access to the policy file. The contents should be shared with members of the investigation so everyone understands the direction of the enquiry and why certain decisions have been made, or not made. This is made much simpler if the policy decisions are quickly transferred onto HOLMES, normally under the document reference of 'D1', making digital access for everyone that much simpler. The log belongs to the investigation and is available to the investigation team, but care should be taken regarding access where sensitive and confidential material is concerned.

An additional 'sensitive' policy file might be required if there are confidential matters and/or material that needs to be protected due to its sensitive nature (eg outlining covert tactics or covert human intelligence source (CHIS) information). If this kind of policy file is created, the level of access must be determined as a safeguard. The first entry of a sensitive policy file may have to state that only the SIO, Deputy SIO and Office Manager are permitted access to the contents. If using HOLMES, restrictive access levels can be agreed and arranged through the account manager.

It is worth remembering that some sensitive material may have to be preserved for a long period of time, including after an investigation has ended. Sensitive documents, important as they are, often end up stored in 'libraries' (ie storage of archived case material), for which long-term access can be difficult to control. Once protected with restrictive markings on a computerised system such as HOLMES, it becomes less susceptible to being lost and there is a clear audit trail of those who have accessed it.

It should be noted, however, that any sensitive policy file must be brought to the attention of the CPS and prosecuting counsel in accordance with the CPIA. This is usually done by direct consultation with the CPS case lawyer concerned.

4.8 **Disclosure**

In most cases, in agreement with the CPS, policy files are not disclosed to any external parties without their consent, or on the instruction of a court order. As a general rule, defence legal teams do not get access to policy files; nor do judges or bereaved family solicitors etc. However, bodies such as the IPCC will usually gain access to them in order to conduct their own investigation.

CHECKLIST—POLICY FILES

- Used for recording key strategic and tactical decisions.

- Contain 3 x elements: (i) decision; (ii) reason; (iii) information known.

- An accurate timepiece is useful for recording precise times decision are made.

- Only one policy file is used per enquiry (plus a 'sensitive' one if used).

- Officer recording decision must sign and date each entry, countersigned by SIO (if different to decision maker).

- Stand-alone or 'other' documents may be referred to in an entry with their sequential indexed number.

- Self-carbonating pages in the file can be removed for speeding up written decisions being transferred onto HOLMES.

- Policy entries should be made available to enquiry teams except those that are 'sensitive'.

- Contents are not usually disclosed to other parties (eg defence teams) unless directed by the CPS or court order.

- They are maintained throughout the entire duration of the enquiry and case disposal.

- Arrangements should be made for the safe and lasting storage of the policy file and any separate sensitive file.

Initial Response

5.1 **Introduction**

The key to a successful reactive crime investigation usually lies in an effective initial response. This involves efficient resource deployment, gathering and recording of accurate and detailed information, making the right decisions, taking the right action and securing evidence. This process starts the very first moment an initial call or report is received by a call taker and continues with subsequent attendance and management of the crime scene(s) and investigation.

The initial response to a serious incident usually becomes the focus of media and public attention (and public enquiries) if things go wrong. This is where a law enforcement agency risks its reputation if mistakes are made, which in turn can have an adverse effect on any relationship with the public, the very source from which assistance is often required.

It is fundamental that all those involved in an initial response adopt the right approach. There is often only one chance to get it right. Initial assessments and decisions made by or fed back to call handlers/resource despatchers and supervisors determines how an incident is graded, treated and prioritised as to seriousness, urgency and resourcing. This is often during a period referred to as the 'golden hour(s)'.

Any assumptions at this crucial stage need to be reviewed, as there can be a tendency to 'buy into' the easy option by treating an incident report as having far less importance than it requires—for example, treating a missing person report as a low or medium risk when it is indicative of homicide or child sexual exploitation (CSE). Precursor or linked incidents that aren't given the importance and attention they deserve to prevent an escalation into something more serious are another example.

One consideration that may not be so obvious when dealing with the initial response to any incident, and of prime importance, is the training and experience of personnel. No opportunity should be lost in applying a methodical and professional approach to a suitable case, even if it turns out to be insignificant. This will afford staff the opportunity of becoming familiar with using key procedures and rehearsing a professional approach.

KEY POINTS

- Checklists are useful references for ensuring nothing is forgotten or missed. Surgeons and commercial pilots use them and the trick is to treat them as guidelines not tramlines. Each case is always unique.
- *'The first 24 hours, the first clue, the first line of enquiry, the first breakthrough . . .'*—in reactive crime investigation the first can mean everything to the chances of success.

5.2 **Teamwork Approach**

A Senior Investigating Officer (SIO) assumes responsibility for investigations into crimes that are of utmost gravity and likely to contain many complex and connected decisions, actions, challenges and procedures. A number of constituent parts need to come together in the initial stages, during which an essential ingredient for success is *teamwork*. This relates to the combined effort between a group of professionals who join forces to produce an efficient and effective response.

Each role and stage of the process connects in a chain that is only as strong as its weakest link. An SIO is not likely to be involved initially, but as soon as they are they must set the tone for a teamwork approach by leading, managing and coordinating activity. Momentum and progress should be consolidated and maintained to provide the foundations for a coordinated investigation. This requires a shared sense of purpose, positive professional attitudes and pooling of skills and expertise.

Effective teams acknowledge those around them who have complementary skills. Effective cooperation and communication with the sharing of information and knowledge help bring everything together to achieve a common goal.

5.3 **'Golden Hour(s)' Principle**

The 'golden hour(s)' principle derives from the medical profession. It is used as a basic rule in major trauma cases, and means that patients who are treated quickly are more likely to make a full recovery.

The same rule applies to the initial response to a reported crime. There are clear benefits in a speedy and effective response, as prompt actions and decisions have far-reaching advantages, which is what the golden hour(s) principle refers to.

The golden hour(s) is a time when evidence is fresh and easier to detect (eg blood is still wet), memories are still sharp, witnesses are likely to be at their most cooperative and offenders nervous or unguarded with any lies and false alibis being at their most vulnerable. This is why it is important to capitalise on all the available investigative opportunities during the golden hour(s).

The initial stage begins after the first report or contact to call management units, public enquiry desks, or via reports to staff or agencies. Correct incident categorisation and handling (be it crime or not) significantly helps produce the best outcome. Many crimes are quickly resolved through prompt and decisive resource dispatch: locating offenders, witnesses, seizing CCTV footage or finding and preserving forensic evidence while still available.

5.4 'Five Building Blocks' Principle

The *Core Investigative Doctrine*[1] and the *Murder Investigation Manual*[2] (MIM) describe the Five Building Blocks Principle that underpins the reactive phase and initial stages of an investigation. Visually, they have been made very simple to remember. (see diagram below). Headings contained within the 'blocks' are self-explanatory and covered within this handbook, particularly when considering the initial actions (see the 'First responders—10 x "golden hour" actions' in Chapter 5.7.2).

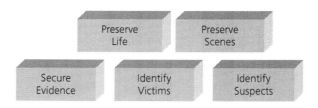

5.5 Call Handling and Recording

A 'call taker' automatically becomes an important participant in the investigation chain and can immediately and positively influence the outcome of an enquiry. Their role in obtaining, receiving and recording vital information, sometimes at the point of first delivery, is vital.

When a call or report is handled skilfully, important information can be obtained to launch and direct initial lines of enquiry. Depending on the circumstances, it is advisable to obtain a copy of any record or log made to review and scrutinise, so that vital information is not missed. For example, if a witness makes contact, any notes made by the receiver are likely to contain a first account of what the witness has seen or heard and this detail should be examined carefully. Information contained in phone messages and recordings can be omitted from incident logs or not relayed correctly; there may also be interim recordings of emergency calls made before being transferred which are also worth obtaining and analysing.

Incident logs sometimes include running commentaries about crime incidents and can reveal useful information about the reportee, as well as being a contemporaneous record of the call taker's actions and decisions, including resources dispatched, other agencies informed, with names, contact details and times. These records are a useful source from which to begin raising initial actions and commence an investigation.

---

[1] ACPO, *Core Investigative Doctrine* (NCPE, 2005).
[2] ACPO, *Murder Investigation Manual* (NCPE, 2006).

5.5.1 **Role of call takers/handlers**

This role is both reactive and proactive. Call takers can be inundated with large numbers of routine calls under high-pressure conditions. Hopefully, they are professional enough to differentiate those of a more urgent nature. Call handlers are not just a channel of communication; they are one of the first to become involved in the very early stages of decision making and the investigation chain.

Call takers are in the best position to make initial decisions, handle and extract useful information and record contemporaneous details. This is the start of the investigative process and the point when a wealth of information and intelligence is available. They are entrusted with the task of identifying, linking and grading important facts and information, such as precursor incidents, that can help solve a case and prevent further serious offending. For example, many serial and dangerous offenders spend time researching their victims, following them and spending time in targeted locations looking for suitable opportunities before they commit a crime. When these matters are reported there is a danger the classic term 'suspicious circumstances' is applied and the importance of the incident goes unrecognised.

Call takers have to classify reported information into categories and determine the level of response. When the initial report has a title attached (eg reported 'suicide'), there is a danger they will automatically be treated as such. This may create a preconceived notion that it is what it has been recorded as, when it might actually be something else (ie homicide). This emphasises the importance of the role of the call taker.

Like all good investigators they should adopt an investigative mindset, using open questions to elicit information and the 5WH principles (Who? What? Where? When? Why? and How?). A call may be the only opportunity to extract information from a caller, who may also be a victim, witness or offender. Most callers have a wealth of information of benefit to the investigation, and need to be asked relevant questions without any hastiness to end the conversation.

KEY POINTS

- Precise words spoken by a reportee may prove vital to the investigation. This information and any recording or logging mechanisms should be carefully checked and in most cases transcribed.
- Call takers and first responders must remember that the person reporting the crime might be an offender and recording what they say is vitally important . . . because the next best thing to a confession is a provable lie.

The capture and review of any emergency call is potentially a vital piece of evidence. The careful transcription (word by word) of the call must be obtained and checked against subsequent accounts or statements made in order to identify inconsistencies. A first account is usually the most accurate and truthful. At times background noise or activity may provide vital clues, and comments made by offenders or victims still at the scene can be captured on record.

A further point of note is the provision of advice on basic scene preservation and evidence recovery wherever possible. It may be difficult to protect crime scenes at this stage; however, advice from a call taker can reduce the risk of contamination and assist in preserving evidence. The person calling may be a crime scene themselves (particularly if they are victims of sex offences). For this reason the call handler should be skilled in forensic awareness and witness care as part of their training and development.

Checklist—Basic call-handler duties

- Create a running 'incident log'.

- Assess type/importance of the information and urgency of response/grade.

- Don't assume the incident is what it is reported as.

- Identify links in calls and information to other incidents.

- Consider whether there are any communication or language issues.

- Prioritise the safety of the caller, victim and other potential victims, and give appropriate advice.

- Obtain as much factual, accurate and detailed information as possible (eg description of offender, direction of travel, vehicle or weapons used).

- Adopt an investigative mindset (and use the 5WH principles).

- Consider the caller may be a victim, offender or significant witness (exact wording used must not be distorted or recorded incorrectly).

- If the caller is a child, only ask questions to gain sufficient information to deploy officers.

- If suspect is present, keep line open to record any evidence.

- Deploy appropriate resources to key points quickly and confirm attendance.

- Deploy any specialist resources (eg scent dogs), armed officers, paramedics.

- Arrange circulations and alerts to adjoining regions/agencies.

- Provide basic advice on preservation of any crime scene (which could be the caller themselves, who may want to clean up, which could destroy evidence).

- Activate any pre-prepared contingency plan (eg one set by an SIO).

- Notify/dispatch a PIP 2 investigator.

- Upon confirmation, inform an on-call SIO.

- Keep all logs, tapes and other documentary evidence.

- Don't provide any investigative details to the media or unauthorised persons.

KEY POINTS

- Call handlers should carefully consider what/where/how/when resources can be best utilised (eg some offenders have pre-planned escape routes).
- Deployment of police helicopters over crime scenes may attract curious onlookers and their downdraught can disrupt outdoor crime scenes.

5.5.2 **Reports to officers/public enquiry counters**

Similar principles apply as to those for call handlers. An added advantage is that the person reporting is likely to be physically present, although some individuals may refuse to provide their personal details. In such a case, the recipient should record all they can about them—full description, clothing worn, who they are in company with, vehicles, direction of travel, etc. This may assist in later establishing their full identity and conducting a follow-up interview (CCTV may also assist).

The reportee could also be involved in the incident or the perpetrator. If there are reasonable grounds to suspect their involvement, then consideration should be given to having them arrested without warrant (eg under s 24 PACE). It is not uncommon for offenders to speak to officers or make reports at or near the scenes of crime, in order to appear helpful, get themselves an alibi, return to find out what the police response is or even offer themselves as witnesses. Some even court the media (eg Ian Huntley during the Soham investigation who voluntarily spoke to the police and media before he was arrested for the murder of Holly Wells and Jessica Chapman in August 2002). This is why it so vital to record as much accurate detail as possible (same rule again—the next best thing to a confession is a provable lie).

KEY POINT

Many public enquiry counters and reception areas are covered by audio and CCTV equipment. Early recovery and viewing might prove extremely useful.

5.6 **Initial Responders**

A major crime scene, particularly homicide, is perhaps one of the most important any officer will ever attend and may happen only once or twice during their service. To begin with, they are the initial investigating officer(s) responsible for making key decisions until assistance arrives. This includes making and relaying an initial assessment back to their colleagues. A whole host of critical decisions and procedures depends upon the effectiveness and professionalism of first responders.

They should be encouraged to remain sceptical of accepting what a call taker or reporting source has labelled an incident. They have to challenge assumptions, believe no one and check everything. In other words they are expected to apply the ABC principle:

> **A**—Assume nothing
> **B**—Believe nothing
> **C**—Challenge/check everything

Attending officers are expected to utilise their practical and investigative skills and good situational awareness (see Chapter 3.2.5) to gain and interpret as much information as possible. Aspects that initially seem irrelevant can gain much more significance later on, so all actions and information must be recorded and if relevant, are always potentially 'disclosable'. Investigators may find it useful to recover the actual recording made of any radio transmissions to confirm exact wording and detail of information obtained and passed on by first responders, and to view any body-worn recording devices, eg camcorders.

Rarely is the first attending officer ever a witness to the actual incident (although they might become a significant witness post-attendance), so they have to depend on what they see and hear plus their training, intuition and good SA—situational awareness (see Chapter 3). Whatever the circumstances, response officers need to remain composed and begin the preliminary investigation. All their senses must come alive, noting what they see, hear, touch/feel and smell (odours, eg exhaust fumes, gas, perfume/aftershave, bleach, alcohol, drugs, tobacco) that may prove useful to the investigation. They are the first members of the investigation team to arrive on site and are in the best position to gather information at a time when it is most likely to be available.

Initial responders (including crime investigators) need to be alert and use their 'sixth' sense to notice things that seem significant and unusual and apply the principle ('Just Doesn't Look Right'). They should try and spot and search for useful investigative material before it gets lost or spoilt, and note, recover or preserve it. Examples could include items of furniture that seem to have been recently damaged, signs of a struggle or unusual neatness/tidiness, trails of blood, unusual behaviour and comments, forced windows and doors, lights that are switched on or off, dry shapes of a missing vehicle set against an otherwise wet road or driveway, or footwear and tyre marks.

Observing and noting what is happening at the time of arrival—such as persons present and the atmosphere and mood (watching the watchers), descriptions, things being talked about or said and who by, persons or vehicles that seem to leave suddenly—this is all part of the bigger picture that needs observing and noting by first responders. It is this type of information that often diminishes quickly and for which there is usually only one opportunity to capture.

KEY POINTS

1. There have been numerous cases in which the person reporting the crime has been the offender. Responders should remember this fact.
2. Initial responders can take images of things they think might be of evidential value but which may be removed or unavailable later for forensic examination (eg injuries on a victim who is found alive but later dies in hospital).
3. People frequently use their own recording devices (eg on smartphones) when they see something of interest. Officers, including SIOs, should be mindful they too may get filmed with the images being quickly uploaded onto social media platforms.

It may be useful for investigators and SIOs to know that a pneumonic often taught and mentioned in manuals of guidance for initial responders to help when conducting initial assessments at incident scenes is SAD CHALETS:

S—Survey (make observations, eg position of a body and any possible injuries)

A—Assess (determine what has happened, eg murder or natural death)

D—Disseminate (relay information to those who need to know)

C—Casualties (determine approximate number and their condition)

H—Hazards (eg terrain, public disorder, weather, dangerous buildings)

A—Access (best routes for emergency vehicles and supporting resources)

L—Location (using landmarks, street names, buildings, etc)

E—Emergency services (present and/or required)

T—Type of incident

S—Safety (all aspects of health and safety risk assessment)

KEY POINTS

1. Initial responders and resource dispatchers should decide what/where/how and when resources should be put to best use, eg if suspects are making good their escape, covering possible exit routes instead of going to the scene.
2. 'Flash' or 'hasty' searches need to be systematic and methodical to swiftly identify and locate useful evidence, victims, suspects or witnesses. Details should be recorded to assist fully managed (eg CSI and forensic) searches later (see also Chapter 6).
3. Public areas and transport links such as taxi ranks, buses, tram and train stations may need checking (including their CCTV systems) and hospitals in cases involving violence.
4. Scene preservation is important; so, too, is tracking offenders and pinpointing their direction of travel. Scent dogs can be used but need deploying early.

5.6.1 Preservation of life

One of the five building blocks is the preservation of life (see Chapter 5.4), and the first priority, if applicable, is always to make a scene safe and preserve life. A rapid response to any crime scene carries an overriding responsibility of searching for and attending to the medical and welfare needs of any member of the public, particularly victim(s). If there is any doubt as to death or possible signs of life, first aid and resuscitation techniques should be administered and medical assistance summoned. Due to significant advances in medical science and emergency techniques, casualties who have suffered serious trauma can often be treated in order to make full recovery.

Only when absolutely necessary should initial responders make an exploratory examination of a deceased person for wounds, injuries or signs of recent trauma, and if so it must be very minor in nature and limited to exposed parts of the body (ie head, face, neck and forearms). The presence of a Crime Scene Investigator (CSI) and Force Medical Examiner (FME) should be considered and in any event it is always useful to take photographs before and after any disturbance and make sketch plans of the scene. Protective gloves should be worn and substantial disturbance of any forensic evidence avoided. The SIO must be notified if this has taken place. Normally it is unnecessary, as the relevant information can be obtained from medical staff who have certified or confirmed death and in so doing will have had a chance to look at the body.

Any attempt to check clothing or possessions for identification (which should be avoided if possible) must be disclosed. This action could either destroy vital evidence or prove misleading by giving, for example, the appearance that a theft/ robbery has taken place.

KEY POINT

Checking for (further) victims, providing first aid and attempting resuscitation are of paramount importance. If there is the slightest doubt, the presumption must be that a person is still alive. Some victims give the appearance of being dead while still alive because their life signs are hardly noticeable, eg in hypothermia cases.

5.7 **Health and Safety**

Crime scenes can pose a range of hazards that, because of the attending spontaneity, require dynamic risk assessments. Examples include:

- Dangerous offenders and/or volatile crowds, difficult onlookers (rubber-neckers), communities or individuals.
- Decomposing bodies or body parts.
- Liquid blood and body fluids.
- Animals, infestations and parasites.
- Fire, water, electricity or gas hazards.
- Drugs and drug paraphernalia, eg syringes, drug production equipment.
- Hazardous chemicals.
- Explosives, improvised explosive devices (IEDs), biological, radiological and nuclear agents.
- Unsafe buildings or materials.
- Firearms and other dangerous weapons.
- Sharp items.
- Difficult terrain or dangerous environments and weather.
- Diseases and poisons.

Generic risk assessments usually exist for attendance at crime scenes. However, wherever possible advice should be sought and personal protective equipment worn if required. At a major crime scene, once cordons are in place, standard protection consists of a scene suit with hood up, face mask, overshoes and protective gloves.

KEY POINT

The SIO should be mindful of staff welfare when checking on first responders who may still be on duty at a crime scene, particularly those who have been guarding cordons for any length of time in inclement weather.

5.7.1 **Preserving crime scenes**

Another of the five building blocks is preserving crime scenes. This can be separated into three key elements known as the 'ISP' principle:

```
I—IDENTIFY
S—SECURE
P—PROTECT
```

All areas relating to a crime scene(s), once identified, have to be sealed and
secured. A key task of initial responders is to prevent disturbance and unauthorised persons entering and/or disturbing and contaminating crime scenes. This
includes supervisory staff, unless there is an urgent operational need. The three
procedures are outlined below and also explained in Chapter 6.

1. **Identify**. Depending on the circumstances, there may be more than one
   crime scene and the initial response may identify and deal with just one of
   a number. The identification of all other potential crime scenes can originate
   from information, observations or CCTV, etc. If there is more than one
   scene, each should be sequentially numbered, eg Scene 1 (S1), Scene 2 (S2)
   and so on. A list of what may constitute a crime scene (such as a location,
   victim, escape route, vehicle(s) used, attack sites, suspects) is outlined in
   Chapter 6.
2. **Secure**. There are a number of ways to secure crime scenes and much depends
   on the circumstances and environment. In serious or complex cases, cordons
   are used with high-visibility tape to mark out the sterile area, and uniformed
   staff restricting and controlling access. Indoor scenes are generally easier to
   secure than outdoor locations, which need more resources to keep sterile.
3. **Protect**. In addition to safety issues, officers should try to prevent any disturbance and interference from the public, media, weather, animals, etc. A common approach path (CAP) should be established for a single access and exit
   route, which needs to be the route least likely to have been used by the
   offender(s).

Any item at a scene can be of evidential value and nothing should be touched
or moved. If, however, something of a physical nature is in immediate danger
of being lost, destroyed or contaminated, steps should be taken to protect or
recover the item to preserve it. Removal should be conducted with minimum
disturbance, carefully recording the exact position and location of the exhibit.
If possible, it should be photographed in position (situ) first. This includes fragile
material such as footprints, blood marks, and footwear or tyre impressions in
mud/soil that may be destroyed by weather. Improvisation may be necessary to
cover and protect items using available 'make-do' objects until the right equipment arrives.

Once preserved and contained, nothing further need be done until a CSI arrives. Other pieces of evidence can be sought and collected, including details such as eyewitness accounts, information offered, house-to-house (H-2-H) and CCTV enquiries.

It is sometimes difficult to determine exact boundaries for scene cordons and preservation. If indoors, the task is much easier; outdoors, however, there are added complications such as the weather, general public, vehicular traffic, terrain and location. As a general rule, it is better to make cordons as wide as possible, using natural boundaries, as they can always be reduced later. It is not always possible the other way around.

KEY POINT

In serious sexual assaults there are specific guidelines for dealing with victims, such as the use of early evidence kits (EEK). This enables first response officers to quickly and effectively recover forensic material from victims before a medical examination takes place that could otherwise be lost.

5.7.2 Golden hour actions

There are different procedures for responding to different types of incidents. The five building blocks mentioned earlier contain useful headings (preserve life and scenes, secure evidence, identify witnesses and suspects) from which to produce a quick guide of ten basic golden hour actions for first responders at serious crime incidents.

Checklist—First responders—10 x 'golden hour(s)' actions

1. Initial assessment—(use ABC principle and senses of sight, hearing and smell), make a situation report using 5WH format (eg What happened? What resources are required? What officer/emergency services safety risks are there? Where? Who? When? Why? How?).

2. Victims—search for, identify, support, attend to and administer first aid where necessary, summon medical assistance. SAFEGUARD their WELFARE.

3. ISP crime scenes and any physical evidence (eg CCTV, weapons, mobile phones, clothing, blood marks, footprints, vehicles, escape routes).

4. Identify entry/exit route with one point of entry and designated CAP and rendezvous point (RVP). Use barrier tape for cordons. Prevent unauthorised access and cross-contamination and commence incident scene log(s).

---

5. Identify persons reporting the crime and potential witnesses; separate and obtain first accounts. Ensure 'first descriptions' are accurately recorded. Consider tactfully treating as crime scene (eg obtaining outer clothing).

6. Identify suspects and consider early arrest. Identify likely escape route/direction of travel and means (eg public transport, car or on foot) and any flash (eg scent dog) searches. Check key locations and confirm identity of those found nearby. Treat suspects as crime scenes.

7. Make initial enquiries (eg H-2-H type) and record all details, including who spoken to, vehicles present and anything that appears unusual at and around the scene. Include descriptions of people and clothing.

8. Intelligence—seek/record all useful investigative information.

9. Victim's family/local community—make contact and establish needs, concerns and expectations—keep informed.

10. Log details and times of all activities, actions taken, when, why, how, where and by whom.

5.7.3 Basic crime scene kits

Basic crime scene kits better equip staff to preserve evidence and minimise the chances of contamination. These should be carried by all operational personnel and as a minimum contain:

- cordon/barrier tape
- 2 x pairs of disposable overshoes
- 2 x pairs of disposable gloves
- scene log forms
- exhibit bags and boxes plus labels
- tape for sealing bags and scissors
- EEK for sexual offences
- first-aid kit
- aide-memoire of actions

5.8 Emergency Responders

Paramedics and fire crews attending scenes require debriefing soon afterwards as they have a habit of leaving to redeploy. They are often the first at incident scenes and create and keep their own records of attendance and involvement, including the circumstances of what they find and what they are told upon arrival. Sometimes they obtain or hear accounts from victims, witnesses and even suspects. In some instances, therefore, consideration may need to be given to treating them as significant witnesses, depending on the extent of what they have seen or heard.

Emergency services personnel are not trained investigators and must be debriefed for relevant information. Details to obtain include how they gained entry to the scene (indoors or outdoors), where they have been and what they have touched or moved. They should be asked questions along the lines of: Who was present? What did they see? What did any victims or witnesses say? What medical intervention was made and what items were left behind at the scene? (ie 5WH principles). In some circumstances they take their own images and create their own records, which could contain valuable information about who was around the scene (eg the fire service may take photographs to assist their own assessment and investigation into a fire, which could contain details of an arsonist, an associate or a significant witness). Some fire and ambulance service vehicles carry their own CCTV which investigators should make a priority to seize and examine.

KEY POINTS

- Medical personnel (eg paramedics) have primacy at crime scenes until victims have been treated (preservation of life is the first priority).
- Medical teams can unavoidably disturb and/or contaminate potential evidence. This should be considered when interpreting a crime scene. Resuscitation devices such as defibrillator pads cause injuries or marks which, together with any discarded medical equipment, need accounting for, including establishing what they have touched (eg leaving blood traces on a light switch they have accessed to try and improve visibility).
- Sensible and pragmatic judgement should apply when seeking to recover trace evidence from emergency services' personnel, clothing, footwear or vehicles, eg ambulances. Local agreements usually provide guidance on what should/should not be retained or impounded for forensic examination. Usually samples can be taken without disrupting the ability of the emergency resources to continue providing a normal service. If ambulances and/or rapid response vehicles are located within a cordon, a path can be cleared for their release and tyre impressions or photographs taken prior to their release or at some later stage for elimination purposes. Normally if victims are placed within ambulances, the only items that should be considered seizing are blankets; it is not sensible to seize equipment needed for other patients, such as defibrillators.

5.9 **Supervisory Officer Duties**

Responsibility for command and control at a major crime scene is usually initially assumed by a supervisory officer. They need to attend quickly to provide assistance and support to initial responders and debrief them. Continuous contact should be maintained with any communications room supervisor and an assessment made as to the nature of the incident and an SIO can check with them to confirm what has/has not been completed.

Checklist—Supervisory officer duties

1. Attend scene, assume command and control.

2. Debrief those in attendance and determine scale, nature and type of incident.

3. Provide situation report to/update control room.

4. Decide whether to declare a critical or major incident.

5. Check any victim's welfare and medical needs are being taken care of.

6. Check and review all responsibilities and 'golden hour(s)' actions of first officers attending have been completed correctly.

7. Establish what disturbance, if any, has been made at the crime scene, eg door/windows locked/open, lights on/off, body moved or cut down, fire on/off.

8. Check all potential crime scenes have been subject to ISP requirements.

9. Check if essential resources are being or have been contacted, eg Senior Detective, CSI and SIO.

10. Identify any health and safety risks associated with circumstances and location and introduce adequate control measures and check/monitor staff welfare.

11. Make assessment of the number and type of resources required, what equipment, other agencies, specialist resources and contingencies is/are required, eg emergency lighting, scene tent, mobile police station, catering, extra staff, firearms officers, public order response teams/tactical advisers, back-up staff, dog handlers, road policing unit, Media Liaison Officer, CSI(s), accredited investigators, local authority departments.

12. Formulate initial plan for dealing with management of the scene and initiate fast-track actions, eg arrest of offenders, scent dog searches, road blocks, circulation of persons, descriptions or vehicles, arrest teams, custody arrangements. (This does not mean the supervisor should enter and review the scene. The least disruption of the crime scene, the better.)

13. Allocate duties, tasks, responsibilities and priorities. Ensure all parties are briefed as to their role.

14. Liaise with any emergency services that may be in attendance and coordinate the combined response.

15. Make assessment and survey of area for correct scene parameters and ensure adequate inner/outer cordons are in place that are staffed and secure.

16. Establish and/or review an RVP and/or forward command post (FCP).

17. Review appointment of scene loggist(s), ensure they are positioned at RVP, fully briefed and equipped with appropriate forms and documentation.

18. Review most suitable entry/exit point into scene, ie least likely/likeliest route taken by offender(s).

19. Check whether there are any other crime scenes and ensure adequate supervision.

20. Ensure collection of details of all those who are/were present (if large crowds, consider use of evidence gatherers and/or visual images—remembering offenders or significant witnesses may still be around).

21. Ensure all staff have recorded their actions and involvement.

22. Ensure next of kin and immediate family of victims are notified of their condition/death and are receiving adequate support from the police (if homicide, arrange suitably qualified Family Liaison Officer (FLO) without delay).

23. Remove unauthorised persons from inside cordons.

24. Ensure any potential witnesses are identified and details obtained.

25. Ensure any exhibits identified are forensically preserved and confirm appropriate continuity relating to finding, location and storage.

26. If victim conveyed to hospital, despatch officer to accompany them to note anything said and ensure evidence recovery (clothing etc).

27. If suspect(s) is(are) in custody, confirm arrangements for custody reception, avoidance of cross-contamination and collection of clothing and samples.

28. Make arrangements for completion of a community impact assessment.

29. Consider issuing preliminary media release and monitor and control media intrusion and interest, ensure no statements given by staff (utilise Media Liaison Officer at earliest opportunity).

30. Identify all staff who have been involved in the initial response and ensure they attend a 'hot debrief' and arrange collection of all their notes.

31. Notify and brief the on-call Senior Investigator and/or SIO.

32. Make comprehensive record of all actions taken and decisions made.

33. Consider logistical resilience in all designated roles and tasks.

34. Consider early allocation of roles to begin investigation management, such as Exhibits Officer, and where the enquiry might be initially run from.

5.10 Debriefing Initial Responders

An important task is to arrange the time and place for a hot debrief of all those involved in the initial response. This should be arranged within the first two to four hours and before any staff leave or go off-duty. This time frame allows the SIO to travel to the crime scene and liaise with the officer in charge (OIC) to ensure all procedures and correct measures are in place. The SIO can then relocate to a debriefing point, which could be a local station or portable command unit in remote cases.

Once more, the importance of the ABC principle is relevant (Assume nothing, Believe nothing, Challenge/check everything). Mistakes and errors can and do happen and it is essential they are discovered quickly. There has to be a clear audit trail of any remedial action taken to demonstrate transparency and honesty of purpose.

Officers attending should firstly complete a debrief sheet outlining their involvement and attach a copy of any notes, pocket/casebook entry or statement which should all be handed in at the debriefing session. It is good practice for the SIO to carry a pack of debrief sheets for distribution (see Chapter 1.5 'Checklist—SIO's basic tool kit').

The SIO, or at least a senior detective, should conduct a structured debrief ensuring all documents and information are gathered. This practice will ensure that every piece of evidence is obtained and secured from the outset. The process can also be used to identify good practice or highlight areas of concern. A record of the debriefing should be made and used to inform any later enquiry team briefing (see also Chapter 9).

KEY POINT

When debriefing, it is *essential* to encourage people to be open and honest. Mistakes cannot be rectified if they are concealed to keep someone 'out of trouble'. Initial responders need encouraging to be truthful and willing to speak up about what actions they did or did not take. Inevitably some won't, which is why it is important to apply the ABC principle.

5.11 Crime Investigator Responsibilities

Investigators should aim for early attendance at reactive crime scenes to assist with the commencement or handover of the investigation. When dealing with certain types of enquiry or serious crime, it may be policy to deploy a supervisor or senior detective to assume the role of Investigating Officer (IO) or Senior Investigating Officer (SIO) and take command. The initial investigator is nonetheless expected to get a full briefing themselves and commence preliminary investigations, obtain and review all the pertinent information and begin a list of actions that have been or need to be conducted. They are often the person initially in overall charge of the investigation.

Initial assessments should determine whether to hand over to a more senior supervisor and/or SIO. Until such time it must be recognised that it is the crime investigator who is in charge of the investigation. Appropriate administration and documentation should be used to begin a basic enquiry management system (see Chapter 7), including statement forms, personal descriptive forms, crime scene tape, exhibit management logs, forensic labels and bags. These are the basis for implementing standard administrative procedures.

Members of the public may have different perceptions of non-uniformed investigators. This can provide an opportunity for them to take full advantage of rummaging around and engaging with members of the public (ie sources of information) who may otherwise be reluctant to speak or to be seen speaking with uniformed staff. Investigators should be skilled and adept at eliciting information from onlookers, 'working the crowd' and getting amongst bystanders and passers-by, watching the *watchers*, amongst whom might be offenders or witnesses. Building rapport with those who may be useful as witnesses, sources of information and potential 'confidential sources' or informants (better known under the Regulation of Investigatory Powers Act 2000 (RIPA) as covert human intelligence sources, or CHIS for short) is a key communication skill. Using intuition and insight like a sixth sense, gut feeling or hunch that says that something or somebody 'just doesn't look right' (JDLR principle).

A comprehensive and useful checklist containing a top-50 bank of initial considerations for crime investigators is contained in an appendix of the *Blackstone's Crime Investigator's Handbook*.[3] If any of the bank of actions are completed or are in progress, an SIO's role is not only to confirm this, but to apply a 5WH-type review process. Reviewing, checking, making decisions, skilfully recording and directing, indicate the necessary process of taking ownership of the investigation that has begun.

5.12 **SIO—Initial Actions**

An SIO is rarely the first person to attend a reactive investigation and is normally notified only after a host of other staff and supervisors have attended, taken action and made important decisions. This means there is much information to catch up on in order to take effective command of the investigation. The first contact will usually be over a mobile phone or radio and establishing good, clear communications are vital.

If an SIO is contacted out of hours (OOH) or at some other inconvenient time, a good tactic is to get the messenger to call back. This allows time to gather thoughts, focus and get ready to take in all the details and think and act clearly.

---

[3] T Cook, S Hibbitt and M Hill, *Blackstone's Crime Investigator's Handbook*, 2nd edn (Oxford University Press, 2016).

Another benefit is to ensure the person who makes the first contact is someone who knows the full facts; time and energy are important and should not be wasted on having to delay and repeat the process.

KEY POINT

A good SIO remains calm, demonstrating professionalism and composure by bringing everything under control. This is done using core skills and attributes and remaining COOL, CALM and DETACHED, which sends out a clear statement of intent of how the investigation will be led.

One of the first actions is to decide who is in charge of the investigation. What must be clearly understood is that as soon as the SIO is notified and begins to get involved, they are assuming command. By dynamically reviewing, checking and giving instructions, the process has already begun of taking ownership of the investigation. This is so even though it may be some time before an SIO physically attends any scene or RVP. It is accepted that certain things may happen while en route that may be beyond their control because they are happening in 'fast time' and at a distance. Also, there may be other (eg silver) commanders in charge of other aspects of the incident which are outside the control of the SIO, eg if the fire service is extinguishing a large fire or a police silver commander is dealing with public disorder or a 'crime in action'-type incident. Nonetheless, the SIO should accept responsibility for and command of the criminal investigation at the earliest opportunity and 'own' that element of the incident.

KEY POINTS

1. If unable to reach a key crime scene quickly, the SIO confirms who is in command and control. Any directions or instructions given remotely should be recorded, stipulating precisely what is required. Until arrival, the most senior investigator or other supervisor is the person making fast-time decisions and needs to keep the en route SIO constantly updated via a communications link.
2. Verbal instructions can be prone to misinterpretation, particularly in highly pressured environments. Instructions must be given clearly and repeated back, keeping an accurate record of what has been agreed and actions raised, who to and when.
3. The process of dynamically reviewing and updating fast-track actions needs to commence quickly. These need to be reconsidered and updated in line with investigative developments and during any handover periods.
4. The SIO is responsible for bringing under control activities that have been initiated during the initial response.
5. A 'hot debrief' of all initial responders should be arranged as soon as possible and before they go off duty.

A note/casebook should be used throughout to log all actions, decisions and relevant information. Initially policy decisions should be recorded, together with times and dates, although these will need to be transferred into a more formal policy file at a later stage. The SIO should try and take a few steps back from the incident itself and remain calm, confident and completely objective. Important instructions must be given to the person who initially took charge. These must be recorded, timed and dated in the case/notebook, together with important contact details of those who are at the scene and with whom the SIO will need to keep in close contact.

KEY POINTS

- A decision should be made and communicated as to who has overall responsibility for leading and managing the investigation.
- A briefing is required before arrival at a scene whilst en route, and again upon arrival. It is best to stipulate when and how often to be contacted and updated. This is a critical period, there are risks from lack of continuity and even temporary loss of direction and momentum if any handover is not managed professionally.
- Discussions about the case should be conducted out of earshot of witnesses, relatives and friends of any victims, the public and the media.
- Careful note-taking forces the SIO to steady themselves, slow down and set a calmer tone for subsequent events at and around the crime scene. It ensures attention is paid to obtaining and recording accurate and precise details that should be delivered in a manner that allows them to be recorded coherently.
- The 5WH structure can be used to obtain relevant information. If facts are provided in a fragmented style, delivery becomes disjointed and more difficult to follow, and notes recorded will also be more difficult to understand.
- SIOs should quickly begin gathering initial thoughts, such as: 'What are we dealing with?' 'What do we know?' 'What do we need to know?' 'Where can we get it from?'.

It is helpful to keep a separate list and running log of important contact names and numbers rather than having to thumb through pages of notes to find some valuable detail that has been written in amongst something else. A printed table kept separately and readily available can be extremely practical, or by using the back of a note/workbook that might reduce the need for separate pieces of paper that can easily get lost. The list might look as simple as this:

Useful contact numbers

Name	Role	Number
Isla Jayne Greaves	Crime Scene Investigator	07562 543121
Wayne Hepworth	Patrol Inspector	02256 890245
Dr. Chris Wright	Forensic Pathologist	01356 978351
Tony Cook	National SIO Adviser	07769 724956

A smart SIO quickly appoints themself a trusty assistant or 'staff officer' (who ensures all policy decisions, information and actions raised are recorded accurately and contemporaneously). Once appointed, they should remain with the SIO at all times and be allocated responsibilities such as fielding non-urgent calls and noting details of initial actions. This role becomes very advantageous at times such as during debriefings and briefings of staff, when care must be taken to ensure details and information are accurately recorded.

Early thoughts should also focus around appointing key people and resources who will be required quickly, for example a Crime Scene Manager, Cordon Supervisor, H-2-H Enquiries Manager, Exhibits Officer, digital forensics team, incident room accommodation and staff, and outside enquiry teams. This is the formation of an initial investigation and management team.

5.12.1 **Scene attendance**

The SIO needs to decide where they are going to initially locate themselves, which may be at a crime scene RVP, a nearby secure facility or other suitable place. If the scene is indoors and well protected, there is no immediate rush to attend and it may be more practical and advantageous to meet staff at a nearby location that has better facilities to receive a full and comprehensive briefing, examine any relevant data and images, and make fuller preparation. It may also be a better way to meet and brief key people who may accompany the SIO to the scene, such as a Forensic Pathologist or Crime Scene Manager.

Where there is an outdoor scene, the SIO should not delay in attending the RVP in order to bring any well-meaning confusion under control, make a full assessment and arrange scene preservation and examination to their satisfaction. The early deployment of a mobile incident vehicle can be useful to act as a temporary control centre. It can also be used for briefing staff, providing valuable shelter and refreshments and acting as a focal point for witnesses, the community and even the media. If dealing with a high-profile incident, the SIO must get to the scene and **take control as quickly as possible,** making themselves highly visible so people can clearly see *who* and *where* the SIO is—demonstrating strong visible leadership. This is one way of applying the ABC principle and ensuring nothing is assumed or taken at face value and everything is properly checked—for example, making sure everyone's details at the scene have been obtained and that all vehicle numbers have been fully recorded. More importantly, the sight of an SIO turning up at the crime scene boosts the morale of staff and reassures everyone that a trusted and competent person is now in charge.

5.12.2 Situational awareness

Crime scenes yield lots of information and evidence. Hearing and reading about an incident and crime scene is not the same as being there, experiencing first hand and getting a feel for the environment, contours and layout of the location where an incident took place (aka situational awareness, see also Chapter 3). This helps put everything into context and perspective and helps make sense of, for example, why a location or victim may have been chosen, eg ease of access or escape route.

Geographical (spatial) and time (temporal) detail for most crimes are very suggestive. Looking around a location (preferably on foot) and scanning the environment from a three-dimensional (3D) perspective helps develop better knowledge and awareness about the crime and offender. This process satisfies one of the primary 5WH questions, ie 'Where?', and good clues usually fall out of this activity from fundamental queries, for example:

Targeted victim?
or
Targeted location?
or
Opportunistic encounter?

Closely examining a scene and surrounding location, geography and the social and demographic makeup of an area helps raise or answer 5WH questions. For example, who else may have been in the area or live nearby? What possible access and escape routes are there? Where are any buildings and places of interest? What are the distances between locations (if more than one crime scene or a series of offences) or the proximity of any key locations, events or hot spots? Where are locations where key nominals live, frequent or have been seen, etc? A good map is always helpful, together with some input from someone who has good local knowledge of the locality and community, and, if it is an older or historic offence, checking to see if the layout has changed (see also Chapter 3.8).

KEY POINTS

- The SIO should try and get to a crime scene and take control as quickly as possible, making themselves highly visible so people can clearly see *who* and *where* the SIO is, demonstrating strong leadership.
- Viewing what is happening at a crime scene can tell a great deal about how the initial response is being/was dealt with and whether important actions are being/have been done properly.

References

ACPO, *Emergency Procedures Manual* (NCPE, 2002)

ACPO, *Murder Investigation Manual* (NCPE, 2006)

Cook, T, Hibbitt, S and Hill, M, *Blackstone's Crime Investigator's Handbook*, 2nd edn (Oxford University Press, 2016)

Crime Scenes, Searches and Exhibits

6.1 **Introduction**

A 19th-century French medico-legal pioneer named Edmond Locard conceived the principle 'every contact leaves a trace', which highlights that everyone who enters a crime scene takes something in with them or leaves traces behind. This is known as Locard's Principle of Exchange,[1] and is one reason why the professional management of crime scenes, searches and exhibits is so important.

One advantage of forensic or physical evidence is that it cannot be affected by faulty memory, prejudice, bad eyesight or preference not to 'get involved'. However, in order to use it evidentially, it must be proved beyond all doubt that the correct and necessary procedures have been applied and managed professionally. This is in order to maintain the 'integrity' of the processes and to ensure the avoidance of interference or cross-contamination. The chain of custody of scenes, exhibits and forensic samples must receive careful attention plus all relevant legislative authorities and powers have to be strictly complied with to ensure that important evidential finds are not discredited.

There is much to be gained from the procedures covered in this chapter. Managed and applied correctly, they will pay dividends for the benefit of an investigation. Outlined are the essential processes of scene, search and exhibit management on which the success of serious and major crime investigations are often so heavily reliant.

KEY POINT

A murder victim is killed once; a murder scene can be killed many times.

6.2 **Identification, Security and Protection (ISP)**

Crime scenes present in a variety of different forms and the list seems to be growing. Any one or a combination from the list below could be designated as a crime scene.

Checklist—Crime scene types

- Location where offence took place.

- Premises that are being searched.

- Vehicle(s) connected to the enquiry.

---

[1] E Locard, *Traité de Criminalistique* 7 vols (Lyons Police Authority, 1914).

- Where a significant object may be suspected of being or is located.
- Victims (their body if deceased, or body part).
- Where a victim was last seen (eg if missing).
- Locations where a victim has been deposited (deposition site) or moved from.
- Witnesses who have come into contact with victims, offenders or related crime scenes.
- Suspects.
- Attack sites.
- Where there is trace or physical evidence, eg footprints, fingerprints or blood.
- Articles connected to victims, witnesses or offenders, eg clothing or weapons.
- Digital items and communication devices, eg computers, wi-fi routers, tablets and phones, gaming machines, virtual (cyber) scenes or cloud storage.
- Premises or places connected with suspects or offences (including offices or businesses).
- Access and escape routes.
- Location(s) where a crime has been planned or has a significant connection.

What constitutes a crime scene is up to an SIO to decide, who may wish to consult experts and specialists for advice. Initial responders may also have already made decisions as to what is/is not a crime scene; if so, these decisions need to be reviewed.

KEY POINTS

1. Crime scenes are allocated a sequential number (Scene 1, Scene 2, etc). Using the terms 'primary' or 'secondary' crime scenes should be avoided so as not to cause confusion and lead to perceptions that one has been treated more preferentially than another. The term 'multiple crime scenes' is safer.
2. Some crime scenes are not what you'd normally expect, eg in a train disaster a signal/junction box may be deemed a crime scene; in corporate manslaughter or death in healthcare setting cases, offices, filing cabinets, ledgers or surgical instruments may become such; or in a suicide/mass murder by an airline pilot, his home address and parents' addresses might need to be treated as crime scenes (eg Andreas Lubitz, who deliberately crashed his Germanwings A320 airbus into the French Alps, killing himself and 149 others on board in March 2015).

Crime scenes may not be uncovered until a physical or forensic search has taken place if not immediately obvious. The sooner this happens, the more chance there is of successful evidential capture. Once identified, crime scenes should be secured and protected from unauthorised interference (including family, friends and relatives of victims, non-essential police/medical personnel, animals, onlookers and journalists). This is to avoid any evidence being altered, moved, destroyed, lost or contaminated. No unauthorised persons should ever be allowed to enter a crime scene except in an emergency, such as to give medical aid or save life, until the arrival of a senior detective and/or the SIO and Crime Scene Manager/Investigator (CSM/CSI). Those persons who do not have a **specific or valid reason** for being inside a crime scene cordon should be regarded as *unauthorised*. Only an SIO or crime scene investigator/manager (with agreement of the SIO) should grant authority to access a crime scene, and this directive has to be clearly communicated to all those at and around the crime scene location.

KEY POINTS

- Medical personnel may have to disturb a crime scene to administer treatment and it is important to debrief them afterwards to ascertain what they disturbed when securing access for their vehicles and equipment and providing treatment. All medical 'consumables' should be left at the scene/on the body.
- When police (or journalistic) helicopters hover close to outside scenes (including air ambulances), their downdraught can disrupt and prove detrimental to crime scene preservation.

6.2.1 **Cordons and scene security**

Security cordons are not only useful for guarding crime scenes, but also protecting officers and staff working inside them, controlling the public, sightseers and the media, preventing unauthorised interference and access (eg by offenders), preventing sensitive activities, conversations and comments being observed or overheard and for preserving evidence and avoiding contamination. Initial responders are expected to arrange scene security at the earliest opportunity by setting up effective cordons as quickly as possible. This can prove challenging and be resource-intensive, particularly if there is a large area to protect out of doors. Nonetheless, at some later stage it may have to be proved beyond all reasonable doubt to the satisfaction of a court that there was no possibility of interference with or contamination of a crime scene, particularly if vital trace evidence links an offender to it.

Cordons can be resource- and time-consuming and usually rely upon overt staff to provide the most suitable and visible resources to make them effective. These officers are effectively the 'visible' element of the investigation and what the public see when they are near the scene or watching news reports. Apart from an essential security and scene sterility function, the cordon officers can influence community confidence (positively or negatively) on how the enquiry is being managed; so they must at all times appear totally professional and remain alert and look interested while on duty at a scene cordon.

KEY POINTS

1. Those engaged in cordon duties should make themselves clearly visible to the public. They are on show and indicative of the level of police professionalism. Unacceptable behaviour from officers looking disinterested or being undisciplined (eg sat in vehicles eating food or reading newspapers) sends out the wrong message and can adversely affect public confidence.
2. Cordon officers should be encouraged to communicate with people visiting, loitering around or passing by as they may hold vital information. They should be warned, however, not to give out too much detail about the incident or investigation without prior briefing or sanction from the SIO, especially to journalists or members of a victim's family.

Early review and assessment of the security arrangements, parameters, position and adequacy of cordons should be made. This should take cognisance of the circumstances of the case and available information, such as entry and egress routes by offenders. Precise scene cordon parameters, when determined, should be recorded and indicated clearly and accurately on a drawing, sketch, plan and/ or map. If any alterations are made to the parameters, then these also need accurately recording, together with the reasons why.

Indoor scenes are usually comparatively easier to secure by the closing of doors and restricting entry into premises, initially by the presence of officers at entrance and exit points. They are usually relatively self-contained. However, most outdoor scenes provide additional complications, such as adverse weather conditions, challenging environments, crowds, animals, traffic, security, media intrusion or elevated observation points nearby. Outdoor cordons should be made as large as possible as they can be reduced later. Restricting access to outdoor scenes can be achieved by the use of metal barriers or cordon tape, vehicles to block entrances, officers and Police Community Support Officers (PCSOs), and some forces may use private security companies to control the outer perimeter and entry/exit points, dog handlers and mounted officers if available (if a large rural area, for instance) to ensure boundary lines cannot be crossed.

Natural boundaries such as hedges, fences and walls can also form part of a cordon, bearing in mind the potential for offenders to have discarded items such as weapons, blood-stained clothing, mobile phones, keys or stolen items over or into them. Road blocks may also be necessary, dependent on the location. Scene cordons *must* be adequately guarded along their entire perimeter to ensure there is no unauthorised access.

Responsibility for managing/supervising cordons should be given to a supervisor who is sometimes referred to as a designated 'Scene Bronze Commander'. Their task is to ensure adequate resources and arrangements are in place for safeguarding the integrity and security of a scene and eliminating unauthorised access. The role includes briefing and continuously supervising all those on cordon security duties. It also includes ensuring that scene logs are completed correctly. Their effectiveness in performing this role may play an important part in proving the sterility and integrity of key exhibits in the prosecution case.

KEY POINT

SIOs and supervisors need to be intrusive when quality-assuring the effectiveness of cordon management and scene security. This can best be achieved by arriving unannounced at cordons and querying with officers about their duties, asking if they have been briefed properly, who is supervising them and checking the content, accuracy and quality of their scene log(s).

There are usually two types of cordons—inner and outer. In some circumstances it may be necessary to set up an additional (third) outer cordon. This would be much wider, covering both inner and outer cordons, and might be needed if there is more than one significant scene within close proximity. On Operation Sumac (linked series of five female homicides in December 2006 near Ipswich in Suffolk), two of the five victims' bodies (Annette Nicholls and Paula Clennel) were located close together and adjacent to a busy country road. At these scenes, both inner and outer cordons were created with an additional (third) outer cordon used to keep the media and public out of both perimeters.[2]

KEY POINT—OP SUMAC CORDONS/SCENE SEARCH

Where bodies were recovered from land, there were obviously more forensic opportunities. In these cases the Police Search Adviser (PolSA), PolSA Coordinator (PolSC) and CSI attended each scene to formulate a joint approach to scene examination and search in agreement with the relevant SIO. This worked well and enabled the PolSC to start planning for the search when the scene was released by the CSI...Cordons at all scenes were made as large as possible. It was recognised that this increased the cost of policing but it was crucial for preserving the integrity of the scenes. Once the scenes were released to PolSA, the areas within the cordon were subject to detailed or fingertip search. The force dog unit was used to search areas outside the cordon. This worked well and provided reassurance that nothing was missed...A clear audit trail was maintained by the search team office

---

[2] See NPIA, (2008) 4(2) *Journal of Homicide and Major Incident Investigation*, 94–7.

regarding which teams had been used on which search, what measures had been put in place to minimise cross contamination and the location, usage and cleaning of equipment. At the end of each day statements were submitted from all staff involved in searching even if nothing was recovered. This provided an audit trail of the whole search strategy.

NPIA Professional Practice, *Strategic Debrief—Operation Sumac* (NPIA, 2008), p. 29

The terms 'hot zone', 'warm zone' and 'cold zone' are sometimes used when referring to crime scenes that involve contaminated areas (eg in terrorism cases). These are areas that are graded depending on how likely they are to pose a threat to the health and safety of anyone located within.

Inner and outer cordons

1. *Inner cordon*—This is a designated area that is closest to where the main examination takes place. It may be where a body lies or the main offence site (eg at an illicit drug laboratory/storage place). The inner cordon usually has quite small parameters and provides a boundary for detailed forensic examinations and must be very tightly controlled. This is where the SIO may wish to consider the use of a large tent or other similar screening equipment in order to safeguard the privacy of the scene, in particular away from onlookers or long-range media cameras or observation and listening equipment (and the use of airborne 'drones' that is becoming popular).[3]

2. *Outer cordon*—A larger containment area covering peripheral parts of the inner scene. It provides a secure area not only for examination, but also preparatory work to be undertaken and the adequate distancing of members of the public and media. This area may also be subject to forensic examination and physical searching, but is unlikely to be as detailed as the inner cordon.

Each cordon must have adequate 'access control' to ensure only authorised people gain entry. The SIO must set adequate policies and clear instructions to cordon officers as to who is to be allowed/not allowed entry, which may differ between inner and outer cordons. This decision is probably best made in consultation with the CSM/CSI and there may well be separate and distinct policies for both. For these reasons, both cordons require a separate scene log to be completed for each (scene logs are covered later).

6.2.2 **Rendezvous points (RVP)**

An RVP is usually the best place to site the person compiling the outer cordon scene log and provide precisely what the name suggests. A suitable location

---

[3] Not all scenes involve offences that are 'against the person' and cordons may be required, eg at places such as illicit drug laboratory/farm at a house.

should be found where all required scene resources can congregate to discuss examination and search tactics. A signed police vehicle that is easily identifiable may be used in the first instance, and if there are good communication systems on board, they can be put to good use while there.

There may be practical and logistical difficulties to consider (such as parking or briefing facilities) from the sheer volume and type of resources required. The SIO may feel it is easier to manage their required resources if they are directed to attend an RVP located at the scene cordon. If specialist services or agencies that bring large vehicles and equipment (eg an underwater or specialist search unit) are involved, then an area needs to be identified where these resources can safely assemble, park, gain access to facilities, brief, change clothing, take refreshments, rest and recuperate, etc, where they will not be impeded by the public or media. In such a case the SIO (and in some cases this may be a requirement of a Gold or Silver Commander) should nominate someone to take control of managing all the necessary arrangements for the resources required at the scene. This may include traffic management officers if there are vehicle and public route diversions involved. These roles are usually designated Bronze roles.

Suitability of RVPs (and secondary RVPs such as forward command post (FCP) used for mobile command facilities and locating Silver and Bronze Commanders, used in major incident response contingency plans) must be a consideration. Risks and safety also have to be considered when locations are chosen, particularly in terrorism cases where suspected secondary devices may have been deliberately placed; in which case any potential RVP will have to be searched before it is deemed safe and suitable for use.

6.2.3 Common approach path (CAP)

A common approach path should be designated and marked out at the earliest opportunity. This should be used as the only route into and out of a crime scene for all those subsequently attending (eg for examination purposes or treatment/ removal of victims). It is most likely the direct route to any victims or premises that will already have been taken by initial response teams including medical practitioners. Wherever possible this same route should be used to also leave the area, unless it becomes clear the offenders have also used that route (eg if eye witnesses or CCTV so indicate or there are footwear marks or other telltale signs). Protective stepping plates are usually used to protect the surface underneath and particularly inside premises, where trace evidence on flooring and carpets may need preserving.

It is vital that details of all those initially attending are recorded so that their route taken can be clarified before the CAP is determined. A sketch plan may be helpful, which can be exhibited and registered as a document (eg on HOLMES). The golden rule is that any CAP established should be along the *least likely route taken by the offender(s) or victim(s)*.

KEY POINTS

1. At outdoor scenes hard-standing or compact gravel-type path areas are better for a CAP as they are more practical to use; they are also easier and quicker to search to render them clear than other surfaces such as foliage or grassland.
2. A CAP may have to be wide enough to enable CSIs and other experts to carry in their equipment and for the removal of any casualties or victims.
3. A CAP should be selected on the *least likely route taken by the offender(s) or victim(s)*.

Checklist—Cordons and preservation

- Both inner and outer cordons are required (ie 2 x cordons).

- Largest possible area should be cleared; parameters can be narrowed later.

- Scene logs should be commenced (one for inner, one for outer).

- For parameters, a quick and objective evaluation can be based upon:

  o location of offence, incident (or victim)
  o likely presence of physical evidence
  o eyewitness accounts and/or information/intelligence/CCTV.

- Outdoor scenes—use can be made of natural boundaries (eg trees, streams, gates, walls, fences, lamp-posts, building lines) as cordon boundaries.

- Consider possible entry/exit route used by offender(s) and victim(s)—and *avoid when determining the CAP.*

- Consider possibility of other linked crime scenes (eg abandoned vehicles or an attack site) that may also need to be preserved.

- Cordon areas should be clearly marked (ie with identifiable crime scene tape).

- Cordons restrict access to nominated authorised persons—this instruction must be clearly communicated to all staff present.

- Outdoor scenes may need early consideration of protective covers or high screens (regardless of weather forecast, to protect dignity of victims from public/media).

- Inner cordons can be grid-referenced to show exactly where items are located.

- Nominate Bronze scene cordon managers to supervise cordon responsibilities.

KEY POINT

In terrorism cases it is not uncommon for secondary devices to be placed for deliberate targeting of responding emergency services and to cause maximum carnage and destruction at places where cordons and RVPs are likely to be located. Any RVPs therefore need to be searched prior to being deemed safe to use.

6.2.4 Displaced residents and vehicles

Some scenes are located in areas that are difficult to contain, such as places where local residents have their homes, possessions or vehicles that then become stranded inside a police cordon. This may include residences or business premises where the placing and security of secure cordons means third parties become victims of collateral interference and are effectively displaced by their restricted access and can suffer significant disruption as a consequence.

Sensible solutions (in consultation with a CSI/CSM) are the solution, such as having vehicles examined by a CSI and recording or photographing of their type and exact position to allow them to be released. When satisfied there is no link to the crime, supervised removal can be arranged. Residents can be permitted to use their rear doors rather than front doors, and if necessary put into protective suits or overshoes to allow access in and out of the cordon. A protectively suited officer should visit each address to explain to displaced residents the reasons for the restrictions and arrangements for their safe movements. An explanatory note from the SIO and/or local policing team, apologising for the inconvenience, might also reduce any frustrations against the police enquiry team. This policy can be included as part of a 'community impact' control strategy (see Chapter 11).

6.2.5 Legal issues—entering and securing crime scenes

The majority of the law-abiding public are usually willing to cooperate and allow access to and examination of crime scenes on their property. They think it is sensible to follow police advice, which may be supported by other agencies such as the fire and rescue service, health professionals or local authority representatives. There are also legal powers conferred in sections 8, 17, 18 and 32 of the Police and Criminal Evidence Act 1984 (PACE) and other legislation to enter premises (using reasonable force if necessary) for the purpose of conducting a search.

In the case of *DPP v Morrison*,[4] a decision confirmed that under common law the police have a power to erect a cordon in order to preserve the scene of a crime. The Divisional Court upheld this rule in this case given the importance of this function in investigating serious crime.

---

[4] *DPP v Morrison* QBD, 4 April 2003; *Telegraph*, 17 April 2003; *The Times*, 21 April 2003.

The case of *Rice v Connolly*[5] previously reaffirmed long-established principles that had not been challenged. It was confirmed that the police are entitled to take all reasonable steps to keep the peace, prevent and detect crime, and bring offenders to justice. It is within these principles that the police are entitled to secure scenes of crime for examination by specialists, forensic scientists, etc. If anyone were to frustrate, hinder or obstruct the securing of a crime scene, they would commit an offence of obstructing a police officer in the execution of their duty. This would include non-warranted staff such as scene investigators who are regarded as investigators under the Criminal Procedure and Investigations Act 1996 (CPIA).

The *Murder Investigation Manual* (MIM) states:

> Where a scene is on private property, SIOs will need to negotiate access with those in control of the premises. Considerable tact and diplomacy will often be necessary for this, particularly where the scene is occupied or controlled by a suspect's family or associates or where the scene requires to be searched for objects suspected of being buried or concealed. If necessary, alternative arrangements should be made for their accommodation until the scene is released. Where a crime scene is likely to have a significant impact on commerce, SIOs should consult their force legal department for advice about the length of time it can be held.[6]

Care must be taken if a crime is released and then, for whatever reason, it becomes necessary to re-apply the cordons and perform searches. Under these circumstances it may be legally safer to apply for a warrant under section 8 of PACE or utilise other sections of the Act to guarantee there is a firm legal basis for further activity at the particular location.

KEY POINT

If the incident under investigation is terrorist-related, the police have powers to impose and enforce cordons under sections 33–36 of the Terrorism Act 2000 (TACT).

6.2.6 **Search warrants**

Due to the intrusive nature and invasion of privacy and human rights, a decision to search a person's home or premises should never be taken lightly. Search warrants are an area where the process can easily be challenged by legal teams and care should be taken not to allow any errors to creep into the application and execution processes. It should be noted that section 8(1) of PACE states that the statutory test is 'reasonable grounds for believing', which is a higher degree of

---

[5] *Rice v Connolly* (1966) QB P414.
[6] ACPO, *Murder Investigation Manual* (NCPE, 2006), 136.

suspicion than 'reasonable grounds to suspect' (eg under section 23(3) of the Misuse Drugs Act 1971). The case of *Redknapp v Metropolitan Police Commissioner* (2008) states:

> Obtaining a warrant should never be undertaken as mere formality because it authorizes the invasion of a person's home…all the necessary information to justify the grant of a section 8 warrant should be included in the information on the form.

Checklist—Search warrants

- Ensure all necessary information to justify the application is included in the information form.

- Anticipate and prepare for the likelihood of questioning by the magistrate/judge.

- Use the information *form* as an aide-memoire for the application.

- Consider anything that may mitigate against the application being granted.

- Ensure any questions and answers during the application stage are recorded (see *R v Sheffield Justices* (2003)).

- Keep a record of any additional material relied upon for the purposes of the application.

- Seek advice from the CPS on sensitive information that may be required for a warrant application process to see if the material can be protected (the court has a duty to record the application process, even if information is given verbally).

- If occupier not present when warrant executed, leave a copy in a prominent position and consider photographing it at that location.

6.3 **Crime Scene Assessments**

The SIO and CSM/CSI and any other specialists and experts (eg the PolSC/PolSA) need to work together as a team to establish and agree what constitutes a scene, the parameters, preservation measures and the physical/forensic searches, tactics and examination and evidence recovery plan. This includes any separate and additional policy that may be required to recover human remains. Once agreed, the strategy and tactics can be recorded and any resulting agreement signed by all parties contributing to it.

A crime scene assessment is usually the precursor to a tactical meeting and the first part of the process. It provides an opportunity to review and check that adequate preservation procedures are in place and for the SIO to get a first-hand 'feel' for the scene and surroundings. It may be some time before images are available and a senior investigator such as an SIO can still exploit every opportunity to apply their own skills and knowledge of the crime scene assessment. They do not need to become overly influenced by experts either such as CSI/CSMs who do not have the same level of training in the law, points to prove, investigative mindset, or the same awareness and knowledge of the wider investigation.

The SIO may also require those who have already been involved at the scene (such as the senior detective who responded and initially took charge) and the CSM to accompany them during a 'walk and talk' (aka 'walkthrough) session through the crime scene, taking great care to prevent any risk of contamination or cross-contamination by wearing protective clothing.

Scene assessments allow for the review of cordons and screening arrangements. In the case of a deceased person at the scene, the assessment process usually includes a Forensic Pathologist. Any assessment can be aided by CCTV coverage and any first accounts from witnesses, paramedics and initial responders. It can also be conducted with the aid of a review of a visual (eg digital-type) recording of the crime scene.

KEY POINT

Scene assessments provide an opportunity to identify physical evidence that may need recovering quickly, not just forensic items such as blood-stained clothing or weapons, but other items and material such as passive data (eg CCTV or ANPR cameras) that may prove vitally important and need to be fast-tracked for rapid recovery and viewing. Dangerous items, such as loaded firearms, would also come under this category and would need closely guarding until they are rendered safe.

6.3.1 **Potential scene contaminators**

A scene assessment should include consideration of potential evidence contaminators or destroyers.

Checklist—Potential crime scene contaminators

- Weather—particularly if the scene is out of doors, blood, prints, body fluids, DNA, etc can be ruined by inclement weather such as rain, frost, snow, wind, direct sunlight and heat.

- Relatives or friends either of the victim(s) or suspect(s), or members of the public wishing to be helpful.

- Suspects or associates—in attempts to destroy or remove any incriminating evidence, or legitimately put themselves at the crime scene and negate incriminating trace evidence that is subsequently recovered.

- Spectators, onlookers, concerned members of the community or general public (eg ghouls with morbid fascination), displaced residents—people who cannot return to their homes for instance, or move vehicles because they are within cordons—may pose a serious threat and problem to scene security.

- Officials, experts or supervisors—people who may think they have a right to enter crime scenes need to be dealt with quickly and the SIO needs to make a decision as to who has or has not got permission to enter.

- Scavenging animals and insects.

- Media—probably the biggest culprits for potentially breaching cordons in order to get pictures and/or interviews (dealt with in Chapter 9).[7]

- Geological disturbances, particularly if the crime is outdoors (eg flooding, landslides, seeps, springs, subsidence, gas emissions, landfill and waste, areas of ground contamination, pollution, weathering and erosion).

6.3.2 Scene maps, plans, sketches and digital images

Detailed maps, plans and digital images of crime scenes and surrounding areas are always extremely useful for assessment purposes and setting parameters. The exact position, scale, proximity and dimensions of locations and objects in context of their location are invaluable. Scene photographs or digital images are good at recording 'close-ups' etc, but a detailed plan or map can show precise locations and context, particularly at complex or large crime scenes. These can also be used for effective communication of detail about crime scene information that is helpful when teams and specialists need briefing. Maps can also be used to delineate search areas. The SIO can also produce their own rough sketches or plans of scenes when they conduct assessments to use as an aide-memoire and for consideration of cordon and search parameters, early hypotheses, conducting briefings, etc. There may be a significant time delay before official maps, plans or images become available, which is when a rough sketch becomes useful.

KEY POINT

A detailed crime scene plan or map should have a relevant title, date, time and orientation, usually given by the inclusion of a north (N) pointing arrow.

---

[7] One tactic to manage the media at crime scenes is to agree with the CSM to arrange 'staged' shots so they can get the images they need.

Aerial photography can assist in finding and recording the exact location of scenes and help make other significant discoveries. Resulting images may provide a valuable tool for briefings and decision-making processes. The SIO may also wish to take advantage of some of the satellite imagery that is now available on the internet.

These types of satellite images can be used to gain a good appreciation of the layout of scenes and their proximity to other significant geographical locations, including buildings and roads, although the time and date the imagery was taken must be borne in mind.

6.3.3 **Digital scene reproduction**

There may be opportunities to produce a computerised digital reproduction and/ or a reconstruction of a crime scene to help gain a better understanding of what took place, in what sequence and how it happened. This can help in:

- formation of hypotheses
- testing individual hypotheses by additional analysis
- producing the most probable reconstruction theory.

Sophisticated computer enhancements, animated reconstructions, 3D models and 360-degree camera angles can recreate a crime scene and check witness timings, distance, etc. These can be used in court to show a jury the most likely sequence of events and positions and the importance of exhibits and forensic samples, or how the evidence combines, to present a clearer picture of fragmented or complex evidence.

6.4 **Crime Scene Coordinators and Managers**

Most large and complex crime investigations have an appointed CSM and/or Coordinator (CSC) if more than one major scene is involved. The status or seniority for these roles may vary according to the nature of the investigation. For some investigations, including most homicide cases, the roles should go to accredited CSMs, although for less serious cases an experienced CSI may be utilised.

Their role involves assessing, deploying and managing staff both from the force crime scene examination unit perspective and also from other agencies. They act as an adviser to the SIO on examination strategies, evidential types, values and prioritisation of exhibits and maintain comprehensive records of scene strategies and contribute to forensic strategies. They are effectively the focal point for all forensic-related enquiries during the examination of the scene and during the subsequent forensic submissions and analysis processes.

The sooner a CSM/CSC is involved, the better managed and more coordinated the investigation will be. For pre-planned crime investigations, involving a CSM at the preparation stage can enable appropriate tactical options to be put into place prior to the execution of searches and for forensic recovery potential to be maximised.

The CSC appointed to an investigation should be the SIO's first point of contact for any deployment of CSI staff. The CSC is also the most appropriately qualified person to deploy additional CSI staff, as they have an overview of all other aspects of the investigation, and are also able to develop appropriate strategies and advice on the most suitable sampling techniques and best practice, and to brief forensic staff and other specialists on behalf of the SIO. A CSM, on the other hand, will direct staff at one particular scene and usually there is a CSM at each scene of 'multiples', with a CSC overseeing deployment of staff across all the scenes.

Checklist—Role of Crime Scene Coordinator (CSC)

- Provide liaison between the CSM and investigation team.

- Coordinate all scenes within the investigation, providing necessary resources.

- Advise the investigation team on the viability of forensic evidence.

- Liaise with PolSC/lead PolSA.

- Liaise with other relevant agencies, forensic providers and specialists.

- Brief relevant persons on scene examination and scientific support matters.

- Accurately record information as prescribed in national and local procedures.

- Ensure compliance with health and safety legislation.

- Provide quality assurance prior to the release of a scene.

- Attend forensic strategy meetings when required.

- Ensure that all aspects of staff welfare are considered.

Role of Crime Scene Manager (CSM)

- Ensure adequate preservation measures have been taken to protect the scene.

- Ensure a scene log has been started and that the officer in charge of the log is aware of their responsibilities.

- Ensure appropriate recording and recovery of potential forensic evidence in line with forensic strategy agreed with the SIO.

- Decide upon sequence of evidence gathering, suggesting other services if required (eg specialist photography, forensic scientists).

- Allocate resources effectively within the scene.

- Update the CSC and SIO at regular intervals and notify if any changes to forensic strategy required (eg if found item requires different approach).

- Liaise with the Exhibits Officer (EO) and offer advice on forensic examination of items.

- Accurately record information as prescribed in national and local procedures.

- Ensure swift submission of items.

- Ensure compliance with health and safety legislation.

- Attend forensic strategy meetings when required.

(See also ACPO, *National Crime Scene Investigation Manual*, Issue 1 (NPIA, 2007), 46–7.)

KEY POINT

CSCs/CSMs can have a big influence on decisions made about crime scenes, forensic strategies and examination priorities and policies. The final decision always rests with the SIO and if there is any doubt as to the advice given, or there is a significant difference of opinion, there is always the option of commissioning a peer review (second opinion) by an independent crime scene expert and/or forensic adviser.

6.5 **Conducting Searches**

Most investigations require some sort of physical search(es) to be conducted. There are many occasions where the initiation of a thorough search operation has had a direct and positive bearing on the quality of evidence recovered. The opportunity to maximise the evidential yield through effective search and recovery processes is an integral part of an investigation and wherever possible it is preferable to utilise the College of Policing trained, licensed and experienced search assets.

A decision will be required as to what, if any, type of physical search is required and how it links into a forensic (ie more detailed and scientific) strategy for an examination of a crime scene, which usually takes precedence. This will be guided by the circumstances of the case. Searching first may inhibit forensic recovery, but a forensic examination is not a search, and therefore items can get missed. The interface between search and crime scene examination must be properly managed, with a clear understanding of which takes precedence and who is responsible for each phase. Unless the person who is conducting the scene examination has received accredited search training (highly unlikely), this phase cannot be considered a search and the use of search-trained personnel may still be required. Similarly, search teams do not usually have the same level of forensic awareness and ability as CSIs. If a search takes place after the forensic examination, it is possible that new evidence and articles may be found and therefore a strategy will be required for dealing with them.[8]

A physical search may be required as an investigative tool for locating:

- victims or suspects
- human remains/body parts
- crime scenes
- physical investigative material (eg weapons, vehicles, stolen property, discarded items, digital data storage devices, CCTV, drugs)
- storage and/or deposition sites
- access/exit routes from a scene
- missing persons
- intelligence.

An initial visual check (IVC) is a preliminary and quick overview for anything obvious (eg a victim or suspect) and to make a rapid and early identification of anything likely to assist the investigation. This is likely to be the subject of a fast-track (golden hour) action. It must be remembered that the preservation of life is always the overriding objective. These checks (searches), however, should wherever possible be systematic, thorough and recorded in detail so they can assist any subsequent more substantial (fully managed) searches. With an initial search there is a potential for compromising any necessary forensic examination due to contamination and disruption, but this may have to be a calculated and accepted risk. Dependent on available timescales, cautious tactics can be adopted and close consultation with a CSI/CSM and/or forensic scientists is advisable.

Physical searching should, wherever possible be intelligence-led and those conducting them need briefing (and later debriefing) fully on the details of the investigation and what the objectives and tactics are for the search, eg what to look for and how to preserve/recover items. Listing items required is important, but there must also be some latitude to allow searchers to use their own initiative to recover anything they consider might be relevant. This is why it is useful for search teams to have a good understanding of the case.

KEY POINT

When conducting searches, it may be necessary to look up as well as look down to see, for example, if anything of significance is located above ground level, eg in trees, on flat rooftops (aerial photography can sometimes assist).

---

[8] See also ACPO, *Practice Advice on Search Management and Procedures* (NCPE, 2006), 164–6.

Anything required for forensic examination when found should, as a general rule, be left in its original position for a decision on how best to recover it. For general items this is normally done by a CSI (in consultation with the CSM or forensic scientist). The examination of large or fragile items may need careful planning. These are decisions made through a teamwork approach between the SIO, CSM/CSI/PolSC/PolSA and specialists, ie everyone working together.

The crime scene assessment (as noted in the previous section) and planning process provides an opportunity to discuss and plan the examination and search sequence and the recovery of specific items, eg cadavers. The crime scene team, CSM, CSI, forensic scientists, forensic pathologist and any other required scientific advisers and experts, such as fingerprint experts, biologists, environmental profilers, digital forensic advisers, anthropologists, and ballistics experts, led by the SIO, must adopt a joined-up approach working towards specific objectives—NOT just for the benefit of individual specialisms. There are a number of considerations that will influence the way in which a search is managed and in what sequence, such as:

- search objectives
- identification of whether it is a search **for** a scene or **of** a scene
- most appropriate resources
- areas to be designated as crime scenes
- parameters of each search
- measures to control the risk of contamination
- appropriate reviews ('plan it—do it—review it').

KEY POINTS

- Cross-contamination is a huge consideration. Ensure those conducting searches have not been in contact with other crime scenes (eg suspects).
- In some circumstances it is necessary to conduct an IVC and recover evidence immediately, balancing risk against opportunity and necessity.
- Outdoor searches provide added benefits of visible reassurance and often become popular images for use in news bulletins (eg fingertip searches). These can be incorporated into community impact control strategies.
- Media and sightseers need controlling, including the witnessing, recording or broadcasting of any recoveries.
- The term 'search' should be prefixed with an adjective that qualifies it, eg 'flash', 'PolSA', 'forensic', 'initial' or 'underwater' search.

6.5.1 Roles of the Police Search Adviser (PolSA), Police Search Coordinator (PolSC) and Police Search Team (PST)

Fully managed searches are far more intrusive and detailed than initial (or hasty) searches and usually conducted by those who are trained and accredited by the

College of Policing. These types of searches are managed under the control and supervision of a Police Search Adviser (PolSA).

A PolSA can:

- advise on all aspects of physical search techniques and specialist assets
- plan, direct, manage and implement searches
- manage Police Search Teams (PST)
- obtain technical resources
- advise on search plans
- maintain comprehensive records of the search.

A PolSA and their PST are invaluable assets who have their own requirements in order to perform their roles. However, they should never be left to work in isolation and must be provided with the necessary information and briefings on developing intelligence. Any search team is an operational arm of the enquiry and must be fully integrated into the investigation. Wherever practicable, the PolSC/PolSA should be invited to partake in enquiry team briefings and cascade information to their search teams—a strong communications link MUST exist between the enquiry team and the PolSC/PolSA/PST.

The SIO retains full responsibility for deciding which persons, premises or areas are to be searched and agrees on the parameters in accordance with their investigative objectives. A PolSA can advise on the best parameters, methodology and techniques, search assets, health and safety aspects, logistical and technical constraints, and which other agencies and specialists are required, eg blood/victim recovery dogs, underwater search, air support, height access, marine experts, confined space teams, use of volunteers.

Role of the PolSC

If there is more than one PolSA involved in search activity, then a Police Search Coordinator (PolSC) may be required to manage and supervise all the various search operations and act as primary link between the SIO and major incident team.

A PolSC is responsible for:

- overseeing all operational search responsibilities
- coordinating multi-venue search operations
- maintaining search role standards and competencies
- supporting resource acquisition
- quality assuring searches and associated documentation.

Role of the PST

A PST works under the supervision of a PolSA and comprises officers who are trained by the College of Policing in specific search techniques for searching persons, vehicles, buildings, areas and routes. Their role is to:

- provide a consistent approach to search tasks
- be better equipped and resourced to provide an effective search response
- produce appropriate records and audit trail relevant to their search
- provide high levels of assurance and raise the probability of success
- provide heightened awareness of health and safety measures and dangerous materials (and liaise with HAZMAT teams).

On requesting a PolSA-led search, the SIO or delegated person from the enquiry team should liaise with the PolSC/PolSA and CSM/CSI in order to discuss and agree the search plan and parameters. The SIO should insist on agreeing a properly recorded formal tactical search plan (also referred to as a 'search strategy document') which should be signed, timed and dated by all parties. The PolSC/PolSA will develop a tactical plan, the aim of which is to deliver the search in accordance with the SIO's search and investigative objectives.

Checklist—Suggested content of tactical search plan

- All information of relevance to the search.

- Search objectives (including specific items sought).

- Search parameters clearly marked out on maps/plans of the search area (with title, scale, north arrow, legend, date and initials/name).

- Reasons why an area is being searched (or not searched) and relevant lawful authority.

- How the search will be conducted, methodology, instrumentation, resources/assets and anticipated timescales.

- Health and safety issues.

- Area, building and/or subsurface or utility plans needed and referred to, including historical and current Ordnance Survey maps, geological maps, local archives and photographs.

- Useful knowledge, information or contacts used (eg local water authority or bailiff when searching canals, rivers or streams).

- Specialist resources and order of (phased) deployment.

- Site reconnaissance to identify logistical or technical constraints (such as points of access, locations overhead or underground utilities which may exclude the use of certain geophysical instruments).

- Standard Operating Procedure (SOP) for the search. This helps to provide a high level of consistency and allow independent peer review.

- Media and arrangements for completion of a CIA.

- How evidence is to be preserved and recovered.

- Ongoing review and reassessment in light of search progress or new intelligence.

KEY POINTS

1. Same staff searching more than one scene means there is the potential for cross-contamination and needs to be avoided at all costs.
2. Good searches are intelligence-led and based on facts or intelligence available at the time. There should be a mechanism for reviewing and if necessary revising the search strategy in light of emerging information.
3. Strong communication links must be maintained between the PolSC/PolSA and the enquiry team to ensure search teams:
   (i) work towards the SIO's objectives
   (ii) are involved in producing and aware of agreed search tactics
   (iii) are kept informed and updated on emerging developments.

6.5.2 Searching premises

During the course of an investigation it is highly probable there will be a requirement to conduct searches of premises that may or may not initially constitute crime scenes. This could include places where an offence has occurred, where there might be evidential or intelligence material, or to locate a suspect, victims, missing persons or vulnerable people. It could also include premises that form part of a proactive search, under power of a warrant, eg to look for evidence and/or link to an arrest strategy.

Adequate planning and preparation for a premises search with identified and communicated aims and objectives is necessary. If a thorough physical search of premises is required, then a PolSA-led PST should be considered. This will ensure a high assurance search is conducted. The SIO should also consider including one of their own investigators to be on hand to advise and assist the search team with their in-depth knowledge of the case and investigative skills. A dedicated EO (Exhibits Officer) will also be required. A CSI should, whenever possible, also be deployed to accurately record the evidence and advise on the appropriate recording/photographing, forensic recovery, packaging, transportation and safe storage of seized items.

The type of premises/incident under investigation and stage of the investigation will determine what the search tactics should entail. For example, the minimum standard required when searching for a person such as an offender or missing person on premises is an 'open door' search. This means that all rooms, outbuildings, lofts, cupboards, wardrobes, etc will be accessed and checked.

KEY POINTS

- Bathrooms and kitchens are popular places to wash away forensic traces and dismember bodies/body parts. Therefore baths, sinks and shower traps should be examined for blood or mesh deposits, together with towels, bath mats, shower curtains, soap and shampoo bottles, and outdoor tap/drain areas.
- Searches should include a visual check for any signs of a struggle, disturbance or clean-up activity.
- Toilets and sinks should be checked for trace evidence in case offenders used them before, during or after the offence, and may have removed any gloves or face coverings in the process.

When recovering clothing and items against set criteria, there must be a clear policy to stipulate what should/should not and how they should be seized. For example, if checking footwear, taking photographs or making drawings to compare tread patterns and markings may avoid having to seize and store too many exhibits. Search officers should be working to a clear examination and retrieval strategy. For instance, when recovering clothing that is to be forensically packaged and sealed, best practice is to get it photographed prior to recovery, and then front and back photographs prior to packaging. Although time-consuming, this negates the need to submit numerous items for assessment to a forensic service provider, and allows the prioritising of certain items as they are more difficult to see or describe once sealed in bags that can only be opened under laboratory conditions. Photographed items should aim to show not just the item but in context with other items and layout, such as blood spray on a wall in context with its position in a room.

KEY POINTS

1. Using someone who is familiar with the premises (mindful of contamination) may help identify anything that is out of place, missing, unusual, or suspicious or any factors (in)consistent with the lifestyle of the victim.
2. Some areas of premises may require specialist equipment and training, eg to search below floors, in lofts or behind walls.
3. Staff should be aware of finding potential vulnerable people such as children prior to and during searches who might need safeguarding. This includes remaining alert to the signs of neglected, abused or sexually exploited children, including those who might have been trafficked (also may apply to adults, particularly in multi-occupancy premises).

When searching premises (eg dwellings) where there are likely to be unconnected third parties, it is worthwhile preparing a displacement plan. People who have no criminal involvement can sometimes get caught up in investigative searches merely because of their association with, presence on or familial link to the premises. Often this can be anticipated in advance and a suitable plan prepared to minimise hardship (such as in a Community Impact Assessment (CIA)) caused by the disruptive and sometimes upsetting collateral effects of a search. On the plus side the search may also provide an opportunity to communicate with such persons, who may be able to assist the enquiry with information.

When reviewing a search after it has been conducted, the total time taken and amount and types of resources can be checked to give an indication of standard and thoroughness. Official documentation should note what, if any, damage was caused during the search and may help plan for or mitigate future compensation claims. If this is a foreseen possibility, then a plan to have a photographic record before and after the entry and search might prove useful.

Cordons erected around search premises will provide protection, enable the search to take place undisturbed and provide safety for those conducting the search. This may be a control tactic for any identified risks where prolonged search operations are required and where the premises are in areas that are hostile to the police, or are connected to hostile and dangerous families and individuals (eg connections with an OCG).

Checklist—Searching premises

Consider:

- Seeking early PolSA advice and other specialists, eg CSI or Hi-Tec Units.

- Using a scene log and cordons (if necessary).

- Health and safety risks (eg dangerous premises, persons or animals).

- Legal powers (if warrant, ensure application process is legally compliant).

- Signs of entry and exit, plus route to and from the premises by offenders.

- Use of specialist search dogs, such as blood, cadavers, attack sites, body parts, drugs, firearms, weapons, explosives or accelerants.

- CAP into/out of premises and cordons to protect procedure and staff.

- Personal protective equipment (PPE) policy, ie face mask, oversuit, gloves, overshoes.

- Stepping plates (being aware of slippery surfaces underneath).

- Exhibit recovery policy (eg photographing and/or forensic examination).

- Utilities, gas, water, electricity—inclusion in safety check.

- Additional lighting requirements.

- Visual/still/aerial/360-degree photography or plan drawing of premises.

- Forensic strategy and resources, eg CSI, experts and specialists.

- At time of entering, whether lights on or off, heating on or off, curtains/blinds open/closed when found, door, window and curtain positions.

- Clothing and footwear checks (potential impressions on mooring and mats).

- Checking for stolen or missing property.

- Specific items related to the case (eg incapacitants or cleaning materials).

- Plan for dealing with associated vehicles/pedal cycles.

- Communication devices,[9] landlines, mobile phones, SIM cards, computers/laptops (specialist recovery advice), tablets, gaming consoles, digital storage devices, DVDs, broadband and wi-fi routers, cameras, cloud accounts, digital wristbands, passwords and pin numbers.

- Satellite navigation, maps, plans, directions, postcodes, travel cards, public transport tickets, taxi numbers, flight and airline travel details, hire car companies, and luggage tags.

- Mail, newspapers, diaries, letters, photographs, newspapers, diaries, address lists, notes, phone numbers, letters, drawings and doodles.

- Financial information, receipts, bank details and statements, credit/debit, cards, utility bills and final demands, loan details, business or appointment cards.

- Signs of any disturbance and broken items.

- Obvious traces of blood, mud or other unusual deposits.

- Items of interest or that appear out of place (unusual clothing or well-cleaned areas in an otherwise untidy house, missing knives) and the JDLR principle.

- Intelligence search (eg lifestyle information, associates and contacts, drug/alcohol abuse, fetishes, associates, places visited, routines, habits, hobbies, reading material, photographs/DVDs, ornaments, medicines, appointment cards, bin contents, social habits and preferred websites).

- Linked premises, gardens, sheds, outbuildings, vehicles or keys that may belong to associated premises/vehicles/lock-ups (search/recovery plan for vehicles).

- Washing machines, driers and laundry baskets (eg for clothing, blood traces or soiling).

- Baths, sinks, showers, water traps, towels, soap, and shampoo containers (evidence of clean-up activity).

---

[9] Sections 50 and 51 of the Criminal Justice and Police Act 2001 (CJPA) grant power when carrying out a lawful search on premises or persons to seize anything for which there are reasonable grounds to believe may be or contain something which it is authorised to search for and it is not reasonably practicable to conduct the examination at the time of seizure from the premises or person.

- Door handles, mats, curtains and carpets for trace evidence.

- Beds and bedding for sexual activity and sexual partners (DNA samples).

- Toilet and sink usage (eg if used by offenders).

- Checking cups, cutlery, glasses, and discarded cigarettes for trace evidence.

- Searching under floorboards, in loft, behind bath panels, inside water cisterns and in other likely concealed areas.

- Searching nearby rubbish, bins, drains and communal chutes.

- Checking what, where and whose possessions are in the premises (may need inventory of all items in premises or certain areas or rooms to account for and prove attribution/ownership of items).

- Checking for obvious missing items (eg if missing person, shower curtain may have been used to wrap up the body; damaged or missing furniture may be indicative of fight or attack; severed communication cables may be significant).

- CCTV covering the premises or nearby.

- H-2-H enquiries around the address for information.

- Contingency for non-case-related finds and offences.

- Plan for displaced occupants or any vulnerable persons discovered, eg children who may require safeguarding or adults who have been trafficked.

- Resilience and welfare for prolonged searches and handover periods.

- Arrangements for fast-tracking important finds.

- Surrounding community impact and potential media attention.

- Checking records are completed afterwards, including total time taken to complete, items recovered and any damage caused.

If a search is being conducted to look for evidential items, under the authority of a search warrant for example, careful thought should be given to determining what items should be included (and not included). As well as looking for an item itself, searchers should be shrewd enough to look for evidence of it having been there even if it cannot be found, eg no mobile phone but a charging lead plugged in to a wall socket or empty delivery box; laptop case or manual and software but no actual laptop; or indentations in carpet where a piece of furniture was once positioned. Searching officers have to be afforded some latitude to use their skills and investigative instincts to spot things that might eventually be of interest to the enquiry (or 'just don't look right'—JDLR principle).

KEY POINT

A Behavioural Investigative Adviser (BIA) or Forensic Clinical Psychologist (FCP) can be asked to review the case and assist with producing a crime scene assessment and/or briefing officers conducting searches on what to look for. (These specialist assets are usually available from the National Crime Agency (NCA)).

6.5.3 **Searching open areas**

Open area searches encompass a wide range of environments and settings, ranging from parkland, rural areas, open fields and spaces, farmland, woodland, remote moorland and mountains to urban streets and estates, town centres and precincts. By their very nature these searches tend to be more complex and larger in scale and can therefore sometimes pose difficulties when defining boundaries and parameters. It is usual for the SIO, CSM and PolSA (plus any other specialists called in) to visit the proposed search site as part of a reconnaissance (scene assessment).

A sensible decision has to be made when ensuring vital evidence is not left outside the search parameters. For example, in the case of a public park, the entire park may not need to be cordoned off resulting in extensive time, resource and cost implications. The focus should be on what is being sought and predicting where those items may be best located. It may be considered proportionate to only search the park's paths and tracks to locate and recover any evidential items discarded by an offender during their escape. Search fatigue and morale are also relevant considerations, eg if searches are conducted over large swathes of open land. Weather conditions and reduced winter daylight hours may also influence the search types and duration.

KEY POINT

Searching large outdoor areas should be 'intelligence-led' and based on facts and information currently available, such as direction of travel, last sighting, noises heard, forensic traces, witness evidence, CCTV.

When conducting searches for concealed and buried items the use of specialist geological and archaeological advice and equipment can be called upon. For example, a forensic geologist will advise on ground conditions (ie soils, rock, groundwater and any artificial deposits) and what could be the most appropriate, cost-effective geophysical detecting equipment for the environment. Once the choice of equipment has been identified, the most effective method for its deployment can then be decided.

Specialist search equipment and resources can be sourced from the National Experts Database and/or NCA National Search Adviser and also via CAST (Centre

119

for Applied Science and Technology—see <http://www.gov.uk/government/organisations/home-office>)[10] and sometimes the military.

Specialist search dogs can be deployed, depending on what items are being sought (most typically scent detector dogs are deployed for drugs, firearms, human blood and remains). Canine assets and specialist equipment should not replace trained staff searchers but can greatly enhance the likelihood of success. The aim should be to use a combination of resources, taking advice on their various benefits and limitations within the specific environment under consideration.

6.5.4 Searches in and around water

Where a search in or around water is necessary, the PolSA will usually seek advice from underwater search units and specialists who have equipment and resources such as robotic submersible cameras and sonar devices. There are a variety of geophysical and other instruments available for searching in lakes, ponds, rivers, streams, reservoirs, canals and other water bodies.

Further advice and guidance can also be sought from experts such as geologists, geomorphologists or marine scientists with regard to water types and quality (eg saline or fresh), flow, discharge and recharge rates, tidal movements, current paths, bathymetry, sedimentation rates and flood plains. Inland and offshore waters are covered by many regulatory bodies, including the Waterways Authority and Environment Agency. Water bailiffs and any other persons who use waterways, such as water utility companies, local boat owners and users, and river and canal cleaners are often good sources of information and expertise for providing local advice useful to search teams. They often know where debris and discarded items get washed up, become entangled or come to rest. Other services such as the fire and rescue service also have specialist capabilities for water searches.

Drowned Victim Detection Dogs (DVDD) can be used when searching for victims of drowning, missing persons and victims of a criminal act. Drowned Victim search is an additional skill for NPCC-approved Victim Detection Dogs and involves searching for the scent emanating from a submerged cadaver. Gas molecules and particles of human skin or tissue are released into water as a result of normal bacterial activity during decomposition. The process may also result in a cadaver floating to the surface. These events result in scent trace being present in and over the water, which a specially trained scent dog can be used to detect and to assist in prioritising a search area.

Consideration should be given to how items (particularly corpses and body parts) are to be recovered and removed from water **in advance** of being found and what forensic evidence recovery (and/or identification) requirements may be required. Once located, dealing with onlookers and the media might also be something to

---

[10] CAST is the name for what was known as HOSDB (Home Office Scientific Development Branch). They are contactable on 01727 816400 and cast@homeoffice.gsi.gov.uk or website www.homeoffice.gov.uk.

be mindful of and may need catering for if and when, for example, a high-profile vulnerable missing person's body is suddenly found when lots of journalists are already in place waiting around the search area. Some degree of subterfuge may be necessary so as not to tip them off to give the recovery plan time to get under way and to ensure that their intrusiveness does not interfere.[11]

6.5.5 Searching vehicles and vessels

Vehicles or vessels can be involved as either a crime scene itself or for transporting offenders or victims to and from crime scenes. UK PolSA and PSTs are trained in and employ methods to systematically search vehicles and vessels, which are over and above what would be conventionally conducted by crime scene or forensic examiners. Vehicles and vessels contain many voids that can be used to conceal evidential material. The search strategy can be aimed at moving proportionally from a non-invasive search (eg using specialist instruments such as x-ray equipment or scent dogs) to a more invasive search of voided areas.

> **KEY POINT**
>
> There are significant health and safety issues involved when searching vehicles and vessels and all such activity must be carefully planned. Specialist search capabilities, eg confined space teams, may be required.

6.5.6 NCA National Search Adviser

The National Search Adviser (NSA) is a resource provided by the NCA,[12] who provides strategic and tactical guidance and support to police forces, SIOs and the police search community engaged in serious and complex crime investigations and 'suspicious' missing person enquiries. Their advice can involve the development of search strategies, tactical plans and the provision of advice including the use of specialist assets. These include:

- complex searches on homicides, no-body murders, missing persons, abductions and mass fatality disasters
- locating human remains, concealed or otherwise
- reviewing previous search activity or strategies on critical or cold cases
- preparing and writing search plans and strategies for SIOs and PolSAs.

---

[11] Alice Gross was a 14-year-old English girl who went missing in London on 28 August 2014. After a month of intensive searching (30 September 2014), her body was found wrapped in a bag, weighted down and submerged in the River Brent. The search had been the largest deployment of MPS officers since the 7 July 2005 London bombings. Her body was found by London Fire Brigade divers. She had been murdered by a Latvian male named Arnis Zalkalns who later committed suicide by hanging himself in a wooded area less than a mile away from where his victim had been found.
[12] Contact number 0845 000 5463.

The NSA has access to experts in all scientific disciplines that are relevant to search, including archaeology, anthropology, biology, geology and the use of geophysics. Additional assets from the UK military and private and commercial enterprise can also be obtained.

6.6 **Releasing Crime Scenes**

A crime scene should always be retained as long as is necessary to allow for all potential searches and forensic examinations to conclude. A decision to release a scene *must* be very carefully considered depending on practical and resource implications and public disruption, eg if situated in a residential or urban area. The SIO and CSC work closely together to make this decision, taking all relevant circumstances into account. A review of the scene examination strategy should firstly happen to ensure sufficient time has been allowed and nothing is missed, both from a prosecution and defence perspective (ie in compliance with CPIA rules).

A significant crime scene must not be released until high-priority main lines of enquiry (MLOE) have been completed, such as interviewing significant witnesses, viewing vital CCTV or interviewing a suspect. Fresh information may emerge that requires putting into context or physically checking at the crime scene. New witnesses might come forward or suspects may disclose information that requires clarification; or forensic experts may want to revisit the scene. Once a scene is released, its sterility and integrity are lost forever. Scene examination needs to be conducted painstakingly and thoroughly . . . so the rule needs repeating: *never release a crime scene too early*.

KEY POINTS

1. Crime scenes may present health and safety hazards not just for the police but for the public. If so, they cannot be released until thoroughly cleansed and deemed fit for use.
2. Never release a crime scene too early.
3. Before release, the SIO and CSM/CSI should conduct a final 'walk through'.
4. Some crime scenes, eg empty premises, can become a magnet for thieves and vandals once security has been removed. Owners must be encouraged to acknowledge responsibility for security and given appropriate crime prevention advice.

6.7 **Scene Administration and Exhibits**

Types of scene administration and documentation vary depending on the force or agency and generally include the following:

- crime scene logs
- scene examination and search strategies/tactics and plans
- search records
- lists and details of exhibits identified and seized
- exhibit recovery methods, packaging, labelling, transportation and storage procedures
- exhibit recording 'books', forms or computerised systems
- sketches, maps and plans indicating scene parameters and cordons, location of victims, exhibits
- CSM/CSI/other experts' notes and their exhibit lists
- other lists and details of exhibits recovered
- photographs and digital imagery (including aerial and satellite imagery)
- images taken independently by attending officers, searchers and experts
- crime scene reconstruction materials
- legislative authorities utilised, correct and accurate formal documentation, and copies of executed/non-executed search warrants and application details
- witness statements made by those making recoveries and seizing exhibits.

6.7.1 **Crime scene logs**

Scene logs are an official audit trail and record of everyone who enters and exits a crime scene. They also prevent unauthorised access and preserve the sterility of a scene. Specifically designed forms are used, which when completed should include details of the person(s) keeping the log, full details of all persons who enter or leave the scene against signature, the exact date and time in and out, the reason for entry, and whether protective clothing was worn. There are usually clear instructions printed inside the front cover of scene logs to provide guidance.

One (and only one) scene log is maintained for each crime scene and cordon, which means there is a separate log for both inner and outer cordons (and another for the third cordon if one is used). All logs, once completed, become registered documents and are submitted into the incident room for examination and processing.

An officer maintaining a scene log is usually positioned at the designated RVP. They do not enter the scene themselves except to save life or arrest offenders. Nominated 'loggists' should record details of all those who physically enter or leave the crime scene (ie the 'sterile' area) including the reasons why and how they entered (ie wearing appropriate protective clothing). Where entry to the scene is authorised and necessary, the cordon officer should ensure that the CAP is identified to them and used.

All entries need to be detailed, accurate and complete. If for any reason the correct log forms are not immediately available, then a pocket notebook or other note-taking format should be utilised, and the same amount of care must be taken even if recording details in this ad hoc way.

All entries need to be detailed, accurate and complete. If for any reason the correct log forms are not immediately available, then a pocket notebook or other note-taking format should be utilised, and the same amount of care must be taken even if recording details in this ad hoc way.

Those maintaining the log must be reminded that they are not to allow any person, including officers of any rank, to enter the cordoned area unless agreed by the SIO and they have a specific reason for doing so and a specific task to perform (eg CSI). Any persons already at the scene when the log is commenced should be added to the log and marked as being 'already at the scene' in the 'reason for entry' column. Where a log has been commenced in a pocket note-book or elsewhere prior to the commencement of the formal log, details should be transferred into the correct scene log form and cross-referenced.

Most scene logs look similar amongst forces and agencies, like the one illustrated here. Further columns can be added for details of who authorised entry, what protective clothing was worn and details of anyone refused entry and why.

Date	Name/Rank/No/ Title/Organisation	Reason for entry	Protective clothing worn	Time of entry	Time of departure

Checklist—Scene logs—common mistakes

- Incorrect forms or none used. Makeshift pieces of paper or a pocket notebook suffice but do not look very professional; whereas if official forms are used then usually the requisite detail is recorded.

- Precise and accurate details not recorded. Each and every box and question on the form is there for a specific purpose. There should be no gaps; for instance, if protective clothing has not been worn, the 'box' should state so and not be left blank. If it is a requirement to note the weather conditions at regular intervals, this should be duly completed.

- Incorrect detail. Attention to detail is vital, even down to the correct spelling of names. Scene logs are entered onto a case management system with all the names of persons attending the scene. Any that are spelt incorrectly will lead to dual registration, fouling up nominal indices.

- Entries not being signed. Some officers feel awkward about asking people who are wearing protective suits to keep signing themselves in and out of scenes. All entries should be made against signature, with no excuses.

- Briefing and supervision. It can be a tedious and thankless task to maintain a scene log and perform security duties. Those tasked need to be properly briefed on the importance of the role, and their log keeping checked at regular intervals by a supervisor to ensure they are completed correctly.

- Handover periods. These need to be recorded as to date, time and persons involved, and professionally managed to ensure consistency and professionalism in approach.

KEY POINT

A sensible approach to log keeping is required. For example, if CSIs are returning to and from their vehicles or equipment that are located just outside the outer cordon on a regular basis, there may be no need for them to be constantly logged in and out as they are effectively still 'in the scene', provided the SIO and CSM are satisfied there is no risk of contamination.

6.7.2 CSM and CSI notes and exhibit lists

Whenever a crime scene exhibit list is compiled by a CSM or CSI during their scene examination, the list (and their notes) should be copied and handed to the EO for checking and processing by the incident room. This is because they may contain details of important items that the SIO needs to be aware of so important decisions can be made and actions raised. The lists should not be left, for example, until a forensic strategy meeting is held, which may be too late to instigate fast-track actions. This rule also applies to any other experts who attend and examine aspects of the scene and may prepare their own exhibit lists, such as forensic providers.

6.8 Exhibit Management

There are correct and proper procedures and processes for the handling, packaging, transportation, continuity and integrity of exhibits—compliance of which must be provable beyond all reasonable doubt to a court of law. Lawyers like to search for mistakes and omissions to get a ruling in their favour when vital evidence relies upon proving the integrity of an exhibit or process.

KEY POINT

Processes, procedures, records and documentation fall under intense scrutiny from legal teams if an exhibit becomes a key piece of evidence in a criminal trial.

6.8.1 'Continuity' and 'integrity'

These are key terms within the context of crime scene, exhibit management and evidence recovery.

> **Continuity**—A continuous, complete and accurate record of all the movements of any evidential material from identification at a crime scene, subsequent recovery, transportation, examination, storage and any other investigative processes until the ultimate destination—production at court.
>
> **Integrity**—The handling, packaging and storage of evidential material that can demonstrate beyond all reasonable doubt that there has been no interference, contamination, cross-transfer, tampering, destruction or loss that could have occurred to the item, either intentionally or accidentally.
>
> **Contamination**—When something is added to an evidential sample from another, either accidentally or intentionally.
>
> **Cross-transfer**—Process in which material from one location, person or item is transferred to another.

6.8.2 **Power to seize evidence**

When not under the power of a magistrate's search warrant (eg section 8 of PACE which allows anything to be seized and retained for which the search is authorised) then section 19 of PACE is often relied upon for a power to seize evidential items which are *on premises*. This power applies to a constable or civilian designated an Investigating Officer (under section 38 of the Police Reform Act 2002, Sch 4, Pt 2, para 19(a)) provided:

(a) they are **on premises** lawfully; and
(b) there are reasonable grounds for believing:
   (i) the item seized is either (1) a thing which has been obtained in consequence of the commission of an offence (s 19(2)): eg stolen items or the proceeds of crime); or (2) that it is evidence in relation to an offence under investigation or **any other offence** (s 19(3)); and
   (ii) that it is necessary to seize it in order to prevent it being concealed, lost, damaged, altered, or destroyed (s 19(2)(b) and (3)(b)); and
(c) the item is not one for which there are reasonable grounds for believing it to be subject to legal privilege (as defined in s 10 (s 19(6)).

The term 'on premises' for the purposes of this power under PACE is one that is extensive and includes vehicles, vessels, aircraft and hovercraft; and any tent or movable structure (PACE 1984, App 1). However, the case of *Ghani v Jones*[13] provides a ruling on the justification for taking articles where no one has been arrested or charged and is not restricted to being 'on premises'. This power should also extend to civilian investigating officers under Schedule 4 to the Police Reform Act 2002. The ruling states there must be reasonable grounds for believing:

---

[13] *Ghani v Jones* Court of Appeal 1969 No 2947 [1970] 1 QB 693.

(a) a serious crime has been committed;
(b) the article was either the fruit of the crime or the instrument by which it was committed or was material evidence to prove its commission;
(c) the person in possession of the article had committed the crime or was implicated in it;
(d) the police must not keep the article or prevent its removal for any longer than is reasonably necessary to complete the investigation or preserve it for evidence; and
(e) the lawfulness of the conduct of the police must be judged at the time and not by what happens afterwards.

There may be occasions when this case ruling is useful, for example when dealing with persons who are potential 'crime scenes' but not under arrest or on premises and items are required from them for examination, such as clothing or personal effects or communication devices.

6.8.3 **Forensic Management Groups and exhibit reviews**

A forensic strategy determines what items are prioritised for examination. This will require a regular meeting to methodically discuss each and every item and exhibit that may be considered suitable for examination. A Forensic Management Group (FMG) can be formed to perform this function and ensure that every available evidence recovery opportunity is used to full potential. This group might be comprised of the SIO/DSIO, CSM, forensic providers and specialists, fingerprint experts, EO, the MIR Office Manager and any internal forensic budget holder. The group can be brought together and tasked with managing all the forensic issues in the enquiry. The meetings should be recorded and actions raised and prioritised from decisions made.

The FMG responsibilities include keeping all seized exhibits under continuous review. This can be achieved by adopting a screening process at regular review meetings whereby each exhibit is rated for both forensic potential and priority. The EO can print off a list of all exhibits and score each one as per the following grid:

F—shows whether the exhibit has forensic potential, then graded with a score of '1–3', 1 being high priority, 2 medium and 3 low priority.
FP—fingerprint examination required.
O/D—other document or exhibit for disclosure only.
O/R—other document or exhibit for research.
O/C—other document or exhibit required for court.

All exhibits graded 'F1' should be discussed at a forensic strategy meeting in order to ensure the appropriate examination is considered. In view of the high costs of forensic examination, it is essential that care is taken to prioritise only those items that may provide a result of significant evidential value.

Further review meetings can be held throughout the investigation to ensure all priority exhibits are fully debated for forensic examination. Minutes of all meetings should be recorded and registered onto HOLMES (or similar). Reasons why they were sent for examination or why they were not should be noted, along with an explanation of all decisions made. Minutes taken can be cross-referenced in the SIO's policy file.

During the early stages of an investigation the FMG should seek to identify *fast-track* forensic submissions that may result in the early identification of a suspect and lead to a speedy arrest. These should be a standard feature and agenda item for discussion at any forensic exhibit meetings.

6.9 Role of Exhibits Officer (EO)

A trained and experienced EO has a pivotal role in a major investigation which is usually performed by an experienced detective or investigator trained in all aspects of exhibit management, including packaging, storage, documentation, and computerised management system together with an up-to-date knowledge of forensic techniques and their applications. They should also be conversant with relevant parts of health and safety legislation, CPIA and PACE.

The EO(s)[14] once appointed usually remain(s) dedicated to the role for the duration of the investigation through to completion of trial and case disposal. They attend briefings and establish a close working relationship with the CSM, CSIs, first officers responding and indeed all the investigating team to ensure that all recovered exhibits are properly handled and packaged, together with the necessary signed labels. They must guard against any risk of contamination or cross-contamination throughout the entire exhibit-handling process. The importance of preserving the integrity of an exhibit cannot be overstated.

The EO should be allocated suitable facilities and accommodation with appropriate storage, freezer and drying facilities, and a computer terminal. This is to ensure all exhibits are kept under close review, particularly those sent for specialist forensic or fingerprint treatment or examination. There should be formal exhibit reviews on a regular basis in order to assess the forensic potential of every exhibit and to check outstanding examination results. It may be useful for the EO to maintain a spreadsheet or other suitable means of representing information for exhibits that have been forwarded for tests and examination.

---

[14] A case may be of such a size and complexity that more than one EO may be required.

KEY POINT

Tracing physical evidence and potential exhibits is important to investigations so the EO may be allocated tasks/actions to check relevant found property records and stores for any items that may be of interest to the investigation, such as knives, blood-stained clothing, footwear, pedal cycles, or mobile phones.

6.10 Use of Specialists and Experts

There are many types of forensic evidence, examination techniques, and experts who may be able to provide assistance in providing supporting evidence. Some sciences are constantly evolving and the SIO and their enquiry team should strive to make the best use of what is available. It is always useful to keep up to date or find out what scientific methods and techniques there are available.

The NCA Specialist Operations Centre (SOC) maintains an Expert Advisors' Database (EAD) which contains details of a wide spectrum of forensic experts. The SOC identifies areas of expertise and forensic experts who may be able to assist in solving major crime. Advisers are available who can help identify and source particular expert advisers. While they do not accredit experts nor offer any guarantees as to reliability or suitability, their database contains up-to-date information on each individual or company as to what they can provide, current CV, who has used them previously and what the outcome was. The SOC can be contacted by email at soc@nca.pnn.police.uk or by telephone on 0845 000 5463.

KEY POINT

If a number of specialist resources and assets are utilised during searches and the processing of crime scenes, then the effective coordination and management of those resources is required via a clear command and control structure.

6.11 Health and Safety Considerations

Crime scenes present a range of hazards that require dynamic risk assessment. Examples of these include:

- liquid blood and body fluids
- items stained with blood or other body fluids
- infestations and parasites
- drugs and drugs paraphernalia (eg syringes)
- hazardous chemicals and poisonous gases
- fires, heat and hot environments
- explosives and improvised explosive devices (IEDs)

- decomposing human remains
- unsafe and collapsing buildings or structures
- firearms and ammunition
- sharp items
- animals and pets
- difficult terrain or environments (eg high-voltage electricity, traffic and weather conditions)
- difficult or dangerous individuals and offenders
- hostile crowds.

Determining scene safety for all investigative personnel is essential to the investigative process. The risk of physical injury must be managed prior to initiating any scene investigation. Generic risk assessments may exist for attendance at crime scenes. However, wherever possible appropriate advice should be sought and personal protective clothing and equipment worn and used when required. In addition to protecting the individual, this minimises the possibility of contamination. At a major or serious crime scene, standard protection usually consists of a scene suit with hood up, face mask, overshoes, and protective gloves.

When dealing with scenes containing blood staining or known infectious diseases, extra care must be taken to avoid hazards and risk from potential blood-borne infections, eg HIV or Hepatitis B. Gloves should always be worn when handling items or persons covered in blood or other bodily fluids. Dried blood is also a hazard as it can enter the body through mucus membranes. Wearing a disposable mask can reduce the risk of inhaling particles. Footwear or other items of police clothing may also need to be decontaminated to avoid the risk of cross-transfer.

KEY POINT

Firearms and explosive devices are per se very dangerous. Firearms must never be handled until they have been rendered safe by a qualified firearms officer or equivalent accredited expert. The same rule applies for any potential explosives or chemicals.

Staff deployed at crime scenes must remain vigilant to spot dangers, think quickly, adapt and take a flexible approach. In extreme cases, they may have to instinctively abandon crime scenes, pick up exhibits or leave a deceased in place because of the severity of the danger or risk involved. Potential threats to members of the public and/or officers in some circumstances may present no alternative. Some priorities override the needs of the investigation and it may not always be possible to keep a crime scene sterile.

Safety of the public and the personnel who are engaged at the scene is at all times of paramount importance and non-negotiable. If there is a conflict of interest between public safety and the investigation, the former always takes precedence, although it should always be the aim to try to minimise the destruction or loss of evidential material. Reasons why any emergency actions were taken should be recorded and made known to the SIO and CSM/CSI as soon as practicable. Actions that have limited the potential for forensic recovery must be justified at a later stage. This demonstrates good standards of integrity and honesty of purpose.

KEY POINTS

1. The SIO, CSM and all supervisory staff should ensure there are adequate safeguards in place for those engaged at crime scenes. Members of search and examination teams may need to spend a lot of time in what might be wet, cold or unpleasant working conditions and provisions should be made for their welfare and safety. Providing warm and dry rest, changing, cleaning, toiletries and refreshment facilities within easy access can make a whole lot of difference when working in a difficult environment and help maintain high levels of morale.
2. Appropriate personal protective equipment (PPE) must always be incorporated into risk management control strategies.

References

ACPO, *National Crime Scene Investigation Manual*, Issue 1 (NPIA, 2007), 46–7
ACPO, *Practice Advice on Search Management and Procedures* (NCPE, 2006), 164–6

7

Investigation Management

7.1 **Introduction**

Professional management of an investigation is paramount to success. There are numerous examples of high-profile cases that have proved unsuccessful. Lord Byford, for example, commented in the famous Yorkshire Ripper (Peter Sutcliffe) case that 'the incident room became overwhelmed by a welter of information', because everything had been stored on handwritten index cards.[1] Even following the introduction of HOLMES (Home Office Large Major Enquiry System), some enquiries struggled to cope simply due to the complexities of managing vast and rapid amounts of information in high-volume cases.

In another example, Operation Fincham, the tragic case in Soham (2002) of the murders of Holly Wells and Jessica Chapman, the HMIC report commented 'the delay in putting into place appropriate mechanisms had an impact on the extent to which the force was able to manage the sheer volume of information which was to descend upon it in connection with what rapidly became one of the largest enquiries of its kind in the UK for many years'.[2]

This chapter aims to outline core roles, responsibilities, strategies, conventions and standard procedures which must be used to manage a full-scale proactive or reactive investigation. There will be an outline not only of roles and processes but of responsibilities that need to come together. These are all necessary and essential administrative methods that enable an SIO to launch and manage investigations successfully. They help provide greater professionalism and accountability for formal requirements enshrined in law, eg disclosure principles under the Criminal Procedure and Investigations Act 1996 (CPIA), and serve as a solid foundation block for any investigation.

There are sections on formulating main lines of enquiry and using investigative strategies; how to deal with information; and action management, including fast-track actions and statement policies. Wherever possible these are all '*must dos*' for SIOs.

7.2 **Setting Up an Incident Room**

A Major Incident Room (MIR) becomes the 'beating heart' of an investigation. Getting one established quickly is key, particularly when a 'crime in action' (eg kidnapping or suspect hunt) is in progress, when it becomes even more important to set up an MIR quickly to support and stabilise administrative and decision-making functions.

MIRs vary considerably and ideally there is one available that is the right size with the right equipment and facilities. When deciding upon the location of a

---

[1] Sir Lawrence Byford, '*The Byford Report*' (1981) HMIC, London.
[2] Sir R Flanagan, '*A Report on the Investigation by Cambridgeshire Constabulary into the Murders of Jessica Chapman and Holly Wells at Soham on 4 August 2002*' (June 2004), HMIC, London. [note: the triage process that Cambridgeshire did eventually introduce became the precursor to developing the modern-day MIR-web that now deals with a high volume of incoming information in a flexible way against criteria set by the SIO (eg Op. Sumac in Suffolk].

MIR a number of factors should be considered. The geographic siting near to the area of investigation and the provision of suitable accommodation is preferable, although it is common for most forces and agencies to have opted for more centralised incident room facilities for reasons of cost savings and enabling multi-incident/collaborative working. The accommodation should include sufficient HOLMES (or similar case management system) terminals, briefings facilities, report writing area, car parking and secure exhibit storage. In more widespread investigations, use can be made of temporary satellite rooms, often in other force areas, fitted with HOLMES connection and ideally some visual (video) or telephone dial-in conferencing facilities.

In the early response phase, a makeshift room may have to be utilised until a suitable MIR is identified and available. If so, the management of any transfer and administrative movement needs to be skilfully coordinated so as not to cause disruption to the enquiry.

KEY POINT

Most police forces run major enquiries on HOLMES through special incident rooms using trained staff. An early decision may have to be taken as to whether an enquiry goes on to HOLMES or an equivalent downsized version (there are effectively three levels of HOLMES: 'full', 'intermediate' and 'minimum'). HOLMES provides an excellent analytical and research facility, plus action/exhibits management and a comprehensive disclosure package that can be cross-linked with other forces. There are enormous advantages in putting an enquiry onto a system like HOLMES as early as possible.

Any case management system, however, must not be allowed to dictate the progress or pace of an enquiry. It is there to assist in its smooth running and to improve effectiveness; management of information is paramount to the success of an investigation. At all times the SIO and their management team must adopt a disciplined approach and introduce monitoring and review mechanisms to check what work the MIR staff are producing through the system. The SIO and investigation team run the enquiry, and HOLMES is there as a valuable tool to assist.

One early function of an MIR is to gather all the original material generated during the initial response phase. Often this involves staff no longer engaged on the enquiry and steps should be taken to collect it at the first (de)briefing held. It is vital to safeguard the integrity of this information, in particular first accounts from key witnesses and any significant comments made by suspects, together with any other 'first hand' material, such as emergency calls, fast-track CCTV footage, ANPR hits and continuity of exhibits. All this information needs to be collected, logged and processed through the MIR.

Checklist—Key roles in an MIR

SIO

Has overall responsibility for the MIR eg allocation, final 'sign off' or 'referral' of actions. Important to note that running an investigation on HOLMES (or manual system) does not replace any of the SIO's responsibilities, despite the role of others listed below.

Deputy SIO (DSIO)

Responsible for conduct of the investigation in absence of SIO, plus any other tasks as nominated (eg dealing with sensitive intelligence).

Office Manager (OM)

Manages MIR staff, ensures systems, procedures and effective running of MIR are maintained. Implements SIO instructions and monitors high-priority actions, reads and assesses all reports and documents, and approves for filing. Maintains awareness of all developments and informs SIO.

Receiver (R)

Usually most up to date in respect of current state of enquiry, as all material coming into the MIR goes through them first. They assess, prioritise and determine the urgency of information, and identify important developments and opportunities.

Action Manager (AM)

Manages and allocates actions. Must have current knowledge of all staff workloads, their skills and experience to inform allocation decisions. Good working knowledge of area useful. Liaises with SIO to examine actions allocated, referred, for referral and pending lists and recognises priorities.

Document Reader (DR)

Reads and examines all statements, officers' reports, interviews and other documents (eg PDFs, H-2-H questionnaires) in great detail. Decides where additional actions need to be raised to progress the investigation in line with the SIO's policy and direction. Assesses importance and priority of documents, producing a summary of contents where necessary.

Action Writer (AW)

Usually an indexer who raises actions as directed (particularly during (de)briefing sessions). Ensures actions are not being duplicated and the originating authority is clearly outlined.

Indexer (I)

(HOLMES database) Indexes all documentation as indicated by R or DR, raising actions as indicated and maintaining designated indexes and categories on the database. Inputs results and endorses documents.

Registrar (Reg)	Usually an indexer tasked with registering documents (ie on HOLMES). Could be separate role if high-volume messaging system utilised (eg in Cat A+ type incident) to ensure documents are entered onto database as soon as possible.
Exhibits Officer (EO)	Records and safeguards all property and material recovered and ensures correct packaging, labelling, indexing and storage of exhibits (see also Chapter 6.9).
H-2-H Coordinator (H-2-HC)	Manages all H-2-H enquiries. Checks documentation and ensures completed correctly with any actions raised through the MIR. Agrees content of questionnaire, level required and parameters of area to be covered with SIO. Supervises and briefs all H-2-H teams.
Disclosure Officer (DO)	Examines and is responsible for disclosure of all material in enquiry. Prepares all schedules for prosecutor and edits relevant material prior to service on defence.
File Preparation Officer (FPO)	Prepares case papers in consultation with SIO, OM, DO and EO. Liaises with prosecutions team. Arranges storage of all case papers and associated material.
Researcher (R)	Undertakes detailed research of HOLMES to seek out important links and information that may be missed by other more specific office roles. Can be specifically tasked by SIO on large enquiries.
HOLMES Account Manager	Ensures compliance with rules and conventions plus MIRSAP. Checks indexing and registration categories and documents.
Typist	Types up documents from original statements, officers' reports, messages, interview transcripts and other documents as required.

Role descriptions are further outlined in the *Guidance on Major Incident Room Standardised Administrative Procedures*.[3] It suggests how some roles can be combined (often referred to as 'double-hatting') when resources are limited. For example, Deputy SIO may be combined with Office Manager or Action Manager; Receiver with Document Reader; Document Reader with File Preparation Officer.[4]

---

[3] ACPO, *Guidance on Major Incident Room Standardised Administrative Procedures* (MIRSAP, (2005), 18–42.
[4] ACPO, *Guidance on Major Incident Room Standardised Administrative Procedures* (MIRSAP, (2005), 58–9.

KEY POINTS

1. Allocated roles and responsibilities should not restrict staff from performing the overarching role of crime investigator. As far as practicable, every team member should retain an awareness of as many aspects of the investigation as possible to enable them to fully contribute. It also helps to place their own roles into perspective by having an awareness of what is happening across the enquiry.
2. Incident room staff need a working environment that allows them to concentrate without interruptions and noise.
3. Desks and in-trays that are always full to overflowing may be indicative of an incident room that is not functioning efficiently (eg due to lack of staff).
4. HOLMES can be used flexibly and the number of staff required will depend on either: (a) volume of work; or (b) the number of staff allocated to conduct outside enquiries (ie who dictate amount of work produced).
5. An incident room remains open until such time the enquiry has formally concluded, and may well be required to remain 'live' for court trials.

7.2.1 **Home Office Large Major Enquiry System (HOLMES)**

HOLMES is a computerised information storage and retrieval system with five major aims:

- Provide an accurate record of the state of the enquiry.
- Determine the current status of the enquiry (eg number of actions generated, messages received).
- Provide an accurate record of all data collected.
- Assist in the cross-referencing of information and intelligence.
- Assist legal decision making and disclosure issues.

HOLMES is still largely governed by a set of standardised procedures termed MIRSAP (Major Incident Room Standardised Administrative Procedures) that stipulate the correct input, processing and accessing of data. No computerised system can ever eliminate mistakes and errors or even malpractice from the enquiry system. Human error must always be borne in mind when relying on the data stored.

7.3 **Resource Management**

Complex and major crime investigations invariably require the management of a large number of staff, including experts and those brought in from elsewhere to assist. There will be considerations such as budgetary requirements (and constraints), technical resources, vehicles, overtime costs and expenses to consider, in addition to ensuring the correct amount and type of resources are sustained.

Requests for the necessary and essential resources are best made in the early stages. This is to ensure as much evidence and information is captured and secured quickly, which in the long term will save time and resources and prevent evidence becoming harder to find or contaminated. Enquiry teams can be reassessed and trimmed back later when resource implications may not be as critical. It is worth keeping a regular check on what resources are available in advance, particularly when undertaking 'cover rota' duties.

Effective management means getting teams to perform to a higher standard than their numbers would generally allow. There are always finite resources available and the SIO should record any staffing problems and when/how they have to balance investigational needs against (non-)available resources. This will afford some protection if a formal review comes later. Provided teams are willing, eager, enthusiastic and dedicated to their tasks—attitudes inherent in good SIOs—success can still be achieved despite staffing limitations. The key is to *get the most out of available staff* by setting focused, achievable and realistic priorities.

KEY POINTS

1. When staff work in pairs it halves the number of resources available. Unless there is a high-risk task, corroboration is required or a complex TIE action needs to be completed, then there is little justification for doubling up teams.

2. Making an estimate of the nature and scale of the investigation helps make informed decisions as to quantity and type of resources required, eg whether it is a Category A, B or C murder, and the gravity of the crime, likely political, community and media impact, etc, which will need regular reassessment.

3. If an enquiry is likely to be protracted, a human resource (HR) adviser should be tasked with monitoring the development and career aspirations of staff, as prolonged attachments can sometimes hinder career progression.

7.3.1 Factors affecting resourcing

In addition to categorisation, there are other factors to consider:

- Volume of work (eg number of victims, witnesses, suspects, crime scenes and material being gathered such as CCTV).

- Solvability factors (forensic, witnesses, suspects or passive data potential).
- Complexity (eg organised crime, specialist area, linked series crime, cultural barriers, unusual modus operandi (MO)).
- Levels of local, (inter)national, political, community or media interest.
- Whether deemed a 'critical incident'.
- Likely cost and competing demands.

7.3.2 **Specialist resources and support**

An SIO will often need to call upon specialist resources to assist their investigation. These could come from a multitude of sources, some of the more common being:

- Crime Scene Investigators/Examiners/Managers and Coordinators (CSIs/CSEs/CSMs/CSCs).
- Forensic and fingerprint experts and service providers.
- Physical search specialists (eg PolSAs/PSTs, aerial support, underwater search teams, CAST, hi-tech digital and computer expertise).
- Imaging and photography expertise.
- Intelligence cells.
- Specialist investigative interviewers.
- Forensic pathologist.
- House-to-house (H-2-H) teams and coordinator.
- Communications/digital media/data investigators and single point of contact (SPoCs).
- Passive data recovery teams (eg CCTV and ANPR).
- Tactical firearms teams.
- Covert operations advisers, assets and teams.
- Other agencies and partners (eg Fire Service, local area health authority, LCSBs).
- National Crime Agency (NCA).[5]

7.4 **Enquiry Team Structure**

Dependent on the type and scale of enquiry, an SIO needs to consider who and what is required and how the investigation team will be structured. There is no 'one size fits all'; however, it is worthwhile giving some early thought to this, and a flow chart is often the simplest way to produce an enquiry-team structure, which may look something like this:

---

[5] The NCA resources are further described in Chapter 10.

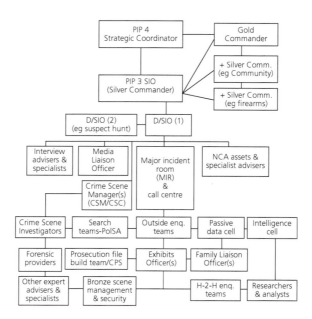

Delegated areas of responsibility can be assigned to any or all of the various tasks and roles, although they must all still report back to the SIO, who must retain overall responsibility for the investigation. This is a management method that allows important areas of responsibility to be delegated. The SIO can discuss and agree policies and tactics and request regular updates on progress.

In addition, the SIO needs to be aware that in some cases there may be other parallel investigations which need to be factored in. Common examples are Serious Case Reviews (SCRs) when a death enquiry involves a child or young person (see Chapter 15), Child Care Proceedings through the civil courts, Domestic Homicide Reviews (DHRs) held in all domestic homicide cases (Chapter 14) and Independent Police Complaints Commission (IPCC) investigations when the death has some prior police involvement. Such reviews are normally set up through the initial multi-agency Gold (Strategic Coordination) Group (aka SCG) meeting at which persons with joint responsibilities may be involved such as Local Child Safeguarding Board (LCSB) members (see Chapter 16). It is important for the SIO to link in with lead members of each group to establish strict terms of reference to avoid duplication of work, the safe exchange of information and appropriate third-party disclosure arrangements in accordance with CPIA.

7.5 **Main Lines of Enquiry (MLOE)**

These are a means of setting and focusing clear investigative priorities that aim to establish the facts, find the evidence, and arrest and convict the person(s) responsible for the offence(s). The SIO can draw up a list entitled 'main lines of enquiry' (MLOE, or LOE) in their policy file that ensure all staff are made fully aware of what they are and in which direction the investigation is headed. This enables the enquiry to remain focused and not get too bogged down with non-urgent actions and enquiries that may be the product of an administration and case management system.

Some main (or key) lines will be obvious and stand out from the information available and the circumstances under investigation—for instance, known key witnesses who need to be interviewed quickly, or potential exhibits that can be forensically fast-tracked for the offender's fingerprints or DNA, or the securing and viewing of CCTV footage that may provide images of the persons responsible. This also allows for important enquiries to be prioritised because they present a pressing need to rule in or out a process that is sometimes commonly referred to as *'clearing the ground from under your feet'*.

In formulating MLOE, the SIO has to consider where the necessary investigative material is likely to come from. The answer normally lies in sources such as:

- Victims and witnesses.
- Suspects (eg admissions, provable lies or implicating others).
- Forensic/fingerprint and other expert evidence (including specialists and experts).
- Passive data (eg CCTV, communications data, ANPR, digital media).
- Circumstantial evidence (ie evidence of circumstances surrounding the offence which provides inferences, eg failing to furnish a credible alibi).
- Intelligence.

When producing MLOE, there is freedom to use all available information and material (eg intelligence) and not just material that is admissible as evidence. All information relied upon must, of course, be evaluated and analysed to determine reliability, accuracy and suitability. This rule applies to all sources of information, whether from witnesses, electronic/scientific sources, or whatever. The ABC principle states:

> A—Assume nothing
> B—Believe nothing
> C—Challenge/check everything

Setting too many main lines of enquiry can lead to low productivity and overload. It is important to determine and judge the relevance and value of available information in order to make judgements and determine the best leads to prioritise. In the initial stages this may need to be done under time constraints, and wherever possible an SIO should try to create 'slow time' to consider and not act too hastily (investigative decision making is discussed in Chapter 3). Setting out the MLOE is a task that needs completing at the earliest opportunity so the investigation is heading in the right direction, correct priorities are applied and best use is made of resources.

The MLOE remains under dynamic review throughout the life of the investigation. There will always be changes. Some inevitably drop away once dealt with, are found to be irrelevant, not leading anywhere or the investigation changes direction altogether. It is advisable to make regular reference to, and entries about, the MLOE in the policy file, together with explanatory reasons as to why some feature and others do not. This is a means of showing good control of the investigation and defendable reasons for adopting or dropping (non-) significant lines of enquiry.

KEY POINTS

- Main lines of enquiry should have rationale recorded against them in a policy entry to explain and justify why they were chosen.
- If there is a significant change or development in the investigation, there should be a re-evaluation of the MLOE.
- MLOE should reflect any resourcing or logistical difficulties.

What the MLOE contain is entirely dependent on the individual circumstances of each case. Some are quite specific, but similar themes appear in most investigations.

Checklist—MLOE examples

- Tracing and interviewing (TI) one or more named significant witnesses.

- Search (physical) of a particular site or area.

- Obtaining a full profile of the victim N1 ('victimology').

- Forensic/physical scene examination and search of ... (Scene number).

- Conducting H-2-H enquiries (in set parameters).

- Intelligence collection (eg identifying intelligence gaps; biographical profile of associates, their activities, habits, methods; open source intelligence; community intelligence; tactical initiatives).

- Determining 'relevant time', eg likely time of incident.

- Determining movements of all persons at scene (1) (between – and –).

- Determining movements of victim N1 (between – and –).

- Determining movements of declared suspects (between – and –).

- Pursuing TIE enquiries.

- DNA or finger/palm print mass screening (or fDNA techniques).

- Establishing motive—eg sexual, financial, hate crime.

- Researching and analysing potential linked crimes or precursor incidents.

- Making use of a communications strategy (eg media).

- Passive Data recovery and viewing strategy.

- Victim management strategy.

- Use of a specific overt or covert proactive tactic.

- Use of an anniversary reconstruction and/or road checks in locality.

- Making use of specialist assets, eg NCA.

An enquiry team needs to be kept fully aware of what is included on the current list and up to date with any amendments or additions (except 'sensitive tactics'). The list can be displayed in a prominent position and/or communicated to everyone on the team (and version-controlled if it changes).

KEY POINT

When determining MLOE, para 3.4 of the CPIA Code of Practice has to be considered, which states that investigators must pursue all reasonable lines of enquiry, whether they point towards **or away** from a suspect (or particular hypothesis).

7.6 **Messages and Information**

Most major enquiries produce an influx of information into the investigation (if not, this needs to be queried) that needs capturing, recording, analysing and evaluating. It must be stressed *the effective management of information is of **paramount importance to the success of an investigation***. That one piece of information that can solve the case and save hours of time, financial cost and resources HAS to be identified and actioned as quickly as possible. Therefore, an effective system must be in place to handle all communications (eg calls, messages and information) that come into the enquiry. Valuable time will be lost, information overlooked, progress compromised and likely sources of information discouraged if information is not managed promptly and effectively.

The usual method of logging messages containing information is via standard printed message forms. These need to be instantly recognisable (for HOLMES there are green, pre-printed forms known as MIR/6) and include all the details of the information, the originator, time and date received, and what has been done. These messages are the lifeblood of an enquiry and have to be monitored and checked on a regular basis (daily as a minimum). Sufficient copies should allow each and every message to be forwarded directly to the SIO if he/she wishes.

A significant line of enquiry may be contained within a message, so the incident room staff and SIO have to be able to identify important information early and in order to do so messages containing investigative information should not be left lying around, eg on desks, in a tray or within a computerised database without being checked for any length of time.

KEY POINTS

1. A dedicated contact number or system is much better than expecting people to remember and quote 'crime' or reference numbers etc when they wish to provide information.

2. Dedicated 'hotlines' need supervision and management. Someone familiar with the enquiry should be tasked with checking them on a regular basis, including any out-of-hours message recording systems when an incident room may be closed. Interpreters might also be required.

Enquiry team members need to know what information they are expected to bring quickly to the attention of supervisors, who in turn must quickly know what to do with it and when and how to notify the (D)SIO rather than waiting for it to pass through administrative processes. An important line of enquiry cannot afford to wait for significant information to be idly ignored when it can be dealt with quickly.

KEY POINT

When dealing with large volumes of messages, criteria for prioritising through the use of the high, medium and low ratings should be introduced and clearly marked on them. If in printed format, the gradings need attaching clearly so they stand out (eg with brightly coloured labels or tags).

7.7 **Use of 'Call Centres'**

When receiving large volumes of messages and contacts from the public, eg where the enquiry is high profile, a dedicated 'call centre' may be required to handle the vast influx of information and a supervisor appointed to manage it. The Gold function is usually responsible for providing and arranging this resource. Facilities such as NMAT2 (National Mutual Aid Telephony), Casweb (casualty bureau weblink) and MIRWeb (major incident room weblink) can provide the ability to deal with the receipt of a mass volume of information remotely through HVM (High Volume Messaging), embedded within HOLMES. Facilities such as those provided by MIRWeb allow for the electronic recording of messages across linked forces directly onto the host force's HOLMES system on a mutual aid basis. This add-on technology was successfully used in the 2006 investigation into the murders of five women in Ipswich and commented upon in the NPIA *Tactical Debrief: Operation Sumac.*[6]

7.8 **Action Management**

Actions are defined as: 'any activity which, if pursued is likely to establish significant facts, preserve material, or lead to the resolution of the investigation'.[7] Quite literally the term 'action' means doing something or performing an activity and is widely used in serious crime investigation and referred to in MIRSAP.

Actions are numbered documents (usually printed out in hard copy from HOLMES) that contain instructions or directions to perform specific tasks and serve as a means of recording, allocating, performing and managing workloads and operational activity that drive an investigation (denoted as A1, A2, A12, etc).

Actions detail specific instructions and a course of action, to whom it has been allocated, time and date, its origin, and the enquiry result. Each one passes through various supervisory check points and roles within the MIR before finally reaching the SIO, who has to make a decision whether to file it as complete, return for rework, or raise further tasks from it.

MIRSAP states:

4.3 **Actions**

Actions are generated from information gathered during the investigation and may be requested by any member of the major incident room. Actions are raised once authorized by any of the following: SIO, D/SIO, Office Manager, Receiver and Document Reader. Actions can be raised and registered by any of the indexers. Each action is given a unique reference, consecutive numbers prefixed by the letter 'A'.

Action management

Action management should ensure that each action:
• Refers to one specific line of enquiry only.
• Does not contain multiple instructions.
• Contains sufficient detail to inform the enquiry officer of exactly what is required.

Associated documentation must be made accessible to complete the task. Action results text completed by the enquiry officer should contain:

---

[6] See ACPO, *Tactical Debrief: Operation Sumac* (NPIA, 2008). Note: with the advent of HOLMES2 version 16 this process may change but will maintain the same principles of how it should assist.
[7] ACPO, *Practice Advice on Core Investigative Doctrine* (NCPE, 2005), 77.

145

- Enquiries made to trace the subject or perform the task on the action requirement.
- Information which is not recorded in any accompanying documentation.[8]

The raising, allocating, resulting and reviewing of actions is the process by which all team workloads and activities are organised and managed. Actions are generated from information received or gathered during the investigation and should be raised and authorised only by specific persons within the enquiry, usually the SIO/DSIO, Office Manager, Receiver, Document Reader or nominated Action Writer at SIO instruction (ie during briefings/debriefings).

Once allocated, actions must be properly supervised, a function normally undertaken by an appointed Action Manager. If this function is done incorrectly, the efficiency of an enquiry will suffer. All allocated actions must remain under constant supervision as to:

- who they have been allocated to and why
- workloads/numbers of actions each staff member has
- length of time allocated (usually 14 days is sufficient time to complete medium/low-priority actions)
- whether the actions are achievable
- skills/training or experience required to carry out the tasks.

It is worth considering the acronym SMARTER—which means all actions/tasks are:

S	Specific
M	Meaningful
A	Achievable
R	Realistic
T	Time-specific
E	Ethical
R	Recorded

The Action Manager must, on behalf of the SIO, maintain an awareness of staff workloads and match skills and experience to tasks. They need to apply effective planning and organising skills to avoid potential problems, such as staff going on leave, courses, and court commitments, to ensure actions are completed in a timely and efficient manner.

---

[8] ACPO, *Guidance on Major Incident Room Standardised Administrative Procedures* (MIRSAP, 2005), 84–5.

> **KEY POINT**
>
> Enquiries are not usually conducted without an 'action' first being raised and
> allocated under the SIO's direction. The SIO/MIR has to remain vigilant to ensure
> all tasks undertaken go through the correct administrative channels in order to
> retain effective control and supervision of the enquiry.

7.8.1 Action abbreviations

The following abbreviations are used when creating actions and on HOLMES:

TIE	trace/interview/eliminate (or Trace/Investigate/Evaluate—see Chapter 8)
TI	trace and interview (or Trace/Investigate)
TST	take statement
TFST	take further statement
RI	re-interview
OBT	obtain
ENQS	make enquiries
NOMINAL	person who is allocated a sequential number (eg N12)
UF	unidentified female
UM	unidentified male
UU	unidentified unknown
PDF	personal descriptive form
AQVF	alibi questionnaire verification form
M	message form (eg M14)
A	action
HP	high priority
MP	medium priority
LP	low priority

7.8.2 Prioritising actions

Priority levels need assigning to all actions raised and allocated. Each one should
be assigned a high, medium or low priority. The parameters for these priorities
are set by the SIO and recorded in the policy file. Suggested parameters are:

High Priority (HP)	Fast-track actions requiring immediate allocation and completion within a tightly defined timeframe.
Medium Priority (MP)	Actions that relate directly to a main line of enquiry.
Low Priority (LP)	Actions that may not currently support a main line of enquiry and may not ordinarily be allocated as a matter of routine.

Not all actions should be given the same priority, eg high or medium, as this defeats the object of prioritising and organising workloads. The whole point of prioritising is to enable the investigating team to devote their time and effort to the most important lines of enquiry. All decisions and markers should, of course, be regularly and dynamically reviewed throughout the course and progress of the investigation.

7.8.3 Early allocation and recording

Most major investigations require similar actions being raised and allocated in order to conduct early important enquiries. In order to speed up this process various templates can be devised that contain a bank of generic actions for use and consideration in order to 'kick-start' an enquiry. These are often referred to as the 'first 50, 60, etc [or whatever amount] bank actions'. They are pre-prepared in order to facilitate the swift allocation and registering, and to act as an aide-memoire.

The sooner actions are decided, recorded, raised and allocated, the easier and quicker it becomes to keep track of and manage the initial and subsequent investigation. Any pre-prepared list or system for having these readily to hand can be a good aid for the SIO. In the initial stages, systems such as HOLMES may take a while to become fully functional. An initial 'manual' or 'paper' version may have to suffice, which can be set in place quite quickly. This will enable any subsequent back-record conversion (say, on HOLMES) to be more speedily organised later on.

In order to commence a quick and simple 'manual' HOLMES-type system, an action management matrix/table/spreadsheet can be introduced almost as soon as the SIO takes charge of the investigation. All essential action details can be entered onto the matrix or spreadsheet in numerical order to keep a record of what activities have been or need to be raised, allocated and completed. As the details of the actions are recorded together with names of whomsoever they have been allocated to, the list can be used as an ongoing log of all the investigative work that is being/has been conducted. This will avoid duplication of effort and hasten any back-record conversion process onto HOLMES. The matrix/table/spreadsheet will also make any handover process that much easier and show what initial actions have or have not been raised and completed. This can then be available to amend/view/send etc digitally. It may also be advantageous to appoint an 'Action Writer' at the earliest opportunity to help record and populate the list contemporaneously.

The SIO must retain an awareness of actions that are being raised on their behalf, eg by an Action Writer or incident room. Increasing the number of actions increases workloads and, once raised, a decision has to be taken as to whether to proceed with them. Only relevant and focused actions that reflect the SIO's priorities and objectives should be raised. Care must be taken to ensure the investigation is not overburdened with tasks that are not going to take the enquiry any further forward. Once raised, however, actions need not necessarily be allocated.

Keeping track of what has been done, by whom, when and where, and what still needs completing can be an onerous responsibility unless a good action management system is implemented. One can be introduced as soon as a (de)briefing session is in progress. The list of tasks can be continuously updated and logged as information is fed in by investigators, which saves precious time as tasks are ready to be allocated immediately. An example follows.

Example—Briefing

Mrs Davies from Number 12, Gould Street, heard what she thought were raised voices coming from outside Number 8 (Gould Street). Her husband, Paul Davies, came home shortly afterwards and told her he had seen a young female with blonde hair standing crying at the end of the street. An ambulance attended and treated a male with head injuries who was lying on the footpath. An unknown hysterical female was trying to administer first aid to the victim before he was taken to hospital. The victim, now known to be Mark George, later died of his injuries.

Actions arising from this initial briefing can start being raised and entered onto a matrix/table almost immediately.

1. TI +TST from Mrs Davies, occupant of 12 Gould Street, who may have heard raised voices coming from outside Number 8 (MP).
2. TI +TST from N3, Paul Davies, occupant of 12 Gould Street, re sighting of young UF with blonde hair standing crying at end of the street (MP).
3. TIE and consider suitability for significant witness status N4 UF with blonde hair standing crying at the end of the street (HP).
4. TI+ TST from ambulance crew who attended victim and consider recovery of any relevant forensic samples and notes made (MP).
5. TIE and consider suitability for significant witness status N5 hysterical UF believed attempting to administer first aid to the victim (HP).
6. Conduct background checks on victim N1 Mark George (MP).
7. Arrange treating of victim's body at hospital as a crime scene (HP).
8. Arrange forensic recovery of all clothing and possessions taken from victim at hospital and obtain an admission blood sample, if applicable (HP).
9. Obtain hospital medical notes for treatment of victim upon arrival (LP).
10. Arrange inner and outer cordons for scene (1) believed to be on Gould Street where victim treated by an ambulance crew (HP).
11. Conduct initial H-2-H enquiries in the immediate vicinity or within sight and hearing of scene (1) on Gould Street (MP).
12. Appoint Family Liaison Officer and fully brief on circumstances and provision of immediate family support and notification of next of kin (HP).
13. Debrief initial responders and arrange collection of unused material (HP).

14. Notify senior local policing commander and consider treating as critical incident. Discuss command and control requirements for enquiry and community impact assessment through the Gold Group Meeting (MP).
15. Check for any precursor or linked incidents (MP).

7.8.4 **Fast-track and high-priority actions**

These are the most effective way of prioritising and allocating urgent and time-critical enquiries. The *Murder Investigation Manual*,[9] defines fast-track actions as:

> Any investigative actions which, if pursued immediately, are likely to establish important facts, preserve evidence or lead to the early resolution of the investigation... Fast track actions are often used during the first twenty-four hours of an investigation, but they may be required at other stages, for example, where another scene is discovered, a significant witness is identified, or a suspect is identified.

Fast-track actions can be applied to reactive or proactive investigations irrespective of whether the crime has been recently committed or not. The *first* chance to obtain material may be the *last*. SIOs must ensure that any new information is brought to their attention quickly so that fast-track actions can be raised and allocated when they are most needed and time-critical.

These are invaluable for complying with the 'golden hour(s)' principles (the initial period where vital actions are necessary). It is, however, important to *review* any fast-track actions that have been allocated or in the process of being allocated. This meets one of the three strands of the important **ABC** principles—('challenge/check everything'). An SIO must be satisfied that fast-track action allocations are based upon valid reasoning and sound judgement to avoid the enquiry taking off in the wrong direction. In the initial stages any critical actions must be reviewed against changing circumstances as and when any new facts and information become available.

A control policy is necessary for how and when updates and results are expected on fast-tracked enquiries. There is little point in allocating high-priority actions if they are not completed and resulted quickly. Clear instructions and direction on when and how to report back is the key. For example, the SIO may stipulate an update or completion on fast-track actions is provided verbally within 24 hours (or less), followed by a more formal (eg written report), within 48 hours.

---

[9] ACPO, *Murder Investigation Manual* (NCPE, 2006).

Checklist—Fast-track examples

- Locate and attend to victim(s) welfare (and related parties, eg safeguarding children).
- Locate and arrest suspect(s).
- Conduct urgent high-priority TIE actions.
- TI/TST significant witness(es).
- Notify next of kin of victim and arrange FLO support.
- Obtain victimology details.
- Identify, secure and protect all potential crime scenes.
- Set initial scene search strategy and forensic examination.
- Implement urgent PACE road checks.
- Locate Passive Data (eg CCTV) sites and preserve/secure recordings.
- Set initial media strategy (eg immediate holding statement).
- Set up a 'fast time' intelligence cell.
- Conduct H-2-H enquiries in line of sight and hearing of incident.
- Initiate covert/overt proactive tactics.
- Arrange/conduct debrief of all initial responders.
- Arrange rapid response with inter agency collaboration (SUDI/C cases).
- Brief senior commanders/partner agencies on any emerging community tension.

7.8.5 Action results

Action results (or reports) are used to learn about and evaluate the outcome of enquiries. They also serve as a means of indicating the effectiveness and competency of that particular investigation. Thorough, accurate and methodical reports portray professionalism and underlie success.

Good reports are indicative of a well-managed and professional approach to the investigation, which is important as they contain potentially disclosable material for the purposes of the prosecutor, defence teams, courts and any subsequent reviews or public enquiries.

SIOs may have their own preferences and styles for the way they prefer action reports to be completed, and for the avoidance of doubt they should spell out to their staff what level of detail they expect. This may include guidance and direction on avoidance of vocabulary that is too vague, such as *'assume'*, *'presume'*, *'possibly'*, *'maybe'*, and phrases such as *'must have'*, *'obvious that'*, and *'no doubt that...'*, ie terms that are too vague and not sufficiently *factual*.

Important rules and standards need to be set so all enquiry team staff are aware of what is/what is not required and acceptable or otherwise. This is particularly important if staff and teams have been assembled or are seconded from different regions, units or agencies.

Checklist—Action reports

- Good reports indicate good investigative work. No amount of rhetoric or waffle can disguise a poor or shoddy approach and outcome.

- The type of language and comments used in social media forums or in text messages should **not** be included in formal reports. Staff should be reminded that improper/inappropriate phrases and opinions made elsewhere (eg on personal devices and forums) are potentially disclosable.

- Opinions in reports should be avoided, eg *'I don't think this person is telling the truth'*, whereas observations and evaluations based on fact and evidence can be included, eg *'there are inconsistencies in their account because of . . .'*

- Facts should be listed in a clear and logical order.

- Accurate details of times, dates and places of any work or interviews conducted, plus full details of any nominals referred to should be included.

- Information cited should be accompanied by an explanation as to provenance and a clear distinction made between hearsay, opinion and fact.

- Any rough notes should accompany reports, for the purposes of disclosure (worth checking—as they sometimes contain more detail than the report itself).

- There must be a true and complete account of all the facts and information, whether or not they fit in with any favoured hypothesis.

- Other relevant information should be included, eg exhibits and property seized, relevant documents and witness statements.

- Clear and concise language must be used; if handwritten, there should be double spacing between lines and easily decipherable words and sentences.

- Witness accounts do not need replicating if contained in a CJS statement or ABE interview which can be referred to.

> **KEY POINTS**
>
> 1. Investigators can sometimes become too preoccupied in fast-moving investigations to complete their reports. If so, SIOs need to ensure they are kept updated by other means, eg through verbal updates or during team briefings.
> 2. Beware of staff 'self-validating' important information, not fully complying with instructions or recording negative results. This may be an indication of work avoidance, trying to get an action filed quickly, being de-motivated or even corrupt practice. Checking and challenging for thorough processes is a MUST (ie to avoid missing an offender or important lead who/which is already 'in the system' (see also Chapter 12).

7.8.6 Action reviews

The SIO and Office Manager should hold regular Action Reviews of both Allocated and Unallocated Actions. Print-outs from a HOLMES account can be used for this purpose to produce a record which can be signed, timed and dated, with any instructions clearly highlighted. This allows a clear audit trail for checking both action lists/queues and ensures that all priority work is being undertaken in accordance with the SIO's policy. This task can be designated to the DSIO depending on their experience, the complexity of the investigation and the volumes involved.

7.8.7 Action filing policy

There is a requirement to determine a HOLMES action filing policy. This directs the level of management checking and supervision of all material passing through the investigation before it moves onto the Disclosure Officer and then filed. Normally at least two levels of supervision are required, those being the Office Manager and SIO, to read and place their signatures against all actions, messages, documents and statements which contain relevant material. All other more routine material can generally be left to a single signatory at the discretion of the Office Manager.

7.9 Current Situation Reports

Current Situation Reports (CSRs) are a useful document usually registered onto HOLMES (if in use) containing important details and updates about an investigation when a case is complex and protracted. The objective is to create a report that provides a clear and up-to-date overview of an enquiry at any given stage. This will be useful for briefing staff, including late joiners, review and cold case staff should the enquiry remain unresolved.

SIOs should ensure work begins on the preparation of the CSR at an early stage in the enquiry and that it is regularly updated as the enquiry progresses. Each and every updated version should be saved, given a further reference number and a 'hard copy' printed off prior to amendment and registering on HOLMES. Responsibility for creating and maintaining an accurate CSR lies with the SIO or their nominated deputy or case/file preparation officer.

Prior to closure of an investigation the case officer should ensure that either: (a) the court result is indicated; or (b) reference is made to a closing review which summarises the current state of the investigation and what lines of enquiry or actions remain outstanding. It is also useful to make reference to an audit list of case material and location of all stored and archived exhibits and where the policy file is kept.

References

ACPO, *Guidance on Major Incident Room Standardised Administrative Procedures* (MIRSAP, 2005)

ACPO, *Murder Investigation Manual* (NCPE, 2006)

ACPO, *Practice Advice on Core Investigative Doctrine* (NCPE, 2005)

ACPO, *Tactical Debrief: Operation Sumac* (NPIA, 2008)

Flanagan, R, 'A Report on the Investigation by Cambridgeshire Constabulary into the Murders of Jessica Chapman and Holly Wells at Soham on 4 August 2002' (HMIC, June 2004)

8

Conducting TIE Enquiries

8.1 **Introduction**

The term 'TIE' (which currently stands for 'trace, interview and eliminate') is an abbreviated instruction and process used as an investigative strategy. It is an investigative tool aimed at identifying those who could realistically be either a witness or offender. The process is an established and accepted technique in the UK that many law enforcement counterparts elsewhere (eg overseas) don't have the benefit of. This is because the UK process allows chosen subjects to be allocated a status that sits somewhere in between suspect and witness; whereas in many other jurisdictions they have to be designated either one or the other.

The use of a TIE strategy is generally used only in the most serious of cases where there is no clear suspect. They are rarely used in simple cases or 'self-solvers' because either they are not needed or are too resource-intensive and intrusive as they have to be justifiable and proportionate. One of the early decisions an SIO might have to make is whether or not the technique is going to be used on their enquiry. Any decision to do so should be considered carefully and if used should feature in the list of main lines of enquiry (MLOE) and explained in the policy log.

Key components of the process involve creating and populating categories and prioritising individuals who are identified from information or research processes during the investigation. Examples of sources that may provide suitable TIE subjects include general enquiries, house-to-house (H-2-H), messages, intelligence research, search activities, forensic results, analytical work and so on. Once a group of subjects has been identified through defined criteria as being suitable for the TIE process, they become the focus of a range of investigative techniques to assist in evaluating what, if any, connection they have to the enquiry. These may include alibi checks, interviews to gain their accounts, and taking samples and fingerprints. In other words the subjects are placed under much closer scrutiny in an effort to ascertain what significance they may or may not have.

Applying a more thorough and determined process to selected subjects helps not only obtain and closely examine their accounts and apply important techniques but also utilise good crime investigation skills. This includes spotting things that seem out of place (or 'just doesn't look right'—the JDLR principle mentioned in Chapter 5.11) such as nervousness, strange behaviour, odd comments, unusual marks on hands/faces or injuries, missing/broken items, disinfectant or putrid smells in premises.

Although there is no 'one size fits all', TIE strategies can be tailored to fit individual cases, and this chapter explains and outlines the basic and fundamental principles. Having a TIE policy is sometimes seen as being complex and challenging, but if used properly can be a very useful and important technique.

8.2 **National Guidance**

ACPO (now National Police Chief's Council) approved guidance relating to TIEs which, although now somewhat dated, is still used and contained within:

1. *Major Incident Room Standardised Administrative Procedures* (MIRSAP).[1] This standardised the terminology and incident room procedures. It also provided the definition of what TIE officially means, ie **Trace, Interview and Eliminate.**[2] Other important points made in this document are that the action should not be returned for additional actions to be raised when verifying the subject's account. Instead enquiries should be completed in their entirety. The document also highlighted the importance of cross-referencing by the MIR to ensure all information available and known relating to the subject is completed (eg if a relative or associate of the subject owns a vehicle type of interest to the enquiry). The document also stipulates the elimination codes 1—6 (see section 8.8).

2. *Murder Investigation Manual* (MIM).[3] The manual makes reference to the problem of over-use of the TIE process, suggesting the lesser option of TI (Trace and Interview) is often more appropriate. MIM states: *'Being in a TIE category does not mean that individuals are suspected of the crime, merely that the group is one which, in theory at least, could contain the offender...* Following enquiries, TIE subjects should be regarded as being either eliminated or un-eliminated from the TIE category, not as being eliminated or un-eliminated as the offender.'[4]

3. *Core Investigative Doctrine.*[5] Updated in 2012 and now incorporated into the College of Policing APP (Authorised Professional Practice), this covered subjects such as prioritisation, elimination criteria and conducting enquiries. It described the use of categories in order to identify persons to be subjects of TIE action, defining these categories as: *'A group of people sharing a common characteristic which is likely to include the offender.'* One paragraph states: *'When carrying out TIE enquiries investigators should be mindful that the subjects may also be potential witnesses...particularly so where they are in a group who may know the victim or offender.'* Like MIRSAP, the doctrine mentioned the HOLMES six-point code for the purposes of recording elimination. It also stated: *'An important principle of TIE strategies is that implication and elimination are always provisional and should be rigorously tested against the material to hand and to any new material that later becomes available. It is good practice to regard TIE subjects as being either implicated or eliminated from the TIE category, not as being as the offender.'*[6]

[1] ACPO, *Guidance on Major Incident Room Standardised Administrative Procedures* (MIRSAP, 2005).
[2] Confusion has arisen with the TIE acronym sometimes being referred to as meaning Trace, *Implicate* and Eliminate. Whatever terminology is used, the procedures remain the same.
[3] ACPO, *Murder Investigation Manual* (NCPE, 2006).
[4] ACPO, *Murder Investigation Manual* (NCPE, 2006), 250.
[5] ACPO, *Practice Advice on Core Investigative Doctrine*, 2nd edn (NPIA, 2012).
[6] ACPO, *Practice Advice on Core Investigative Doctrine*, 2nd edn (NPIA, 2012), para 6.8.7, 140.

8.3 **General Considerations**

TIE processes are intrusive because they need to be, which may leave some subjects feeling they are under suspicion. This may conflict with objectives aimed at securing the willing cooperation of individuals, witnesses, victims' families, groups and communities. Cultural and language barriers may provide further confusion. Therefore there may be a need to tactfully explain the process (avoiding use of organisational or legal jargon) and what each element means and why it is necessary. Using investigative processes are always that much easier when there is willing agreement and cooperation from those affected.

The Human Rights Act 1998 (HRA) is one further consideration when conducting TIE enquiries. Intrusive elimination activities may lead to potential breaches of human rights and the Article 8 legal right to respect for private and family life. A breach is only permissible if absolutely necessary, proportionate and justifiable and in the interests of national security, public safety, economic well-being of the country, prevention of crime and disorder, health, morals or protection of the rights and freedoms of others (HRA, Article 8). Each TIE criterion needs to be justified and necessary, eg if there are no fingerprints at any crime scene, there may be no justifiable reason to take them as part of the elimination process.

KEY POINT

To comply with the HRA, designated categories that lead to the inclusion of individuals as TIE subjects and elimination processes have to be justifiable, proportionate and necessary.

TIE actions need to be carefully managed and only raised either directly or in the name of and under the authority of the SIO because of:

- time and resources—two officers are often required to complete them
- research—required to produce risk assessments/control strategies
- high standards of investigation—required, otherwise mistakes can occur with offenders being wrongly implicated or eliminated
- intrusiveness—enquiries need to be intrusive for TIE subjects
- close scrutiny—by judicial and review processes
- audit trails—must be clear and transparent links to information sources and reasoning as to how and why they are being conducted
- powers and legal basis—care must be taken to ensure that tactics employed are kept within legislative frameworks and not in breach of safeguards such as PACE.

8.4 **Meaning of Terms**

The term 'TIE'—'Trace', 'Interview' and 'Eliminate'—has been around for a considerable time and sometimes get confused, although the acronym 'TIE' is referred to extensively in major crime investigations and on systems such as HOLMES. The NPCC Homicide Working Group (HWG) crime business area sub-group commissioned a research project group in 2015 which made a recommendation that the meaning of the terms be changed ((2015) 10(2) *NPCC Journal of Homicide and Major Incident Investigation*). These are outlined as follows:

TRACE (remains the same)	This term remains the first part of the process. It means conducting research on the subject, confirming residence details, description, warning markers, place of work, places frequented, identity, previous convictions, associates, intelligence checks, risk assessments, build profile, etc. The SIO should determine/agree what 'trace' enquiries should entail.
INVESTIGATE (changed from 'Interview')	Has a wider meaning than merely 'interview', though this remains an important part of the process. Should include a much wider range of tactical options, eg search/seize material, obtain descriptive details, take samples (eg DNA or fingerprints), conduct surveillance, check mobile and digital devices, obtain communications data under RIPA, look for things out of place (marks, injuries, odd behaviour, changes of routine or appearance), conduct alibi checks and corroborate movements.
EVALUATE (changed from 'Eliminate')	Extended to include both 'eliminate' and 'implicate' (ie from the category, not offence). Involves analysing results of investigation process, including verification of alibi and application of alibi codes 1–6, assessment of evidence/intelligence/information and determining relevance of the subject to the enquiry. Can incorporate making recommendations as to what, if any, further action is required or review priority of the action.

8.4.1 **'Persons of interest'**

The term 'person of interest' (or POI) has entered investigation language and is used by some and not others. However, the term 'POI' has never been officially defined or recognised in any nationally approved manuals or College of Policing APP. Neither has it been formally included as a category on HOLMES.

The term POI could feasibly refer to anyone who fits somewhere in between a witness and TIE subject, TI or TIE subject, or suspect and TIE subject. It could also be used to describe key witnesses, sources of information and those identified by Crimestoppers or nominals requiring further research. It could also be viewed by the criminal justice system as having been a means of circumventing the legal safeguards of PACE.

It seems more likely, however, that investigators who use the term do so as a substitute for and equivalent of a 'TIE subject'. If so, then a clear communication to all those engaged on the enquiry team and any others who have an involvement will be required for the avoidance of doubt.

KEY POINT

The term 'TIE' stands for a process and instruction, not title or status. Some investigators commonly use the term 'TIE subjects' or just TIEs' (eg *'How many TIEs have we got?'*). Others prefer to use the term 'Person of Interest' or 'POI' for short. It is best to clarify or confirm what the terms in use are and mean when drawing up a policy and briefing those who will be conducting the enquiries and processing outcomes. If the enquiry is part of a linked series non-standard terminology may cause confusion amongst staff who come from different regions.

8.5 **Recording TIE Policy**

Devising a TIE policy is an early consideration, with the associated decision and reasoning recorded in a policy file entry. The strategy should be well considered and clear in its purpose. An example follows:

Policy File Entry (Number)

TIE Strategy

This is a serious offence and in the absence of a clear suspect it is intended to introduce a process of tracing, investigating and evaluating carefully selected individuals who are of potential interest to the inquiry. This shall be achieved through the use of TIE actions.

The purpose of this strategy is to introduce a process aimed at more closely investigating selected individuals as to their possible connection with the offence under investigation.

TIE subjects/actions will be identified/raised from specific groups (or categories) of individuals created under selected headings that are considered to be of significance. These groups are considered to have the potential to contain the offender(s) or witnesses and will be recorded on the HOLMES database under their category headings, which are as follows:

(categories—see para 7.4)

Individual TIE actions shall be raised for all persons falling within the aforementioned categories and include a requirement for obtaining the following:

(eg samples—eg fingerprints, personal descriptive details and buccal swabs)

On conclusion of the enquiries each action will be evaluated and a determination made of whether the nominal can be allocated a MIRSAP elimination code of 1–6.

It is important not to allow terminology to become confused or misinterpreted. For example, wrongly substituting the term 'subject' with the stronger term 'suspect' presents obvious complications and legal challenges. Careful checks should be made to ensure the correct wording is consistent in official records and documents used by other agencies that become involved in the investigation, including representatives of the Crown Prosecution Service (CPS). A TIE 'subject' is something entirely different to a 'suspect', for which different processes apply, such as arrest, cautioning, custody detention, legal representation and formal interview under the Police and Criminal Evidence Act 1984 (PACE).

A TIE strategy/policy decision should record (perhaps in a 'stand-alone' document) the SIO's specific requirements as to:

- why the strategy is required
- what the objectives are
- who will conduct the enquiries, where the resources will come from and if any additional resources such as interpreters will be required
- who the subjects are, why they have been chosen (ie TIE categories) and how they have been prioritised
- what the TIE allocation policy is (eg how many per officer/team)
- how nominals should be traced and what information and research is to be completed
- what the elimination/implication policy and criteria are
- when, where and how interviews will take place
- what the pre-prepared interview plan is, including topics to cover and relevant time parameters
- what documentation is required (eg PDFs for all subjects, photographs—full body or facial)
- what risk assessment criteria is (eg research requirements, always two officers, supervisory officer to monitor)
- what samples are required (eg fingerprints or DNA buccal swabs)
- what search requirements are necessary (eg search premises, property and vehicles) and the type and extent of search (eg forensic, PolSA hi-tech digital specialist) and legal powers
- what the seizure policy is (eg clothing, footwear, pedal cycles, laptops, phones, tablets, satellite navigation) and legal powers
- what case-specific requirements are necessary (what to check for or collect)
- what the refusal-to-cooperate policy is
- what to do if necessary to caution and arrest (eg reasonable grounds arise from a significant find during search or admission made)
- when action results should be completed and returned for checking
- how outputs/outcomes will be reviewed and (re)evaluated and who by.

Some investigations require consideration of particular case-specific checks when conducting TIE actions, some examples being:

1. offenders who may have suffered injuries (eg cuts to hands and fingers when holding a knife blade) then visible checks for and questions regarding such injuries can be included
2. arson or explosives offences, checking to see if subjects have any burn marks or injuries from close contact with an ignition or chemical source
3. child abuse or IIOC offences being investigated, checks for items and environment seen in the background of recovered images.

8.6 Constructing Categories

A TIE category is a group of people likely to share common characteristics with the offender. These common characteristics depend entirely on the case circumstances. Each category is defined by discriminating factors that match those of significance to or profile of the offender, such as age, gender, ethnicity, description, movements, forensic profile (eg DNA or fingerprints), use of or access to locations and types of premises, vehicles, lifestyles, and criminal background, etc.

Categories are case-specific and the more narrow and focused they are, the better; otherwise they can become over-populated and difficult to manage. For example, not using sufficiently tight and focused time parameters for a category aimed at identifying and eliminating persons who were present at an outdoor urban crime scene, may produce too many individuals to interview and eliminate.

When creating likely profiles of offenders and characteristics of offenders to include in TIE categories, specialist advice can be sought from Behavioural Investigative Advisers and/or Forensic Clinical Psychologists. Their academic research and practical expertise can provide a more scientific and specialist approach to the selection of characteristics and criteria for determining TIE categories.

Checklist—TIE category examples

- Aged between (x) and (y) years with access to scene (1) between...and...(time parameters).

- Aged between (x) and (y) years who were within scene (1) or vicinity of scene (1) (as defined) between...and...(time parameters).

- Previous convictions for similar offences and/or modus operandi (MO) (eg knife or sex offences within a defined period and locality).

- Last person to see deceased victim alive or who found their body.

- Similar physical characteristics or profile to the offender(s).

- Used or had access to type of premises, specific location, vehicle or other mode of transport.

- Named as being involved (eg via intelligence reports, information messages or ongoing work via the enquiry teams or other sources).

- Registered sex offenders (RSOs) and dangerous or violent offenders.

- Suffering with a current mental health condition and residing within a (named) district.

- Identified by partner agencies as being of concern within given locality.

- Recent prison releases or bail hostel residents (including tagged offenders).

- Known associates of or persons closely linked to victim.

- Close relatives of victim.

- Males/females of certain profile residing within (stated proximity).

- Committed or attempted to commit suicide or self-referred to a mental clinic (within stipulated time and area parameters) post-offence.

- Sought treatment for certain types of injuries (eg burns if arson or gunshot injuries if firearms-related) or sexually transmitted disease.

- Anyone else at the SIO's discretion.

A list of categories relies upon how much is known about the circumstances of the crime and profile of the offender. As an enquiry progresses, the SIO should review the validity of each TIE category and where necessary adjust or downgrade some of the actions created to just trace and interview (TI).

The SIO needs to be mindful that a separate policy for TIE actions may also be created within HOLMES to be used by indexers and will probably contain details of parameters that define terms such as 'vicinity of the scene' or 'alibi times'. These need to be identical to and mirror those referred to in the SIO's policy file (eg time parameters for TIE of all persons at scene (1)). It should also be noted that this means there are other categories on HOLMES other than TIEs and they must not become confused with one another.

KEY POINTS

- As a general rule, the more TIE categories a subject fits into, the more likely they are to be the offender and should therefore be prioritised.
- The category entitled 'Anyone else at the SIO's discretion' should not be routinely used without justification and only then via a policy file entry and instruction from the SIO, ie not incident room staff.

8.6.1 Defining the 'scene' and 'vicinity of the scene'

In addition to the usefulness of defining a 'scene' for determining parameters and cordons for the purposes of forensic examination and searching (see Chapter 6), this process can also be applied for TIE purposes and indexing on HOLMES. The SIO determines not only what constitutes the parameters of the scene, but also the 'vicinity' of the scene. This enables TIE categories to encapsulate a wider area that is of significance to the circumstances, eg to cover entrance and exit routes. For example, a category may stipulate: 'TIE all persons within scene (1)', or 'TIE all persons within the vicinity of scene (1)' within a defined timescale.

8.6.2 Prioritising categories

Where there are a large number of TIE subjects/actions, they need to be prioritised. Investigative priorities always remain dynamic and are regularly reviewed as they may change on a regular basis. Regular action reviews (especially TIEs) on HOLMES with MIR staff need to be performed to monitor and determine progress and prioritisation. This also facilitates a check on workloads to ensure they reflect the SIO's requirements and investigative direction.

8.6.3 Scoring matrix

To assist in prioritising TIE subjects and focusing resources, a scoring matrix can be introduced. This caters for certain criteria that are specific and directly applicable to the case circumstances to provide a numerical score against which the list of TIEs can be hierarchically prioritised. An SIO may wish to enlist the services of key members of their team to assist with and contribute to this process, as it can be complex and challenging.

Certain facts and features can be used in the scoring process. For example, in a case which has a positive scene-specific fingerprint or DNA profile, any TIE subject who is not recorded on the respective national IDENT1 or National DNA Database (NDNAD) and therefore not eliminated, can be made an early priority for the elimination process.

KEY POINT

Behavioural Investigative Advisers (BIAs) available from the NCA can be useful for assisting with and providing advice and expertise on drawing up a TIE scoring matrix and also setting/populating categories.

TIE scoring matrix example

The following example relates to a hypothetical case in which a 72-year-old male victim was found battered to death at his home address between 1.00 pm and

3.00 pm on a weekday afternoon. There was no sign of a forced entry. He had recently retired and was believed to keep large amounts of money in his home, some of which was subsequently found to be missing. He resided alone and had very few associates or close family. A TIE scoring matrix for subjects contained within the categories (which would be geographically specific) may look as follows:

CRITERIA	SCORE (1–10)
Previous intelligence or conviction for burglary in a dwelling	(5)
Previous intelligence or conviction for aggravated burglary, violence or similar offence (eg street robbery, theft from the person)	(9)
Linked to the victim or relative or associate of the victim	(6)
Linked (offending, intelligence, family member, known associate, stop-checks or otherwise) to geographical location of offence	(6)
Previous conviction for daytime offending	(4)
Known to target or select elderly or vulnerable victims	(8)
Linked to the offence through high-grade intelligence	(10)
TOTAL	

Scoring matrix dos and don'ts

DO:

- Provide explicit direction on 'operational definitions' of what is meant by each of the terms, eg 'daytime offending'.
- Test the matrix to ensure the right persons are coming out with the highest scores who are expected to be there.
- Seek help where possible, particularly from a BIA.

DON'T:

- Consider it an easy or quick task; weighting scores are vital and if incorrect could waste resources with the true offender being overlooked.
- EVER eliminate anyone/anything using this process; it is a means of PRIORI-TISATION only.
- Score everyone with the same points—the idea is to distinguish and prioritise.
- Ever reuse a prioritisation matrix—it should be re-done on a case-by-case basis.

8.7 **Interviewing Subjects**

Conducting interviews is a standard TIE process important as any other and the precise method should be prescribed and agreed by the SIO who may wish to seek advice from an accredited PIP2 interview adviser. It may be decided, for example that all TIE interviews are digitally (video) recorded on DVD, on an audio device or contemporaneously on notes signed by the subject. These tactics would be aimed at safeguarding the accuracy and integrity of the interview process, an important factor, as TIE subjects can later develop into suspects or witnesses. What subjects say during an interview might be something that can be used in evidence, particularly when considering the principle that the next best thing to a confession is a provable lie.

Consideration should be given to adequate planning and preparation around the interviews to ensure there is consistency and the best approach is adopted. The preferred venue for interviews should be considered and it may, for example, be preferable to invite a TIE subject into a police station where there are better facilities and fewer interruptions, or other suitable premises where the process can be conducted uninterrupted. Alternatively, interviewing them at their home addresses may allow officers an opportunity to see them in their own habitat with the added benefit of being able to observe their lifestyles and living environment simultaneously.

Accredited interviewer advisers (Tier 3/PIP 2) can be used to help plan and prepare for interviews and support and assist those conducting them. This will ensure a higher level of professionalism and maximise evidential opportunities. A consistent list of points to cover may also prove useful.

Important areas to cover in an interview should form an important part of the planning and preparation. Relevant time parameters of the offence/incident (particularly for alibis) and the aims and objectives will guide the construction of an interview plan. If the subject has already been interviewed or their comments have been captured elsewhere, eg on an officer's body-worn camera, this material should be checked beforehand by the officers conducting the TIE interview. TIE subjects can also become important witnesses and be given a relevant status (eg SigWit—see Chapter 13). Whether there is a need for interpreters might be another consideration.

KEY POINTS

1. A structured interview plan should be an integral part of a TIE strategy in order to maximise evidence-gathering opportunities.
2. Some TIE subject interviews may result in them being assessed as SigWits and therefore merit interviewing under specific conditions (see Chapter 13).
3. Negative responses should always be captured such as: '*I have not been there*' ... '*I do not know (name)*' ... '*I cannot remember where I was*' ... '*I have never had sexual contact with* ...'

8.8 **Elimination and Implication**

A point worth stressing is that the term 'elimination' has always meant to eliminate from the category, **not** the investigation (see also section 8.2). This fact often gets confused or misunderstood. For the avoidance of doubt it will be repeated once more—elimination means from the TIE category and not the offence under investigation. For example, if an offender's DNA profile is discovered at a crime scene, the elimination policy would include obtaining DNA samples from all TIE subjects. Any sample that didn't match the scene profile would mean the subject can be eliminated from the category for persons matching the profile. This, however, does not necessarily eliminate them from the offence as there might have been more than one offender.

The second point refers back to the terminology mentioned in section 8.4. The term 'eliminate' has previously meant just that (ie in the TIE process). This should, however, also provide an opportunity to do entirely the opposite—ie potentially implicate them. Therefore any of the 'old' terminology used in this section, because it is contained in rules and conventions for HOLMES and MIRSAP, should be construed as meeting both requirements.

In order to eliminate or implicate a subject, it is necessary to set criteria to compare against. Agreed criteria and accompanying methods will not only help in satisfying the needs of HOLMES and MIRSAP elimination recording criteria, but can also be used for the purposes of prioritisation when reviewing inconclusive TIE actions. Care must be taken to ensure the codes and criteria are completed correctly. The categories are:

Elimination Code 1:	Forensic elimination
Elimination Code 2:	Descriptive elimination
Elimination Code 3:	Alibi by independent witness
Elimination Code 4:	Alibi by associate or relative
Elimination Code 5:	Alibi by spouse/partner/common-law partner
Elimination Code 6:	Not eliminated

SIOs, incident room staff and managers determine and agree from the returned Action report what level of elimination from the list applies. An important point about this criterion is that these markers can be changed depending on new information if it becomes available, for example if an associate changes their initial alibi account or it is disproved.

KEY POINTS

1. Any requirement to obtain samples or conduct checks and enquiries as part of a TIE process must remain under review and be included as a standing agenda

> item at any forensic strategy meetings or action review meetings to ensure the elimination criteria remains relevant, justifiable and necessary.
> 2. A policy is required to ensure all samples obtained are examined in a timely fashion, in order to assist in eliminating or implicating TIE subjects.

8.8.1 Forensic elimination (Code 1)

In the majority of cases there is the potential for a crime scene examination to reveal useful marks, trace evidence or material to eliminate against. These might be finger or palm prints, DNA profiles (through the taking of an elimination buccal swab or fingerprints), footwear marks or vehicle tyre mark impressions. Other items such as mobile phones or other digital communication devices may also allow for a forensic examination process to help in the elimination process.

When determining what samples to obtain, it is wise to be initially cautious and obtain them (eg fingerprints and DNA swabs) even though, at the time, no forensic results may be available to compare against. This is because some examination results may take time to complete and only become known a considerable time later when it is too late to obtain them. However, the justification and necessity requirements need to be clearly outlined if this policy is to be adopted to comply with human rights principles.

Whenever tyre or footwear marks are involved, a visual screening policy can prove practical. This is to help limit the unnecessary seizing, storage and examination of items that are not clearly similar to the make, style, type, pattern or tread of those being sought. Expert advice can assist in making this decision and, if necessary, details or photographs issued to enquiry staff to compare against. This process should be supported by Crime Scene Investigators (CSIs) who have more expertise to evaluate any doubtful tread patterns and check for potential blood or body fluid staining to support the screening process.

The cost of taking samples needs to be borne in mind, which may be considerable if high numbers are obtained (eg buccal swabs). This may include not just forensic examination costs, but also the time it takes to obtain them and the processing time within the incident room exhibit system and storage implications.

KEY POINT

Care must be taken when deciding to eliminate against forensic samples found at crime scenes. There may be other offenders involved who didn't leave any forensic traces. This is why the term 'elimination' means from the category and not always the offence. Also, some offenders commit offences (plan, arrange, conspire, etc) without ever being present at the location where the offence took place.

Retention and destruction of DNA samples

Legislation under the Protection of Freedoms Act 2012 (PoFA) was introduced in 2013, which states that DNA samples must be destroyed as soon as a DNA profile has been satisfactorily derived from the sample (including the carrying out of the necessary quality and integrity checks) and, in any event, within six months of the taking of the sample.

The Act applies to samples taken under PACE Part 5 powers or with the person's consent. A voluntary sample refers to anyone supplying a sample by consent and not being required to do so under PACE powers or as a condition of employment.

The previous position was that if a volunteer provided a sample, they would be asked to sign an agreement to: (a) provide the sample; and (b) agree that the profile derived from their sample would be used either for a one-off search relating to a particular investigation or loaded permanently onto the NDNAD. In either case, the sample and profile would be kept until the investigation was complete. If the person agreed to their profile being permanently loaded onto the NDNAD, PACE stated that they could not later withdraw that agreement (PoFA now reverses this).

There is an exception to the requirement to destroy DNA samples within six months, other than those that fall under CPIA,[7] provided by section 14 of the Act. This allows the police to apply to a magistrates' court for longer retention of the sample, if this is thought necessary to meet a possible challenge by a defendant to the validity of the process by which the profile was derived from the sample.

Section 17(6) of the Act states that samples taken from a person that relate to another person do not have to be destroyed. This means that any samples taken from a person to find DNA from a second person (such as swabs from medical examinations, fingernail scrapings, swabs of bite marks) are not covered by the Act. Nor does it apply to samples taken from a victim after death that do not fall under the Act; therefore there is no requirement to destroy these.

8.8.2 Descriptive elimination (Code 2)

Descriptions of offenders can be obtained from witnesses, CCTV, height or physique analysis, etc and used as factors for elimination. A careful decision needs to be taken, however, when deciding what importance should be attached to the accuracy of any description, particularly where features such as height and

---

[7] The Protection of Freedoms Act of 2013, ss 1-25 cover DNA and fingerprint non-retention. The Act was in response to the 2008 judgment of the European Court case of *S and Marper v UK*. However, section 146 of the Anti-social Behaviour, Crime and Policing Act 2014 allows samples to be retained for the purposes of disclosure under the Criminal Procedure and Investigations Act 1996 (CPIA) and its associated Code of Practice. This is provided that any sample taken under the CPIA is not used for any other offence other than the one it was taken for and that once the CPIA requirement has expired, it is destroyed,

build are concerned. Unusual physical characteristics such as distinguishing marks or accents can also prove misleading if wrongly assessed or faked by offenders. Personal features such as the colour of a person's skin can sometimes also be difficult to confirm with any degree of accuracy, eg under poor lighting conditions. A person who is seen to have a walking limp or peculiar gait on CCTV, for example, can prove misleading if they are in fact concealing a large weapon under their clothing.

It may be included as a requirement in the TIE criteria for the taking of a person's photograph (either facial or full body). This is so that the true description of that person can be used for comparison purposes and the avoidance of doubt.

Personal descriptive form (PDF)

A PDF is referred to in MIRSAP and used to provide descriptive detail for elimination purposes and identification. The form provides prompts for obtaining relevant detail, such as vehicles owned and used, and contact details. The form does not have to be exhaustive and can be amended to include other case-specific detail.

KEY POINTS—PDFs

PDFs should not be regarded as an administrative burden as used intelligently, they can provide invaluable descriptive information from which analysts/researchers can identify potential suspects and eliminate unidentified persons. SIOs should, at an early stage of the investigation, establish PDF criteria. The completion of PDFs can be time consuming and, therefore, SIOs should avoid the routine, blanket approach of obtaining PDFs unless it cannot be avoided. PDF criteria should be set against known facts, for example, if the evidence suggests the offender was a male in his twenties, the SIO may determine PDFs will be taken from all males interviewed between the ages of 14 and 45 years, thus excluding other males and females. Where PDFs are required, it is essential that a thorough briefing is given to investigators. Particular attention should be drawn to the fact that descriptions and clothing worn relate to the day of the incident rather than the day the form is completed. Similarly, care should be taken when recording details of vehicles owned or used by the interviewee and, where possible, officers should check the facts carefully.

ACPO, *Murder Investigation Manual* (NCPE, 2006), chapter 10.

8.8.3 ALIBI elimination (Codes 3–5)

Alibis are a fundamental part of an elimination process, provided time parameters are kept tight. The process can sometimes prove quite time-consuming and intrusive, as follow-up enquiries invariably involve others being interviewed. The reliability of alibis is always a major consideration, which is why they are subcategorised into three further elimination codes dependent on the relationship to the subject and significance in terms of reliability.

Some police forces have created their own forms for the purposes of conducting and recording alibi details, with a space for recording not only the personal details but signatures of confirmation. A decision is needed as to whether a witness statement is required from alibi witnesses, which may extend the process even further but may prove useful at a later stage if the alibi can be disproved or changes.

Setting alibi times

TIE subjects can be asked to account for their movements during alibi times set by the SIO. These should coincide with significant events applicable to the investigation determined by, for example, witness information, CCTV or, in homicide cases, the 'time of death' indicating when the offence is likely to have occurred.[8] Time parameters may need to be wide enough to include other factors, such as events before or after an incident that may also be significant. However, the wider the times are, the more effort is required to alibi a subject over a longer period.

Alibi times need to remain under review and react to information that may reduce the time periods, in which case some individuals who may have fallen within the initial periods may no longer be of relevance.

Enquiry teams should include in the alibi verification where the TIE subject was during the relevant times and details of any person(s) who can verify their movements, ie alibi witnesses, who have to be seen and interviewed. Their details are recorded and signed by the alibi witnesses as proof of verification. Alternatively, if the witnesses do not confirm the subject's alibi, then it is a good idea to record this in a witness statement.

8.9 **Search Considerations**

Included in the TIE process may be a requirement to search for and seize certain items. The legal power to do so has to be confirmed, which may be by consent, legal power or search warrant (if there are sufficient grounds and justification). Searches may involve home addresses, other linked premises, vehicles, vessels or other linked premises (eg garage, land, gardens, adjacent building, work premises). Powers to seize items need to be considered, such as under PACE or common law (see also *Ghani v Jones* (1969) in Chapter 6). Such a search may include seizing items such as:

- communications devices—check for (in some cases, seize) all communications data devices,[9] such as mobile phones, computers, tablets, laptops, routers, digital recording and wi-fi devices, gaming devices, and all contact numbers, passwords, websites, email addresses

---

[8] For 'time of death', see Chapter 14.

[9] Sections 50 and 51 of the Criminal Justice and Police Act 2001 (CJPA) grant power when carrying out a lawful search on premises or persons to seize anything for which there are reasonable grounds to believe may be or contain something which it is authorised to search for and it is not reasonably practicable to conduct the examination at the time of seizure from the premises or person.

- types of clothing, jewellery, and foot and head wear
- items that are specific to the investigation (eg types of adapted weapons, damaged or burnt clothing)
- vehicles, vessels and pedal cycles
- intelligence information (as well as evidence) and links to others, documents, photographs, anything indicating lifestyle habits, etc.

In some cases where it is known there has been some biological material shed by, say, a victim (eg if there was any blood loss) or a firearm was discharged and there may be traces of firearms discharge residue, there may be a possibility it may have transferred onto the offender or their possessions. Checks for items that might be receptors of such trace evidence should therefore be included as part of the TIE process—items such as clothing, jewellery, rings and watches, shoes, mats and door handles, and bedding. Advice can be taken from a CSI or scientist on what to look for and how to recover it.

Instructions and guidance are required on to how these searches are to be conducted, under what authority and to what extent and level. It may be that a forensic-style search is required with the presence of at least a CSI or Forensic Scientist, hi-tech digital specialist or is PolSA-led, dependent on the circumstances. If so, these need to be planned in advance with the appropriate resources made available (including an Exhibits Officer (EO)) and legal authority if necessary. Like any other search, these have to be executed thoroughly, methodically and within the law (see also Chapter 6).

8.10 **Refusal Policy**

A 'refusal policy' should be set to provide guidance in the event of a refusal by TIE subjects to be interviewed, provide information or samples, hand over items, permit a search or even provide their details.

Checklist—TIE refusal policy

1. Ask and note reason for refusal and request signature against notes made.

2. Ascertain whether DNA/fingerprints/photograph already held or other agency (identity verification on initial provider may be required).

3. If previously obtained, ascertain level of verification of identity.

4. Create intelligence database entry (eg PNC/PND requesting the obtaining of photo/fingerprints/DNA and cross-referencing with enquiry/incident room interest).

5. Consider possible grounds for search warrant/further action.

6. Immediate referral back to the SIO/management team for decision.

Checklist—TIE process requirements

All or any of the following may be considerations for inclusion in a TIE strategy:

- Alibi between stipulated time parameters (witness statement).
- DNA buccal swab (with consent form).
- Finger and palm prints.
- PDF.
- Photograph.
- Items/property checking/seizure policy.
- Search policy (eg physical, PolSA or forensic).
- Method/mode/place of interview.
- Refusal policy.

TIE checklist:

- TIE strategies are a useful investigative tool but not suited to every enquiry.
- TIEs are resource-intensive and intrusive and need managing effectively.
- TIE subject and category nominations should be supported with good reasons.
- Correct terminology should be used, ie 'TIE subject' not 'suspect'.
- TIEs should not be used if sufficient grounds to grant 'suspect' status.
- TIE actions may reveal witnesses as well as offenders.
- Categories need to be case-specific.
- TIE policy should state clearly what enquiries are to be conducted and how.
- Interviews need to be planned carefully and use made of interview advisers.
- Enquiries need to be carefully planned with specific instructions as to elimination criteria, place and mode of interview, points to cover and what the process is for taking samples, searching and seizing requirements.
- Alibis should be checked thoroughly against set time parameters.
- Elimination enquiries include opportunities for implication.
- TIE actions should be completed and checked methodically and thoroughly, for eventual sign off by the SIO.

References

ACPO, *Guidance on Major Incident Room Standardised Administrative Procedures* (MIRSAP, 2005)

ACPO, *Murder Investigation Manual* (NCPE, 2006)

ACPO, *Practice Advice on Core Investigative Doctrine*, 2nd edn (NPIA, 2012)

NPCC Homicide Working Group (HWG), (2015) 10(2) *NPCC Journal of Homicide and Major Incident Investigation*

9

Managing Communication

9.1 **Introduction**

Over the course of an investigation an SIO communicates with very many different people, groups and audiences, in many different situations, in many different ways and for many different reasons. Having good communication skills is one of the key prerequisites for the role and needs to be demonstrated at all times throughout the course of an investigation. The way in which communication is managed can have a significant impact on the outcome.

Using modern methods of connecting with and reaching out to people are now routine for law enforcement which has opened up many new enterprising opportunities. Initiatives for utilising social networks and digital platforms have been opened up, such as making instant announcements about crime and incidents in local communities and also for the public to provide their information. Local policing regularly uses digital electronic applications to inform local people about important announcements, stating what their priorities are and what they are working on. This has presented new opportunities for investigative communications and at the same time created added challenges for managing and controlling information dissemination, as the public share information in the same way.

Exploiting traditional methods of communication, such as the 24-hour news cycle and across and between internal staff and enquiry teams effectively, are equally significant. The focus in this chapter is on what could be construed as the more traditional methods of communication. Nonetheless, they should be a consideration for inclusion in most communication strategies. The topic of (de)briefings is included simply because they remain an extremely valuable tool for staying connected with an enquiry team, demonstrating good leadership and ensuring everyone shares and has access to important information and detail.

The philosophy of any good communication strategy is to aim to facilitate good channels of communication both inside and outside the law enforcement organisation through the effective exchange of information. The chapter that follows contains useful advice and content on managing communication that can be of benefit to investigations and improve the overall effectiveness of the SIO.

9.2 **Channels of Investigative Communication**

In most investigations there is usually a 'media' strategy. However, an SIO should look to expand their list of options to include 'media' as but one of a range of options or 'channels' to form part of an overarching communication strategy. For ease of reference these can be sub-divided into two distinct categories: internal and external.

9.2.1 **Internal communication**

Examples of internal communication channels are as follows:

- Conducting briefings and debriefings.
- Internal publications, bulletins, emails and circulations.
- Presentations and chaired meetings.
- Current situation reports (CSRs).
- Case management systems and policy files.
- Reassurance messages.[1]
- Contingency (or response) plans.
- Local, regional and (inter)national intelligence systems and bulletins.
- Dedicated intelligence cells.
- Poster-type and leaflet distributions.

9.2.2 **External communication**

- Briefings for and meetings with external partners and agencies.
- News media management.
- Social media and networking platforms.
- Digital methods and electronic means (eg Bluetooth circulations and appeals).
- Websites, eg those specifically created for a particular investigation or case.
- Publicising and managing contact methods with the enquiry team.
- Multi-agency communication protocols and Memorandums of Understanding (MOUs).
- Poster and leaflet campaigns (eg mobile electronic notice and appeal boards).
- Reconstructions, BBC Crimewatch, anniversary and publicised appeals.
- Community engagement via public meetings and local policing teams.

The examples under the two category headings are not exhaustive and a degree of initiative and creativity can be applied to introduce and exploit as many useful communication channels and opportunities as possible. Making the most of what modern technology can offer is a must.

KEY POINT

An external communications strategy may need to cater for planned or casual encounters with the public by enquiry team staff, either on or off duty.

---

[1] An internal reassurance message might be required if a suspect is at large and has threatened to attack officers and/or is regarded as extremely dangerous dangerous (eg member of an organised crime gang (OCG)).

9.3 **7 x Cs of Communication**

Some very straightforward rules can be applied to any or all of the elements of communication including during day-to-day communicating over the course of an investigation. According to the 7 x Cs rule,[2] all communication needs to be:

1.	Clear	Making understanding simple, giving clarity using simple and straightforward language, avoiding jargon and buzzwords.
2.	Concise	Brevity saves time and avoids repetition, is more appealing and comprehensible— by sticking to the point.
3.	Concrete	Good reasoning and logic to the message so recipients have a clear picture of what they are being told.
4.	Correct	Information provided should be accurate and precise, without guesswork or speculation.
5.	Coherent	Meaning logical and simple to understand with all points being relevant and properly joined up.
6.	Complete	Ensuring audiences and recipients have all the information required to make sense of what they are being told.
7.	Courteous	Being friendly, open and honest, considering other viewpoints and respecting/ adapting to diverse audiences.

These simple rules can be adopted for any or all of the communication methods described in the remainder of this chapter.

9.4 **Conducting Briefings**

In a major investigation the term 'briefing' usually refers to occasions when all staff, the SIO and their management team attend a structured meeting during which instructions and direction are given and information is exchanged. This might happen either once or on many occasions during the course of an investigation, or prior to a pre-planned operation (eg for searches and arrests).

Briefings are a key part of a communication strategy; it would be extremely difficult to manage and control an investigation effectively without them. They are a means by which information is disseminated and shared, ideas, tactics, and hypotheses exchanged, progress discussed, updates provided, tasks allocated and feedback gained. Matters of interest and developments can be discussed, good work praised, problems spotted, issues raised at short notice and poor standards identified. Overall they provide the vital communications link that allows an

---

[2] Adapted from an idea by S M Cutlip and A H Center, *Effective Public Relations: Pathways to Public Favour* (University of Wisconsin, 1952).

SIO to engage with their operational teams so everyone can participate in and contribute to decision-making processes that are driving the investigation.

Briefings are also opportunities to foster good working relationships and engender team spirit, gauge morale and make staff feel valued and part of the decision-making process. Team members can get together after being out on enquiries or just get to know one another and any new members, including specialists and experts, who can be welcomed and made to feel part of the team.

KEY POINT

Investigative briefings are an important means of providing, capturing and sharing information and engaging with the team. They provide an opportunity for an SIO to demonstrate effective control and direction, which is the language of leadership.

Briefings and debriefings can also be a good asset to the action management process. Having an action writer present is a way of taking/maintaining control of the enquiry and creating and recording actions for prioritising and allocating. This allows the management element of the enquiry to keep pace dynamically and speed up any necessary back-record conversion on the case management system.

The contents of briefings are a key component of the investigative process. Apart from discussing the information and material currently available, they provide a good forum for collective discussions and to fill in any missing information from the 5WH matrix. The SIO can use team briefings to share intelligence and discuss the 'what we know, what we need to know' principle (see Chapter 3, Figure 3.3).

Briefings also serve as a subtle means of facilitating supervision and accountability, as updates and progress results can be requested in an open forum to the SIO in the presence of team managers, supervisors, peers and colleagues. Questions, opinions, suggestions and requests for clarification of any concerns and issues that arise can and should be encouraged, emphasising the rule that there is no such thing as a 'stupid question'.

Regular briefings should be held and in the early stages of a complex enquiry sometimes twice-daily depending on the circumstances, then maybe once a day thereafter. All those involved in the investigation should be invited to attend and the lead always taken by the SIO or Deputy SIO in their absence.

A high proportion of debriefs and briefings involve cases that result in court proceedings. The content of operational briefings material falls within the ambit of the Criminal Procedure and Investigations Act 1996 (CPIA). It is the responsibility of each individual involved in a criminal investigation to ensure that any information that may be **relevant** to the investigation and is not listed elsewhere is recorded and retained. This applies to any conversations or discussions and, therefore, applies to all debriefings and briefings. It includes any observations relating to the investigation and any notes or accounts made/received. Therefore all that is said or recorded is subject to disclosure rules and care must be taken that any information discussed is factually correct.

KEY POINTS

- It is useful for the management team to have a prior meeting (and incident room staff, if appropriate) to agree relevant policies and parameters, such as alibi times, initial main lines of enquiry (MLOE) and objectives for the investigation. These can then be announced at the briefing, creating a good impression of managerial efficiency (and to avoid heavy debating or signs of disunity among the management team during the initial briefing).
- If there is a handover from one SIO and/or investigative team to another, they should be invited to attend the initial briefing so that important issues can be explained and continuity maintained.
- There must be a focus on positive aspects of the case, and the SIO's style of delivery and content will have an important impact on the morale of the team. Use of strong points rather than too many negative ones should be the focus (ie the 3 x Ps principle mentioned in Chapter 2.5).

9.4.1 Planning and conducting briefings

As a general rule, anyone involved in the investigation or who may be able to contribute is invited to briefings (or team meetings), depending on the subject matter (eg if sensitive issues are to be discussed, attendance may need to be restricted). However, briefings can also be subject- or activity-specific, such as forensic searches or arrest operations, when not everyone may need to be present. Everyone should be warned in advance to know what is expected of them, particularly if they have inputs to provide. They should also know the time and location of the briefing with a message that, with very few exceptions, attendance is mandatory.

The SIO needs to carefully plan and prepare prior to conducting briefings. They should be armed with all the important facts and information that need providing to their teams. The 5WH format is often useful as a template to structure the way subjects and areas are covered (eg what happened, when, how, who the victim is, why it happened, where), together with an agenda that is focused and structured. If practicable, the agenda and any useful material such as association charts, maps, photographs, diagrams and timelines should be made available. Content should be kept inclusive by ensuring anyone is encouraged to actively participate and propose items for inclusion. The agenda for an initial team briefing may look like this example.

Briefing agenda

No Subject

1. Introduction of SIO/DSIO and management team.
2. Outline of case circumstances.
3. Background information, victim, their associates and community details.
4. Current and emerging MLOE (including high-priority actions).
5. Explanation of victim/witness/suspect management strategies.
6. Outline of family liaison and communication strategies.
7. Forensic update, searches, H-2-H, CCTV (ie all applicable investigative strategies).
8. Allocation/explanation of key roles, enquiries and actions.
9. Relevant policies (eg TIE criteria).
10. Risk-assessment decisions and control strategies.
11. Administration issues (eg duties, (de)briefing times).
12. Q & A (question and answer session).

KEY POINT

There are recognised briefing models in the UK police service such as:

- IIMARCH model (information, intention, method, administration, risk assessment, communication, human rights and other legal issues).
- SAFCOM (situation, aim, factors, choices, option, monitoring).
- The National Briefing Model.[3]

Whichever format is used should always highlight the SIO's objectives for the investigation/operation.

Briefing venues need to be adequately equipped, with sufficient space for all attendees to be comfortable, observe, speak and hear. It may be necessary to find a suitable location and room that is fit for purpose. If large numbers are expected, this may pose a problem. Some training establishments have lecture theatres or large conference facilities that can be utilised, bearing in mind parking facilities and adequate security may be required.

There may be a need to show maps, plans, digital images, etc, and a requirement for basic equipment such as marker boards, flip charts, analytical charts or projectors that can display visual images such as CCTV, crime-scene shots or aerial photographs. Other diagrams or scenes may need to be illustrated to

---

[3] ACPO, *Guidance on the National Briefing Model* (NCPE, 2006) and also cited in <https://www.app.college.uk/app-content/operations/briefing-and-debriefing>.

explain the position of victims and witnesses etc, which can then be added to and built up over time. Good facilities and equipment make a briefing appear more professional and are simpler to follow.

The SIO should take good notes during the briefing and/or arrange for a contemporaneous record of the proceedings. Good listening skills are essential; one way of proving that information provided has been fully received and understood is to paraphrase the main points and repeat them back to confirm understanding and accuracy. Active listening is a communication skill in itself and one that must be encouraged amongst all those present. Body language and atmosphere can provide a good indication of levels of attention, concentration and understanding.

In certain circumstances it may be prudent to audio or digitally record key briefings in order to capture precise detail and the nature of the content, which can then be used for briefing those who are absent if necessary. This is a process regularly undertaken in major operations, such as those involving tactical firearms or for policing large-scale public events when detailed information, instructions or risk assessments are provided. One drawback might be that recording the process may make certain attendees reticent about making an active contribution.

Sufficient time should be allowed for briefings. Some may last as long as 1–2 hours depending on the nature of the enquiry. If so, allowances should be made for comfort breaks. Attention spans dwindle after a time and it is necessary to maintain everyone's 100 per cent focus and attention throughout the entire process.

The SIO must skilfully control the proceedings, ensuring everyone contributes, with an equal amount of time allowed for those who wish or need to do so. Those who come with preconceived ideas of particular theories and views should be encouraged to 'suspend judgement' so they can consider the opinions of others and alternative theories (ie investigative mindset). The proceedings need to be managed so there is no over-speaking, everyone is allowed to concentrate and hear, and proceedings are kept on track and do not go off at tangents. *Time management is critical* to ensure the briefing/meeting does not become tedious nor dwells on irrelevant issues by remaining focused.

The appropriate use of humour can be a good thing, as it lifts team spirit and encourages good listening. However, there should be no room for sarcasm, pessimism or derogatory and inappropriate remarks which do not create the ideal environment for a briefing and may dissuade people from making a contribution.

KEY POINTS

- Interruptions must be prevented and distractions eliminated by choosing a secure environment with restricted access. A notice should be placed on the door stating an important briefing is taking place. The SIO should avoid being called out to see people or answer urgent calls. This can be avoided by nominating someone to screen calls and visitors on their behalf with an instruction not to be disturbed unless vital, informing those present to do likewise and to *switch mobiles to silent/vibrate*.

- When requesting updates, staff should be selected at random to ensure they are paying attention (as opposed to sequentially).
- The SIO takes the lead and effectively manages the briefing, remaining at all times in control and adhering to the agenda, insisting that all contributions are *relevant and precise*.

There is one other important rule, constantly referred to in this handbook and known as the **ABC** principle: **A**ssume nothing, **B**elieve nothing, **C**heck/challenge everything. It cannot be assumed that information provided in briefings is always entirely accurate or that a task has been completed thoroughly. For example, if an enquiry team states they have tried everything possible to trace a TIE subject and failed, it should not be assumed that obvious possibilities have been considered—for example, early morning visits or checking neighbours either side of the last known address for sightings or information. There is always the requirement to challenge and probe.

KEY POINT

If sensitive or confidential information is provided and discussed at briefings, it may be necessary to get all those present to be indoctrinated and to sign an inclusion agreement (aka confidentiality agreement) beforehand to ensure they maintain professionalism and formally agree not to share or leak confidential information, particularly over social media platforms.

Checklist—Briefings

- Use a suitable venue with adequate space, facilities and equipment.
- Prepare and circulate an agenda.
- Allow sufficient time and manage it strictly.
- Invite the right people and ensure everyone attends.
- Have no distractions—all phones and radios to silent or switched off.
- SIO should positively lead, control and manage against priorities.
- Sketch plans and digital images can serve as a useful visual aid.

- SIO must set the right standard and tone by speaking confidently, always looking keen and interested, projecting enthusiasm and energy.

- Content should be relevant avoiding dominating, monotonous or extraneous contributions.

- General reports/updates/feedback should be taken randomly to retain attention.

- Apply the ABC principle—probe and question.

- Remain cautious about summary interpretations of what subjects or witnesses have said; always check the actual wording of statements and reports afterwards.

- Remind staff there is no such thing as a stupid question.

- Appropriate humour can be useful and encourages active listening.

- Briefings are a good forum for giving praise/recognition, gauging progress and focusing on task, team and individual needs (see Chapter 2).

- Check levels of understanding of important information, policies and MLOE.

- Make good use of props such as marker boards, flip charts, maps and plans.

- Appoint an Action Manager to raise/allocate actions during briefing.

- Beware of embellishments from those eager to impress.

- Make an accurate record of the content and attendees.

- Identify and communicate risks and appropriate control methods.

- Identify any welfare needs.

- Invite others to make them feel part of the team, eg representatives of the Crown Prosecution Service (CPS), forensic scientists, pathologists and local officers (who can also play an active part by explaining the policing environment, points of law or scientific evidence).

- If sensitive information is discussed, attendees can sign an inclusion agreement.

9.5 **Conducting Debriefings**

Debriefings are aimed at obtaining detailed information from those who have been involved in an incident response. They facilitate obtaining a chronological breakdown of events and actions as they occurred, who did what and the outcomes. Debriefings are an early opportunity to capture important and significant information or evidence post-incident response. These are sometimes known as 'hot debriefs' and a wealth of information can be gleaned from the golden hours period when some staff may also be witnesses or need to hand over vital exhibits or information.

Wherever possible, conducting debriefings should not be delegated. Unless impracticable they should be conducted by the (D)SIO. The timing of a debrief will depend on individual circumstances, and fulfilling this requirement might have to compete with other urgent responsibilities.

The primary objective is to identify what actions have been taken and by whom, and to capture all possible information that can assist the investigation—for example, details of potential witnesses, useful observations or comments from bystanders, information and opinions regarding possible suspects, suspicious circumstances that may be linked, any persons or vehicles of interest and important intelligence.

Checklist—Debriefings

- Debriefs are an important early requirement.

- Task should not be delegated unless in exceptional circumstances.

- Those involved in the initial response should be required to attend.

- Attendees should have completed notes, pocket books, etc before attending to avoid any collusion (ie 'pooled memory') and compromising integrity.

- Proceedings should be recorded if possible.

- Relevant documents and exhibits should be handed in.

- Details of actions taken and a résumé of roles should be provided.

Extra points for the SIO

- Make notes contemporaneously for immediate reference purposes.

- Nominate an action writer to raise relevant actions *during* the process.

- Recognise those who have been on duty for a long time and take account of the need to debrief them as soon as possible (this may involve overtime payments to retain staff on duty—but it will be money well spent!).

KEY POINTS

1. Debriefings should produce a package of information, documents and raised actions suitable to feed into the case management system (eg HOLMES).
2. Pre-prepared debriefing pro formas can be utilised for distributing, completing and collection.

9.6 **Media Management**

The press and broadcasting media can have a positive or negative affect on investigations and prosecutions. Journalists and reporters can cause disruption at crime scenes, block access points, and seek out and interview victims, their relatives and key witnesses, and influence public perceptions.

The mass media cannot be ignored and have to be managed, otherwise they will wreak havoc not only by criticising the authorities, but by sourcing their own information and 'experts'. They can quickly mobilise and dispatch outside broadcasting teams and use whatever means necessary to capture information and newsworthy material. Within a short space of time local, national and even international media agencies spring into action. Some eyewitnesses contact media agencies directly (and via the internet, uploading their stories and pictures) with what they have seen or recorded and speak about their perceptions of events.

Fortunately the needs of serious and major crime investigations and those of newsrooms and journalists are equally compatible, as both require something from each other. Journalists and reporters usually want to participate in mutual arrangements whereby they obtain essential information and updates they need and the SIO can use them to make important announcements and appeals. Without such arrangements it would be more difficult and costly to solve crime, gain public trust and confidence, reach out to witnesses, suspects and communities, and demonstrate openness, transparency and accountability.

If an incident or circumstances are of grave public concern or interest (eg vulnerable victim, celebrity, part of a series of crimes, child abuse/sexual exploitation, vulnerable missing person), then media attention is likely to be more intense. It must be remembered, however, that after a relatively short period (usually around 10 days or so—aka the '10-day rule') the media usually begin to refocus upon any negative aspects they can find based on an assumption that this is what makes a good story. This is when they tend to look for potential faults, mistakes and blame for what happened or didn't happen that might have.

This means there has to be a proactive approach to managing the media by working with them and providing accurate and regular updates of information. Otherwise they may conduct their own enquiries and reach and broadcast/publish incorrect or inaccurate information and wrong conclusions that do not assist in gaining public support. Misrepresentation or incorrect, biaised facts, opinions and negativity can damage a communications strategy and destabilise public and political relations. Such negative comments might include:

- speculative *links* to other offences/incidents
- critical comments about the *location* where the incident took place
- assertions about *motive* or *cause* behind an offence/incident/operation
- negative assertions about the details of victims, witnesses or offenders
- claims about mistakes made by the investigation team or initial responders.

KEY POINTS

1. The media work on the principle there is a public appetite for negative news stories. If allowed, they will make the investigation the target for their headline stories for all the wrong reasons, which can be avoided by proactively working with them.
2. Remember the '10-day rule'—usually the time when the media focus on point (1).

9.6.1 Proactively using the media

The media can actively support an external communication strategy by:

- keeping the public informed with accurate and timely information
- disseminating information quickly to large audiences
- helping the public understand what investigators are doing and why
- making appeals for information and witnesses
- identifying victims and/or establishing their last movements
- tracing named suspects
- tracing the whereabouts of missing persons
- increasing public/political confidence
- providing reassurance and advice
- developing good external relations
- providing positive publicity for the investigation and organisation.

The media can be used to urge suspects to hand themselves in by indicating the investigation is drawing closer to arresting them. Publicity can be used to appeal to the consciences of those who may be shielding offenders or knowingly withholding information. One tactic is to mount appeals highlighting precise locations closely connected to potential suspects or witnesses (eg opposite their home addresses). The power and influence of the media should never be underestimated.

It is not uncommon for reporters to be taken along on overt operations. There have been numerous 'fly on the wall' type documentaries depicting overt policing operations and routines. This is another tactic for increasing publicity. Controlled pre-verdict media briefings are also considered good practice with released material being distributed under embargo agreements to achieve maximum impact and publicity while protecting the integrity of the court proceedings. These are good examples of working with the media.

A decision must be made as to who should provide media interviews. In the early stages, it is very often a senior officer (eg Chief Officer) who fronts the media and gives reassurance to the public. This provides the SIO with some time and space to get on with the investigation without being interrupted to spend valuable time giving interviews. If there is an OCG element to the case, then it may be part of a risk control strategy to keep the SIO out of the public spotlight for their own safety.

9.6.2 **Initial media management**

Not every encounter with the media occurs at major or serious incidents or crime scenes. Yet this is when things can usually go wrong. An appreciation of the likely risks and implications is important, particularly for early responders who have initial command and control and possible contact with the media.

The media tend to get notified relatively quickly when serious incidents occur and can often descend on the scene soon after. They may already be present if reporting on another event nearby. Determined reporters can present awkward challenges for responding officers, especially if TV crews, bulky vehicles and technical equipment block or commandeer valuable space and obstruct access and egress routes. Reporters invariably try to get as close as possible for the best shots and hunt around seeking witnesses and information. They try and record all events and activities at the scene, which may include police and emergency services activity, casualties, victims, crime scene evidence, or even fatalities.

In order to manage and control them, secure cordons must be quickly put in place around scenes to keep the media (and public) out. This is done not just to preserve and protect the integrity of the scene but also keep the media from interfering with the investigation. This may include the use of large portable screens to keep certain items and activities out of the line of sight (eg casualties and victims).

KEY POINTS

- Media have a right to be present at crime scenes provided they are in public places AND outside of cordons. In public places, there is no power to require them to leave or confiscate equipment. If there is a problem with the proximity of the media and public to the scene, the best solution is to extend cordons, not threaten to arrest or report journalists and photographers for obstruction.
- The Contempt of Court Act 1981 forbids the use of any publication in the media which may impede or prejudice a fair trial. This, however, only applies during the time legal proceedings are 'active'. Schedule 1 states that criminal proceedings become 'active' at the time a summons is issued or person is arrested without warrant (where a warrant is issued, proceedings cease to be active once 12 months have elapsed without the suspect's arrest).

The media can be effectively managed through a designated Media Liaison Officer (MLO, or similar title) who assumes control by directing them to an agreed location suitably positioned away from important activities (ie a media briefing point, see next section). This is where and how they are best controlled and can be regularly updated with information that satisfies their needs to inform the viewing and listening public.

9.6.3 **Media briefing points**

Despite cordons, media crews will attempt to get into the best vantage points to take shots of scenes and surrounding activities. Media representatives come from a wide variety of agencies and although the majority may be well known and trusted, others from less well-known ones must be treated with caution. If there is more than one crime scene, this compounds matters further and they will be even more difficult to control. The best option is to arrange a suitable briefing point. This is normally sited where journalists can still see some amount of activity, but there is less interference with the investigation and serves as a place where enquiries can be fielded and formal briefings held. MLOs and/or the incident commander/SIO should consult with the media to negotiate with them if it is felt that any distressing images have been obtained and may be published or broadcast. Broadcasting codes of practice discourage the use of inappropriate images, although there are no formal powers of censorship.

9.6.4 **Holding statements**

An initial holding statement allows the 'buying of time' while a more informed response is prepared. It usually includes the following detail:

1. Confirmation that (named agency) are investigating an incident.
2. General location of where it occurred.
3. Initial indications as to nature of any investigation (eg suspicious death or vulnerable missing person).
4. If a death has occurred, arrangements for a post-mortem.
5. If an incident room has been opened, location and contact details.
6. Initial appeal for witnesses/information/assistance.

KEY POINTS

1. In the initial stages, discussing specific details about an investigation should be resisted. Limited knowledge and incorrect facts become magnified and later hinder the investigation. Staff must be reminded not to discuss the case with the media too—any requests being channelled through to the SIO/MLO.
2. Details of victims should not released, and if deceased, not until after formal identification and/or next of kin have been notified.
3. There is the option of seek willing cooperation from the media by explaining there is a proactive phase (eg arrests) and any release of information by them (eg suspect names) could jeopardise the operation.

9.6.5 **Role of the MLO**

Media interviews can take up a substantial amount of time and often there is not just one agency but many with representatives coming from a variety of different television companies, large and small radio stations and press journalists, including freelancers. They all want that exclusive one-on-one interview which can become repetitive, time-consuming and burdensome.

Media Liaison Officers (MLO—aka 'press officer') can manage the demand on behalf of the SIO. They usually link into a wider communication strategy which also caters for focusing on targeted audiences. MLOs play an active coordination and liaison role. This is not only for media and communication activities, but also good publicity for promoting and managing the professional image of the organisation. MLOs operate at both strategic and tactical levels, communicating with external agencies and providing support to operational staff. This occurs both 'back stage' in facilitating preparation and 'front stage' in acting as an important buffer and conduit between the media and the investigation. Media relations are, by and large, more professional when managed by MLOs, who are an invaluable asset. MLOs assist in formulating media strategies and are usually adept at finding the right form of words and choosing the most appropriate methods and timing for external communications.

Creative ideas are often better discussed and developed jointly, and it is the job of the MLO to spot or create media opportunities or use local contacts to improve their usage. They can monitor the media and gauge reactions, level of interest, and accuracy of story lines in order to anticipate misinterpretations and negative reporting. This serves as an early warning mechanism to give ample opportunity to react and produce a response. Knowing what has been or is going to be published or broadcast can positively influence media activity.

It is best to engage the services of advisers at the earliest opportunity. Most have extensive knowledge, appropriate training and journalistic experience. Once engaged they should be included as integral members of the enquiry team and kept briefed and up to date as the enquiry progresses. They are able to maintain an awareness of local reporting methods and reporters, and will know when there are quiet and busy news days or other events to consider. They will also probably know which reporters can be trusted and which to be wary of.

Most importantly, they are able to offer support and protection for the SIO to fend off unwanted media interest and attention and help formulate the right content and words prior to interview. They collate all the media publications for the use of the enquiry team and for disclosure purposes later at court, as it is not uncommon for legal teams to make challenges about what has been said in the media, particularly when quoting facts provided by the SIO. Such material is generally made available to a victim's family and relatives, should the need arise.

Checklist—Role of the MLO

- Preparation and dissemination of information for communication.

- Analysis of media reporting.

- Liaison with and management of journalists and reporters at crime scenes.

- Checking and logging information distributed to journalists.

- Mediating over and arranging interviews, media facilities/opportunities.

- Monitoring all media coverage to check accuracy and interpretation.

- Assisting in development of an overarching external communications strategy.

9.6.6 Devising a media strategy

The *Murder Investigation Manual* (MIM) states the purpose of a media strategy should be:

- Establishing circumstances of the incident/bringing any offenders to justice.
- Controlling police interaction with the media.
- Maintaining public confidence in the police.
- Minimising impact on public fear of crime.
- Generating confidence in the investigation team.
- Maximising publicity opportunities in the search for information.[4]

The policy should include a requirement to monitor all news media outlets, which may be linked to the intelligence-gathering function. Swift action may be required to correct inaccuracies in media reporting, and a review of the strategy will then be required. A carefully formulated strategy can be linked to a list of objectives (eg filling information gaps) indicating what media appeals are necessary, how they can be communicated and when, where, why and by whom. Specific investigative requirements may need to be catered for, such as requests for sightings of a particular vehicle, or witnesses who may have something pertinent for the investigation.

A good media strategy remains dynamic, flexible and tailored to individual circumstances as things develop and change as the investigation progresses. It has to cater for and make the most of overt activities or significant events, eg arrests, searches, execution of search warrants, significant dates or anniversaries, court appearances, potential criticism of enquiry, connected incidents, to raise public interest and support.

At certain times during an investigation it may be a deliberate tactic not to engage with the media until information or comment is requested. This may be

---

[4] ACPO, *Murder Investigation Manual* (NCPE, 2006), 22.

because the SIO is not ready to provide any details. If so, then a response must be prepared which is often referred to as an *'If asked'* position, which means it has been agreed what will be said should the media request information.

9.6.7 **Consideration of victims**

It is important to consider the impact media reporting can have on victims, including their close family/friends and local community. A communications strategy takes account of liaising, consulting and keeping victims or their next of kin and family informed wherever practicable prior to any statement being released. They should be consulted on releases of information that may impact on them or their reputation or well-being and given support to prevent excessive media intrusion beforehand.

It is a continuing responsibility (normally via the Family Liaison Officer (FLO)) to keep the family of a deceased person informed of developments to ensure they are aware and briefed before any formal release of information, pictures or case updates. This includes being provided with copies of formal media statements *in advance* of publication, unless this is practically difficult or impossible; in which case the notification should be given as soon as possible. The SIO should be mindful of balancing the requirement to appease media demands for information and releases (eg holding an immediate press conference at the scene) alongside safeguarding the best interests of victims and relatives.

Sometimes sensitive facts have to be disclosed to the media for the benefit of the investigation. For example, a victim may have had numerous personal relationships and it may be important to make this clear in order to encourage previous partners to come forward for elimination. This may not be very pleasant for a deceased's next of kin and family and would need careful planning with the FLOs.

Previous convictions of the victim, or their lifestyle and background, are other examples. One option is to reach a compromise and balance the negative side of the victim's character against the positive, eg how good she was as a mother and carer for two young children as a single parent (despite working in the sex industry). Efforts to maintain the support of the family and sympathy of the public are of paramount importance.

Releasing details of victim(s)

Any decision to release details of a deceased victim should not be made without the authority of the SIO. As a general rule this should not be until:

- victim has been formally identified
- immediate family have been informed
- deceased's family have been notified of an intention to release basic details.

KEY POINT

When details are released about a deceased victim they have to be factually correct. This particularly applies to spelling or pronunciation of a person's name. Getting these important facts wrong can cause serious embarrassment and unnecessary distress, and possibly sour relationships.

9.6.8 **Types of media interviews**

Whatever the type of media, whether print, radio, TV or internet, etc, interviews generally have the following levels of engagement:

- **Formal**: pre-arranged with an interviewer who is likely to have prepared questions and researched areas to discuss.
- **Pre-recorded**: provide an opportunity to pause and re-record comments that haven't come across well or have been said badly (provided the interviewer agrees). Sometimes for convenience they are recorded over a phone link. The main disadvantage is they can be edited and important messages, such as public appeals and 'hotline' numbers, get left out.
- **Live**: more pressurised, as there is only one opportunity to get it right and the interviewer can stray from the agreed areas and ask awkward questions that are difficult to avoid because the broadcast is 'live'. Favoured method in 'breaking news' headlines on 24/7 bulletins. Not for the faint-hearted or inexperienced, although there are benefits because important content and messages cannot be edited.
- **Press conferences** (aka 'media facilities'): traditional method of allowing a large number of media representatives to hear the same message simultaneously to save time. Used for significant announcements that are likely to attract a lot of media interest. Prepared statements can be read out and members of the public such as victims' relatives may appear on them. Question and answer sessions can be added if appropriate at the end.

The golden rule is to clarify beforehand what type of interview is being conducted and to establish whether it is live or pre-recorded, and prepare accordingly, remembering that live interviews require more preparation because of what they are.

KEY POINT

Any superficial, casual, or friendly nature and approach by journalists may lull interviewees into becoming 'off their guard' and saying something they (and the SIO) later regret. Absence of note-taking or recording devices may betray a true intent to use the comments or produce a distorted version. These are also known as 'off the record' interviews and must be avoided at all costs. It is safer to treat everything as being 'on the record'—the reporter may be trustworthy, but their news editor might not.

9.6.9 **Preparing for media interviews**

It is always advisable to establish what an interviewer wants out of an interview, what topics they intend to cover, how long it will last and any other likely questions. Equally it must be clear what the SIO wants to achieve from the interview including any topics they *do not* want to talk about. In order to anticipate lines of questioning, it is worth considering that the interviewer, like good investigators, will make good use of the interrogative pronouns (5WH).

The media have their own agenda and may wish to ambush or catch out the interviewee with certain lines of questioning. This is when it is useful to apply the tactic of *turning negatives into positives*. When an interviewer focuses on any negative aspects, the interviewee should seek to turn the topic back into positive ones. For example, an interviewer may comment on how an enquiry has been running for a number of weeks and there has been no progress. This can be positively turned around by a response stating how many people have been interviewed, statements taken, how many searches, H-2-H enquiries or forensic examinations, etc have been conducted.

KEY POINTS

- Prepare for a media interview by having **3 x key messages** at the ready and in possession for quick reference and last-minute rehearsal.
- Think and prepare carefully about the objectives of the interview and rehearse delivering it (which is what professionals do).
- Highlight the 'It's probably nothing' syndrome by encouraging people to let the investigation team decide whether their information is relevant or not.

Using appropriate language

Using plain 'everyday' language while giving interviews comes across far better than organisational jargon, buzz phrases and acronyms. Frequently used internal terms such as 'intelligence-led policing' (ie. what does *un*intelligent-led policing look like?) or 'partnership approach' are not easily related to by members of the public and sound too official. Only clear, simple, plain and understandable everyday terms the general public understand should be used (as per the 7 x Cs rule mentioned earlier). For example, 'females' are women; and 'males' are men. Everyday language reaches out to the public a lot better than official terminology or clichés. The best way to get people's interest and support is by using language they understand and can relate to.

Inappropriate language must always be avoided to safeguard against offending certain sections of the community and not recognising diversity, such as faith and culture. The use of discriminatory, prejudicial or exclusive language indicates a lack of professionalism and encourages the exclusion, devaluing and stereotyping of groups or individuals. Correct terminology is important, together with a strict adherence to organisational guidance and policies.

KEY POINT

Subtle messages can be hidden amongst the wording of appeals, especially if a particular subject is being targeted. Behavioural Investigative Advisers and Forensic Clinical Psychologists (available through the National Crime Agency) can be put to good use in helping develop and phrase messages aimed at specific persons or themes.

9.6.10 Holding back information

It is usually advisable to be totally open and honest when delivering messages about an investigation via the media, but sometimes it can also be tactically advantageous to withhold unique features or information. This can be justified for particular investigative or interviewing reasons. Unusual features of a modus operandi (MO) is such an example when there is a specific manner in which an offence was committed, how many bullets were fired, blows struck, what part of the body was hit, how a scene was entered or left, what items were taken/left, what type of weapon was used, words uttered to a victim, etc.

Such tactical decisions need to be made early and recorded in a policy log. To safeguard the integrity of the tactic, the SIO may have to withhold the information from the enquiry team to prove it could not have been leaked, either wittingly or unwittingly. The security and integrity of the storage of any withheld material may have to be proved to the satisfaction of a court at subsequent proceedings, particularly if an offender or key witness volunteers information that has been deliberately withheld (therefore increasing its probative value). It may have to be proved beyond all doubt that there was no possibility that withheld information was leaked and therefore could only have been known by the true offender.

This tactic is aimed at proving the veracity of an offender's guilty knowledge, involvement or confession. It also helps eliminate those who may wish, for whatever motive, to wrongly admit their responsibility or mislead the enquiry. It can eliminate other information from intelligence or evidential sources that can be proved to be inaccurate (eg from CHIS).

There may be instances where releasing information would breach a duty of confidentiality or contravene statutory requirements or national guidance (eg naming rape victims). These need to be carefully considered in line with relevant legislation and guidance. In difficult, sensitive or exceptional cases the matter should be referred to a senior grade (eg at Chief Officer level), who makes a strategic decision. A 'Gold Group' may need to be formed, comprising senior officers and community representatives and other agencies, to discuss and agree a media and community impact strategy. Such is the importance in serious cases, particularly critical incidents, of getting the right message across in the right manner at the right time.

> **KEY POINT**
>
> It may be prudent to tell the media why certain details are being withheld. For example: 'We would not wish to reveal details at this time as it might prevent us from tracing and arresting the offender', or 'For operational reasons we cannot reveal information at this stage'. This is better than saying 'no comment' or refusing to answer, which may appear dishonest or untrustworthy.

Disclosing v withholding

For (disclosing)	Against
Identifies offender(s)	Allows destruction of evidence
Locates the suspect(s)	
Identifies victim(s)	Makes victim(s) more vulnerable
Gains publicity/witness appeals	Compromises operational tactics
Maintains media/public interest	Negatively affects relationship with the victim/family/community
Warns public of any dangers	Causes unnecessary fear and distress
Maintains trust/provides reassurance	Dilutes guilty knowledge from admissions
Prompts offender reaction	Offender(s) may reoffend
Provides crime prevention advice	May create 'copycat' offences
Prevents media speculation	May create more media interest/intrusion
Appeals to consciences	Alerts offender(s) to police activity
Corrects misinformation	May affect fairness of trial process
Triggers activities or comments	Need to plan/resources to capture material

9.6.11 Timing of appeals

Releasing information via the media must be timed carefully to produce maximum benefit for the investigation. It may, for example, be linked into other trigger (eg covert surveillance) proactive tactics. Any release of investigative material, however, such as pictures or CCTV, must not compromise witness interviewing strategies by contaminating or influencing recollections. It may be worthwhile seeking the advice of the CPS if in any doubt about the legal implications on identification procedures, for example of photographs or details of possible suspects (although sometimes parts of images can be obscured/pixellated).

To generate maximum publicity, it can be advantageous to make appeals that coincide with significant events, such as the arrest of offenders, execution of search warrants, court appearances or anniversaries of incidents. Attaching appeals to these links can help generate media and public interest. Media publicity can be coordinated with other operational activity aimed at identifying or arresting key witnesses or suspects.

The wider news agenda must be contemplated by scanning to see what other newsworthy events or stories are taking place that may compete for attention. These could be major sporting or political events and anything of a local nature that would occupy the headlines. Publication deadlines may be something else to consider, particularly if it is important to include a popular local media outlet that is not printed or published daily.

KEY POINTS

- Timing of information, messages and appeals can link into significant lines of enquiry or proactive tactics.
- Chronological events and developments can enhance media attention, eg the arrest of suspects or the finding of crucial CCTV footage.
- Information releases must only occur *after* victims (and close family of deceased victims) have been notified (though not practicable in every case).
- Check what other events are competing for media attention.

9.6.12 Generating media interest

There is certain criteria by which news producers and gatekeepers (editors and sub-editors) select events to report in their news. Matters that are judged 'newsworthy' include things such as the specific characteristics of an offence or incident, the location, the victim's age, status, background and vulnerability, linked or series crimes, and race/hate motives. Some stories or incidents become major headlines from the outset, while others are just not considered newsworthy. Both of these extremes have implications for the communications strategy either in engaging with the media or getting them interested in sending out required messages.

Incidents involving major crime, such as murder and child sexual exploitation or death of a child, usually attract a substantial amount of media interest per se, especially in the first few days. Thereafter interest tends to diminish, although some particularly newsworthy cases sustain media interest. Not all offences, however, attract the desired level of attention, and in these circumstances the challenge is to capitalise on media interest and publicity.

The media like to incorporate unusual features or anything that adds value or drama to their stories. For example: CCTV footage; pictures of offenders; artists' impressions; details of missing articles (eg clothing); reconstructions; horrifying injuries; personal appeals from a victim's family or close friends; dramatic emergency calls; pictures of raids; or specialist units in action, such as underwater searches. All these 'extras' make stories more appealing because they appear more dramatic and interesting. They can therefore be used to tempt media agencies into (re)running an appeal. Care must be taken, however, not to breach any copyright protection on photographs, maps and plans.

Checklist—Publicity-gaining examples

- Use of electronic and mobile 'advertising' placards or screens.
- Full-size upright models or 'cut-outs' of victims placed in public places in order to attract attention (eg victim holding or stating an appeal).
- Celebrities and sports personalities supporting appeals.
- Modern social media outlets and websites that attract certain audiences.
- Use of publications to target specific communities, eg gay/lesbian communities, or professional journals to help identify unusual physical features, characteristics of victims or suspects.
- Simple leaflet drops in targeted geographical locations.

To gain publicity, media messages, posters and leaflets need to be 'hard-hitting'. Here are some examples that have proved useful in major investigations:

- 'We know people saw what happened...do you want those responsible to get away with it?'
- 'What if he was your brother, boyfriend, or mate...?'
- 'We know people are scared, we can help and work together on this...don't let them get away with it.'
- 'Please help the police find my killers' (underneath picture of victim).

9.6.13 Partner agencies

The police normally act as lead agency for crime matters and a coordination point for all media releases from other agencies that may also be involved in an incident response and/or investigation. It is good practice for all parties to be kept apprised of media statements and are given an opportunity to contribute. Partners should, where appropriate, be involved in formatting joint press releases (eg local authority or CPS). It must first be discussed and agreed as to who has primacy in providing the information.

Good liaison ensures nothing is released that could compromise an enquiry or relations between various agencies. This may involve close working arrangements or perhaps even co-location. There may be a need to seek external advice and guidance from bodies such as IAGs regarding specific community issues and formulating the wording of media responses. This may be a vital strategic requirement, as badly chosen wording can have a dramatic effect on community relations.

9.6.14 Reconstructions

A communication strategy may include reconstructions in order to rekindle public interest in events and tease out important memories and information. These are a worthy tactic for consideration and serve as a high-impact method of getting messages across, raising the profile of the investigation and assisting public recollections. They can also be used in internal communication messages, such as when providing electronic briefings and presentations about the case.

BBC's *Crimewatch* and any similar localised crime-appeal programmes have proved an invaluable means of attracting public support. They can reach out to a large audience, are very professional in their approach and do everything possible to get the right message across. This is more of a collaborative-type approach to solving the crime, rather than just running a news story. The BBC production team are very experienced in assisting with appeals and meeting focused objectives.

These types of appeals, however, can and often do produce large amounts of information, all of which has to be assessed and potentially investigated; which is why large appeals and reconstructions need to be as focused as possible. Well-intentioned but misleading information coming from the public can take up valuable time and resources. For example, where appeals are for sightings or the whereabouts of suspects, the outcome might be possible sightings all over the United Kingdom and overseas, some of which may prove difficult to ignore.

9.6.15 Locating suspects

Where a suspect has been positively identified but their location is unknown, a media appeal may assist in appealing for help in locating them and/or requesting them to surrender voluntarily. However, consideration needs to be afforded to:

1. Safeguarding the integrity of identification evidence (advice should be taken from the CPS and/or an organisational legal adviser).
2. Risk in breaching human rights (eg right to a fair trial).
3. Dangerous individuals being provided with an opportunity to make a name for themselves by taking advantage of the added notoriety and publicity.

[Note: This type of tactic usually requires authorisation at the highest level (ie Chief Officer) and may be the subject of a decision by a Gold group and close monitoring by a consequence management cell as a critical incident.]

Checklist—Media handling dos and don'ts

The dos...

- Take full advantage of an MLO.

- Be clear about the aims and objectives of the media interview.

- Retain control by refocusing on the issues the SIO wants to talk about (and repeat messages as often as possible).

- Ask what type of questions will be asked beforehand to enable preparation.

- Prepare and rehearse thoroughly—identify and remember **3 x key messages**.

- Research any current 'hot topics' in the media. Think what else is current and could have an impact on the line of interviewing.

- Remember the questioner will also use the 5WH principles.

- Stay relaxed, confident, and always sound very *positive, positive, positive* (3XPs).

- Watch body language—when on camera a person cannot **not** communicate.

- Be confident, not nervous—treat the interviewer as one individual and ignore how many others may be watching or listening.

- Adrenalin is useful for producing excitement and stimulation—use it as an advantage.

- Check appearance, hair, tie, etc (if on camera) before the cameras start rolling.

- Check what material is displayed in the background and remove inappropriate or confidential material.

- Ignore noise and/or activity taking place off-camera.

- Look at the person interviewing, not the camera (unless directed otherwise).

- Use the 7 x Cs of communication—straightforward, simple, everyday plain language, *not* police-speak, jargon or waffle.

- Be clear about what topics can and cannot be discussed (eg pending or ongoing court cases, or sensitive issues).

- Steer clear of giving personal views on subjects—know organisational policy and stick to the party line.

- Ensure victim/family is/are informed before any release is made.

- Ensure messages are clear and strong, stating exactly what is needed from the public (ie do not just appeal for 'general information'—be specific).

- Never say 'No comment'—it sounds suspicious. Explain reasons why a question cannot be answered, or information released (useful alternatives are 'It is too early to say...', or 'That will be looked into as part of the ongoing investigation...', or simply 'At this stage we are still unsure...').

- Avoid comments that imply guilt or innocence—never discuss the evidence.

- Use cognitive prompts wherever possible (eg such as a major sporting event).

- Emphasise the importance of all information, no matter how trivial (highlight the 'It's probably nothing' syndrome).

- Remember to state contact details of the investigation team (have them written down).

- Ensure there is an appropriate (eg answering-machine) recorded message and policy for regularly checking the incident room contact system, if giving out to the public or media.

- Inform the media as soon as possible when a suspect is charged. This helps to prevent the possibility of them inadvertently breaching the Contempt of Court Act and jeopardising the case. Confirm the name, date of birth, address, full details of charges and court date.

- Consider giving positive crime prevention advice along with reports of crime and offer public reassurance and help ease the fear of crime.

- Publicise good work, particularly heroics or important events such as court results.

- Use interesting facets of the case to gain extra publicity and interest from the media (eg CCTV footage, heroics).

- Try and turn negatives into positives.

- Keep full control of the interview and keep switching the subject back to the topics the SIO wants to talk about.

The don'ts...

- Allow junior staff to provide information or interviews about the incident to members of the public or media without being authorised.

- Fidget or sway on or stare at feet.

- Stare directly at the camera (unless doing a 'down-the-lens' interview where the reporter is at a different venue).

- Drop your guard and make 'off the cuff' remarks as the microphone could be still switched on.

- Answer questions on topics someone else should be answering (eg local policing issues).

- Respond to the reporter's questions with just 'Yes' or 'No' answers.

- Let the reporter try to put words into your mouth or try to get you to agree to what they are saying. (Instead use phrases such as *'well, that's one point of view, but from our perspective...'*)

- Lower your voice or appear disinterested—always look and sound confident, enthusiastic and in control.

- Ever criticise the criminal justice system or other agencies.

9.7 **Community Communication**

Most communities rely upon public bodies such as the police to protect them. Simultaneously, public bodies might need to rely upon communities' support and cooperation to provide effective services such as the prevention of criminal acts and enforcement of the law. Therefore communications with the public and local communities should aim to be reciprocal, remembering that effective communication may need to take account of barriers such as language, culture, fear or mistrust.

The Community Impact Assessment that is discussed in Chapter 11.9 is one way of assessing whether the communication strategy is effective enough and whether it is meeting these objectives. Just like victims, communities also need regular updates of information and usually depend on what they see and hear from the news media. Neighbourhood and community support teams are integral to the process of getting the right and timely messages out, which is why it is important to ensure they too have an effective channel of communication with the enquiry team and if necessary are invited to attend and contribute to team meetings/briefings whenever possible.

References

ACPO, *Guidance on the National Briefing Model* (NCPE, 2006)

ACPO, *Murder Investigation Manual* (NCPE, 2006), 225

College of Policing, *Briefing and debriefing* (online, 2013) <https://www.app.college.police.uk/app-content/operations/briefing-and-debriefing> (accessed 13 September 2015)

Cutlip, S M and Center, A H, *Effective Public Relations: Pathways to Public Favour* (University of Wisconsin, 1952)

Core Investigative Strategies

10.1 **Introduction**

Core investigative strategies comprise of methods and tactics that form part of an overall investigation plan. Each strategy contributes an element to the plan in order to achieve an overall objective. In short, the purpose of an investigative strategy is to:

- define aims and objectives of how it will contribute to the investigation; and
- identify and outline the most beneficial and appropriate tactics that are likely to establish significant facts, reveal or preserve evidential material and lead to the successful resolution of the investigation, taking into account resources, priorities, time scales, cost, achievability, justification and proportionality.

Each strategy is a way of linking and grouping activities under certain investigative themes and headings. While some are given separate chapters of this book on their own, eg searching, managing victims, witnesses, suspects and pursuing TIE actions, the remainder are covered in this chapter.

Checklist—Investigative strategies

- Suspect management[1]

- Witness management[2]

- TIE enquiries[3]

- H-2-H enquiries

- Managing crime scenes and searches[4]

- Passive data (eg CCTV and ANPR)

- Intelligence management

- Communication management[5]

- Victim management[6]

- Communications data and social media

- Financial investigation

- Proactive overt and covert investigation

- Specialist support and expert advisers.

---

[1] See Chapter 12.
[2] See Chapter 13.
[3] See Chapter 8.
[4] See Chapter 6.
[5] See Chapter 9.
[6] See Chapter 11.

Inevitably overlaps will occur between various strategies, as some, if not most, cross over one another. For example, a strategy to conduct house-to-house (H-2-H) enquiries may also be referred to in a witness trawl strategy; or digital communications data requirements may be included as part of a search strategy. There may also be similarities in policies, for example, geographical parameters for the H-2-H enquiries may share similar boundaries to those for the CCTV trawls. Processes, considerations and even roles may also bear close correlation (eg H-2-H and CCTV Coordinators).

KEY POINT

An investigative strategy contains overarching aims and objectives under which sit a group of activities, tactics and actions that are likely to establish significant facts, reveal or preserve evidential material or lead to the successful resolution of the investigation.

Investigative strategies are discussed and agreed (eg at meetings and briefings) between the SIO, management team and enquiry staff (ie the team approach). Expert advice and support may be required for some of the options such as Interview Advisers, Media Liaison Officers, Police Search Advisers (PolSAs), forensic and hi-tech crime experts or Crime Scene Investigators/Managers (CSI/CSMs). Clear aims and objectives should be recorded and agreed for each strategy and relayed to those working on them. For example, the objective for an intelligence strategy may be 'to obtain all possible intelligence regarding rival criminal associates of the victim to help establish who was responsible for the offence'.

It is advisable to assign ownership for a specific strategy to an individual and/ or teams. Those with supervisory responsibility are usually best placed to take on large or substantial projects, including the Deputy SIO. Those nominated should be involved in setting the objectives for the strategy and be in no doubt as to how the SIO expects them to be completed. For example, CCTV (passive data) collection and viewing is allocated to a nominated supervisor and team to undertake the task and provide regular updates on progress. This decision is then recorded in the policy log together with terms of reference, aims and objectives, agreed methods, parameters, staffing and resource levels.

Each individual strategy requires its own specific meeting or discussion, if not several over the course of an investigation. These are usually led and facilitated by the SIO (or Deputy in their absence) to begin with, with an agenda and contents minuted/recorded. The purpose would be to gather together key staff involved in or useful to the particular subject area to discuss, determine and set/ review the tactics, progress and policy. For example, in the 'communications data strategy' meetings, the SIO and Deputy probably meet with a team such as Communications Data Investigator(s), Digital Media Investigator, single point of contact (SPoC) and senior analyst.

Investigative strategies remain under dynamic review to ensure they are relevant, appropriate and kept on track. Investigations are usually fast-moving and frequently require subtle changes in direction and priorities; investigative strategies need to reflect and remain supportive of any such amendments or shifts.

> **KEY POINT**
>
> Investigative strategies can be delegated to designated staff to project manage who may require various subject-matter experts and specialists to assist and support them. The SIO, however, still retains 'ownership' of the strategy and is ultimately responsible for it, regardless of who might be the chosen lead, and retains the right to make any final decisions.

10.2 **Strategy Implementation**

Each strategy will contain key tactics, actions and activities. A list of individual key 'actions' can be compiled to provide specific detail and instructions about tactical activities required for achieving the strategic aims.

> **Example 1**
>
> **Nature of tactical action**
>
> 'Arrange house-to-house enquiries and report on exact areas to be covered as authorised by the SIO with a plan of the parameters' (H-2-H investigative strategy).
>
> **Example 2**
>
> **Nature of tactical action**
>
> 'Arrange fingertip search of scene (1) and obtain statements from officers involved' (search investigative strategy).
>
> **Example 3**
>
> **Nature of tactical action**
>
> 'Obtain itemised billing for mobile (number) believed used by suspect's girlfriend N34 (name) for period (date) covering all outgoing calls' (communications data investigative strategy).

In a large and complex strategy, one option is to register all details in a 'stand-alone' policy document with relevant action numbers listed alongside each activity. Any such document must be version-controlled, entered onto the case management system (eg HOLMES) and cross-referenced to an entry in the main policy file.

10.3 **House-to-House (H-2-H) Enquiries**

Conducting H-2-H enquiries can be used to:

- identify suspects, witnesses and victims
- gather local information and intelligence
- obtain investigation-specific material and information
- support a communication strategy (eg appeal for witnesses, provide public reassurance or give crime prevention advice)
- identify passive or digital communications data sources (eg CCTV or wi-fi)
- facilitate a mass screening exercise (eg DNA or fingerprints).

A combination of the above is usual. There will also be case-specific requirements with a list of questions or topics to cover when speaking to occupants and visitors.

H-2-H is a useful tactic that can be used in nearly every major crime investigation, but to be effective must be conducted methodically, thoroughly and without undue delay. In a high proportion of cases a victim is known by the offender and resides within close proximity of the place where the offence occurred. It is always feasible that a H-2-H enquiry may uncover such an individual.

KEY POINT—IMPORTANCE OF H-2-H ENQUIRIES

Amanda (Milly) Dowler was a 13-year-old schoolgirl when she was abducted in broad daylight on her way home from school and murdered in Walton-on-Thames, Surrey, on 21 March 2002. Her body lay undiscovered in a rural area until 18 September 2002 and it wasn't until 23 June 2011 that a convicted serial killer named Levi Bellfield was found guilty of her murder. A key piece of evidence was at the time of the murder Bellfield resided at an address in Collingwood Place, very close to the point where the abduction occurred. Bellfield had resided just 50 yards from where Milly Dowler was last seen but, as the media put it, 'escaped the net when police knocked ten times at his rented flat without getting an answer but made no enquiries of the landlord as to who lived there'.[7]

10.3.1 **Location parameters**

An SIO needs to be familiar with geographical locations in order to set realistic and relevant parameters for the H-2-H enquiries. It is best practice to visit, walk around and view the surroundings at key locations. If a H-2-H Manager is appointed, they should accompany the SIO/DSIO during the process. Each road, street, house, flat, business premises, or other building and premises of interest needs to be identified and duly included. Areas where people are known to 'sleep rough', gather frequently or congregate should also be considered.

[7] C Davies, 'Milly Dowler: Did police mistakes let Levi Bellfield kill again?' *Guardian*, 24 June 2011.

A detailed street/area map comes in very handy for marking on the boundaries of H-2-H parameters, which can later be registered as an official 'document'. This is better than attempting to provide verbal or written descriptions of the chosen areas and can be linked to a policy file entry explaining the reasons why and how the tactic is to be used. Natural boundaries can help determine parameters, such as roads, streets, rivers, walls, paths, railway lines, natural borders and fences.

Large areas should be divided into zones or phases in order of priority (phase 1, 2, 3, etc). This helps the teams that are conducting the enquiries to understand what the most important areas are to meet the SIO's objectives and allocate time and resources accordingly.

To help determine parameters, good use should be made of all available intelligence and information. Local officers, PCSOs, special constables, etc and members of the community (ie community intelligence) who may have specific local knowledge can be asked to contribute, which adds qualitative detail to the task. Looking at a map or location does not always provide sufficient local information to work with, for example knowledge of local shortcuts, meeting places or locations where vehicles and stolen cars are abandoned. Other resources such as Geographical Profilers[8] can be considered to help determine parameters and priorities.

KEY POINTS

1. Some addresses included in H-2-H parameters may have other significance, eg associated with significant witnesses, victim's family members or TIEs. These will be subject to other strategies and actions, and it looks unprofessional for different staff to keep visiting the same addresses for different reasons at similar times. Good management and coordination is necessary to avoid this happening.
2. Walking around and inspecting a locus is the best method of ensuring no areas or premises are missed, eg flat 2b hidden out of sight at the rear of or directly above house number 2 (or small take-away or shop), or those premises in an adjoining street that have rear windows overlooking the crime scene.

10.3.2 Fast-track H-2-H enquiries

A valuable tactic is to conduct early and/or initial H-2-H enquiries (often called 'flash' or 'hasty' H-2-H) during the 'golden hour(s)'. Staff can be quickly directed to addresses within the **line of sight** or **hearing** of crime scenes. Even if specific parameters have not been determined, it still means general investigative material can be obtained sooner to generate early lines of enquiry. Accurate records need to be kept of any premises visited or persons spoken to, including negative responses. This is always best supported by full H-2-H when resources allow.

---

[8] Geographical Profilers are available via the NCA.

A good way to establish what could be accomplished during fast-track H-2-H is to concentrate on areas where an offender may have been and consider locations as per the LEASH acronym:

```
L—Lain in wait
E—Egress routes
A—Access routes
S—Line of sight
H—Line of hearing
```

An outline of what questions to ask or what information is required will need to be compiled. However, in the initial stages officers can simply make general requests for information at each address visited and to each interviewee—what did they see? What do they know? What have they heard? Good use of open questions is always the best policy to avoid single and closed answers such as 'yes' or 'no'.

KEY POINT

Information obtained during H-2-H enquiries should be accurately recorded and, if possible, signed by the person spoken to and countersigned by the officer.
A first account may become important if a subsequent witness statement is required, particularly if the witness disengages or becomes reluctant.

10.3.3 Phased H-2-H enquiries

Phase one usually includes visiting all dwellings and premises in the immediate vicinity (eg of Scene 1) as determined by set parameters. These parameters can remain under review and get extended or reduced as the enquiry develops. A policy log entry should be made outlining the reasons and specific details of each phase, for example:

Phase (I) H-2-H

This is a densely populated residential area in (location) and all these addresses have been deemed as directly overlooking scene (1). It is anticipated there will be a good level of cooperation from members of the public in this area given the nature of the investigation. The initial addresses for phase (I) are listed below.

2–12 Glendon Court

89–115 Avondale Gardens

70–96 Avondale Gardens

98–126 Avondale Gardens

1–11 Glendon Court

2–10a and 10b Castlebrook Terrace

10.3.4 **Policy and documentation**

Alongside a H-2-H strategy should be specific instructions and policy that cover any or all of the following:

- Identifying, determining and stipulating parameters.
- Identifying and nominating most appropriate (ideally trained) resources.
- Determining whether a dedicated coordinator role will be utilised.
- Specific questions and topics to be covered.
- Documentation to be used and completed (eg questionnaires, PDFs and occupancy details).
- Details of any information *not* to be given out (eg specific details about the incident under investigation or victim).
- Timing of enquiries and number of visits required (eg 'initially 2 visits will be made, one in the daytime and one in the evening').
- What and how information should be relayed back to the incident room (eg 'all significant information will be passed directly to the Receiver in the form of a message form; any high-priority information must be relayed to the Receiver and/or SIO without any delay').
- When witness statements should be recorded (eg 'statements should be taken in line with the SIO's designated statement policy').
- A 'no reply' and/or 'not at home' policy (eg if no response on 2nd or 3rd visit, do a leaflet drop, research enquiries by intelligence cell, enquiries with neighbours or occupants of nearby other premises, raise to a T/I action, or simply vary times for return visits—but must *always* include informing the SIO).
- Consideration of interview advisers to help formulate questionnaires.
- Geographical profiling/analyst to assist with determining location parameters.
- Policy to manage any language or cultural issues.
- Consideration of capturing 'nosey-neighbour'-type information to confirm occupant numbers and details.

KEY POINTS

- Multi-occupancy, sub-let premises or transient communities might need a policy decision to obtain fingerprints and photographs of all occupants to help confirm their identities and presence (eg where there are numerous foreign nationals in cramped living accommodation).
- H-2-H enquiry questionnaires should be intelligence-led to accommodate specific information, eg where loud voices or screams are believed to have been heard at a particular time and location.

In most forces there are standard forms for recording H-2-H information, which are usually stored in folders for ease of reference, eg a street form with space for a number of addresses. Having gained access to an address, the enquiry team officer endorses the street form with the total number of questionnaires required and outstanding for the number of persons at the address. There is also a house occupant form and the all-important questionnaire template.[9]

H-2-H questionnaires

Case-specific questions should be compiled and used as part of the enquiry team package. The golden rule is that using open questions is always better than using closed ones that require one-word (yes/no) answers. Questionnaires should be bespoke and regularly reviewed to ensure they ask the right questions in line with changes and developments in the investigation.

Questionnaires should be considered 'dynamic' in nature as information flows often necessitate amendments to questions being asked.

H-2-H sample questions:
1. Where were you between (time/date) and (time/date)?
2. What did you see or hear in the area of (address/location) during these times?
3. What vehicles do you own, use or have access to?
4. What vehicles have you seen in the vicinity of the address of (location) between (dates and times)?
5. Where were any of those vehicles in (3) and (4) above during these times?
6. What do you know about an incident that took place at that location?
7. What do you know about the occupants of that address?
8. Have you any knowledge of CCTV photographic or recording devices fitted or used at either this address or nearby?
9. What other information might you have that could assist the enquiry?

KEY POINTS

- Questions should be worded carefully to avoid closed ones, eg Q. 'Do you own a white van?' A. 'No' (yet the occupant might regularly use one that belongs to someone else such as an employer).
- If using terms such as 'suspicious' (eg 'did you see anything suspicious?'), the term needs explaining as to what it means and refers to.
- Sentences should not contain more than one question and topic.

Leaflet drops and social media (eg use of Bluetooth technology) can also be an effective method of covering a large area to request public assistance. These leaflets must include enquiry team contact details should a member of the public respond to the request and, depending on the demographics of the area, may have to be multilingual.

---

[9] Sample documents can be found in ACPO, *Practice Advice on House to House Enquiries* (Centrex, 2006).

10.3.5 **Identifying suspects**

Where a suspect is believed to live, work or frequent can be a specific requirement of H-2-H enquiries. H-2-H is a sure way of achieving this objective and a technique of particular importance on major enquiries when intelligence-led mass screening for DNA or fingerprints is being conducted or considered. However, it is not uncommon for close associates and even family members to conceal offenders or provide misinformation so they avoid detection; therefore good application of the ABC principle is necessary.

Usually both suspect and witness enquiries are conducted simultaneously, to avoid alerting potential suspects who may be in the area who can then make good their escape.

H-2-H enquiries can also be useful at or nearby suspect addresses, eg during arrests or house searches for useful information about movements, vehicles, habits, associates, that might prove useful to the investigation.

10.3.6 **Identifying witnesses or victims**

H-2-H can be used to try and identify:

- those who may have witnessed anything of relevance
- victims (eg in series offences or reluctance/fear to report)
- connected events, such as an encounter, attack, disposal site, getaway vehicle stolen or abandoned
- people in or around the vicinity of a crime scene at the relevant time
- sightings of the victim or offender before or after the event, eg along the likely entry and exit routes of the offender(s)
- sightings of or information regarding relevant property, eg clothing or items of significance that may have been disposed of
- persons seen elsewhere (eg on CCTV).

KEY POINT

Offenders tend to be less careful away from crime scenes. This is where they may be noticed while changing or discarding clothing, dropping or concealing weapons, hiding stolen property or their means of transport, or meeting up with accomplices before and after the offence, etc. Once known, these locations are good places to mount H-2-H enquiries to try to identify witnesses.

10.3.7 **Community reassurance**

H-2-H visits can be used as part of a communication strategy to deliver important messages to the public. Visits can incorporate the distribution of relevant crime prevention or personal safety advice. Any reassurance messages should remain consistent with those contained in a media (ie external communication) strategy. Enquiries can also be used to measure and gauge public reaction, and local policing teams can be consulted to assist in completing the task.

KEY POINT

A temporary mobile incident vehicle situated at or near an important crime scene can serve not only as a base for H-2-H teams, but also to provide public reassurance and community engagement, making it much easier for locals, commuters and passers-by to drop in and offer assistance.

10.3.8 'No reply' policies

At some addresses there will inevitably be no response and a consistent policy needs to be implemented to manage the problem. There are various options available, ranging from repeat visits (if so, how many and at what times and by whom?) to contacting occupants by other means, such as phone calls or leaflet drops/calling cards. While there are resource and time implications for making re-visits, this is always the best option as some residents may need persuading or reassurance to respond or engage.

10.3.9 H-2-H coordinators

In larger investigations, a H-2-H coordinator is an optional extra for managing and supervising all H-2-H enquiries. They can be co-located at a temporary mobile incident vehicle (or caravan) at or near a chosen location/crime scene so they are close to their teams and enquiry locations. Their role is to ensure enquiries are conducted thoroughly, information is properly recorded and fed back to the incident room with no further action being taken (eg follow-up enquiries) without prior approval, and that any significant information is fed into the incident room without delay.

The coordinator ensures staff engaged on H-2-H enquiries are kept fully updated and briefed, and keep updated themselves by regularly attending enquiry team briefings to cascade information back to their teams. There has to be a two-way flow of information between H-2-H teams and the incident room. It is important their staff remain highly motivated and made to feel an integral part of the investigation. The SIO should occasionally drop by and speak to the coordinator and their teams whenever down at the crime scene or in the area to show appreciation for and interest in their task and to stress how important it is. This also presents an opportunity to dip-sample the records being completed.

The H-2-H coordinator should be supplied with a dedicated communications link (eg mobile phone or office number), details of which can be left at any premises where there is no response. This allows people to contact the coordinator directly rather than the incident room to arrange a return visit etc.

Checklist—H-2-H enquiries

- Identify key locations for H-2-H enquiries (eg crime scene, deposition site, exhibit locations, routes taken, suspect's home/place of arrest).

- Identify and record parameters and policy.

- Formulate an investigation-specific questionnaire (use open questions) and a 'no reply' policy.

- Fast-track H-2-H enquiries are those during the golden hour(s) period, ie anywhere within *line of sight or hearing* of the chosen crime scene(s).

- Prioritise and phase H-2-H enquiries where necessary.

- Determine what forms are to be used (eg PDFs and house occupancy).

- Consider form of approach (ie some people/communities may prefer a non-uniformed visit).

- Set a visits policy (eg two evening visits then leaflet drop where no reply).

- Consider extended area for mass leaflet distribution with contact details of the enquiry team.

- Coincide H-2-H visits with trigger events, such as arrests or anniversary of incident (eg exactly one week or month after) for maximum impact.

- Mobile incident vehicles are a useful focal point for the public and a convenient base for H-2-H staff.

- Administration must be methodical and completed forms submitted timely.

- High-priority (HP) information should be fast-tracked for the SIO's attention.

- Planning and preparation may be required for 'multi-occupancy'-type premises, language barriers and foreign nationals.

- Dedicated coordinator role can manage the process and supervise teams.

10.4 Passive Data

The term 'passive data' is one referred to in both the *Murder Investigation Manual* (MIM),[10] and the College of Policing, *Authorised Professional Practice*.[11] It generally means information that is obtained from automated/mechanical systems, hence the term 'passive'.

---

[10] ACPO, *Murder Investigation Manual* (NCPE, 2006), 94–5.
[11] <http://www.app.college.police.uk/app/passive data generators>.

Checklist—Passive data sources (examples)

- CCTV

- Images and data (eg captured on laptops, digital cameras, wi-fi routers, mobile smartphones and tablets)

- Body-worn camcorders (eg worn by officers)

- Financial information

- Communications data

- Voice-recording systems

- Customer information (eg customer loyalty cards)

- Electronic access systems

- Satellite navigation and goods vehicle tachographs

- Automatic Number Plate Recognition (ANPR) and speed cameras

- Electronic tagging devices, and fuel cards

- GPS tracking devices (eg covertly fitted to vehicles for/by OCGs)

- Insurance 'black boxes' (eg those fitted to young drivers' vehicles)

- TV viewing boxes and game consoles (eg SKY TV box)

Devices, images, data or equipment have to be seized quite quickly in order to prevent destruction, loss or overwriting. Fortunately, most officers instinctively look for and seize any CCTV they can lay their hands on. Passive data can provide compelling evidence and it should be a priority in every investigation. CCTV can show the nature and severity of offences and identify suspects and witnesses, (in)consistencies in accounts and forensic or scientific opportunities, such as identifying crime scenes.

There are practical issues to be mindful of:

- Variety of recording systems and video file formats in existence.
- Storage and viewing of material, ie if large amounts of data are recovered.
- Criminal Procedure and Investigations Act 1996 (CPIA) means all data recovered has to be examined for any material which is 'relevant'.
- Range and type of images vary greatly and usefulness often depends on the standard of equipment and recordings (eg some systems overwrite and are rotated on a regular basis to make them cost-effective).
- Date and time stamps can be inaccurate.
- Audit trails must be strictly maintained, particularly when copies are made and original seals are broken (ie integrity).

- Some external agencies have strict protocols governing how and when recordings may be handed over.
- Data protection must be considered.
- Integrity of systems must be checked to ensure they have not been the subject of any virus or tampered/interfered with.

Two passive sources most commonly used in major investigations are CCTV and Communications Data.

10.4.1 Closed Circuit Television (CCTV)

CCTV in investigations is of enormous benefit and routinely sought and treated as a high priority alongside other evidential gathering considerations such as witnesses and forensics.

As well as recording the actual commission of an offence, CCTV may also capture persons en route to/from committing crimes, or engaging in other activities of interest to the investigation. Some recordings may show that an alleged incident did not occur at all, or corroborate witness accounts and disprove alibis. CCTV and ANPR is also good for corroborating and tracking movements and routes taken by victims and suspects, and in some cases for identifying people who may be following or travelling with them or nearby.

A number of police forces have invested heavily in this strategy by creating dedicated units for finding and/or recovering CCTV. These contain specialists who have the best training and equipment. Some have recruited staff who are particularly gifted with powers of recognition and extremely skilled and capable at recognising and spotting people (aka 'super recognisers') in amongst complex and high-volume images.

10.4.2 CCTV policy

When setting a CCTV policy, the following should be considered:

Checklist—CCTV considerations

- Objectives (eg to trace suspect's movements before and after the offence).
- Parameters and priorities for CCTV trawls and viewing.
- How CCTV will be located and recovered, by whom and when (systems with limited storage overwrite quickly).
- External communication policy (appeals for CCTV recordings and systems).
- Specifying locations to be checked for systems (eg shops, cash machines, fuel stations, town centres, supermarkets, pubs and clubs, private properties and businesses, public transport areas, public car parks).

- How checks are to be made, ie whether a visual check will suffice or if some form of H-2-H type enquiries should be made to ask if there are any hidden systems or recordings.

- Direction on when/when not to view CCTV at the premises prior to recovery (to determine relevance) and who should/should not be present (ie witnesses).

- How CCTV is to be retrieved (dependent on type, eg analogue tapes/digital hard drives).

- What is to be noted, eg camera angle, position, type of equipment (eg if time-lapse or continuous), location captured in the image, and the terrain immediately around it to identify blind spots.

- How accuracy of time and date are to be checked (eg with the speaking clock).

- Documentation policy (eg completion of a recovery form for each and every item outlining precise location and reasons why/why not recovered).

- Legislation and powers (eg sections 8 and 19 of PACE, data protection, CPIA).

- Policy for safeguarding continuity of exhibits and provision of continuity statements.

- Viewing policy.

- Resources, facilities and equipment required.

- Disclosure and preparation of CCTV footage for court purposes.

- Retention and disposal policy.

KEY POINTS

- Early retrieval of CCTV is often vital as some systems record continuously over previous material, sometimes in a 24-hour cycle. Recovery has to be made a fast-track and golden hour(s) task.
- A minimum initial viewing objective should be to identify any CCTV recordings that show the offence being committed.
- CCTV can be viewed in position to see what is recorded that may be relevant. If anything useful is in immediate danger of being recorded over and lost, a recording of the recording might be a safe option, eg on a smartphone camera.
- CCTV can be used post-offence to see what offenders were wearing and may subsequently be missing having been worn at the time of the offence.
- CCTV can be used for reconstruction purposes, eg to compare a suspect's vehicle with one caught on a camera at a significant time and location.
- Swift evidence is good evidence, but it is not always good policy to take more than is needed. If parameters for collection are set too widely, there is a danger of being overwhelmed by too much irrelevant material to view.

Time parameters need to be wide enough to cover periods known as the 'relevant time' for the investigation, recognising that if they are too wide, they will slow down the recovery and viewing processes. However, intelligence may suggest that in some cases offenders, victims and witnesses may have been at the scene beforehand or afterwards.

The method of physically removing CCTV recordings needs clarification to ensure the best evidential product is obtained. Instructions on when and whether to shut down the recording system (if still in use), how to check the position of cameras, time and date accuracy will need clarification, and this is where expert advice and experience is needed, and specialist or dedicated CCTV units come in very useful (and ideally are available/deployable at short notice).

Checklist—CCTV trawling/retrieving/viewing objectives[12]

Trawling

- Specify times and location parameters (dynamic reviews).

- Confirm list of possible locations (eg local authority control, public transport hubs, private systems, car parks, public buildings, cash machines, fuel stations, body-worn and vehicle-mounted cameras).

- Consideration of CCTV teams and coordinator.

- Legal responsibilities (eg CPIA, Data Protection Act 1998 and PACE).

Retrieving

- Whether to view in position (prior to retrieval).

- Policy regarding checking accuracy of time/date.

- Consideration of overwriting period.

- How much recording to take (time parameters).

- How to manage hard-drive systems.

- Refusal policy.

- Relevant existing partnership MOUs (eg local authority, British Transport Police (BTP) systems).

- Practical considerations (eg removing systems from public vehicles).

---

[12] See also <https://app.college.police.uk/cctv>.

- Continuity and integrity of evidence.
- Storage requirements.

Viewing

- Creation of master and working copies.
- Dealing with poor-quality systems and images.
- Selection of staff with requisite skills and correct equipment.

Viewing objectives

- Identify offence being committed.
- Identify related events, significant incidents, persons or vehicles.
- Identify offenders.
- Identify anyone entering or exiting a significant location.
- Identify routes taken/not taken.
- Identify victims, suspects or witnesses and their behaviour, movements and actions (ie before, during and after).
- Assist in the implication or elimination of persons in a TIE category.
- Corroborate or negate accounts.
- Identify crime scenes, evidential items/exhibits and forensic opportunities.
- Establish and confirm timescales and for time-lining purposes.
- Prove association or links to specific items (eg mobile phone usage).
- Identify sightings of relevant vehicles and who is in them.
- Identify reconnaissance activities.

The purpose of viewing seized material is to identify anything which is of use to the investigation and record it so that it may be considered for inclusion as evidence or intelligence. It must be determined by policy as to what material should be viewed and what should be simply retained, which will be influenced by the aims and objectives of the strategy and parameters set.

It may be beneficial for viewing staff to visit the areas from where the CCTV is recovered and images taken. This will help to familiarise themselves with the relevant locations, visualise where events have taken place and put things into the context of the wider area.

KEY POINTS

- There are legal considerations when considering how CCTV might be utilised to identify unknown persons (contained within section 3.82 Code D and Annex E, PACE Codes of Practice 1984).
- Guidance on the best ways to disseminate CCTV evidence to internal personnel, external partners, the public via media, poster or social network means, and individual and group viewing of images for identification purposes is contained in *Practice Advice on the Use of CCTV in Criminal Investigations*, chapter 7.[13]

10.5 Communications Data and Social Media

There has been a rapid expansion and increase in the use of communications data (CD), social media, networking and the internet via computers, tablets, wi-fi, cloud storage, smartphones and other devices such as online gaming systems. The world of global communications has changed exponentially and produced a significant impact on all areas of law enforcement. What was once viewed as simply 'telephony work' in investigations has become far more complex and reliant upon a wider variety of skills and tactics.

Mobile data can take many forms—anything from conventional images, text messages, photographs to voice over internet protocol (VOIP) and voice over wi-fi (VOWI). There is a broad range of evidence that can be retrieved from suspects' and victims' mobile devices. Data items including emails can be critical to helping create links and patterns in a criminal investigation. In a digital age, there is a plethora of communication between friends, family and associates using sophisticated devices. This is something that forensic analysts and investigators must use to their advantage, as information and data recovered can reveal a great deal about activities, life patterns, behaviour and personal relationships. The tone of a text or voice message can reveal valuable information, as can the retrieval of GPS (Global Positioning System) and GPRS (General Packet Radio Service) data.

Social media is a major communications contributor and facilitator. It is inconceivable these days for any person not to make some use of social media or the internet. Digital traces and footprints left by using (meta) data and programme files that store information have become a major boon to crime investigation and law enforcement; from posting location information, compiling and uploading on websites, to tagging people on social media sites.

Social media examinations can offer a wealth of information about a person's lifestyle, thoughts, behaviour, movements, intentions and beliefs. This doesn't have to incorporate criminality per se, though it has created new opportunities for criminals to communicate via the 'dark web/net' to commit and arrange criminal activity, identify and trace victims, cause serious harassment (labelled

---

[13] ACPO, *Practice Advice on the Use of CCTV in Criminal Investigations* (NPIA, 2011), chapter 7.

'cyber stalking') and create enemies (through online competitive gaming and in virtual communities). In some cases, it might have been possible to prevent serious offences being committed had closer monitoring of social media taken place (eg some notorious spree and serial killers reveal their psychological state of mind and criminal intent prior to the commission of mass murder, terrorism and other acts of violence). This is why it is so important to identify what profiles and usage of digital communications an individual has, particularly offenders and victims.

Investigating cybercrime is a national priority, which indicates the level of importance placed upon the use of the internet and communications data to commit serious crime. The majority of investigations now involve some element of communications data information, and a strategy should be devised to capture and evidentially exploit it. Traditionally, communications data strategies have focused on the use of fixed line and mobile devices (formerly known as 'telecommunications data'); advances in technology and usage mean modern investigators and SIOs need to be aware of and knowledgeable in the latest and varied types of digital communications that are in use.

SIOs need to know about the rapidly expanding growth and increasing capabilities in speed and functionality of digital devices and applications when considering a communications data strategy. Fourth generation (4G) phones have very fast data-streaming capability that allows videos to be shared in real time as they are being recorded. This means recordings made of crimes as they occur can be instantaneously uploaded onto the internet. The implications of this on victims, witnesses, victim's families, relatives and on communities could be severe if it occurs at the time of or very soon after a crime is committed and before an investigation begins.

KEY POINTS

1. SIOs need to be aware of and increase their knowledge in the digital dimension and incorporate it into their intelligence-building and investigative strategies. The key message is 'think digital'.
2. They also need to demonstrate good leadership qualities by changing cultural attitudes resistant to moving with the times and those who proudly boast about their lack of understanding of new technology.
3. People routinely activate their portable cameras and recording devices when they see something of interest. This may also include images of initial responders at incidents and crime scenes, and also the manner in which staff conduct themselves, professionally or otherwise.

Most investigations now benefit from having communications and digital data specialists who are taskable with getting the best evidence and intelligence from this important line of enquiry. This should be treated as an investigative strategy in itself under the control and direction of an appointed lead or supervisor with a team that would probably include the Communications Liaison Officer (CLO), Digital Media Investigator (DMI), Communications Data Investigator (CDI), SPoC, researchers and an analyst.

10.5.1 **Types of communications data**

Storage of digital information has changed. Hard drives, CD/DVDs and USB sticks are not the only places where material can be stored as 'cloud' and 'remote' computing are popular. This means physical presence of evidential material may be more difficult to find and secure as it may be in another part of the world, making it more challenging to find and legally recover. The existence of 'virtual crime scenes' are a phenomena that may have to be tackled.

Social networking and internet usage must be linked with most if not all other strategies mentioned in this chapter. A search strategy, for example, should incorporate looking for digital devices and gadgets that may store or transmit data, some of which (eg tiny micro sandisk 'SD' drives) may be difficult to find and checks should be routinely made at premises for broadband and wi-fi connection. Examples of digital media and communications are:

- phones and SIM cards, computers (tablets, desktops and laptops) and printers, games stations, e-readers, browsing MP3 devices, remote (application) controlled appliances (eg building security, utilities, media players)
- entries and images on social networking sites (that can be made quickly and easily shared via most 3/4G smartphones)
- devices containing digital data and memory
- use of location data (GPRS/GPS) that record a device's position
- wi-fi systems and routers that facilitate internet access and record devices in range
- cloud storage of digital information (and 'virtual' crime scenes)
- virtual worlds (eg use of avatars) and 'virtual' financial transactions (eg through Linden dollars and bitcoins)
- Internet Connection Records (ICRs)—catered for within the proposed Investigatory Powers Bill 2016.

Different types and usage of digital media present new opportunities and challenges. Social networking can be a friend or an enemy, as the safety and security of victims' families, witnesses, the investigating organisation and investigators can be placed at risk from the careless use of social networking on the internet.

Investigative strategies that deal with victims, suspects and witnesses usually include background research requirements. Collection plans for this information must include detail about online and social media presence (not just criminal activities) and usage of/access to digital media and communications data—eg what social networking and internet sites they use, what devices they possess, how, where and when they access the internet, and how and where they store digital information.

KEY POINTS

1. Most law enforcement officers carry smartphones with built-in cameras and mobile access to the internet and social networking. Advising on (non-)professional usage at crime scenes is necessary as well as debriefing anyone who might have taken images.
2. Digital communication profiles and usage of any persons connected to an investigation should be a routine line of enquiry.
3. Search strategies and evidence collection plans need to incorporate digital communication devices, passwords and pin codes and storage systems (eg 'cloud' storage).

10.5.2 Using data evidentially

The majority of communications data once obtained can be used evidentially. Attribution of a device remains important, ie proving a person was using the device at the time of a significant communication. This can be done through possession or use at the time of recovery, device content and usage, forensic and fingerprints, supportive CCTV, covert observations, witnesses or analytical products.

Confidential and covert techniques can prove useful, and at times supply crucial information that can assist the investigation of high-end serious crime. If this data is later required evidentially, there are set criteria which must be adhered to (the CDI will advise on the criteria and the process for this, and will be involved in the gathering and presentation of the evidence). Communication service providers (CSPs) can provide data that cannot be used evidentially and the CDI is able to advise in relation to this.

KEY POINT

Communications and digital data devices may also provide traditional opportunities for providing conventional trace and transfer evidence such as blood, fingerprints or DNA.

10.5.3 Proactive use of social media intelligence

OSINT (open source intelligence) and SOCMINT (social media intelligence) can be used proactively for operational advantages and as part of an external communications strategy, eg for publicising public reassurance or giving safety advice. Social networking sites are used extensively by some of the biggest law enforcement agencies, eg New York Police Department, the FBI and UK NCA who all use Twitter to circulate 'wanted' details and photographs to the general public. Many UK police forces do this routinely also.

10.5.4 **Role of Digital Media Investigator (DMI)**

This role is an evolution of the Telecommunications Liaison Officer (TLO) and includes the coordination of covert and overt digital media inputs into an investigation, such as communications data, open source material, eg from the internet, and digital forensic recovery and examinations.

Checklist—DMI role and duties

- Proactively advising the SIO from an investigator's perspective on present or emerging tactical opportunities for exploiting all digital media and communications data.

- Being aware of all aspects of the wider investigation and investigative strategy.

- Working closely with the analyst (if appointed) to examine data and seek out information and evidence of use to the enquiry.

- Working with expert analysts, SPoCS, open source and digital forensics teams to develop the technology and data strategy within the overall investigative strategy.

- Advising on and/or managing any 'virtual' crime scenes.

- Performing role of or advising on role of 'Digital Forensics Manager' (similar to a CSM).

- Coordinating covert and overt CD-related activities across the investigation team and the intelligence cell to ensure that the firewall between the sensitive and non-sensitive is maintained.

- Using expert advice of the SPoC, open source and digital forensics teams in ascertaining what CD to obtain and how best to do it in order to streamline the application process and acquisition of specific CD as highlighted in the technology and data strategy.

- Working with the analyst to coordinate their needs from CD alongside other sources of intelligence and evidence.

- Acting as professional applicant for CD and controlling the volume and relevancy of the data requested.

- Advising on exploitation of 'OSINT' and 'SOCMINT'.

- Providing support for the investigation in the area of communications data.

10.6 **Use of Intelligence**

Intelligence cells can be established quite quickly to capitalise on early research and information development opportunities to meet the operational intelligence requirement of an investigation. While it is desirable to use resources comprising of suitably trained staff, initially this may not always be practicable.

The SIO may therefore have to rely on whoever is initially available with the requisite skills and knowledge to conduct urgent intelligence checks in 'fast time' and feed the required information into the enquiry. The SIO may want dynamic research conducting to fill information gaps when seeking and posing the important 5WH questions such as those mentioned in Chapter 3.6.

10.6.1 Role of an intelligence officer/cell

An intelligence officer (or cell) is appointed to obtain and develop information and intelligence as part of the overall strategy. Depending on the scale and type of enquiry, the size and nature of the intelligence potential will vary. In some instances one person performing the role will suffice; in others there may be a number of intelligence officers, dedicated researchers, an analyst and internal assistance from specialist officers from a dedicated intelligence unit from within the organisation. Linkage may be also required across regional, national or international agencies.

The intelligence strategy, once determined, is outlined either in the policy file or within a separate registered document. As with all other investigative strategies, this should be regularly reviewed and updated, together with an agreed list of the closed and open sources that should be exploited and accessed.

The SIO should insist that an important requirement of their intelligence cell is to be *proactive* as well as reactive in order to be of maximum benefit. The cell needs directing to be mobile as well as static in seeking information of interest and in establishing useful contacts from which information can be gleaned. This function involves much more than sitting behind a computer screen analysing digitally available material. Intelligence officers have to put themselves out to find information, meet and speak with people to establish/maintain useful contacts (remaining aware of status drift towards CHIS (covert human intelligence source) status). They must ensure that any useful contacts remain aware of their intelligence requirement, ie the one set by the SIO which remains dynamic as the enquiry progresses.

Checklist—Intelligence officer/cell responsibilities

- Research of victims, suspects and witnesses (including social media profiles).

- Preparing intelligence briefings, packages and updates.

- Preparing CHIS tasking requests and liaising with any dedicated source units.

- Partaking in or managing proactive covert surveillance activities.

- Liaising with local, regional, national and international intelligence agencies.

- Researching TIE subjects, locations, incident logs and crime pattern analysis.

- Researching H-2-H information.

- Researching significant messages and information received.

- Sanitising information and putting it into the correct format for dissemination.

- Researching prison intelligence and releases.

- Liaising with other agencies for information sharing opportunities.

- Producing a regular enquiry intelligence bulletin.

- Any other intelligence functions at the SIO's discretion.

KEY POINTS

- Intelligence cell strategies are limited only by their own imagination.
- Intelligence collection is the responsibility of all investigators on the enquiry, not just those in the intelligence cell.
- Open sources of information are widely available, but may not be accurate, reliable or as valid as closed sources. Care must be taken not to leave a 'digital footprint' indicating that an LEA has had access.[14]

10.6.2 Role of Intelligence Cell Manager

To get the best use out of a cell, it may be worth appointing a person to take overall charge of managing the intelligence strategy and performing the role of Intelligence Cell Manager. Role holders are responsible for day-to-day supervision of the cell and ensuring any relevant or new intelligence is brought to the attention of the SIO and enquiry team. They ensure relevant intelligence is disseminated to enquiry teams in a timely fashion and always at briefing sessions or other suitable times, and fresh intelligence is registered within the enquiry (eg on an intelligence or information form for appropriate actions to be raised) and an audit trail is maintained for disclosure purposes.

Wherever intelligence is being shared between internal and external agencies, terms of reference or protocols need to be adhered to or drafted and agreed. This may form part of an existing Information Sharing Agreement (ISA) and the task delegated to the Intelligence Cell Manager.

It is a consideration that the intelligence cell receives copies of all messages that enter the MIR. An optional function of the intelligence cell is to research the information contained within the message, eg any named subjects, addresses/ locations or vehicles.

---

[14] As cited in College of Policing, *Intelligence collection, development and dissemination* (2015) <https:// www.app.college.police.uk/app-content/intelligence-management/intelligence-cycle/> (accessed 28 July 2015).

An intelligence cell policy must stipulate when and how intelligence meetings are to be held, for instance on a weekly basis or more frequently depending on the requirements of the SIO and needs of the investigation.

KEY POINT

Where there are regular intelligence feeds, an Intelligence Officer can be tasked with preparing a running log in simplified format containing a résumé of all available intelligence, together with evaluation codes. This can then be distributed to the enquiry teams and updated on a daily/weekly/bi-weekly basis for ease of reference.

Checklist—Intelligence cell strategy

To support the SIO and enquiry team in:

- exploiting and managing all intelligence

- developing and providing strategic/tactical intelligence, advice and information

- providing the SIO and enquiry team with intelligence briefings and updates

- disseminating intelligence collated during the investigation

- adhering to requirements of disclosure rules.

To provide assistance in:

- history and background checks, compiling sequence of events and other analytical products in respect of the victim, associates, witnesses, scene, suspects, timelines, TIEs and any other subjects or requirements at the SIO's discretion

- producing research profiles—victim, witnesses and suspects

- preparing and providing intelligence packages/running logs

- managing communications data intelligence

- developing intelligence from covert sources

- preparing any covert RIPA 'authority' applications

- exploiting useful open (eg social media) and closed sources (eg police, NCA, Her Majesty's Revenue & Customs (HMRC), UK Border Agency (UKBA), financial or prison intelligence, Driver & Vehicle Licensing Agency (DVLA), BTP)

- arranging local and national circulations.

10.6.3 **Setting the intelligence requirement**

The SIO and enquiry team should be in an early position to identify intelligence gaps which need filling which forms the basis of the intelligence requirement. An analyst can be tasked with helping in this. The intelligence requirement should always remain dynamic and focused not only upon priorities but also on other key information and research to service the needs of the investigation (eg risk assessments for TIE subjects). The intelligence requirement should remain under continual review and any amendments recorded by the SIO.

The SIO should try to avoid information overload. When requesting information, specific terms and parameters should be recorded in the strategy and/or policy log. For example, if a victim had an extensive criminal background: '*the SIO requests all intelligence logs held by (source) that mention the victim between (date) and (date)*'.

The intelligence collection plan is part of the intelligence strategy and must be updated regularly to ensure any gaps and additional sources are identified. The collection of intelligence must always remain in accordance with human rights principles, ie justifiable, proportionate and necessary. Some thought must go into the methods of collection, which may need to involve resources required for the intelligence cell, such as an analyst and researcher(s).

KEY POINTS

- A communications strategy should link into the dissemination and requirement of important information for which further detail or development is required, eg within bulletins or briefings. Local officers or those with particular knowledge of an area or community should be invited to partake in team briefings and encouraged to contribute as part of the team, eg officers who work in or who have particular responsibilities for specific areas.
- Opportunities to collect community intelligence need to be identified, such as having officers around at times and locations where good sources of information are likely to congregate, eg at school opening/finishing time when local people are dropping off or collecting their children.
- In April 2015, the UK joined the Schengen Information System (SIS) which is an EU-wide IT system enabling Schengen member states to share real-time information on persons and objects of interest. This includes persons wanted for extradition or missing persons and adults/minors at risk. This information is available via the Police National Computer (PNC) and Warnings Index, or a SPoC (named SIRENE Bureau) housed within the National Crime Agency.

10.6.4 **Research levels**

As part of an intelligence strategy, the intelligence officer/cell is required to conduct research for background details of certain nominals (eg TIEs or suspects). Intelligence searches should be conducted according to a grading system (or levels) set or agreed by the SIO. As there are numerous amounts of research and databases potentially available from which searches can be made, a degree of consistency is required. When the research is requested on a nominal (named/recorded subject), the level required should also be stipulated. For example:

Level A   Basic search criteria
Level B   Intermediate search criteria
Level C   Specific search criteria
Level D   Advanced search criteria

Each level becomes more detailed as it goes up the scale. The search criteria should be fixed according to the requirements of the investigation and range from local checks, such as crime-recording systems, the police national computer (PNC), local intelligence systems, the PND and HOLMES, stop/search records, summons/warrants, HMRC, finance companies, NCA, Europol, and Interpol.

Nominals for research should be agreed as part of the intelligence strategy and discussed with and clearly communicated to the intelligence cell. For example, in a case where there is no declared suspect, a policy decision could indicate research to identify all recorded offenders or individuals who fall into one or more of the below mentioned category examples some of which may be included in or as a TIE category:

• Convictions for offences involving weapons.
• Convictions for burglary in dwellings.
• Convictions for drug-related offences/sex offences.
• Known to have mental health problems.
• Recorded as subjects for multi-agency public protection panels.
• Aged between...and...and have links to...
• White males (IC1) who have identifying marks or features.
• Known offenders who have current or previous residence in...
• Occupants of bail hostels within location of...
• Registered homeless within postcodes of...
• Males previously issued with harassment warnings in...
• Male offenders released on licence or serving suspended or community sentences between...(date) and...(date).
• Male employees of...(eg victim's place of work).

10.6.5 **Covert sources of intelligence**

There are a number of sensitive sources of covert intelligence that cannot be mentioned in any great detail for reasons of confidentiality. The tactic of covert intelligence gathering can link in with a proactive covert strategy and is governed by the provisions of the Regulation of Investigatory Powers Act 2000 (RIPA) (and draft Investigatory Powers Bill 2015/16), for example:

- covert surveillance and other covert operations
- CHIS (source) information
- Covert Internet Investigator (CII) tactics
- prison intelligence (through Prison Intelligence Officers (PIOs))
- communications data
- Technical Support Units.

10.6.6 Sensitive or 'need to know' information

'Need to know' is a security principle which means the dissemination of certain classified information should go no wider than is required for the efficient conduct of the tactic and enquiry, and should be restricted to those whom the SIO deems appropriate and have the requisite vetting clearance level. A balance must be struck between making information widely available to maximise potential benefits and restricting availability to protect the security of sources, techniques and information. Put simply, there is a distinction between 'need to know' and 'like to know'.

Information held on a case management system (eg HOLMES) is mainly non-sensitive, but some information may be confidential (or even secret). Confidentiality usually relates to the origin of the material. For example, information obtained from CHIS or from other types of covert deployment would usually attract a general protection in law from disclosure. This is known as public interest immunity (PII). Such information **may** be protected (at the discretion of a court judge) if it can be argued that disclosure would harm or endanger the source, or would be against the public interest in future law enforcement activity (eg compromise a sensitive tactic).

The SIO liaises with the DSIO and Office Manager to agree levels of access to confidential or sensitive material registered on HOLMES. Any decisions should be recorded in the SIO's policy log. Some information may be deemed so sensitive that it needs to be kept in secure storage throughout the duration of the enquiry and cross-referenced in the sensitive policy file (see Chapter 4.7). This is entirely at the SIO's discretion, remembering that access levels can be pre-set on a HOLMES database (with only designated persons able to view policy), which reduces any risk of misplacing or losing sensitive information.

KEY POINT

Sterile corridors or **firewalls** must be implemented to protect the source of covertly obtained (aka red zone) material and maintain strict rules of confidentiality when sharing and disseminating intelligence, both internally and externally.

10.6.7 **Recording sensitive intelligence**

Intelligence logs (aka 5x5x5 forms) have a restricted handling code accompanied by a risk assessment and stipulated conditions as to the reasons why it may be unwise to disseminate any further or to act on the information. This position can change and logs re-graded in consultation with the SIO and the originator. If this occurs, the case management system should reflect this, showing both ratings, relevant change details and reasons why.

Any sensitive documents are usually afforded the protection of 'Official-Sensitive', 'confidential' or 'secret' markings. The SIO should agree at the start of each enquiry, whilst setting the intelligence strategy, which persons or role holders are afforded access to any such material, either loaded onto database or otherwise.

10.6.8 **Intelligence dissemination and sharing**

It is highly likely there will be an accrual of intelligence that is of benefit to other units or agencies, either internally or externally. An intelligence strategy can cater for a means of feeding and sharing useful information into other appropriate intelligence systems. The intelligence officer/cell can be tasked with exchanging relevant intelligence with all other interested parties and departments, which should be duly recorded. A risk assessment may be necessary before some types of intelligence are disseminated to ensure they are handled appropriately.

10.6.9 **Intelligence disclosure policy**

Policy is not only required to comply with the CPIA rules, but also to ensure that *all* material is correctly gathered and, where necessary, sanitised before being listed on the disclosure schedule. Suitable arrangements are needed to guarantee that all relevant material is collected either from sensitive, confidential or other sources.

Heavy reliance is sometimes placed upon those not directly connected to the enquiry but who search for and furnish all the relevant material related to the enquiry from other sources (eg CHIS controllers and/or RIPA Authorising Officer). The SIO has to be proactive in gaining the full cooperation of the role holders for compiling accurate lists and gathering together all the relevant documentation for disclosure and any PII hearings.

KEY POINT

Relevant intelligence (including covert or sensitive material, particularly if it comes from other agencies unconnected to the investigation) has to be traced, made available and presented in a suitable format to the Disclosure Officer and Crown Prosecutor/special case worker. Any PII (public interest immunity) preparatory material and schedules need closely supervising, as mistakes tend to prove very costly, with the potential to inflict irreparable damage on a prosecution case (ie for failing to disclose or incorrect disclosure).

10.6.10 **Analytical support**

Analysts (and their researchers) are important members of an enquiry team as analysis forms part of the intelligence cycle[15] (direction, collection, collation, evaluation, analysis and dissemination) that allows intelligence material to be processed. There are a variety of analytical tools they can use that can be applied, such as association charts, consanguinity chains (see Chapter 11.6.3), timelines and sequence of events (SOE), comparative case analysis (including serial offending), subject and risk analysis, mapping, flow and frequency charts, and storyboards. They can also help in hypotheses building/testing and inference development to help draw conclusions, making predictions and aiding problem solving and decision making (see also Chapter 3). Analysts can also be utilised for preparing interview schedules and they could even be considered for involvement in any 'downstream monitoring' process.

Once appointed to a case, analysts should attend and participate in operational briefings and sometimes management meetings. They can be shown appropriate crime scenes in order to familiarise themselves with the offence under investigation and ideally are co-located within the incident room as they need to become part of the team and have easy access to relevant material and a HOLMES terminal if necessary. This should not preclude them from having access to their own specialist equipment such as large printers located elsewhere.

Whenever practical and as soon as material becomes available (eg witness statements), it should be provided to them so they can begin work without undue delay. Their work can be expertly plotted and charted using specialist software and technology that makes the interpretation of information so much easier to present and understand. This may eventually form part of the evidential case as an exhibit (ie not just as an intelligence product) and analysts can be treated as professional witnesses. If not used as a witness, they may be invited to attend case conferences, prepare jury bundles of analytical evidence and, while a case is in session, be on hand to support and advise the prosecution team, and analyse the case as it progresses, particularly witness testimonies.

KEY POINTS

- Appointment of an analyst and their terms of reference is recorded in the policy log. As the case develops these may be subject to review and amendment. If so, new terms of reference should also be recorded.
- Only the SIO/DSIO or intelligence cell managers task the analyst/researcher. Other staff must not commission them to do tasks without seeking permission.
- Key is knowing *what* to ask an analyst to do, so a basic understanding and appreciation of what they can produce and tools and products they have at their disposal is advisable.

---

[15] As cited in College of Policing, *Research and analysis* (2014) <https:app.college.police.uk/app-content/intelligence-management/analysis/> (accessed 28 July 2015).

10.6.11 Analyst—terms of reference

The SIO should discuss and agree with the appointed analyst clear terms of reference. These must mirror the current priorities, and main lines of enquiry. The terms of reference (TOR) cover topics such as:

- aims and objectives
- data sources to be accessed and relied upon
- analytical products requested and software that can be utilised
- parameters and limitations
- timescales and reporting mechanism.

The analyst should be able to advise the SIO on what analytical products they can produce and all the topics contained within the above list. These may need reviewing and amending as the enquiry progresses.

All tasks allocated and work completed should be recorded on actions to keep an accurate record, which should reflect what is contained within the analyst's terms of reference.

> **KEY POINT**
>
> *To assist in understanding the various strands of the investigation, the analysts developed a time-line document for easy reference. In the event this ran to 99 pages. It was subsequently described by the Principal CPS lawyer as the single most useful document that came out of Operation Fincham.*[16]

10.7 **Financial Investigation**

There are significant benefits from seeking financial information as an investigative strategy. This type of information can reveal details about a suspect or victim's lifestyle, financial profile, and the identification and use of significant transactions. It can reveal suspects and witnesses from evidence of them making financial transactions or being present at significant times and locations. Financial information can be developed and analysed to establish patterns and trends, fill intelligence gaps and contribute to intelligence profiles.

The assistance of a Financial Investigator (FI) should be considered in all major investigations. Financial data may assist in giving an indication of motive, debt or even financial stress. Persons cannot exist without leaving behind some kind of 'financial footprint', be it the victim, suspect or witness. This information can be used to identify:

---

[16] Sir R Flanagan, 'A report on the investigation by Cambridgeshire Constabulary into the murders of Jessica Chapman and Holly Wells' HMIC, June 2004, Ch 5.72.

- offences (including money laundering)
- suspects, witnesses, victims, missing persons (and to locate)
- association with others and/or links to places and premises
- information around a person's location and movements
- use of services such as phones, transport or other amenities and facilities
- motives
- lifestyles and habits.

Financial data may have been created in one, two or all three areas of the Problem Analysis Triangle (see Chapter 3.8.5), ie victim, offender and location. For example, the creation of financial data by both the victim and offender at a certain location may be the evidence that links them together. Third parties who leave some financial data may also become useful witnesses.

Financial data may indicate motive, such as personal gain. Valuable lines of enquiry can be developed by identifying a credit/debit card used to top up a mobile phone, or examining till receipts in retail premises, or use of ATMs (automatic telling machines) to see who was at or near a crime scene (as suspect or witness).

Searches of premises or vehicles should include checks for financial information that may help build a picture of a person's lifestyle or generate additional lines of enquiry (eg money suddenly going in or out of a bank account). There is a vast amount of information available in the financial world and investigators must have clear objectives when seeking it that are appropriate and beneficial to the enquiry. Vague and non-specific requests, such as 'obtain a financial profile', are not helpful.

KEY POINT

Financial data can be gathered from family and relatives of victims, during H-2-H enquiries (eg details of financial outlets in the area such as ATMs or general stores that have a small cash-dispensing service) and during covert proactive operations.

10.7.1 **Tournier Rules**

Accredited Financial Investigators (AFIs) under the Proceeds of Crime Act 2002 (POCA) are permitted to make pre-order enquiries to financial institutions under the Tournier Rules.[17] These permit disclosure of information to law enforcement agencies that would otherwise be a breach of contract between the institution and their customers. Financial data may therefore be disclosed in the following circumstances:

- for the protection of the public
- for the protection of the institution's own interests

---

[17] *Tournier v National Provincial and Union Bank of England* [1924] 1 KB 461.

- under compulsion by law
- with the consent of the owner.

This material is gathered by AFIs and is supplied for intelligence purposes only. If it is to be adduced into the evidential chain (including questioning during interview), a production order is required, hence the term 'pre-order enquiries'.

10.7.2 **Suspicious Activity Reports (SARs)**

A SAR is an information report on what a financial institution considers to be suspicious transactions, eg money laundering. This information is made available to the police in order to assist investigations and help identify assets that have been obtained through criminality. Local policy usually dictates how this information is collected.

The rules for disclosure extend to a wide variety of financial sectors, ranging from high-value dealers (eg cars and jewellery), tax advisers and the legal profession, to real estates, security deposit box companies and gambling agencies.

10.7.3 **Proceeds of Crime Act 2002 (POCA)**

This legislation provides for the obtaining of production orders, search and seizure warrants, account monitoring orders, customer information orders and restraint orders (POCA, parts 2 and 8). The orders require the signature of a Crown Court judge.

This legislation should be considered in any major investigation where there is an opportunity to seize any assets that may have been the proceeds of crime. The type of information or material that may provide this opportunity needs to be a consideration across some of the other strategies, particularly when searching premises. Part 5 of POCA, for example, provides a power to seize any cash if it is believed to be a means of disrupting any criminal acts (eg drug- or gang-type activity).

10.8 **Proactive Investigation**

Proactive (overt and covert) investigation strategies require the initiation of some action rather than merely reacting to and investigating a crime(s) that has already been committed. This may include catering for continuing criminal activity, targeting suspected offenders, dealing with a 'crime in action' (eg ongoing serial offending where there is a pressing public interest to detain the offender(s) as quickly as possible) or targeting a particular kind of crime where the offenders have not been identified.

Proactive strategies are not confined to covert operations such as surveillance. A range of overt proactive options to prevent, detect or disrupt crime may be available which an SIO might wish to use as a multi-purpose function or as part of subterfuge and disruption tactics. Examples include executing search warrants or mounting high-visibility patrols or road checks. Other proactive options might include dealing with threats to life (TTL) in kidnap cases or managing dangerous offenders. Complex investigations may require a fully integrated approach with the use of a number of different techniques dependent on the type of investigation and level of crime.

10.8.1 Contingency plans

A proactive contingency (or trigger) plan is to prepare for if and when further offences are committed or incidents of interest to the investigation occur. The aim of the plan is to ensure there is an appropriate response to reported incidents that may include capturing evidence and conducting specific actions required by the investigation. Contingency plans need to include protocols around call-out procedures and notifications for enquiry teams, and any other specific roles and responsibilities, eg Exhibits Officer, forensic examination and physical searching, CCTV viewing and recovery, specialists (eg ballistics examination), and victim and witness care arrangements. All these requirements are likely to be 'golden hour' tasks.

The purpose of a contingency plan will differ with each investigation, but generally such plans are put into place for the following reasons:

- prevent further offences
- provide public reassurance
- maximise investigative and forensic gathering opportunities
- identify and apprehend offenders.

The plan may benefit from being divided into three sections to cover the roles of: (1) call taker (instructions on receipt of report what and who to deploy and notify, where and when); (2) initial responders (detail regarding what action to take in addition to general response duties and actions required specific to the investigation; and (3) crime investigators, in addition to general responsibilities to include what the investigation and SIO may require from them, eg notification and call-out procedures.

Ensuring that a senior investigator and/or the SIO are notified at the earliest opportunity is essential. The whole point of a contingency plan is to reduce the risk of required actions not being taken; but in order for them to work they need effective planning and communication. Consideration should be given as to the best way to brief call takers, response officers, investigators and other specialists that are required. This should be incorporated into a communication strategy.

10.8.2 Proactive covert tactics

Covert investigative tactics can be used for a number of reasons and to meet specific needs and objectives. They can be conducted using human or technical resources or a combination of both. Generally speaking, it is best to obtain tactical advice from those who have sound knowledge of the various options that might be available, particularly those who work in or have good knowledge of serious and organised crime investigation. There are many different options and a degree of creativity is often beneficial to make best use of covert assets and options. They should not always be viewed as a stand-alone intelligence tactic either as they can complement other options, such as physical searching, scene identification or as part of an arrest strategy.

Preservation of tactics is essential to 'future-proof' their effectiveness and minimise risk of compromise. Knowledge of certain methods is restricted even within law enforcement circles and this is an equally important consideration for an SIO. Specialist advice and assets utilised have to be made subject to the principle of 'need to know' (as opposed to 'nice to know') and have to be carefully managed throughout the duration of the enquiry and beyond.

Added considerations when using covert tactics are as follows:

- They are often resource- and cost-dependent.
- They produce a product that needs properly analysing (which might be a large task with lots of information to manage).
- Products need to be the subject of special Crown Prosecution Service (CPS) casework and PII hearing.
- Disclosure rules always apply and, despite PII protection, a trial judge might feel duty bound to declare covertly obtained information to the defence (jeopardising or safeguarding the tactic and source).
- Some tactics can be time-consuming and prolong an investigation.
- There is a risk that intelligence gained might be inaccurate and take the investigation off in the wrong direction.
- Some criminals are wise enough to deliberately feed misinformation into an investigation via covert tactics to frustrate the investigation.
- Tactics need carefully protecting on a 'need to know' basis.
- Safeguarding a covert tactic might become burdensome and long term.
- Strict legal provisions need adhering to.

Article 8 of the European Convention for the Protection of Human Rights (ECHR) provides a right to respect for private and family life, and covert investigation at whatever NIM level has to be pre-authorised and closely scrutinised. Any evidence obtained by these infringements is often compelling, so defence tactics at trial may seek its exclusion by questioning the integrity of the process and challenging adherence to the procedures. This includes not just authorisation and the actions of operatives, but also the disclosure obligations under the CPIA.

Balancing a defendant's right to a fair trial alongside the management of sensitive material is challenging and may necessitate a PII hearing to prevent certain information being disclosed. Early consultation with the CPS is essential.

Covert processes can be time-consuming, involving tasking and coordination, pre-application feasibility studies, detailed risk assessment, planning for contingencies (including compromise and its consequences), and preparing and submitting applications. This is a task often allocated to the dedicated intelligence cell. The cell is also usually tasked with managing the covert product and is a very important responsibility. This is because intelligence received might be of such significance that if correct or incorrect could take the investigation off in the right or wrong direction. It is often the interpretation of precise wording contained within covert intelligence products that can become crucially important.

Wherever possible, SIOs should anticipate the need for covert activity early and identify relevant issues by querying:

- What is the least intrusive method of securing such evidence or information?
- What are the legal enablers or constraints?
  — RIPA
  — Police Act 1997
  — Human Rights Act 1998
  — ECHR—Articles 2, 6 and 8
  — CPIA
  — Investigatory Powers Bill 2015
- What is the time frame for the operation or is a unique window of opportunity available?
- What resources are required (are there sufficient trained and accredited staff available)?
- What equipment and funding is required and available?
- What are the risks to the organisation of (not) deploying the tactics?
- What are the risks to the staff of deploying the tactics?
- What are the risks to the public or specified third parties?
- What are the risks to the subject of the investigation?
- Will the methods breach ECHR, Article 8(1)?
- What is the justification for breaching ECHR, Article 8(2)?
- What is the risk of collateral intrusion and how will this be managed?
- How will the covert methods be protected at trial?
- What advice should be sought?

It is only by asking and answering these 5WH-style questions that an authorisation can proceed and a tactical plan be developed and implemented.

KEY POINTS

- SIOs considering covert tactics should seek advice from relevant specialists.
- Intelligence relied upon to justify a covert operation and application should be received in a permanent and tangible format (ie on a formal document) as verbal communications can be open to mistakes or misinterpretation.
- A RIPA Authorising Officer is a useful source for advice.

10.8.3 **Human Rights Act 1998 (HRA)**

The HRA was introduced to safeguard citizens from intrusions by the state into their privacy and rights. There are, of course, legal powers that allow law enforcement agencies and some other public bodies to breach these rights under certain provisions. There are important fundamental rules that must be clearly understood and followed to ensure that investigations, particularly when covert methods are used, are conducted without unnecessary or unfair intrusiveness.

The most relevant articles are:

Article 2: *Right to life*
Article 5: *Right to liberty and security*
Article 6: *Right to a fair trial* (**often cited by defence lawyers during court trials**)
Article 8: *Right to respect for private and family life*
Article 14: *Prohibition of discrimination*

Human rights principles that are incumbent on all investigations are outlined in the table below.

Justification (legality)	The interference with an individual's Article 8 rights is justifiable only if it is necessary and proportionate. This is stipulated in statutory grounds ie s 28(3) of RIPA (prevent or detect serious crime).
Necessity	The breach must be the only and most suitable way to achieve the objective after other alternatives have been considered.
Proportionality	The activities must be proportionate, which involves balancing the intrusiveness of the activity on the subject and others who might be affected. The activity will not be proportionate if it is excessive in the circumstances. This must remain under scrutiny and dynamic review to comply with the principles of the Act.
Collateral intrusion	Refers to the risk of intrusion into the privacy of persons other than those who are directly the subjects of the investigation or operation (third-party damage). Measures to reduce or eliminate unnecessary intrusion into the lives of those not directly connected with the investigation or operation should be included and dynamically monitored. This may include certain sensitivities in a particular area, location or community.

Source: Codes of Practice pursuant to s 71 of the Regulation of Investigatory Powers Act 2000 (RIPA).

10.9 **Specialist Support and Expert Advisers**

Some extremely useful national resources are available from the Crime Operational Support (COS) and the Serious Crime Analysis Section (SCAS) located within the NCA. These assets can be of enormous help and support to a major investigation and should be considered as early into the investigation as possible.

Specialist Operations Centre (SOC)	Serious Crime Analysis Section (SCAS)
Crime Operational Support (COS)	UK Missing Persons Bureau (MPB)
National Injuries Database (NID)	CATCHEM database

These units and resources provide information, advice and specialist support to crime investigators and UK law enforcement agencies. Their core business is focused mainly around serious crimes, such as murder, rape, abduction, serious sexual offences or other crime-related critical incidents. Support to the SIO and enquiry staff is arranged through regionally based teams with extensive investigative experience, specialist skills, knowledge and expertise.

Specialist Operations Centre (SOC)	Single point of contact for police forces and key partners requesting advice and support in relation to specialist research, crime investigative and covert law enforcement advice and witness intermediaries. Also manages and provides a gateway to the Expert Advisor's Database.
Crime Operational Support (COS)	Focuses on sharing and dissemination of good practice, offering tactical and strategic advice through deployable assets such as National PIP4 SIO Advisers and Crime Investigative Support Officers (CISOs). Subject-matter experts and specialists, such as Behavioural Investigative Advisers (BIA), Forensic Clinical Psychologists (FCP), geographical profilers, and national advisers on topics such as search, investigative interviewing, family liaison and forensics can be made available to investigations at no extra cost.
National Injuries Database (NID)	See Chapter 14.13.
Serious Crime Analysis Section (SCAS)	National unit for identifying any potential emergence of serial killers and rapists at an early stage in their offending. Collates detailed information relating to behaviours and features exhibited in the more serious of sexual offences.
UK Missing Persons Bureau	See Chapter 14.18.
Centralised Analytical Team Collating Homicide Expertise and Management (CATCHEM)	A database that holds details of all child murders/homicides committed in England, Wales and Scotland, from 1 January 1960 to the present date. This includes females under the age of 22 years and males under the age of 17 years at the time of death. It also includes details of long-term child missing persons, attempted murders and some cases of child abduction. The database utilises historical data to analyse current cases, and assists with statistical profiling of probable characteristics of an unknown offender, as well as comparative case analysis to identify potential links between offences.

10.9.1 **Expert advisers**

Some investigations may require the assistance from experts who are outside the mainstream of forensic support that is readily available. Specialists and experts may be needed for elements of an investigation that are unusual or even obscure and pose unique challenges. There are experts willing to provide expert opinion on all manner of subjects, such as entomology (insects for establishing time of death), palynology (plants and botanical links to persons and items), podiatry (examination of feet), archaeology and anthropology (search for and recovery of human remains), knots and rope, clothing, geophysics, facial mapping, diatoms from bodies in water (to establish if person alive when entered water), digital reconstruction and so on, even plastic bin liners (eg when used to wrap or conceal body parts and corpses).

However, the use of 'experts' can pose significant challenges—for example, determining how experienced they are, how current their knowledge is, how many times they have successfully given evidence, what their qualifications are, how they present their evidence, what they have in place for avoiding cross-contamination, and not least of all—cost. The Specialist Operations Centre (SOC) within the NCA maintains a national register of experts to assist in sourcing experts in a large variety of specialist subjects. They also keep details of their CVs and information from when they may have been used in the past, who by, when and what their contribution was like. This is to assist in deciding whether to use them or not. The database does not grant accreditation, but a lot of the guesswork can be taken out of the process when requiring expertise that is not available through the usual channels.

KEY POINTS

- When using experts and specialists, an SIO should never be intimidated by what their levels of knowledge and qualifications suggest, nor be afraid of challenging them on their opinions and probing the reliability of their conclusions. The ABC rule should always be applied.
- Experts tend to be good at coming up with answers provided they are asked the right questions.
- Experts (including forensic pathologists) often take their own notes and some take photographs at crime scenes. These need to be declared to the SIO and are potentially disclosable. They may also contain material of significance to the investigation.

References

ACPO, *Murder Investigation Manual* (NCPE, 2006)

ACPO, *Practice Advice on Analysis* (NPIA, 2008)

ACPO, *Practice Advice on Financial Investigation* (NPIA, 2006)

ACPO, *Practice Advice on House to House Enquiries* (Centrex, 2006)

ACPO, *Practice Advice on the Management and Use of Proceeds of Crime Legislation* (NPIA, 2008) <https://www.app.college.police.uk/app-content/intelligence-management/intelligence-cycle/> (accessed 28 July 2015)

ACPO, *Practice Advice on the Use of CCTV in Criminal Investigations* (NPIA, 2011)

Adcock, S, 'Financial Investigation: SIO Considerations' (2010) 6(2) *Journal of Homicide and Major Incident Investigation*

College of Policing, *Research and analysis* (2014) <https:app.college.police.uk/app-content/intelligence-management/analysis/> (accessed 28 July 2015)

Harfield, C and Harfield, K, *Covert Investigation*, 3rd edn (OUP, 2012)

Victim Management

11.1 **Introduction**

'Being a victim of a crime is a very clinical, very personal and very blunt experience that never leaves you' (Baroness Newlove,[1] 2015). Victims, including their close family/relatives and sometimes wider communities, can be on the receiving end of a wide range of atrocious criminal acts such as homicide, physical injury, rape and sexual offences, high-value crime, extortion, terrorism, high-value fraud, sexual exploitation, trafficking abduction and other serious offending. These sufferers need and deserve the full support of and help from those investigating and prosecuting crimes committed against them. Sometimes this responsibility gets pushed down the list of priorities or forgotten in and amongst other competing demands.

Fortunately, a greater emphasis has been placed upon identifying and supporting victims (one of the five building block principles—see Chapter 5.4). High-profile cases, public enquiries, a new code of practice and the appointment of a Victims' Commissioner have led to a significant step change in the approach to victim welfare. Nowadays it is expected they come first and get properly listened to and treated in a respectful, sensitive and professional manner, without discrimination and afforded a fair chance of recovery.

New obligations placed upon the police and other prescribed services by the introduction of the Victims' Code of Practice means it is mandatory that victims, including relatives of deceased persons, are treated with respect, professionalism and dignity. Any failure to do so produces secondary victimisation and potential litigation opportunities. There is also a risk of reputational damage and loss of public support.

The SIO plays a pivotal role, not only in leading the investigation, but in taking a strategic and tactical perspective. This is to ensure help is provided not only for victims and their next of kin, but also enabling local policing and partnership teams meet their objectives in maintaining good relationships, particularly when incidents affect vulnerable or hard-to-hear/reach groups.

There may well be some overlap with some of the contents detailed within Chapter 13, as sometimes victims may also be witnesses. Nonetheless, this chapter aims to cover some of the significant and important considerations that need to be included as a victim management policy/strategy. Having a thorough and robust policy as part of the investigation plan will significantly help strengthen (or weaken) relationships with victims and the general public. This chapter is dedicated to increasing awareness and professionally managing this important element of an investigation.

---

[1] Baroness Helen Newlove, UK Government Victims' Commissioner, speaking at PIP4 CPD seminar, College of Policing, Ryton, 13 May 2015. Her 47-year-old husband Gary had been murdered in August 2007, Warrington, Cheshire, after confronting a gang of youths found vandalising his car. They kicked him repeatedly in the head and are now serving time for murder. See also <http://www.victims commissioner.org.uk>.

KEY POINTS

- Investigating major crime involves providing support to victims, their families and sometimes communities. Taking the right approach helps foster healthy and trusting relationships, encourages greater assistance with ongoing and future investigations, and gives victims a better chance of recovery.
- If victim or community relationships become strained or unhealthy, urgent remedial action may be required. The situation may even become 'critical' and the formation of a case-specific NPCC-led Gold group may be necessary.
- Details (and in homicide cases, their photographs) of victims should always remain uppermost in investigators' minds. After all, this is the person they are seeking to get justice for.

11.2 **Code of Practice**

A Code of Practice for victims of crime in England and Wales was published in October 2015 by the Secretary of State for Justice.[2] It forms a key part of a wider Government strategy to transform the CJS and put victims first. It strengthens an aim to treat victims of crime in a respectful, sensitive, tailored and professional manner without discrimination.

Victims can decide if they do not want some or all of the information or services they are entitled to under the Code, or that they want to opt out at a later date. These services on offer are tailored to individual needs and circumstances and can be discussed with whoever is the service provider. It should be noted that victims can opt back into receiving services under the Code at any time while the case is under active investigation or prosecution.

Chapters 1 to 4 of the Code apply to organisations such as all police forces in England and Wales, the British Transport and Ministry of Defence Police, the CPS and the CCRC.

Chapter 5, however, applies to agencies that have a narrower remit and specialised roles in the context of criminal proceedings due to them focusing on specific types of crimes or offences. These are agencies such as the Health and Safety Executive, Serious Fraud Office and National Crime Agency.

The Code contains a list of key entitlements (not all are applicable) that most victims of criminal conduct in England and Wales are entitled to. These entitlements are summarised as follows:

- Enhanced service for victims: (a) of serious crime; (b) who are persistently targeted; or (c) who are vulnerable or intimidated.

---

[2] *Code of Practice for Victims of Crime: Presented to Parliament pursuant to section 33 of the Domestic Violence, Crime and Victims Act 2004* (HM Stationery Office, October 2015, or see downloadable version at <http://www.gov.uk/moj>). It implements relevant provisions of the EU Directive 2012/29/EU establishing minimum standards on the rights, support and protection of victims of crime; Directive 2011/92/EU combating the sexual abuse and exploitation of children; and Directive 2011/36/EU preventing and combating the trafficking of human beings.

- Needs assessment to help establish what support is needed.
- Information on what to expect from the Criminal Justice System (CJS).
- Referral to support organisations, if required.
- Information and updates about the investigation and case disposal details (including time, date and location of any court hearings).
- Make a Victim Personal Statement (VPS), and have it read aloud at court if defendant found guilty.
- Seek a review of the police or CPS's decision not to prosecute in accordance with the NPCC and CPS Victims' Right to Review Schemes.
- Support from a Witness Care Unit (WCU) if required as a witness.
- Arrange a court familiarisation visit, enter through a different entrance from the suspect, supervised attendance and access to the prosecutor to raise any queries about the case (where circumstances permit).
- Be informed of any appeal against the offender's conviction or sentence.
- If offender sentenced to 12 months or more for violent or sexual offence, opt into the Victim Contact Scheme (VCS).[3]
- Apply for compensation under Criminal Injuries Compensation Scheme.
- Receive information about the Restorative Justice Scheme.
- Make a complaint about information and services not received.

The Code defines a victim as:

1. A natural person who has suffered harm, including physical, mental or emotional harm or economic loss which was **directly** caused by a criminal offence (in England and Wales); or
2. A close relative (ie spouse, partner, relatives in direct line, siblings and dependents of victim) of a person whose death was directly caused by a criminal offence (in England and Wales).

Enhanced entitlements are also outlined in the Code for victims in certain categories. These include (i) if the victim is from a serious crime; (ii) is persistently targeted; or (iii) is vulnerable or intimidated (as per criteria of the YJCE Act 1999 sections 16–17). In these circumstances victims are entitled to have (where appropriate) information about special measures explained; be referred to a specialist support organisation; receive information on pre-trial therapy and counselling; and if a case is concluded without charge, be informed if the case is re-opened. A bereaved close relative of a victim who has died as a consequence of criminal conduct is entitled, under the Code, to have a Family Liaison Officer (FLO) assigned (where the SIO deems it appropriate).

A duty to conduct a needs assessment at an early stage falls upon the listed agencies (eg the police) to which the Code applies, and in particular to decide whether victims fall into one of the three priority categories for enhanced services. An SIO would be wise to ensure all their teams are aware of the requirements

[3] If offender is under 18 years of age, a Youth Offending Team may contact the victim to seek their views prior to sentencing if they are not receiving support under the VCS.

of the Code and to appoint a suitably experienced officer to act as a Victim Care Officer (VCO) for each victim at an early stage of the investigation, and determine whether they fall into one of the three categories for enhanced entitlements.

11.3 **Victim Support**

SIOs should assume that victims of serious crimes require significant support and this needs to be a constituent part of a victim management strategy. Support, of course, includes mounting a professional investigation and bringing offenders to justice.

Some victims, however, may have the added trauma of being a witness and providing evidence against their offenders. The Code referred to in section 2 states they have certain entitlements, such as updates on the case progress. For this they are better served with a single point of contact (rather than a succession of different faces) for regular and consistent updates on the progress of the investigation. They may also need support during and following a court trial.

There is no 'one size fits all' for victim support. Some may need a wide range of varied assistance depending on their individual circumstances. In some cases, for example, they may require psychological support; in others, it may be financial or welfare protection or a combination of any of these.

In serious investigations, support may be required from specially trained officers such as Family Liaison Officers (FLOs), Sexual Offence Liaison Officers (SOLOs) and Domestic Violence Officers/Coordinators. There are a also number of voluntary organisations that can help support victims. Joint working arrangements and protocols should enable SIOs/investigators make prompt referrals after an assessment of need, which has the dual benefits of allowing the enquiry team more time for investigations and protecting the public.

There are a number of support providers for victims of crime such as:

- Victim support (<http://www.victimsupport.org.uk/support>, contact phone number 0808 1689111)
- Sexual assault referral centres
- Social services
- National Health Service
- Crown Prosecution Service (CPS)
- Criminal Injuries Compensation Authority (CICA)
- Child Victims of Crime (CVC)

11.3.1 **Registered intermediaries**

Registered intermediaries are specialists who help people with communication difficulties. The Code states that although they were originally intended to help vulnerable witnesses give their best evidence in court, they can also assist victims

247

when they are being interviewed to help them communicate their evidence. This facility is available via the NCA Specialist Operations Centre (0845 000 5463).

11.4 **Victim Engagement**

Police officers are often the first officials to interact and engage with victims. This places them in a unique position to help them cope with the trauma of the crime and restore a sense of dignity, security and control. Depending upon the circumstances, victims cannot always be afforded the full attention of initial responders, eg if a crime is ongoing or there is some evidence that needs securing and protecting (which might also be on the victim). However, as soon as possible the focus of attention should be on the victim and their needs, and it must be a fast-track action to ensure the provision of support has been/is being provided.

Approaching victims appropriately helps gain their trust and cooperation and will largely depend on the individual type of offence, person and victim (eg vulnerable, such as children and young people or elderly; those in difficult family relationships; those with disabilities, mental illnesses or language/cultural barriers). Most, however, have similar basic needs, such as the need to feel safe, express their emotions and have confidence in and understanding of the investigation process. They also need to have faith in any offers of services they want, such as welfare support or ongoing medical assistance. Establishing rapport with victims and explaining the support and investigative processes in simple terms they will understand is important. These duties need to be handled professionally in order to convince victims they should fully engage with and trust the investigation and criminal justice system.

An assessment of the police/victim relationship should be an ongoing process. If there is a failure or it falls short of the required standard, the SIO needs to take an active involvement in establishing why and how this has happened and consider remedial action. Working and engaging successfully with victims is crucial, particularly if there are multiple victims and offences and assistance is required, not only from them themselves but others and the wider community, who may also need convincing to engage with the investigating team.

KEY POINTS

1. Being insensitive to victims inflicts a form of secondary victimisation, whereas engaging with them in a respectful and supportive manner provides more benefit not only for them but also the investigation.
2. Some victims conduct their own 'open source' research on investigators and agencies to help them decide whether to engage. This can be anticipated by, for example, assessing if there is any poor or adverse publicity that may cause

---

concern (eg adverse publicity, criticism of poor service given to other victims), or through victim background enquiries.

3. If victims are also significant, vulnerable or intimidated witnesses, there will be further evidential status considerations (as dealt with in Chapter 13).

11.4.1 Child victims

Engaging with children who may be the victims of sexual crimes such as child sexual exploitation (CSE) needs very careful management, particularly when this comes at a time when there may be potential evidential opportunities as well as safeguarding their welfare. The welfare requirement always takes precedence and some protection powers may need to be considered (eg under section 47 Children Act 1989—see Chapter 16.3). Reassurance is important for convincing them they haven't done anything wrong themselves. Like the initial engagement with any other victim, everything they say should be carefully noted and recorded, including their condition and demeanour, noting precisely what they have been asked as well as their response (avoiding at all times using any leading or closed questions or suggestions). Good use can be made of open questions using terms such as...'Tell me...', 'Describe...' and 'Explain...' (ie not to jeopardise any future prosecution). These should be kept very brief and aimed at checking on welfare, identifying offences, suspects and immediate evidence capture opportunities (eg forensic).

Some child victims may not always present as victims, for example, missing persons. Those who regularly go missing from local authority homes may be victims of CSE and when officers deal with them upon their return this needs to be borne in mind. Looking for evidence of alcohol or substance abuse, new clothing, jewellery or gifts and money, wearing inappropriate clothing and cosmetics, etc may be indicators of them being abused, yet they may not know it themselves. It should be strongly considered whether they have been a victim of crime during the period they had gone missing (see also Chapter 16.9).

KEY POINTS

1. Whenever speaking to child victims, consideration should be given as to who else is present at the time, and who could be a witness or offender.
2. An initial account might be the only one a victim ever offers so this needs to be recorded accurately.

11.5 Victim Enquiries

Victims should always be afforded a high status in an investigation. For this reason, on a HOLMES database they are usually referred to as Nominal One (N1). They are not only of importance because of their entitlement to support, but also because they can provide information that can help solve the case. Therefore a victim strategy not only needs to incorporate a comprehensive support plan, but also seek out what evidence they may have to offer and any necessary facts or information to assist the investigation. This will include details about themselves, their habits and associations, lifestyle and behavioural patterns to help provide clues as to why they were targeted and became victims—often referred to as 'victimology'.

This may have to include making personal and intrusive enquiries and approaches to useful sources of information, such as their family, close friends and acquaintances. This process requires tactful management as it may also necessitate a search of personal belongings and/or room, house, etc to look for vital information and possessions that may offer up clues. Reasons for doing so have to be carefully explained, outlining the routines of the procedure and how it may prove beneficial to progressing the investigation.

The purpose of victimology is to establish links between the suspect, victim and crime scene, along with generating investigative opportunities and useful lines of enquiries. Enlisting the services of an interview adviser to plan what is needed in respect of victimology may reduce the amount of times the family or victim may need to be seen. Initial preparations should be based around the 'what we know and what do we need to know' principle (see Chapter 3.7). This will also enable obligations under the Victims Code of Practice to be adhered to by the right categorisation of victims/witnesses and applications for any special measures applied for.

Obtaining details about a victim's background, lifestyle and the sort of person they are/were usually features in the SIO's MLOE (main lines of enquiry) as a 'fast track' action. If they are a missing person, it may even be necessary to obtain recent photographs of them. It is an unfortunate by-product of being a victim that investigators need to delve into their personal lives to look for clues. What was going on in their lives at the time of or immediately before an offence/incident can and often does generate new leads. It may be helpful to enlist analytical services to identify and examine links amongst associates, family trees, movements, timelines, communications data and social media contacts, etc. In most cases information seeking to obtain the necessary rich picture about a victim is not restricted to relying upon close family and relatives. For example, teenagers do not usually let their parents/carers know about everything they get up to, but this sort of information might be available from their close personal friends.

KEY POINT

A line of enquiry for 'victimology' purposes is to ascertain who knows most about them. This same person, however, could also be the offender. Therefore it may be significant to the enquiry if they have not been seen or made contact with the victim or their family and friends since the offence occurred.

Checklist—Victimology

- Full and detailed personal description (and recent videos or photographs).

- Home address, previous addresses, work address, places frequented.

- Occupation(s), trades and skills, education, training, qualifications, employers and employees.

- Marital status, current and previous relationships and partners, children, siblings, relatives and family tree.

- Friends, associates and colleagues (and recent visitors or persons they came into contact with).

- Vehicle ownership, usage or access.

- Lifestyle, reputation, character, appearance, personality, previous convictions, current criminality, previous incidents of note, employment, habits, personality, hobbies, likes and dislikes, drug abuse or other vices, secrets, sexual preferences, risk-taking likelihood, vulnerabilities, political and religious views, any extreme behaviour and use of online forums/dating websites.

- Routines, daily activities, places visited (including travel, holidays, overseas visits) preferred routes and modes of travel.

- Timeline of movements, where they've been, who they came into contact with and when, last known movements, when last seen and what they said or did and their mood at the time.

- Significant personal possessions, mobile phones, laptops, tablets, gaming machines (including passwords), where they kept money and valuables, who knew about and had access to their belongings, any missing items or safe/secret storage areas.

- Medical background details of doctor (GP), any illnesses (physical or psychological), levels of fitness and health, surgical operations or other treatments, prescribed medicines, deformities, unusual marks, scars, tattoos or piercings, dental history and details of dentist, cosmetic treatments.

- Specific queries such as, if female, whether they have ever been pregnant or had a termination, sexually transmitted diseases, etc (note: it is important that this is recorded properly, including consideration of section 41 of the Youth Justice and Criminal Evidence Act 1999—restricting evidence or questions about their previous sexual history, subject to exceptions for rape and sexual offences).

- Digital profiling information, social media usage, devices, storage (eg cloud computing) virtual communities and sites used/visited, identities used and passwords.

- Financial information, banking details, accounts, savings, valuables, investments, debts, regular payments, earnings, loans, credit/debit cards.

- Whether they made a will or were insured and if so what was in them that may be of interest to the enquiry (eg in homicide cases).

When searching premises connected with a victim (eg one that is deceased), it may be necessary to compile a full inventory of each and every item. This will enable the list to be checked against any items later found to be missing. The SIO may want a Police Search Adviser (PolSA)[4] to be used for the search. The search can also include looking for association through forensic trace evidence (eg on bedding), which is particularly useful if close associates and sexual partners are going to be of interest.

KEY POINTS

1. Examining a victim's bedding and mattress can reveal DNA evidence to show who they may have been sexually involved with.
2. H-2-H enquiries can be utilised to assist in gathering information about victims as to their lifestyle, movements, habits, associates, reputation, etc.

11.6 Family Liaison

In some cases victim support sometimes needs to extend to their immediate families. According to the Victims' Code of Practice (see Chapter 11.2), close relatives of a deceased victim are entitled to receive services as victims of serious crime. It defines close relatives as: spouse, partner, relatives in direct line, siblings and dependants of a person whose death was directly caused by criminal conduct. In law enforcement terminology, support to these persons is commonly referred to as 'family liaison'.

Family liaison becomes necessary when an investigation involves homicide, suspicious death, mass fatality, road death or any incident where it might enhance the police management of the enquiry or if it is deemed 'critical'. This can prove to be one of the most challenging and demanding areas of responsibility. The most significant relationship an enquiry team has to develop is the one with families of the deceased at what is the most difficult and distressing time of their lives. Expectations, demands and accountability levels are extremely high. These responsibilities must be managed and performed professionally throughout the investigation and in most cases the unique relationship can last many years.

---

[4] The role of a PolSA is described in Chapter 6.

The MoJ Code of Practice for Victims of Crime (2013) states:

In addition to the entitlements outlined above (i.e. paragraph 11.2), if you are a bereaved close relative of a victim who died as a result of criminal conduct, you are **entitled** to: (i) have a Family Liaison Officer (FLO) assigned to you by the police, where the Senior Investigating Officer considers this to be appropriate. This will happen in the majority of cases; and (ii) be offered accessible advice on bereavement and information on available victims' services by the police.

11.6.1 Family liaison strategy

A family liaison strategy can directly link into a victim management strategy and should appear near the top of a MLOE list. An effective and comprehensive strategy must be recorded as policy and include all aspects of the FLO relationship and tactical planning for maintaining close contact with the victim's family and keeping them apprised of progress and developments. An overarching objective should be to increase benefits to the investigation by servicing needs of the family for information and support.

A main component of the strategy is to keep the family constantly updated whenever and wherever possible. Victims' families need accurate and regular information on progress of the investigation, plus answers to any of their queries. The likelihood is these will be similar to the type of 5WH questions the enquiry team are working on (eg what happened? why did it happen? who did it? how did they do it?).

Families are reliant on the police for information, otherwise they may have to depend on rumour, gossip, news reporting and social media. Public conjecture and supposition may not be helpful to them or the investigation, which can be corrected provided it is done swiftly and they are encouraged to feed any further information into the enquiry. Mutually interdependent lines of communication must exist.

Checklist—Objectives of a family liaison strategy[5]

- Analyse needs, concerns and expectations of a victim's family in order to identify all relevant and realistic action that should be taken in the context of their human rights.

- Work with the family in order to comply with their right to receive all relevant and up-to-date information about the incident and its investigation (subject to the operational needs of the investigation).

- Gather material from the family in a manner which contributes to the investigation and preserves its integrity (eg victimology).

---

[5] Also cited in ACPO, *Family Liaison Officer Guidance* (NPIA, 2008), 5–6.

- Provide information to and facilitate care and support for the family, who are themselves secondary victims, in a sensitive and compassionate manner in accordance with the needs of the investigation.

- Secure and maintain the confidence and trust of the family, thereby enhancing their contribution to the investigation.

KEY POINTS

- Information should not be provided to a victim's family before being confirmed as factually correct. It is better to explain that information isn't currently known or available than having to apologise later because what they were told initially was incorrect. Misinformation makes the enquiry team appear unprofessional or untrustworthy.
- Providing information to families is a fine balance if they are key significant witnesses to a homicide. This will need careful consideration and policy recording in order to maintain the integrity of the investigation.

11.6.2 Family identification and notification

Identification of a victim's family is treated in the broadest sense. It generally includes partners, parents, guardians, children, siblings, members of the extended family and any others who may have had a direct and close relationship with the victim. This becomes complicated by split marriages, ex-partners and children dispersed across geographic locations, or when a victim is associated with a particular cultural or lifestyle diversity. For example, if the parents of a victim were separated or divorced, communication with each would need to be managed tactfully so as not to show undue favour to one and not the other.

Under the Code of Practice for Victims of Crime, families are entitled to nominate a family spokesperson to be a single point of contact to receive such services. However, if the family cannot choose a family spokesperson, the SIO must choose one. Where there are divided families, more than one set of FLOs may need to be appointed in order for the obligations under the Code to be satisfied.

11.6.3 Death notification

Where there is a death investigation, every reasonable effort should be made to locate and notify the deceased's next of kin as quickly as possible. All attempted, failed, delayed or unsuccessful attempts need to be recorded with reasons. Particulars regarding completion of the task should also be recorded, in particular the time, date, place and method.

The physical task of notifying a next of kin or close family relative about a death can be difficult and traumatic to perform; and if the death is being treated as suspicious, it is a task usually left to the police. This needs to become a fast-track action to eliminate any undue delay and prevent the next of kin (NOK)[6] finding out through their own means (eg rumour, gossip, news bulletins or through the rapid spread of information via digital media and social networking systems).

Other pressing matters might seek to occupy the SIO's attention, such as scene management, witness interviews or arresting suspects. But the death notification must remain one of the most important. Even if the media withhold details or have some uncertainty about a deceased's identity, there are many ways a dead victim's relatives can find out before the police get chance to inform them. By making their own enquiries, the next of kin may begin contacting emergency numbers or attend at scene cordons, hospitals or enquiry desks seeking information. If so, they need to be dealt with tactfully, respectfully and soon.

Variables such as the time of day and day of the week, as well as confirmation of the victim's details and location of the next of kin and their geographic position, state of health and determining who to inform and order of priority, all place specific demands on the notification plan. SIOs need to plan carefully how these problems are to be overcome.

Carefully selected officers should be chosen to deliver a death message. As a rule, if there is a spouse, the spouse or, if a child, their parent should be notified first, and their wishes regarding other notifications respected. This becomes complicated by fragmented families and relatives, so any choice of one over another may need to be justified and explainable. A consanguinity[7] chain may assist in determining who should be notified and in what order of priority.

The way this task is performed will almost certainly influence any future relationship between the police, enquiry team and the family/relatives of a victim. When, where and how the message is delivered, what is said, to whom and by whom are key factors; this is a moment in their lives they will never forget.

Confirmation is required that the message is delivered to the right person(s). There should be attempts to establish if there are likely to be any specific considerations, such interpreters or disability. Those who deliver the message must be well prepared and able to cope with the subsequent response, which may range from raw emotion, anger, disbelief and shock to an outpouring of grief.

The manner in which the message is delivered clearly needs to be tactful. Having a liveried police vehicle pull up outside a relative's address may not be welcomed and privacy should be respected. If, however, using 'plain-clothes' staff to deliver the message, they need to identify themselves convincingly.

---

[6] 'Next of kin' refers to the person or person's most closely related to an individual by blood, marriage or legal ruling.

[7] Consanguinity refers to blood relations and being from the same kinship as another person or descended from the same ancestry.

The wording and manner of the notification is what really matters. There is little point in being vague or trying to make the news sound any less devastating than it already is. Saying a person 'is no longer with us', or 'has passed away' or using religious terminology is generally to be avoided. The deceased person's next of kin need to hear exactly what has happened so they are absolutely clear, eg '*I am very sorry to have to inform you that (name) is dead/or has been killed*'. Simple language using straightforward terms is what works best for the avoidance of doubt.

Before delivering the message, the family should be seated (to prevent accidents) and clarification sought as to where the officers should sit (so they don't choose the wrong place, ie victim's regular chair). They should be asked how they wish the deceased to be referred to and when leaving, the delivering officers should impress on them that they should have confidence in the police and their investigation. Before leaving, the family should be informed of exactly what happens next, why and when, and who their police liaison officers are and how to contact them.

KEY POINTS

1. Many families claim being informed about the death of their loved ones is the most traumatic event of their lives; and those who deliver the message say it is one of the most daunting tasks to perform. Careful thought and planning needs to go into managing this process—there is only one chance to get it right.
2. Recording what the families have been told and by whom is an important responsibility, in particular for the appointed Family Liaison Officer so they know exactly what message has been delivered. It is best that this information is submitted into the Major Incident Room for their attention and registering.

11.6.4 **Family Liaison Officers (FLOs)**

The appointment and role of the FLOs is recorded by the SIO and forms part of the family liaison strategy. Their role is not to comfort or counsel relatives, but to assist and support them wherever possible, and most importantly to assist the investigation. The family's main requirement is usually for the police to quickly resolve the case and arrest any offenders, news of which tends to give the most comfort of all. What is important, also, is that the primary role of a FLO is that of an investigator.

FLOs maintain a comprehensive log of all their dealings and involvement with the family and meetings and instructions from the SIO. Some forces have logbooks designed solely for this purpose with carbonated tear-out sheets; other forces have electronic forms. However the logbooks are developed, it is important they are frequently submitted so incident room staff can have early sight of their contents.

FLO logs must be kept relevant and focused and they should be checked and properly scrutinised. There is usually a space for a supervisor's signature on the log and the SIO should nominate a person to maintain close supervision of the content. This should be the responsibility of the appointed Family Liaison Coordinator/Advisor (FLC/FLA). FLO logs may at some time become disclosable to agencies such as the Independent Police Complaints Commission (IPCC) and/or subsequently the family, who may put their own interpretation on the meaning of entries made. The logs are not the place to record opinions about personalities and individuals.

An important part of the FLO role is a requirement to obtain details for an ongoing family/police *relationship assessment*. The FLO should continuously update the SIO so that a critical assessment of the relationship can be monitored throughout the investigation to check there are no ongoing or anticipated problems. The FLO should also comprehensively record any complaints or concerns the family may have and bring them to the attention of the SIO at the earliest opportunity.

The FLO should in consultation with the SIO, FLC and interview advisor discuss any special measure applications needed to be applied for should any of the family members be identified as vulnerable, intimidated or key/significant witnesses. This is to comply with the obligations set out in the Victims' Code.

A further important role for the FLO is to obtain a 'victim personal statement' (VPS) from an appropriate family member. This is seen as a significant opportunity for the family to outline to a court the true effect and devastation that a loss of life has had on the family. This document is normally placed before the trial judge prior to sentence and either read out in court or referred to in passing sentence.

The amount of detail provided to a family must be determined on a case-by-case basis, although a summary or overview of the evidence is normally sufficient. However, care must be given when a close family member is also a significant witness in the case, which may restrict discussion and contact with that individual.

The police must not be seen to encourage or influence a witness in any way. A further pre-trial meeting with the family is normally held by the SIO to discuss the court process and the presentation of evidence at the forthcoming trial. It is important that the family do not discover a significant or distressing piece of evidence for the first time during the actual trial itself. Care again must be given to avoid discussing evidence with a family member who is also a significant witness in the case. Meetings with the family normally continue throughout the trial process and at its conclusion, usually with the SIO, Crown Prosecution Service (CPS) and Crown Counsel when issues and procedures can be discussed and explained in more detail (again these are obligations set out in the Victim's Code).

257

KEY POINT

It is important the *SIO in person* holds periodic meetings with the FLOs and FLC (ie face to face) to maintain direct communication with them, show support and discuss any concerns for either them or the family. This is in addition to their contact with any appointed Family Liaison Coordinator.

Checklist—Role of the FLO

- Act as conduit between the SIO, enquiry team and victim's close family.

- Ensure families are included as partners in the investigation and provided with as much timely information as possible.

- Ensure families are treated appropriately, professionally, with respect and in accordance with their diverse needs.

- Obtain information about the victim (victimology).

- Keep the victim's family updated on progress of the investigation and any significant developments or events (eg arrests, searches, finds, provided SIO has agreed to the disclosure).

- Provide reassurance the investigation is being conducted diligently and expeditiously.

- Give or facilitate practical support for members of the family.

- Feed back threats or concerns the victim's families have for their personal safety and welfare.

- Arrange and escort the family for formal identification of their relative's body.

- Assist the family and pursue the early release of the body following first and second post-mortem examinations.

- Convey any requests for organ donation to the SIO.

- Ensure they are made aware of any material taken from the body that has been preserved for further examination. Written authority should be obtained as to the return or disposal of this material to include preferred means of disposal.

- Gather antecedent information and evidence of identification (FLOs should not usually interview a family member as a significant witness or as a TIE (trace/ interview/eliminate) subject unless there are exceptional circumstances).

- Record information and intelligence provided by the family and submit it to the incident room.

- Offer victim/family information and advice re supporting agencies and facilitate access to medical services for severe trauma cases.

- In line with national policy, refer all cases of murder to the Victim Support National Homicide Service within the first 24 hours at homicide.referrals@victimsupport.cjsm.net.

- Closely monitor and apprise SIO on relationship between family and the police.

- Deal with any requests or complaints made by the family, eg visiting the crime scene (these should be brought to the attention of the SIO).

- Establish liaison with the Coroner's Office and assist in the arrangements for release of the body following final post-mortem, including any Human Tissue Act issues.

- Consider funeral arrangements and refer to SIO for arranging police attendance, eg SIO/DSIO, plus delivery of flowers and suitable message of condolence from enquiry team.

- Liaise re any media issues and try to protect them from unwarranted intrusion.

- Notify family of any intended media releases in advance of them being released.

- Assist the family in liaison with any other statutory body involved in investigating the circumstances of the death, eg IPCC, Serious Case Review or Domestic Homicide Review.

- Implement an agreed exit strategy (which normally includes a handover meeting with a victim support agency) in line with the SIO's policy.

- Maintain or resume contact with the family prior to and throughout the criminal justice process including any appeal processes, judicial review, Coroner's inquest or reopening of the investigation.

- Act as a conduit between the SIO and CPS to ensure the family are made aware of any changes or reduction in charges made and facilitate a meeting to fully explain the rationale for any decisions made.

- On instructions of the SIO, obtain a 'victim personal statement' from the appropriate family member and present it to the trial judge on conviction via the CPS.

- Update the SIO or FLC in relation to any changes in their circumstances that would have an impact on their deployment.

11.6.5 FLO appointment

In selecting and appointing an FLO a number of factors need to be considered:

- Role of the FLO is as an investigator and for this reason they should be PIP level 2 trained and accredited (or working towards accreditation).
- Needs of the family should be considered, eg the deployment of officers who reflect the culture, lifestyle, religion or gender of the victim (as far as is practicable)

or, for example, when dealing with a child murder, a non-English-speaking family, a gay/lesbian victim, etc (though the SIO should beware of any temptation to match culture and lifestyle at the expense of training and skills—competence is first and foremost, as the FLO response can be supplemented with assistance from cultural specialists etc if necessary).

- FLOs should be deployed in pairs with one taking the lead role. It is not always essential that both should be present on each and every visit, unless corroboration is required or a risk assessment determines it should be so.
- Scale and nature of the incident—there may be a need for multiple FLOs because of multiple victims and the level of media/political attention (and a resilience requirement to cover annual leave commitments etc).
- Training, previous experience and frequency of recent deployments.
- Current workload, commitments and availability (especially if not full-time FLOs).
- If they have suffered themselves any recent bereavement or trauma.
- Necessary equipment required (eg vehicle and mobile phone).
- If there is a 'suspect' in the family and what additional risk this poses.
- If they have previously arrested family members or have had previous contact and link with them or reside or work nearby.

11.6.6 **FLO deployment**

FLOs are deployed at the earliest opportunity after a risk assessment has been completed, though initially a fully trained FLO may not always be immediately available. If so, then experienced officers should be temporarily allocated the responsibility to liaise with the victim's family and commence a vital line of communication and support (as a golden hour task) until such time trained FLOs can be deployed. Those nominated this important task should treat this as their primary responsibility and not get involved in witness interviews, other enquiries or evidence recovery, etc.

During the golden hour(s) period, the victim's family are at their most vulnerable and distraught. It is also a time when they will form early opinions about the investigative response and handling of the case and the very people they are putting all their hope and faith in. They must be treated with the utmost sensitivity and given support **as soon as possible**. This is also a time when their relative (husband, wife, son, daughter, etc) may be lying dead within a protected scene or area where the family cannot enter and whom they cannot (at that time) see, touch or hold. The reasons for this (ie scene protection and preservation) MUST be tactfully explained to them.

If the SIO is not in a position to make early or initial contact with the family themselves, eg because of other pressing commitments, they should personally brief those nominated to ensure they know exactly what is required and the importance of the task. This briefing should be recorded in the policy log. A handover process can follow later, with trained FLOs being briefed on the precise action taken and information supplied to the family.

KEY POINTS

- Victim's family needs to be notified as quickly as possible and without delay. If trained FLOs aren't immediately available, the task must be nominated to someone else under the SIO's direction (a golden hour task).
- SIO should aim to make contact with the family as soon as possible to establish a good early relationship with them.
- If the family are not allowed to see or touch their deceased relative, ie for reasons of scene preservation, the reasons must be tactfully explained.
- Golden rule is to treat the victim's family with respect from the outset.

11.6.7 **FLO briefing**

Recognised good practice is for the SIO to meet and brief the FLOs prior to their deployment, discussing in detail the family liaison strategy, incorporating details of previous contact, their likely expectations and how they will be managed.

Checklist—FLO briefing

- Current known details about the circumstances of the incident and what is already in the public domain, eg rumour, media reporting and social networking.

- What the family already know.

- What information can be given to them.

- Background details of family and victim (including cultural, lifestyle and religious details).

- Known tensions or breakdowns in the family.

- Where the deceased lies and, if within a protected scene, why the family cannot enter and see them.

- Whether formal identification of the victim has been completed, who by, where, how and current location of the body and viewing procedures and facilities.

- Investigation set-up and details of incident room, contact numbers, names of SIO/DSIO.

- Whether any arrests have been made.

- Whether a post-mortem has been completed or when one is scheduled.

- Precise details of what can be released about cause and manner of death.

- Whether the family can visit, see or touch the body, what restrictions there are (if any), and what are likely timescales for release of the body for burial purposes.

- Whether anything known about the victim's lifestyle, drugs, convictions, etc and how any sensitive details are going to be handled (eg circumstances and nature of the victim's death and revealing a lifestyle the family may be unaware of).

- Role and responsibility of the Coroner.

- If deceased person was not alone when the incident occurred and if they were with other members of the same family, the FLO must be made aware of their location and condition.

- Fast-track tasks/actions (eg victimology, items required).

- Resources and equipment allocated (eg vehicle, mobile telephone).

- Reporting chain, supervision and support mechanisms (eg SIO, DSIO, FLO Coordinator).

- Expectations, attendance at briefings, regular contacts, submission of reports.

- Referral to the Homicide Service—agreement or refusal.

- Anything to be provided, eg bereavement pack, FLO leaflet.

11.6.8 FLO welfare

Being an FLO is an arduous and emotionally draining role. There is a statutory duty of care to ensure the safety of all officers and staff, including FLOs. The SIO should complete and record a risk assessment which includes control measures to cover risk or potential risk caused by people, action/activity, location and environment. This remains under dynamic review during the course of the investigation and should be included in the strategy. There is a nationally approved form in use for this process that should be agreed and signed by the SIO/DSIO, and the forms should be available via local force arrangements.

The SIO has an ongoing responsibility to look after the welfare of their FLOs. Regular contact and meetings should always include checks on their wellbeing and they should be encouraged to report any emerging problems immediately.

11.6.9 Suspect/ TIE in family

If there is the potential for a suspect to be amongst members of the victim's family, an increased level of risk assessment is required. Regardless of individual force policy or preference that may stipulate the required numbers of FLOs to be deployed on an investigation, if there is a suspect 'in the family' it must *never* be a single FLO in these circumstances—always two for safety reasons.

When deployed under these circumstances, care must be taken to ensure the FLOs don't stray into a role which is similar to that of a covert human intelligence source (CHIS). FLOs are always overt investigators and subject to the requirements of the Police and Criminal Evidence Act 1984 (PACE), the Criminal Procedure and Investigations Act 1996 (CPIA) (disclosure rules), the Regulation of Investigatory Powers Act 2000 (RIPA) and human rights considerations. The SIO may therefore wish to plan ahead for how any intelligence and evidence gathering is going to be managed resulting from the FLO's interaction with a family which contains potential suspects.

Decisions should be duly recorded regarding the deployment of FLOs in these circumstances. The level and amount of disclosure of information given to both the FLOs and the family must be controlled and reviewed to prevent undermining the prosecution case. FLOs should not be utilised for the purposes of arrest or searching.

If necessary to apply a TIE process to a subject who is a member of the victim's family, the method of approach will need to be reflected in the FLO strategy (although the FLO should not normally partake in the TIE process).

11.6.10 **Media intrusion**

If journalists and news reporters are keen to report on a serious and 'newsworthy' incident, they will undoubtedly try their level best to interview and photograph family and friends of the victim. In some instances (eg high-profile cases) the media become a major threat, with high levels of intrusion and interference, and even harassment and distress to close relatives. At other times the family may enjoy and encourage media attention, something that warrants close monitoring and controlling wherever possible.

The SIO, FLOs and MLO (Media Liaison Officer) must anticipate in advance and *act quickly* to control any likely media intrusion to the family and relatives of the victim. The family must be given support and protection, and any statements or media appeals from the family should be tightly controlled in order to prevent any compromise of the SIO's communication and media strategy.

The family may also approach or be approached by people who wish to act on their behalf, such as solicitors or community interest representatives. The SIO should be aware that sometimes well-meaning people disrupt or affect the important communications link between the enquiry team and the victim's family. Intermediaries may also have a different agenda to the family and/or police. While the family's wishes are always of uppermost importance, the SIO may wish to outline their concerns and seek advice from local policing commanders and/or the Gold Commander or independent advisory group (IAG) wherever possible.

11.6.11 **SIO contact with family and relatives**

The SIO makes contact and arranges to visit a victim's family (alongside the FLOs) as soon as practicable. This personal touch cannot be overstated. It is always good practice to develop and nurture the relationship with a victim's close family to ensure their needs, hopes and expectations are properly considered. This relationship must be dynamically maintained and reviewed throughout all stages of the investigation, covering significant events such as:

- initial response and media coverage
- media headlines on the case or investigation
- significant overt activities such as mass searches
- arrest of suspects
- release or charging of suspects
- release of a victim's body
- funeral arrangements
- court appearances and pre-trial issues
- criminal trial phase (conviction or acquittal and sentence tariff reviews)
- Coroner's court hearings
- post-trial issues, (renewed) media coverage and appeals
- long-term contact arrangements
- referral to the Criminal Cases Review Commission (CCRC) or IPCC
- cold case re-investigation
- similar offences that may occur, particularly in the same area/city/town.

It should be stressed to the close family that the designated FLOs are important members of the enquiry team. If the SIO does not acknowledge this, it may be that for the rest of the enquiry the family will want to engage only with 'the boss' and unnecessarily try to commandeer the SIO's valuable time. The FLO is a vital link between the SIO and the family, and this is what they are trained for and how it should be. This does not prevent the SIO/DSIO from visiting the family regularly as and when appropriate, but the family should not directly contact the SIO. If this happens, the FLO has been bypassed, which is incorrect.

No opportunity should be wasted in keeping a good relationship going, creating a good impression and keeping the family involved (such as helping to distribute publicity posters) and regularly updated. One suggestion is for the FLOs to offer and arrange a guided tour of the incident room and to meet members of the enquiry team, remembering to remove things the SIO may not wish the family to see (eg details of sensitive lines of enquiry or post-mortem photographs). Once arranged, staff should be briefed beforehand and directed on what they can and cannot say if asked.

Another option is to let the victim's family meet and have a discussion with certain members of the enquiry team or specialists. For example, if a large-scale search has been made for a missing person, victim's body or body parts, the family may be allowed to meet the search teams (eg underwater search teams) to hear first hand the strenuous efforts that had been made, how the operation had been conducted and how any hazards and obstacles had to be tackled.

11.6.12 **Managing expectations**

There are high hopes and expectations to quickly find and charge offenders, and the SIO must be careful not to raise the expectations of the victim's family and relatives too much. This is particularly important if the case is complex or going to be difficult to resolve quickly.

An SIO can easily become drawn into a moral obligation to solve a case often through a mixture of professional pride and emotional pleas from the victim's family. This will naturally produce disappointment, and sometimes resentment if good news is not immediately forthcoming.

While the SIO should never appear overly pessimistic or negative about the likelihood of a successful outcome, they must remain totally honest and realistic regarding the difficulties and complexities of the investigation. Some cases are hard to solve, and for one reason or another, securing that vital piece of evidence may not happen as quickly and easily as would be liked.

The SIO and CPS should ensure the family is made aware of any changes or reduction to any charges made. This will normally be undertaken at a confidential meeting with the family, often chaired by the Crown prosecuting counsel to fully consult and explain the rationale for any decisions to be made. This will be particularly relevant if an alternative charge from murder to manslaughter has to be considered based on the statutory defence of 'loss of control' or other defence on the grounds of 'diminished responsibility'. Clearly any reduction in the charge will have a significant effect on any likely sentence; therefore a careful explanation of the legal position must be provided.

11.6.13 **Needs of family versus needs of investigation**

There are occasions when an SIO cannot pass information on to the victim's family for fear of compromising the investigation. For example, planning to deal with suspects or staging arrests when such details need to be treated confidentially to safeguard the element of surprise and evidence recovery opportunities. On these occasions it is entirely understandable and justifiable not to inform the family beforehand.

The aim should be to strike a balance between the competing needs of the investigation and those of the family. In consultation with the FLO and/or FLC, there should be a plan for briefing the family so not to have any potential compromise and an explanation at a later stage as to why the information was withheld. If explained that it was for the good of the investigation, they should normally understand. This decision and procedure should be recorded in the policy log with accompanying reasons.

11.6.14 Subsequent post-mortems and body release

Early release of a victim's body is always of primary concern to a bereaved family, and the SIO and FLO should have this at the forefront of their thoughts when dealing with them. An import aspect of any investigation is the completion of a second (or subsequent) post-mortem, which the Coroner may authorise at the request of a defence legal team following a person being charged. In cases where no offender has been identified or charged, a further independent post-mortem may be ordered to be conducted within 28 days.[8]

It should be the priority to help families through the grieving process. This includes consideration of cultural and religious beliefs held in certain communities, eg Muslim and Jewish, where burial normally occurs within 24 hours or as soon as possible after death, which might not be possible due to the ongoing investigation.

The SIO and FLO should actively pursue an early resolution to all post-mortem examinations and ensure that the body can be released to the family in order to allow the funeral to take place as speedily as possible. It is vital, however, that the family is made aware of any material taken from the body that has been preserved for further examination. Families should be asked if they wish to wait to receive the body complete, which could take a long time in some cases, eg if a separate detailed examination of the brain is required. In paediatric cases delays may be even longer (see Chapter 15). In order to address this issue, the FLO should obtain a written authority from the family as to the decision to either return or dispose of this material and to include preferred means of disposal. In particular, close liaison with the Coroner in relation to the Human Tissue Act should be undertaken. Any records relating to actions on behalf of the Coroner should also be submitted into the incident room for registering and retention.

11.6.15 Returning personal possessions

The return of property such as personal possessions (eg necklaces and rings) is something that can comfort a grieving family. The SIO and CSM/forensic experts should expedite and prioritise any victim's personal possessions that need to be examined so they can be swiftly returned (provided they are not required as court exhibits). The reasons for any prolonged retention of personal items belonging to the victim need to be explained to the family. It should also

---

[8] See Home Office Circular 30/1999 Post Mortem Examinations and Early Release of Bodies.

be considered how the family would like property to be returned, eg cleaned and properly presented. Health and safety issues must be taken into account. Discussion in relation to return/destruction of property should be recorded and retained.

11.6.16 **Family liaison exit strategy**

An exit strategy is always part of an entrance strategy, ie the entry level contains a list of objectives and when those are achieved an exit must be considered. Victim's families often become very attached, close to and reliant on their nominated FLOs and it is not in their long-term interest for recovery and moving on with their lives to maintain permanent FLO contact. Resources in any event would not permit.

Exit tactics, however, need careful handling to avoid damaging relationships. It becomes a gradual process, planned well in advance and conducted tactfully rather than abruptly. Good use can be made of other organisations, such as the Homicide Service, after withdrawal of the FLOs. It is worth pointing out quite early on that the FLO will at some point have to return to normal duties, although in some instances it may be a long time before this actually happens.

Where there is a trial pending, the case officer who has eventual responsibility for the case file process (normally an experienced investigator) can be substituted to keep the family updated with progress and developments in the case (including any post-trial contact). However, the FLO will be required to assist the family during the trial process and be available to support them at court if they wish to sit through the trial.

Consultation with Witness Care Units, Homicide Service and Court Witness Service will occur as per protocols agreed with the Homicide Service. This is so it can be ascertained what support and facilities are needed for the family who may wish to attend court during any trial process. The SIO should be part of the decision process around these arrangements and ultimately agree what, if any, role the FLO has in this.

11.6.17 **Family Liaison Coordinators and Advisers**

Most police forces have an appointed FLC. Those should have attended a coordinators course and will be responsible for the strategic or tactical support to FLOs and SIOs. The FLC can assist the SIO in appointing FLOs and in particular matching the right FLO, with due regard to their skill and experience level, to the deployment. They assist in providing advice around complex cases or multiple deployments. They can also provide assistance around risk assessment, strategy and support organisations both locally and nationally. They manage and brief the FLO during times when the SIO is fully committed.

The FLC should be briefed by the SIO and then task the FLOs directly around the aims and objectives set out in the strategy before reporting back. The management of documentation should therefore be supervised by the FLC and this ensures the speedy feed into the incident room of any statements, logbooks and updates to risk and relationship assessments. The FLC should be monitoring the performance of the FLO and report to the SIO any adverse impact on family liaison.

Some forces also have a number of trained coordinators who are also sometimes referred to as Family Liaison Advisors (FLAs). They provide the same operational capability as the FLCs but do not have the overall force responsibility. They are, however, used to provide operational advice and support on a daily basis and are trained in the same manner as the FLC and deployable when the FLC is not operationally available.

11.6.18 National Family Liaison Advisor

This NCA-enabled role is aimed at providing operational support to forces and agencies in relation to all family liaison matters. They can help in complex investigations and where there are suspects within the family or other sensitivities. They can also assist in the development and delivery of family liaison strategies at both strategic and tactical level. They can be reached via the National SIO Advisor or through the Specialist Operational Support Unit at the NCA.

11.7 Independent Advisory Groups (IAGs)

Most forces have recognised the benefit of community advice and guidance in major crime investigation. Service delivery is normally arranged through processes that make use of IAGs (and also local policing team meetings and networks). IAGs on the whole have been provided with relevant and regular training and practical inputs to ensure they have a clear understanding of a police response to major crime. They are universally acknowledged as an effective means of working with members of the community to solve problems, in particular dealing effectively with critical incidents.

They were largely introduced following criticism outlined in the Macpherson Report of 1999 into the death of Stephen Lawrence. The report highlighted the need for the police to engage with black and minority ethnic communities in order to provide feedback on how policing policy affects those communities. IAGs are now used across the UK and form a vital part of the efforts to maintain trust and confidence in the police service.

IAGs are made up entirely from members of the public. They represent the views from a wide range of local communities and provide lay advice and feedback on all issues of policing, ranging from strategic advice on local operational policy to tactical advice in dealing with critical incidents and major crime investigations. In the event of a critical incident or during the course of a major crime investigation, the SIO may access the relevant IAG via the locally agreed protocols.

The role of an IAG in a homicide investigation is contained in section 18.4 of the *Murder Investigation Manual* (MIM):[9]

> To review the investigative strategy and advise the SIO on relevant diversity issues which may impact upon, or be affected by, the crime itself and any subsequent police action. In addition to providing investigators with an understanding of community issues they may, in some instances, act as a conduit to the community to prevent rumour or misinformation from damaging the investigation and the police relationship with the community. SIOs should, however, exercise caution if attempting to use the IAG as a means of communicating with the community. IAGs act as a voice for the community and the role of community members is to represent particular social groups to the police. Attempts to reverse this role and turn IAG members into police representatives within their own community may cause significant difficulties for the individuals concerned, and impact on their willingness to participate.

11.7.1 **Objectives of IAGs**

Each force or agency will have its own objectives for IAGs. Here is a summary of the usual ones:

- Assist in improving the quality of service provided to all members of the community by offering independent advice on aspects of investigations.
- Assist in identification of institutional discrimination with recommendations on how to tackle such issues and promote diversity and equality.
- Inform on issues that affect local communities.
- Work towards improving and building upon constructive relationships between communities and the police.
- Help towards increasing the public's trust and confidence.
- Advise on critical/major incidents.

An IAG member can be a useful asset in the progression of the investigation, but the SIO/Gold Commander must establish key objectives from the outset. They must clearly understand what their role is and not be allowed to become directly involved in the investigation or become compromised as to confidentiality, particularly if they are obtaining information (in which case they may stray closely towards CHIS status).

An adviser can give guidance on cultural issues of the community involved, advise on communication with family members and witnesses within the community, and provide strategic advice on policy, including the impact it may have on that particular group. However, they are not investigators, mediators, advo-

---

[9] ACPO, *Murder Investigation Manual* (NCPE, 2006).

cates or intermediaries. An adviser should not be asked to speak to witnesses or be allowed to attend a crime scene during the early stages of an investigation without the approval of the SIO. In all cases a risk assessment should be considered and recorded in order to ensure the safety and welfare of the adviser. These further guidelines can also be useful:

An IAG adviser can:

- give strategic advice about the policing of the incident
- advise on the impact of the incident in the relevant community
- advise how particular police activities are likely to be perceived
- provide details of people who may be able to assist in community issues
- comment on how policies may affect communities and cultures, in particular when dealing with members of the victim's family and witnesses.

An adviser should not:

- visit the crime scene during the initial response stage of the investigation without the authority of the SIO (if this is considered, then a fully documented risk assessment must be completed first)
- speak directly to witnesses or attempt to persuade them to give evidence
- speak to the media on behalf of the police or be used to validate tactical decisions made by the SIO
- make enquiries or investigations on behalf of the SIO.

11.8 **Critical Incidents**

The term 'critical incident' (CI) is used to describe any incident where police action (or inaction) may have an impact on the confidence in the police of victims, their relatives or the wider community. There are very few murders or serious crimes that will not fall into the category of a 'critical incident'. Early recognition and declaration as such will ensure the correct command and control procedures are quickly activated to assist in dealing with the incident more effectively. The term 'critical' may apply to a local area and/or a whole force or region.

Critical incidents cover a wide range of possibilities and are, however, not just restricted to murders. Other incidents, local or national, such as the arrest of CSE offenders, high-risk missing persons, political interest, or policing errors and misdemeanours can be included. It is the personal perception that matters and some seemingly minor criminal acts may assume enormous significance to members of the public. Traumatic events can also affect entire communities (such as the mass fatal shootings carried out by Derek Bird in Cumbria in 2010, and the abduction and murder of 5-year-old April Jones in Machynlleth, Wales, in 2012), producing feelings of insecurity and vulnerability.

Critical incidents are often the consequence of major incidents. The event itself is dealt with operationally, using the policy, procedures and tactics laid down for each type of incident. A critical incident response incorporates this, but also enables an SIO to deal with all the other aspects of the incident and the context in which it occurs.

Critical incident management (CIM) is all about restoring public confidence and applying the principles of the National Decision Model (see Chapter 3.5.3). The aim should be to address broader family and community issues, deal with long-term consequences and make clear who is responsible for what. Clear lines of control and accountability are inherent in critical incident management.

The decision to declare a critical incident can take place at any time during the various phases of the investigation being dealt with. This identification may occur as early as the first contact received by a call taker. It may also be applicable and appropriate when the incident is being attended either by the initial officer or later by an SIO. It is a means of focusing on all the 'critical' aspects of an incident and consequent decision making, eg how family liaison support or community impact are to be addressed and managed effectively.

KEY POINT

The NPCC definition of a 'critical incident' is:

Any incident where the effectiveness of the police response is likely to have a significant impact on the confidence of the victim, their family, and/or the community.

Deeming an incident as 'critical' requires a large application of professional judgement. If it is decided this term and status applies, then the circumstances should be given special priority and consideration as to how they are managed and subsequently controlled. Basically, any incident, pre-planned or spontaneous, can become a CI and early recognition through community intelligence, environmental scanning, internal communication processes, monitoring of media outlets and situational awareness will assist in making an assessment of public reaction. Each incident is assessed on its own merits and when such a declaration is made the response plan needs to swiftly identify the cause and strategy to rebuild public confidence.

'Effectiveness' in this context means the measure of the professionalism, competence and integrity of the initial response—for example, if a victim's family are aggrieved at the level of family liaison support they have received. The term 'significant impact' can be felt by individuals, the family and/or community, and the SIO must make a decision as to whether to declare a 'critical incident' on this basis. 'Confidence' refers to any long-term effects on police relations that may have resulted from the incident.

It may be that as an investigation develops and more information becomes available, the decision to deem an incident 'critical' will need to be reviewed and monitored continually. An example is when community confidence in the police response or the incident itself drops and becomes critical as the investigation develops. As a general rule, certain circumstances can become a critical incident at any time, ie in the present, in the future or even something from the past.

11.8.1 **PIP Level 4 Advisers**

A Gold Commander who has overall responsibility for managing the response to a CI may wish to utilise a PIP 4 accredited investigator (see Chapter 1.4) to provide support for the strategic and tactical management of the investigation. This offers the opportunity to have a suitably qualified and experienced individual to take responsibility for the strategic decision-making element of an investigation and provide advice and investigative support to the SIO and Gold Commander. They provide a much-needed middle tier of management and expertise that fits in between the SIO, chief officers and senior commanders, taking pressure off the SIO who is then able to get on with the tactical elements of the investigation. Policy logs and good record keeping are vital elements for both the PIP 4 and SIO, including the Gold Commander in a CI-type situation.

11.9 **Community Impact Assessments**

Major or critical incidents are subject to a great deal of scrutiny from the media, the public and diverse local communities. The effectiveness of the initial response from not just the police but all agencies is likely to have a significant impact on the confidence of victims, families and/or the local community.

In most cases of homicide and other major crime incidents, or where an incident has been deemed 'critical', a Community Impact Assessment (CIA) should be drafted. They are applicable to any pre-planned as well as spontaneous or unexpected activities and events that may also be identified as potential critical incidents, eg arrests being made in high-tension or sensitive areas, or in consideration of 'not guilty' court case verdicts.

This is a means of applying some element of 'consequence management' on community relations. The purpose of the CIA is to cater for and manage the impact, particularly on those of a minority or vulnerable make-up. It draws upon analysis of available intelligence and in doing so creates new knowledge and perspective, which in turn becomes a source of information. The impact of an incident is dependent upon a range of factors including the interrelationships that may exist between areas that make up a community, thus creating a range of potential hotspots in which impacts and tensions may develop and emerge. Some particular incidents can and do lead to high levels of fear and tension, and in some cases a backlash and victimisation of those perceived to be connected.

The fundamental principles and considerations are:

- Incumbent to acknowledge the impact any major investigation may have upon local communities and vulnerable/minority groups.
- Identification and assessment of any impact lies with the police service, generally in collaboration with external agencies.
- Primary responsibility is that of the local policing Commander and/or the most senior officer with direct knowledge of and responsibility for the area.
- Paramount the CIA is considered early, particularly with certain communities ('initial assessment' being made usually within four hours of discovery).
- Concerns of a victim's family need to be adequately and sensitively addressed, as they may represent a valuable mediating influence within the community.
- Crucial that the impact assessment is based on evidence and intelligence, is objective and capable of withstanding scrutiny.
- The CIA should be a standing item on the SIO's management team agenda.

The assessment is informed through effective community engagement and consultation with IAGs and community representatives, partner agencies and local policing teams. The completion of a CIA is a strategic means of considering the extent of any adverse effects on communities and recording what actions are taken (if any) to reduce and manage or control the impact from a policing and partnership perspective, thereby maintaining public trust and confidence.

KEY POINT

Fostering good relationships with local communities, ie those in the area in which the investigation is focused, is not only good for winning support and cooperation, but also raises and maintains morale amongst the enquiry team.

A CIA is a contingency plan that will effectively facilitate and record the dynamic assessment and control measures for any community tensions. These can be created or affected by not just local but also regional, national and global events.

It is very important to work alongside the local policing commander who has a wider responsibility for engaging with the community. The local commander will not want to damage working relationships or partnerships that will have been carefully nurtured. Unfortunately, critical incidents have the potential for upsetting the equilibrium and disrupting everyday business. In many scenarios the response phase to a major or critical incident can be relatively short in comparison with the recovery phase, which in some cases can take weeks, months or even years.

References

ACPO, *Family Liaison Strategy Manual* (NPIA, 2003) as amended by ACPO, *Family Liaison Officer Guidance* (NPIA, 2008)

ACPO, *Murder Investigation Manual* (NCPE, 2006)

ACPO, *Practical Advice on Critical Incident Management* (NPIA, 2007)

Ministry of Justice, *Code of Practice for Victims of Crime: Presented to Parliament pursuant to section 33 of the Domestic Violence, Crime and Victims Act 2004* (HM Stationery Office, 2015, or <http://www.gov.uk/moj>)

Ministry of Justice, 'Getting it Right for Victims and witnesses' Consultation paper CP3/2012 (HM Stationery Office, 2012)

Suspect Management

12.1 **Introduction**

A primary objective for an investigation (and one of the five building blocks—see Chapter 5.4) is the identification of those suspected to be responsible for committing criminal offences. This incorporates management of all connected processes such as making arrests, gathering investigative material, securing evidence, custody and detention, conducting interviews, bringing charges and building a case file for court proceedings. Wherever possible, these processes require careful strategic and tactical operational planning with consideration of:

- methods of identifying suspects
- for what, when, why, how, where and who is to be arrested
- legal powers and organisational policies
- maximising physical and forensic search and evidence recovery
- managing detention arrangements and custody time limits
- planning, preparing and conducting investigative interviews
- reviewing investigative material that has been obtained
- charging and processing procedures
- determining what evidence is to be used in a prosecution case.

The focus of this chapter is to cover important tactical elements of suspect management. These begin with the identification and arrest of suspects. There is an examination of the issues surrounding a decision to declare 'suspect' status, the making and timing of arrests, detention and interviews and recovering forensic evidence from suspects, before moving on to some practical points on ways to conduct effective proactive hunts for suspects.

12.2 **Suspect Identification**

Suspects can be uncovered through a variety of means such as witness interviews, forensic evidence, passive data collection (eg CCTV), admissions, information and intelligence, analytical work, proactive overt or covert work and prompt actions taken at or near a crime scene. Any one or more of the main lines of enquiry or investigative strategies and tactics can point to the identity of a suspect(s) and that is mainly what they are aimed at.

The SIO may wish to produce a 'stand-alone' policy that outlines various methods in which suspects (if not already known) can be identified. Some of these may appear similar, if not identical, to those discussed in Chapter 13 for identifying witnesses:

Checklist—Suspect identification

- Initial response, physical searching surrounding the scene(s) and road checks.
- Witness and CHIS information.

- Matching descriptions through identification and facial recognition techniques (eg PND has a facial search capability).

- Victimology enquiries.

- Conducting TI/TIE enquiries.

- House-to-house (H-2-H) enquiries.

- Forensic results.[1]

- General physical searching.

- Passive data collection.

- Communications data.

- Information and intelligence.

- Checking custody, prison release, stop/search and medical data.

- Proactive overt and covert tactics.

- Suspects 'in the system' (eg HOLMES).

- Offering rewards (see Chapter 13.3).

KEY POINTS

- Prompt and decisive initial action can lead to locating and arrest of offenders.
- Check local hospitals for if an offender is injured, particularly if sharp weapons or fire are involved (eg wounds, scorch or burn marks to skin, eyebrows).
- Suicides or attempts post-incident can be checked against known suspect details (eg DNA, fingerprints and description) in case offenders (post-offence) take their own life (beware of them choosing obscure/distant locations).
- Post-offence, offenders sometimes revisit their victim's attack or body concealment/deposition site, or attend their funeral or burial site (eg for their own curiosity, guilt or morbidity), and tactics can be devised to capture these moments for the benefit of the investigation.[2]

---

[1] Never assume a person with previous offending has had their DNA or fingerprints taken and entered onto a UK database; they may be registered in another country.

[2] Colin Ash-Smith stabbed to death Claire Tiltman in January 1993 and attended her funeral a month later. He was convicted 21 years later in 2014 after a change in the law allowed the use of bad character evidence. He had gone on a spree of attacks against women across Kent during midnight walks armed with knives hunting for victims and bragged about his attacks in his diaries.

> - 'Lone wolf' (lone actor) type offenders have their own personal motives, and although rare, they tend to be well organised and not easily identifiable through conventional means.[3]

12.3 **Suspects 'In the System'**

There are a number of historical high-profile cases in which the suspect's details have been already known and sat within the case management 'system' but not having been recognised as such.[4] Linkage not being made or the importance and significance of information going unrecognised can and sometimes does occur. Human error or unprofessionalism can mean that a vital piece of information is not correctly recognised and dealt with.

This type of information and mistakes need to be discovered in order to identify lines of enquiry that can lead to the identity of the suspect. The longer a case continues and the more data is accumulated, the greater chance there is for a suspect's details or evidential links to exist within an enquiry system. Having large amounts of information to manage increases the risk of an important piece of information or detail being missed.

There are a number of ways a person or piece of information can get overlooked or wrongly excluded. Elimination criteria itself might wrongly do so if, for example, the description used to eliminate against is too prescriptive, such as an offender being described as between 5'8" to 5'10" and a TIE subject who is 6'0" wrongly ruled out). A piece of information about the sighting of a suspicious car in the area may not be followed up and dealt with properly; or a negligent officer may fail to make diligent enquiries to check an alibi: there are numerous ways a vital line of enquiry may get missed.

The best way to avoid this is by rigorous processes and paying attention to detail. High standards of professionalism and scrutiny must be insisted upon to reduce the possibility of mistakes. Thorough checks and supervision and quality assurance of information, messages, reports, action results, priorities and relevance and elimination decisions require the ABC principle (Assume

---

KEY POINT

The importance of incident room staff being able to work efficiently, concentrate and study each and every item cannot be overstated. Distractions such as noise, disruptions, excessive visitors, inadequate premises and equipment and a poor working environment need to be identified and managed properly to avoid mistakes.

---

[3] Ukrainian-born student Pavlo Lapshyn murdered 75-year-old Mohammed Saleem in April 2013, while acting alone and for racial hatred. He would have been difficult to catch had he not tried to cause an explosion at a mosque soon after committing the murder.

[4] For example, the 'Yorkshire Ripper' Peter Sutcliffe case; or Operation Minstead, featuring a masked sexual predator from south London dubbed the 'night stalker' aka Delroy Grant.

nothing, Believe nothing, Challenge/check everything). Sloppiness MUST be avoided at all costs.

12.4 **Declaring 'Suspect' Status**

A decision to declare 'suspect' status on any named individual(s) is a defining moment. It amounts to a formal declaration that the enquiry team is focusing on a particular individual (or plural) and needs careful management. Such a decision can only be based upon solid justification and sound rationale, supported by reliable investigative material (see paragraph 12.11.3). The decision needs to be carefully scripted in a policy entry (and status changing/registering on HOLMES if applicable).

The term 'suspect' implies there are reasonable grounds to suspect a person's involvement in an offence. It affords certain protection and rights under the Police and Criminal Evidence Act 1984 (PACE), including legal advice and a caution before questioning. It is important not only to declare suspect status when appropriate (and there needs to be justification for doing so), but also sometimes to explain why a person is not being nominated suspect. This assists in defending possible accusations of circumventing legal rights.

Suspect status is only declared when:

- tangible evidence or investigative material exists to link a person to an offence, eg physical/forensic evidence, eyewitness testimony, CCTV
- circumstantial evidence exists of sufficient strength to provide reasonable grounds for suspicion based on known facts or information
- strong intelligence is supported by properly graded and evaluated material (ie using the 5 x 5 x 5 intelligence rating system).

If too many suspects are declared, arrested and eliminated, this gives the impression there is little or no idea who is actually responsible. It can also produce contradictory or undermining evidence when the real offender(s) is/are eventually arrested and charged and face(s) prosecution. Formal declaration of a suspect is invariably picked up on by the news media and/or community because it is viewed as a highly significant development. Hopes and expectations increase towards a successful outcome, and if people are being arrested as suspects only to be later released without charge, this is inevitably viewed negatively.

When the time is right and there are sufficient grounds for doing so, the SIO should be bold enough to make the tough decision to declare suspect status. This is a highly significant development and one that lifts the morale of victims, their family, the local community, senior officers and the enquiry team.

When making decisions about declaring suspect status, it is important to be consistent. This means the same criteria and standard must be applied to all potential suspects to show that there has been consistency in approach to decision making.

KEY POINTS

1. The term 'suspect' is not to be confused with the term 'subject'. These terms are sometimes confused, not only internally but by the media, courts, lawyers and judges. Any misunderstanding needs quickly correcting.
2. Investigative material relied upon for declaring suspect status needs to be accurate and reliable—any verbal accounts/witness summaries/intelligence relied upon should be subject of the ABC principle.

12.5 **Suspect Background Enquiries**

The word 'suspectology' has crept in to compete with its partner term 'victimology' in regular usage. The study of suspects is nothing new, as research into a person's background, history and behaviour has always been a useful tactic. It can assist, for example, when considering a motive and answering the 'why?' question. The background of a suspect helps in establishing why a person might have targeted a victim, eg if they hold a grudge. Why a particular location was chosen might also link in with where a suspect lived or have been linked to at some stage in their lives.

A study of patterns of behaviour can give indications of changes of mood or habits and routines. For example, a boyfriend regularly calls or texts his girlfriend and, following her disappearance, doesn't attempt to make contact at all. Or a suspect disappears after an incident or changes their routine, eg in order to avoid the attention of the police. For this reason an intelligence requirement is to establish who is not where they should be post-offence.

12.6 **Legal Powers**

Amendments to PACE made by the Serious Organised Crime and Police Act 2005 (SOCPA) mean arrests can be made for **any** offence provided certain conditions apply. For an arrest to be lawful, the arresting officer must have:

1. Reasonable grounds to **suspect** an offence has been committed, and the person committed it, or they were in the act of committing, or were about to commit the offence; AND
2. Reasonable grounds to **believe** ('believe' demands a higher standard than 'suspect') arrest is necessary for one or more of the specified reasons (known as the 'necessity test') to:
   (a) ascertain the person's name
   (b) ascertain the person's address
   (c) prevent the person causing physical harm to themselves or suffering physical injury

(d) prevent loss of or damage to property

(e) prevent an offence against public decency

(f) prevent an unlawful obstruction of the highway

(g) protect a child or vulnerable person

(h) prevent any prosecution being hindered by the disappearance of the person in question

(i) allow a prompt and effective investigation of the offence or of the conduct of the person in question.

The prompt and effective investigation condition may be satisfied if there are reasonable grounds to **believe** that the person:

- made false statements or statements that cannot be easily verified
- may steal or destroy evidence
- may intimidate, threaten or make contact with witnesses; or
- needs to be interviewed to obtain evidence.

Where the suspected offence is indictable, this condition may justify arrest if there is a need to:

- enter and search premises occupied or controlled by the person
- search the person
- prevent contact with others or take fingerprints, footwear impressions, samples or photographs for comparison purposes.

12.6.1 **Code 'G' of PACE**

On 12 November 2012 a revision of PACE (Code G) was implemented demanding more detailed consideration of the necessity test by arresting officers than was previously required. Arresting officers must consider facts and information tending to indicate the person's innocence as well as their guilt (including whether any use of force was lawful and reasonable), and consider practical alternatives to arrest, such as street bail or conducting a voluntary interview with the suspect.

Each case must be decided on its merits according to the circumstances existing at the time, using professional judgement and discretion concerning the necessity and proportionality of arrest. The importance of recording decision making for future scrutiny cannot be underestimated.

Necessity to arrest and necessity to interview are two separate issues; therefore if arrest is not considered necessary, a suspect could be interviewed voluntarily under caution.

Code G now clarifies the situation of what to do if a 'volunteer' leaves the interview before its conclusion, having been told (under Code C) they are not under arrest and are free to leave at any time. Leaving the interview could now justify arrest (under Code G) if there is a necessity to continue questioning, but this must be judged on the circumstances existing at the time.

Necessity to arrest should be kept under continuous review during the interview. Circumstances could change making arrest necessary, eg threats made to others necessitating arrest to prevent physical harm, or denials requiring corroboration necessitating detention for a prompt and effective investigation (these are not exhaustive examples).

Voluntary interviews should be planned and conducted as thoroughly as for a person under arrest. Attendees should not be treated with any less consideration than an arrested person. It is the interviewer's responsibility to ensure any vulnerability is identified and appropriate safeguards are in place, including any requirement for an appropriate adult, interpreter, etc. Voluntary attendees also have an absolute right to outside communication and legal advice.

12.7 **Planning and Conducting Arrests**

This activity is often referred to as 'executive action' and may attract a separate operational name of its own, depending on size and scale. It is preferable, if practicable, to thoroughly prepare and produce an operational plan before arrests are made. A research (profile) package should be prepared containing all the suspectology-type details (see earlier section). This will include, in addition to the usual name, date of birth, description, photograph, etc, a detailed analysis of known associates and criminal background, modus operandi (MO) and any warning indicators. This task is often delegated to an intelligence officer/cell within the enquiry team.

Background information on suspects may show links to other premises, such as where they work or frequent (eg a social or health club). These may also need to be considered for searches or location checks. The profile should contain information about previous bad character, eg outstanding case files, previous offending, current intelligence, lifestyle, associates, similar-fact evidence. Interviewers may later wish to introduce this information during the interview process.

KEY POINT

Making arrests for serious offences usually attracts media and public attention. This provides an opportunity to elevate the status of the investigation and re-engage with those from whom information is required. Any witnesses (or other victims) who have been previously reluctant to come forward may do so upon news of an arrest. Plans should cater for any such investigative opportunities created.

12.7.1 **Risk assessments—vulnerable suspects**
It may be necessary and sometimes essential to produce an assessment of associated risks prior to arrests being made, particularly if a suspect has mental health

issues or is under suspicion of offences that may render them susceptible to harming themselves. Such offences may, for example, relate to child abuse (eg offering and viewing/possessing indecent images of children (IIOC)) which can leave suspects feeling sufficiently isolated and vulnerable through feelings of guilt, shame or concern about negative reactions from their families, friends and communities. So much so they consider taking their own lives.

Article 2 of the Human Rights Act 1998 (HRA) states everyone's right to life is enshrined in law. This means there is a duty of care to all suspects and a responsibility for managing potential risks of suicide or harm following intervention. In some cases, this duty may have to extend to those closely related to suspects (eg their immediate family). It has been concluded that there is a link between suicides and spells in custody.[5]

Potential risks can be identified via a suspect intelligence profile and it needs to be determined what systems or sources are to be checked in order to introduce appropriate control measures and contingencies. This MUST include relevant information about a person's medical history (physical and mental) or if they have previously self-harmed/attempted suicide. It should also include details about their immediate family and close relatives who may, as described earlier, also become vulnerable. If the offence is one that may create a suicide risk due to their occupation (eg if they are in a position of trust—POT—by nature of their occupation or role), then this needs to be included as part of the research. This information is required not only to safeguard the physical arrest phase and safer management of the process, but also the safe detention of the suspect during their time in police custody and upon release.

There are other agencies that can assist if risks are identified. If, for example, there is a suicide risk, then a healthcare professional is often better qualified to make an assessment (eg NHS community psychiatric nurse). An individual's own family and doctor are also useful for providing information and support. Organisations such as the Samaritans can also provide help and advice.

KEY POINTS

- Risk management when dealing with certain types of offenders or offences (eg IIOC) can be a complex and challenging task that may be better suited to a coordinated and multi-agency approach.
- Concerns need to be brought to the attention of the Custody Officer upon arrival at a custody suite. Support should be extended beyond release if risks are identified.
- Bail can be refused under s 38(1)(a)(6) of PACE if a person is charged and there are reasonable grounds for believing detention is necessary for their own safety and protection.

---

[5] See R Teers, 'Deaths during or following police contact: statistics for England and Wales 2013/14', IPCC research and statistics series: Paper 27 (2014).

Checklist—Suspect intelligence profile

- Name, age, date of birth.

- Other names/aliases used or known by.

- Full physical description.

- Known intelligence (UK and overseas).

- Recent photograph.

- Current residence.

- Details and layout of location of arrest (eg owner, other occupants, risks and hazards, children, pets, likely substance abuse, hiding places, outbuildings and gardens, access and exit points, previous police visits and outcomes, local community and neighbourhood details).

- Vehicles or vessels owned, used or accessed.

- Other premises and places frequented.

- Known associates and their profiles including descriptions.

- Criminal history including MO and behaviour upon arrest.

- Current intelligence, including details from other relevant agencies.

- Warning indicators, eg use of violence, weapons or access to firearms or holder of firearms licence, alcohol or drug abuser, animals at address.

- Previous responses and behaviour in police interviews.

- Family details and any related vulnerable persons.

- Medical information.

- Risk assessment to identify vulnerabilities (particularly around known mental health issues and self-harming/suicide risks).

12.7.2 Arrest team operational briefings

Those involved in arrest operations, including specialist resources such as Crime Scene Managers/Investigators (CSMs/CSIs), should be briefed beforehand by the SIO or nominee. An operational 'order' or briefing document can be circulated beforehand using a recognised structure such as IIMARCH or SAFCOM.

Effective communication through good briefings usually has a positive effect on success (see Chapter 9). Questions about roles and responsibilities should be encouraged and dealt with at a briefing. All documents and records used and referred to are subject to disclosure rules and care must be taken to ensure briefing material is not inadvertently left at any target premises or elsewhere (eg in vehicles or in public places).

An operational plan and policy file entry justifying an arrest strategy may benefit by inclusion of 5WH topics such as:

- Who—who the person is that is being arrested.
- What—what offence they are being arrested for and the primary objectives.
- Why—why they are being arrested (justification).
- Where—where the arrest will take place.
- When—exact time, day and date.
- How—how the arrest will be conducted.

These topics can be expanded to cover and explain further detail, such as what searches are to be conducted upon arrest, what forensic considerations need catering for, where suspects will be transported to, who by and how, what the reception plan is at the custody suite, and who the interview teams are.

Checklist—Arrest and search operation—briefing agenda

1. Introductions.
2. Command and control (eg Gold, Silver and Bronze).
3. Operational objectives.
4. Details of investigation.
5. Current situation report.
6. Details of the suspect(s) and recent photograph(s).
7. Details of premises and others expected to be present.
8. Relevant intelligence and information.
9. Legal powers (entry and arrest) and method of entry.
10. Security and preservation arrangements while operation in progress.
11. Search and seizure: items sought and how they will be dealt with.
12. Intelligence-gathering requirements.
13. Contingencies for dealing with unrelated offences discovered.
14. Neighbourhood checks, eg H-2-H around site of premises targeted.
15. Detainee transportation, custody reception and interview.
16. Fast-track action management (arising during operation).

17. Administration (eg warrants and search records).

18. Roles and responsibilities (arrest and search teams).

19. Risks assessment and control measures.

20. Communications (airwave radios and contact numbers).

21. Criminal Procedure and Investigations Act 1996 (CPIA) material instructions.

22. Community Impact Assessment and/or media control.

23. Debriefing arrangements.

Silver control-type facilities or command and control centres are good to have in place for arrest operations. Local policing teams should be informed and tasked with managing any community impact issues. A Gold Commander may be required to cater for any strategic policing matters (depending on the scale of the operation).

Arrests and searches provide opportunities to conduct other enquiries, including speaking to people at premises who could be witnesses or useful sources of information. Neighbours and visitors can be spoken to at the same time to see if they have any useful knowledge, such as suspect movements, habits, associates, and vehicles used. This might include conducting targeted H-2-H enquiries at neighbouring premises.

12.8 **Timing of Arrests**

Usually the sooner suspects are arrested, the less chance and opportunity there is for them to destroy or contaminate evidence or interfere with witnesses. There may also be financial and resource-saving benefits in reducing costs by avoiding lengthy investigations. A duty of care for safeguarding the welfare and safety of the general public needs to be an overriding factor.

Where there is an opportunity to make an *early arrest* based on available information, then usually it should be made. The closer to the time the offence was committed the arrest is made, the greater an opportunity there is to recover forensic evidence or any other useful items or material by using the element of surprise as an advantage. It also prevents offenders from disappearing, concocting alibis, interfering with witnesses, destroying evidence or committing further offences. It provides victim and/or community reassurance, increases faith in the investigation team and prevents any temptation for people to 'take the law into their own hands' (vigilantism).

However, the most advantageous time, date and place to make an arrest will depend largely on individual circumstances. There are a number of key factors that may influence the decision, for example coinciding an arrest operation with a tactic to try and approach potential witnesses, who may be withholding information for fear of intimidation. There may also be a practical consideration of having to trace a suspect's whereabouts in order to effect the arrest or complete some covert work to 'house' them beforehand.

The 'golden hour(s)' principle suggests offenders who are spoken to closest to the time of the offence are more likely to make mistakes when fabricating stories because they have had less chance to prepare. Consequently people are more likely to be truthful when interviewed soon after offending. This is also a time when they are less able to claim they 'cannot remember' what they were doing or where they were at the material time, because the time difference between offence and arrest is minimal.

An immediate arrest decision may have to take account of a number of factors:

- Does the suspect pose a serious risk to victims, witnesses or the general public?
- Is there a likelihood they will commit further or more serious offences?
- Are they likely to destroy, conceal or falsify evidence and impede the investigation?
- Is further surveillance or other covert means of evidence gathering necessary?

There are, of course, other ways in which to conduct searches of premises without the need to make formal arrests, such as by search warrant. Section 8 of PACE as amended by sections 113 and 114 of SOCPA provides the grounds and procedure to be followed when applying for a search warrant for an indictable offence. It also provides a power to seize certain evidence.

12.8.1 Delaying arrests

It may be advantageous not to arrest immediately if such a course of action would frustrate other enquiries. Delaying an arrest may also reduce the need to pre-charge bail a suspect and provide a better position from which to conduct a meaningful interview and reduce delay in bringing a case to court.

There are other reasons for delaying, eg when trying to increase evidence recovery opportunities. Another reason might be if there are multiple suspects and it is better to make simultaneous arrests to limit opportunities to dispose of evidence and collaborate after being alerted to police interest. A delay may then be necessary in order to synchronise multiple strikes. A further reason to delay might be to enable suspects to unwittingly 'assist' by leading the investigation to evidential locations or where victims are (eg in missing person or kidnap cases).

> **KEY POINT**
>
> A policy decision is needed to explain the reasons and justification for any delay in making an arrest. The decision has to remain under continuous review and may have to be defended if an offender commits further offences or places the public, communities or staff at greater risk of harm that could otherwise have been prevented.

One of the complications when delaying an arrest is that a suspect can be disadvantaged by not being afforded their statutory rights (eg being cautioned and allowed access to independent legal advice) should they be spoken to in the normal course of an investigation. This does not mean that where there is no reasonable suspicion a person cannot be treated as a witness or TIE subject, but once they are deemed a 'suspect' they cannot legally be interviewed until being properly cautioned as either a voluntary attender at a police station or under arrest. Adequate control measures will prevent this from occurring.

A structured 'hot' debriefing of all staff involved in arrest operations ensures evidential and intelligence-gathering opportunities have been fully utilised and all relevant information received and scrutinised (see also Chapter 9).

Checklist—suspect arrests

1. Arrest, reception and detention

- Nominate appropriate officers to make the arrest (decide if independent of interviewing officer or one and the same).

- Determine exact wording of arrest.

- Decide if arrest will be recorded (if so, ensure it is reviewed afterwards).

- Determine custody suite (convenient location with good interview and downstream monitoring facilities) and if separate locations (or separate wings/custody areas) for multiple suspects.

- Decide on mode of transport to custody office (independent staff are usually best to avoid accusations of interference en route; vehicle will need searching before and afterwards).

- Ensure correct procedures followed for recording any unsolicited comments/ significant statements and they are not encouraged.

- Brief custody staff so they know reason and correct wording for the arrest, grounds for detention and any risks identified, eg known medical history.

- Brief any nominated PACE reviewing officers.

- Appoint officer to act as liaison with custody office and coordinate activity (particularly if multiple arrests).
- Plan for recovery of forensic exhibits and biometric samples from suspects and nominate people unconnected with enquiry to obtain them (*avoid cross-contamination—sterile areas/cells*).
- Ensure swabbing and sampling kits available (eg firearms residue kits).
- Plan for recovery of suspect's clothing and footwear—ensure replacements available.
- Consider suspect's religious beliefs/faith considerations and plan for appropriate replacement clothing, dietary and religious requirements.
- Plan for medical examination of suspect and brief/debrief the surgeon involved (request body mapping on a diagram).
- Plan for early photographing of injuries or unusual features.
- Plan for fingerprinting of suspect (eg livescan facility).
- Ensure adequate communications link between arresting officers, custody suite and incident room (SIO) to monitor progress.
- Ensure all details of information provided by detainee (eg addresses, intimation details) and possessions are relayed to incident room for appropriate decisions (eg mobile phone examination, house/vehicle key checks, diaries).
- Arrange home address search plan and consideration of treatment as crime scene (if not done so already) and any other linked addresses of interest.
- Consider family liaison strategy, media, and community impact re details and news of the arrest.
- Plan for custody extensions and warrants of further detention (WOFD).

2. Debrief agenda

- Comments and replies made, including significant statements.
- Details of persons present and visitors.
- Potential witnesses and sources of information.
- Search results and exhibits seized.
- Fast-track actions required.
- Investigative material and intelligence gathered.

- Completion and collection of evidential statements from all staff involved before going off duty and relevant disclosure (CPIA) material.

- Administration—completed search records and executed warrants.

- H-2-H results and documentation.

- Welfare/health and safety issues.

- Risk assessment monitoring and evaluation.

- Any wider safeguarding issues for vulnerable persons, eg children.

- Victim, local community and media impact and information assessment.

12.8.2 Significant statements

As a rule suspects must not be interviewed except at a police station (PACE, Code C, 11.1). An interview is defined as the 'questioning of a person regarding his/her suspected involvement in a criminal offence'. If, however, a suspect becomes talkative and spontaneously comments about the offence without prompting or insists on providing unsolicited comments, once the caution has been administered these comments must be carefully noted. Voluntary comments or 'significant statements', as they are called, may contain vital information or evidence about the offence under investigation. Denials can also form part of the subsequent interview strategy when considered in the context of other evidence.

A *significant statement* includes anything that appears capable of being used in evidence against the suspect and in particular an admission of guilt (PACE, Code C, 11.4A). The term derives from Part III of the Criminal Justice and Public Order Act 1994:

> A significant statement or silence is one which appears capable of being used in evidence against the suspect in particular a direct admission of guilt or a failure or refusal to answer a question or to answer it satisfactorily which may give rise to an inference.

Suspects should be asked to sign a record of any such statement after reading and agreeing it as an accurate and true account. Any refusal to sign should itself be recorded, together with the reasons, including any areas the suspect considers inaccurate. Significant statements should be incorporated into the subsequent interview plan to confirm and probe further during the interview under caution.

When planning arrests, an officer should be nominated to record in writing any significant statements and unsolicited comments, and to maintain a contemporaneous record until the suspect has been booked into custody. Any comments made can be of value to subsequent formal interviews, and denials when arrested also form the basis of a challenge when presented later. If arresting officers are wearing body-worn cameras, these comments become even more significant.

> **KEY POINT**
>
> Few people remain silent or composed when being informed they are under arrest for a serious offence. Arresting officers should be encouraged to note exactly what suspects say in response to being arrested and how they react, Suspects should, wherever practicable, be afforded sufficient time to comment after they are told they are under arrest by allowing a suitable pause before being led away. An option is to video-record the arrest which can provide impactive evidence.

12.8.3 Urgent interviews

Arrested persons must not be interviewed except at a police station or other authorised place of detention. This is unless delay would be likely to lead to:

- interference with or harm to evidence connected with an offence
- interference with or physical harm to other people
- serious loss of or damage to property
- alerting other suspects not yet arrested, or hindering the recovery of property obtained as a consequence of an offence.

If any of these criteria is satisfied, an 'urgent interview' may be conducted, eg questioning to locate and recover a victim, missing person, weapon or firearm discarded by a suspect before anyone finding it is caused harm. Critically, questioning must cease once the relevant risk has been averted or the necessary questions have been put (PACE, Code C, 11.1). Urgent interviews should therefore not be used to ask evidential questions about other lines of enquiry.

When planning arrests involving urgent interviews, consideration must be given to practicalities, including the method of recording, such as contemporaneous notes or portable recording/audio equipment. Seeking advice from an interview adviser beforehand is always a wise option.

When a detainee requests legal advice at the police station, they cannot be interviewed until they have received it, unless the grounds above apply, and authorisation has been provided by a Superintendent grade or above (not necessarily independent of the investigation).

KEY POINTS

- Should the criteria apply, PACE allows urgent interviews to be conducted away from the police station if necessary, such as at the location of arrest. There is no reference in the Act to any authority being required in such circumstances.
- At the police station, after legal advice has been requested, urgent interviews *must* be authorised by a Superintendent (or above) using the caution '*You don't have to say anything but anything you do say may be given in evidence*'. This means adverse inferences cannot be drawn from the interview.
- Urgent interviews are infrequently used except in serious cases such as serial murders, suspicious missing persons, kidnap, abduction and terrorism cases (ie crimes in action). They are always likely to be closely scrutinised by legal teams and courts.

12.9 Suspects as Crime Scenes

Suspects are always considered as potential crime scenes and a rich source of evidence to prove or disprove their involvement. Time scales between incident and arrest will vary in each case and, as stated earlier, the sooner the arrest and detention, the better the chances of trace evidence recovery.

Apart from fingerprints, DNA, clothing and footwear, a suspect can provide a wealth of forensic evidence from transfer of hair, blood, semen, paint, soil, gunshot residue, glass fragments, fibres, pollen, etc. The most needs to be made of evidence recovery opportunities that may link a suspect to a crime. This should be catered for in the pre-arrest planning stage.

It can be advantageous to obtain samples or seize clothing at the point of arrest rather than wait until arrival at a custody centre. Firearms discharge residue in particular needs to be recovered as soon as possible after a firearms-related incident, and in some cases the covering of exposed areas such as the suspect's hands is necessary to increase the likelihood of success. Advice can be taken on all forensic recovery matters and contamination avoidance from an expert such as a CSM/CSI during the planning stage.

It can also be useful to have a suspect medically examined by a medical examiner upon arrival at a custody suite. Checks can be made for blood, cuts, scratches, burn marks or other injuries (eg marks on the hand from the recoil firing mechanism of a semi-automatic handgun). A full body-map profile can also be completed and any marks found recorded and photographed. A medical examiner should be debriefed afterwards to see what, if any, comments the detainee made during their examination.

KEY POINT—POLICY FILE ENTRY

Example of a suspect forensic evidence recovery plan:

Decision: Any persons arrested on suspicion of being involved in the offence of (x) will be subject to the following evidence collection plan:

- *Full length photography in clothes they were arrested in.*
- *Medical examination to identify and photograph any marks and injuries.*
- *Swabbing of hands and any blood or injuries.*
- *Clothing and footwear seizure—to be taken over paper.*
- *Blood and urine samples to be taken.*
- *Hair combings, hair samples and fingernail scrapings to be taken.*
- *Detainee (suspect) to be kept under constant observation and placed into a sterile cell until such time that forensic capture is complete.*

Reason: To find and preserve forensic evidence that might be of benefit to the investigation.

It should be noted that if any third party brings or sends clothing to the custody suite for a detainee, those items should also be checked to see if they are of significance to the investigation.

12.9.1 Strip searches

A strip search is the removal of more than a person's outer clothing. It is authorised by a Custody Officer when considered necessary to remove an article which the detainee would not be allowed to keep because it may present a danger to themselves or others, might be used to assist escape or (more importantly to the investigation) be evidence relating to an offence. The conduct of strip searches is covered by PACE Code C, Annex A.

12.9.2 Taking samples from suspects in custody

Intimate samples

Section 62 of PACE creates a power to take intimate samples from persons in police detention. Examples include anal swab, pubic hair, nose swab, wound swab, penile swab, urine:

(1) Subject to section 63B an intimate sample may be taken from a person in police detention:
    (a) if a police officer of at least the rank of inspector authorises; and
    (b) if the appropriate consent is given.
(1A) An intimate sample may be taken from a person who is not in police detention but from whom, in the course of the investigation of an offence,

two or more non-intimate samples suitable for the same means of analysis have been taken which have proved insufficient:

    (a) if a police officer of at least the rank of inspector authorises; and

    (b) the appropriate consent is given.

(6) The duty imposed by subsection (5)(ii) above includes a duty to state the nature of the offence in which it is suspected that the person from whom the sample is to be taken has been involved.

(9) In the case of an intimate sample which is a dental impression, the sample may be taken from a person only by a registered dentist.

(9A) In the case of any other form of intimate sample, except in the case of a sample of urine, the sample may be taken from a person only by:

    (a) registered medical practitioner; or

    (b) registered healthcare professional.

If consent is refused without due cause, then in any subsequent proceedings adverse inferences may be drawn by a court, judge, or jury (section 62(10)).

The suspect must be made aware of the possible consequences and be reminded of his entitlement to free legal advice.

Non-intimate samples

Section 63 of PACE as amended by section 10 and Schedule 37 of the Criminal Justice Act 2003 provides powers relating to the taking of non-intimate samples. Examples include saliva, head hair, mouth swab, nail cuttings.

(1) Except as provided by this section, a non-intimate sample may not be taken from a person without the appropriate consent

(2) Consent to the taking of a non-intimate sample must be given in writing.

(2A) A non-intimate sample may be taken from a person without the appropriate consent if two conditions are satisfied:

(2B) The first is that the person is in police (or NCA) detention in consequence of his arrest for a recordable offence.

(2C) The second is that—

    (a) he has not had a non-intimate sample of the same type and from the same part of the body taken in the course of the investigation of the offence by the police or NCA, or

    (b) he has had such a sample taken but it proved insufficient.

(3) A non-intimate sample may be taken from a person without the appropriate consent if—

    (a) he is being held in custody by the police [or NCA] on the authority of a court; and

    (b) an officer of at least the rank of inspector authorises it to be taken without the appropriate consent.

(3A) A non-intimate sample may be taken from a person (whether or not he is in police detention or held in custody by the police (or NCA) on the authority of a court) without the appropriate consent if—

(a) he has been charged with a recordable offence or informed that he will be reported for such an offence; and

(b) either he has not had a non-intimate sample taken from him in the course of the investigation of the offence by the police (or NCA) or he has had a non-intimate sample taken from him but either it was not suitable for the same means of analysis or, though so suitable, the sample proved insufficient.

(3B) A non-intimate sample may be taken from a person without the appropriate consent if he has been convicted of a recordable offence.

(4) An officer may give an authorisation under subsection (3) only if he has reasonable grounds—

(a) for suspecting the involvement of the person from whom the sample is to be taken; and

(b) for believing that the sample will tend to confirm or disprove his involvement.

(7) The duty imposed by subsection (6)(ii) includes a duty to state the nature of the offence in which it is suspected that the person from whom the sample is to be taken has been involved.

Note: The Criminal Justice Act 2003 expanded police powers to re-take DNA samples without consent from detainees provided the two conditions in 63(2B) and (2C) are complied with.

KEY POINT

Any necessary authorities should be obtained or planned for in advance, plus the attendance and briefing of a qualified medical examiner and CSI if required. All requirements should be made clear to exploit evidence-gathering opportunities.

12.10 Detention Times and Warrants of Further Detention

Planning and preparation takes cognisance of how long detention proceedings are likely to take in order to plan for exceeding custody time limits. This should identify in advance which (PACE) duty senior officers are likely to be tasked with the responsibility of considering extending any custody time limits and/or authorising the taking of intimate samples. This will enable them to be fully briefed and prepared with the facts of the case and likely requirements.

Custody time limits need close monitoring throughout the entire period of detention. The use of a live-running 'timeline' of events and activities for each and every detainee will be useful and nominating an officer to assume responsibility for monitoring and updating it. Ideally this is the same person who is nominated to supervise and manage the detention and interview process on behalf of the SIO to ensure everything runs smoothly and efficiently. This information is then used as the basis for any warrant of further detention (WOFD, under sections 43/44 PACE) hearings (for detention from 36 to 96 hours) to show enquiries are being progressed diligently and expeditiously.

When dealing with WOFD, wherever practicable the SIO/DSIO should appear in person to make the application If this is delegated, the person who attends court to apply for the warrants must be well briefed and aware of all the circumstances of the investigation and any likely areas of contention. It is very important, particularly if they are someone who is not directly involved with the investigation, they are involved in team briefings post-arrest and kept updated on evidential finds or intelligence updates. It may also be useful to have the interview adviser present when the WOFD hearing takes place. It should be noted that at these hearings the defence legal team may wish to extract information about the investigation and evidence which may not have otherwise been declared in formal interview.

KEY POINTS—'WOFD'

- Applications are made at the time officers are sworn to give evidence. This is important when managing applications involving multiple suspects who are appearing separately, to ensure their detention time does not expire before the application commences.
- If granted, the time of the WOFD commences when it is signed by the magistrate.
- Planning a WOFD should consider the logistics and time frames involved, eg it is often prudent to make early applications, taking account of the court's availability.
- Applications have to be authorised by a Superintendent or above.
- Contingencies should include a 'wash up' interview with the suspect(s) before the WOFD application to ensure all critical questions have been put to them in case further detention is refused.

12.11 Suspect Interviews

Investigative interviewing plays a big role in arrest and detention strategies. While there are specialists and advisers who may assist in professionalising the process, the SIO *must play an active role* in not only devising a suitable interview plan, but also in its implementation, supervision and dynamic management.

Appropriate and skilled officers who are to be tasked with conducting the interview(s) need selecting. It should not just be a case of choosing a person who is trained and 'next on the list' for doing a complex interview, but rather choosing people based upon their skills, experience and suitability. Reserve officers should also be chosen in the event of unforeseen circumstances.

Trained and accredited investigative interviewers fall broadly within three different categories and are all now under the PIP II-level specialist criteria (previously known as Tier 3 or Tier 5). These are:

1. general interviewers (eg serious and complex investigations)
2. specialist interviewers (eg child interviews) and those trained and competent in major crime suspect interviews
3. interview advisers (strategic adviser and coordinator for SIO).

Not all major and serious crime investigators are accredited as above, so the selection of the right staff to conduct interviews is vitally important. Often a combination of three of the categories above may be required in a major investigation (ie 1, 2 and 3).

The interview process is a phase where detailed and careful planning is required which needn't wait until the time of arrest. Once a suspect is identified the planning can commence immediately by highlighting key investigative material that can be used in any subsequent suspect interview.

A briefing should be provided to interview teams (particularly if they are not completely conversant with the investigation), and if necessary they should be given a familiarisation visit to the crime scene. This may be of assistance if admissions are made or detail provided by the suspect that requires an appreciation of significant locations.

The PEACE framework of investigative interviewing is used as the basis for structuring interviews, which should not be misconstrued as a means of producing long and sometimes irrelevant interviews:

> **P**—Planning and preparation
> **E**—Engage and explain
> **A**—Account, clarify and challenge
> **C**—Closure
> **E**—Evaluation

Aims and objectives for interviews should be agreed and separated into 'phases' if there are different areas to cover. Separate objectives can be set for each phase, eg if there is DNA evidence to put the suspect with the victim, the aim of the first phase may be to establish whether the suspect denies ever being in contact with the scene or victim. When the DNA evidence is revealed during later phases of the interview, it then makes it more difficult for the suspect to allege innocent contact.

Disclosure items need to be agreed and decided, and the structure and timing of the disclosure process may be crucial for getting the most out of the interviews. Whenever investigative material is put to the suspect (eg witness evidence, DNA, or fingerprint evidence at a scene), the timing, method and wording of any disclosure becomes extremely important. The SIO should consider appointing a separate disclosure officer to deal specifically with all the disclosure for the interview and thus take away this onerous responsibility from the interviewing officers.

It is good practice and sometimes essential to 'downstream' monitor interviews on a visual or audio link, depending on what equipment is available. Suitable custody facilities can be selected that provide the best possible facilities. The SIO and Interview Adviser (if applicable) should be within easy reach of the interview location so that any matters arising or developments can be easily and speedily discussed.

Any interview plan *must remain flexible* throughout the process, which is why the SIO/DSIO needs to be involved in monitoring the process. It may be important to review, restructure and amend the interview plan as things progress because of things said/not said by the suspect or admissions made, or changing attitudes and opportunities. Some training methods tend to focus on delaying all 'challenges' (as per the PEACE model) towards the end of the interview. This may not always be the best approach if there is an opportunity to get a good point across at the right time and maintain the momentum and focus on a particular topic or line of questioning. To summarise, while interviews need to be structured, they should also remain flexible depending on the circumstances and how the interview develops.

KEY POINTS

- Enquiry teams need to be available plus the incident room staff during suspect interviews. Any information obtained can then be researched and fast-track actions allocated. For example, it may be important to speak to witnesses while a suspect is still in custody and prevent collaboration or the concocting of alibis.
- Interview plans remain flexible and adapt to how a suspect is behaving and reacting, allowing good timing for the introduction of key points and investigative material.

12.11.1 Planning and preparation

The planning of a suspect interview takes cognisance of a number of factors. While flexibility is always key, a structure is needed for the interviewers to follow which is agreed by the interview adviser and SIO.

Based on a timeline of events around the incident under investigation, the various planned phases can be split into three periods:

1. BEFORE INCIDENT (relevant time parameters)	2. DURING INCIDENT (relevant time parameters)	3. AFTER INCIDENT (relevant time parameters)
Topics to cover	Topics to cover	Topics to cover
Investigative areas	Investigative areas	Investigative areas

Without these phases, interviewers can stray off track, whereas the structure ensures they remain focused on specific times and events. This is important if it is necessary to compare and contrast accounts from multiple suspects concerning their movements, actions, etc within similar time periods. These periods are explained as follows:

1. Before the incident. Investigative topics to be covered within this phase help establish potential motives and also significant lines of enquiry. This is often referred to as 'background' but it does not always follow that this has to be historical. It may include key dates leading up to the commission of the offence where it is important to investigate the degree of planning that took place. Other topics that could be included are a suspect's lifestyle, associations, character, ownership of items, and use of websites. Relevant topics are identified during the course of the investigation and informed by the nature of what other investigative material has been covered. For example, in the case of forensic samples being recovered from a crime scene, it must be established whether a suspect had legitimate access or been in contact with them prior to the incident.

2. During the incident. This is where an interview usually starts and where a guilty person is most likely to feel uncomfortable. It contains the most significant detail relative to the offence and where accounts need close probing. It is also, of course, the best place to allow early accounts and detail to be introduced by innocent persons. Relevant time parameters might have to be set wide enough to cover this period. Depending on the circumstances, this may include a time that captures events immediately leading up to and coming away from the offence in question.

3. After the incident. Topics relevant within this phase are determined by the timing of the arrest of suspects. For example, if a suspect is arrested at the scene or relatively soon afterwards, there will be no 'after period' as the time parameters for the 'during' phase should incorporate this. However, if there are several days between the commission of the offence and the arrest, then this is a key area to be covered. A suspect may well have made admissions to others; or their activities may generally be significantly different to their normal behaviour; or they may have taken steps to cover up their involvement, eg by disposing of property. In the case of a historical enquiry, this is still an important area but the level of detail that would be expected to be covered will have to be more realistic.

12.11.2 **Initial accounts**

Before a detained suspect is interviewed to an agreed plan and structure, or during the first interview, it is beneficial to ask them what they have to say about the allegation. This provides an early opportunity to offer up an initial explanation and any important information, such as admissions or details that could eliminate them or help identify co-offenders. It is unlikely any 'challenges' will be used during this phase of an interview strategy so very little or no planning is required.

This type of interview is useful if it is going to be some time before a person is formally interviewed, eg if they are arrested spontaneously and an interview plan and team need to be prepared. During the first interview a detained suspect can be given an early opportunity to provide an account (provided it is conducted at a police station under the proper provisions of PACE with a solicitor present, on tape, etc) that could lead to important information being disclosed (which could be to their own benefit as well as the investigation).

KEY POINT

An initial interview of an arrested suspect under PACE at a police station is aimed at giving them an opportunity to provide an early explanation in response to the allegation, which is entirely different from conducting an 'urgent interview'. This may assist not just in implicating but also eliminating them.

12.11.3 Challenges

This is a phase that requires careful thought and planning as to how it is managed and when to introduce it, remembering that remaining flexible is the key to a successful interview. It is where selected investigative material is introduced and the suspect asked for comment and explanation, affording them an opportunity to comment. This should not be an opportunity for case theories or suggestions to be introduced, but can include topics and areas of significance that may be at odds with what has been stated by the suspect. It is important the strength of the material is not misrepresented or overstated and it is made clear to the suspect what is being alleged. For example, it may be an account from a witness, a CCTV image, telephone data or forensics placing a suspect at a crime scene.

12.11.4 Investigative material

Mention of this term has been made frequently within this chapter and other areas of the book. The CPIA definition of 'material' states: 'Material of any kind including information and objects which are obtained in the course of a criminal investigation and which may be relevant to the investigation.' Potential sources from which investigative material can be obtained include:

- victims
- witnesses
- suspects
- locations and crime scenes, eg forensic material

- property recovered from searched premises
- passive data generators, eg CCTV, communication devices, computers, financial records
- intelligence sources.

In a criminal investigation there is usually an intention to seek and gather investigative material to progress the enquiry. If a prosecution follows, this may or may not become evidence. Therefore when dealing with a suspect's legal adviser prior to or during an interview, it is important to resist using the term 'evidence', eg when asked what 'evidence' the enquiry team has that implicates their client in the offence for which they are to be interviewed. This is because at this stage it will be uncertain what will/will not be treated as evidence until formal agreement by the CPS.

KEY POINT

When dealing with a suspect's legal adviser prior to a suspect interview, it is advisable to use the term 'investigative material' as opposed to 'evidence'. This term covers a far wider range of possible sources that may/may not become evidential material used in any subsequent prosecution case.

Checklist—Suspect interviews

- Prioritise and coordinate interviews (multiple suspects).
- Facilitate a briefing and scene familiarisation visit for interviewing officers.
- Agree nature of allegation and any 'points to prove'.
- Have 'suspectology' detail available.
- Consider any requirement for use of interpreters.
- Examine records/tapes of previous interviews with suspect(s).
- Check custody records for relevant information provided by suspect.
- Consider any 'significant statements'/pre-interview comments.
- Consider what investigative material is to be used during interview.
- Consider monitoring of interviews.
- Consider initial interview to gain suspect account.
- Decide on structure and the three phases.
- Determine what disclosure will be provided, how, when and by whom and content and format of pre-interview briefing (legal adviser).

- Determine what exhibits required for interview/sign labels for continuity.

- Review arrest strategy (impact on interview process).

- Note any requirements for 'appropriate adult'/potential mental health issues.

- Consider witnesses (vulnerable/intimidated/significant) and impact on disclosing their evidence.

- Determine method of recording suspect interview (DVD/audio).

- Consider all PACE issues (custody times/refreshment breaks).

- Identify objectives and areas for clarification (ie SIO's agenda).

- Consider use and timing of 'special warnings'.

- Determine 'no comment' or 'prepared statement' interview strategy.

- Have staff and necessary resources on standby for fast-track actions.

- Determine whether separate interview required for evidence of 'bad character' (under 'previous misconduct' provisions of Criminal Justice Act 2003).

Checklist—Post-interview considerations

- Debrief interview team(s).

- Analyse and evaluate interview process.

- Analyse and evaluate information from interview(s).

- Assess what impact any information provided has on the enquiry.

- Ensure any necessary fast-track action(s)/further enquiries allocated.

- Consider and review further interview strategy.

- Consider welfare of suspect/interview team(s).

- Maintain close liaison with/update CPS.

12.11.5 Intelligence interviews

The objective of an intelligence interview is to obtain information about criminal activity other than the offence(s) for which a suspect has been arrested. They do not fall within the PACE definition of an interview and are not conducted under caution or recorded. Most organisations have individual policies for balancing the integrity of an investigation in progress whilst exploiting the opportunity to obtain potentially actionable information from an intelligence interview. Considerations include not conducting the interview until after the investigation phase has concluded, using officers not connected to the investigation (usually intelligence staff or CHIS handlers) and managing the content of the custody record so the safety of a detainee who agrees to an intelligence interview is not compromised.

12.12 **National Investigative Interview Adviser**

In complex cases involving multiple suspects or where witness testimony is likely to be key, the services of the NCA National Investigative Interview Adviser and their cadre of deputies is available. They can provide advice and guidance on the interviewing of suspects, victims and witnesses across a broad range of criminality with particular reference to PACE Codes and national standards. This includes:

- advice and support in establishing interview strategies
- advice and support regarding planning and preparing interviews
- analysis of interviews
- analysis of written statements
- debriefing of overall interview process
- assistance in reviewing interview processes
- assistance in maximising the interview products in subsequent processes.

The adviser works closely with SIOs and interviewing officers to develop bespoke interview strategies. They also contribute to the implementation of the NPCC Investigative Interviewing Strategy, incorporating development of the Professionalising Investigations Programme (PIP), and the delivery of training (email <soc@nca.pnn.police.uk> or tel. 0845 000 5463).

12.13 **Suspect Hunts/Crimes in Action**

Some cases require time, effort and resources in order to locate and arrest known outstanding suspect(s), particularly if there are a large number of offenders and/or the suspect(s) is/are deemed to be dangerous and a high-risk threat. A high-level search for an outstanding suspect may also mean that a 'crime in action' is in progress requiring both reactive and proactive strands to the investigation.

These typically occur in offences such as kidnap and abduction, terrorism, serial homicides, high-risk suspicious missing person enquiries, or serious physical or sexual attacks where multiple victims are targeted. If the offenders pose a high level of risk to public safety, there will be an urgent operational need to quickly trace and arrest the offender(s), if known.[6]

---

[6] Operation Purple Wave in Brentford, West London, in August 2014 was such an example, when missing 14-year-old teenager Alice Gross was murdered by a missing Latvian suspect named Arnis Zalkalns. Neither could be traced after a huge police operation until both the deceased bodies of the victim and the suspect (murder/suicide) were found some weeks later.

These types of incidents are the supreme test due to widespread public and media attention, and can place the designated SIO in the 'eye of a storm'. Early intervention and capture of those who are declared suspects and who place the public and police at high risk needs to be a primary objective to prevent any escalation and commission of further offences. These operations are time-critical and become more intense the longer they continue.

In proactive arrest operations (particularly those engaged in the hunt for dangerous and/or armed suspects) large amounts of assets and resources may be required, such as covert teams, arrest and search teams, firearms tactical intervention teams, intelligence cells, specialist communications data advisers, hostage negotiators, coordinators from other regions, forces and agencies, media advisers and the National Crime Agency. They are major operations that require dynamic consequence management.

A Silver control room with a designated Gold, Silver, Bronze (GSB) command and control structure may be necessary with the SIO (and/or PIP 4) or their nominated deputy playing a key role in all Gold group meetings and decisions and maintaining an involvement in arrest tactics (especially evidence recovery and suspect processing). Such operations require fast-time control, management and rapid decision making with the essential communications structure, case management system and necessary assets and resources at the ready. They usually require plenty of resilience for the host force (maybe even mutual aid) and SIO/DSIO plus enquiry team on 24/7 duties.

Firearms are an added consideration if believed used/carried by the suspect(s), and a firearms tactical adviser and independent accredited firearms Silver Commander will be required to command and manage the tactical firearms operation (and in some instances authorise the use of firearms in spontaneous emergency situations). Planning and preparation for 'strike arrests' must be properly coordinated with the SIO/DSIO working closely alongside the firearms Silver Commander to ensure that evidential needs of the investigation are considered.

KEY POINTS

- If suspects are armed and/or dangerous, public safety is always of paramount importance, followed closely by the safety of officers and then suspects.
- Contingency plans need to be prepared for when arrest(s) are made, such as a nominated hospital for suspects who are in need of treatment and a risk assessment indicates they require an armed round-the-clock police guard to protect them from rivals or vigilante groups (this may also apply to witnesses who need to be protected once an arrest is made).
- Suspect management and evidence collection plans need preparing in anticipation of arrests being made.
- Interview strategies should be pre-prepared to ensure the investigating team is ready to go once the suspect is arrested.

- If a GSB structure is utilised, the SIO should insist on having their role and responsibility (and that of others in the command structure) clearly outlined and agreed, preferably in writing by the Gold Commander, so ensuring there are clear lines of accountability and everyone knows who has responsibility for what.

12.13.1 **Change of mindset**

Crimes in action and high-level suspect hunts amount to an investigation becoming proactive rather than merely reactive. The mindset of the SIO and their enquiry team needs to recognise the subtle change in priorities, as the locating and arrest of the suspect becomes the main priority over and above the preservation and recovery of evidence. Intelligence that can assist in making a speedy arrest may have to take precedence over traditional investigative considerations, such as finding and preserving evidence or conducting forensic tests.

For example, if a mobile phone is recovered the analysis of which could quickly produce useful lines of enquiry to help locate a suspect, then a dynamic decision will be required as to which takes precedence (forensic evidence versus fast-time intelligence). This is where the dynamics change, ie from a traditional reactive investigation. If the public are at risk, the operation becomes a 'fast-time' enquiry and reacting to developments and creating arrest opportunities takes precedence.

In these operations, the SIO adjusts their aims and objectives and adapts to the faster tempo of proactive decision making, actions and requirements (see also Chapter 3.2). Objectives and directives need to be well communicated to staff to ensure everyone is aware of what might be, for some, a different and more dynamic working environment. The objectives should be prominently displayed for everyone to see in order to convey a clear message; there is no luxury of 'slow time' when public safety is in jeopardy.

12.13.2 **Contingency/trigger plans**

If there is a high-level suspect hunt and a crime is in action, then it is best to have a pre-prepared plan for when a suspect is found and detained. This will otherwise occur at the least convenient time when it is more difficult to get hold of key resources. There may be more than one area to cover in the plan, for example forensic recovery, search and seizure. As a general rule there should be at the very least recorded policy and direction as to what a development should trigger as and when it arises. This may include:

Checklist—Contingency plan

- SIO/DSIO to be notified immediately.

- Rapid deployment and effective management of suspect detention and associated evidence gathering, samples and preservation.

- Scene(s) to be identified, secured and preserved, confirmed and quality assured by a CSI supervisor (CSM).

- Implementation of pre-arranged physical search and forensic examination.

- Communications strategy and media liaison plan.

- Exploitation of any fast-track evidence-gathering opportunities such as CCTV.

- Initial suspect interview plan (eg emergency interview to save life).

- Early H-2-H enquiries.

- Community impact assessment.

- Notify/brief FLOs (where appropriate).

- Brief PIP 3/Gold Commander.

References

ACPO, *Practice Advice on Core Investigative Doctrine*, 2nd edn (NPIA, 2012), 105
Teers, R 'Deaths during or following police contact: statistics for England and Wales 2013/14', IPCC research and statistics series: Paper 27 (2014)

13

Witness Management

13.1 **Introduction**

Witnesses are one of the most vital assets to an investigation and their evidence can play a significant role in the outcome of a case. The term 'witness' relates to anybody, except a suspected offender, who is likely to give evidence at court. However, the definition is not restricted to direct eye or ear witnesses; it can include those who provide circumstantial evidence to implicate or eliminate suspects and testimonies provided by professional and expert witnesses.

Victims can also be witnesses if they provide valuable information about crimes committed against them. A person reporting a crime should always be treated as a potential witness, as should call takers/handlers and initial responders who may be the very first to corroborate, see, hear or receive vital evidence at an early stage in the investigation (ie 'golden hours').

Encouraging members of the general public to step forward and provide testimonies, however, is not always straightforward. Fear and mistrust can be difficult barriers and perceptions to overcome, particularly if there is little or no chance of finding evidence from other sources such as forensics. Any assistance from willing witnesses must therefore be managed carefully so as not to lose their willing cooperation. This chapter covers some of those important processes.

KEY POINT

Witnesses are defined in s 63 of the Youth Justice and Criminal Evidence (YJCE) Act 1999 and s 52 of the Domestic Violence, Crime and Victim's Act 2004 as: 'any person called, or proposed to be called to give evidence in the proceedings.'

13.2 **Tracing Witnesses**

A main line of enquiry is usually to capitalise on all opportunities to trace, interview and take statements (TI/TST) from witnesses. Influential factors are likely to be the circumstances, location, timing of the incident and type of victim, offender and community. This information indicates the type of witness likely to be available and where they might be found. For example, offences that occur in the early hours of the morning may point towards delivery staff, night workers, party-goers, taxi drivers and trades people who are likely to be around at that time of the day.

Like any other area of investigation, a degree of initiative and skill is required. One of the core competencies of an investigator is the ability to communicate with different sorts of people and diverse communities (see also Chapter 9) in order to root out facts and information and win their trust. This may occur at crime scenes, during general enquiries, on visits to houses, shops and premises, over the phone, on social media sites, or during overt activities—basically at every opportunity. Each case is different, but the principles are the same; investigators must be encouraged to remain proactive and alert in looking for opportunities to find, communicate with and obtain evidence from witnesses.

Scientific methods are available that can assist in identifying witness-seeking opportunities, such as analysing association charts to indicate people and places linked to victims and suspects. Anonymous reports from people who have offered information can also be examined closely—for example, when listening to recorded calls directed into enquiry teams for background clues on likely identities or places of origin. Some witnesses make contact and withhold information until they gain sufficient confidence, eg stating they have 'heard something' when they have actually witnessed it.

KEY POINT

Activities to trace witnesses must begin quickly when people are willing and cooperative, events still fresh in their minds and their evidence uncontaminated. Feeling strongly about what they know or have witnessed may reduce over time or if third-party bad influences dissuade them.

Checklist—Witness identification tactics

- During initial response phase (including briefing officers engaged on crime scene cordons for potential witness approaches). If details refused, descriptions should be noted (including vehicles) to help trace them or use questionnaires (pro formas) to record details when there are large numbers to manage.

- Deploying evidence-gathering/mobile visual units at scenes to record those present, particularly where large numbers are involved.

- Checking journalists/media reporters/websites for witness indications with uploaded information or pictures.

- Members of public who may record and upload details of incidents from their phone/cameras onto social media forums.

- Making appeals and giving out positive messages and reassurance about safeguarding welfare and confidentiality.

- Publicising a public hotline, contact method/number/website.

- Using programs that can identify who is active on social media platforms and commenting about incidents under investigation.

- Appeals through other means, eg at public meetings, high-visibility patrolling, street briefings/surgeries, distributing posters, leaflet drops and electronic billboards (in appropriate languages).

- Conducting house-to-house (H-2-H) enquiries.

- Conducting TIE enquiries (may reveal witnesses as well as suspects).

- Passive data collection (eg CCTV, ANPR, body-worn/vehicle-mounted cameras).

- Checking financial transactions in specific areas to see who might have been present (eg using ATM machines or making purchases).

- Enquiries in local public places (eg shops, bars, transport routes to/from scene)

- Locating a mobile incident vehicle at or near an important location/scene.

- Staging reconstructions, road checks or anniversary events as appeals.

- Using cognitive prompts (eg offence occurred when important sporting event played, or at time of popular TV programmes).

- Via a family liaison strategy (see Chapter 11).

- Community liaison, local officers and partner agencies.

- Intelligence gathering (eg use of covert human intelligence source (HUMINT/CHIS) tasking).

- Placing markers on records of potential witnesses.

- Searching premises or important sites and locations.

- Analysing related incident logs and messages, listening to call-handling recordings and having them transcribed to ensure all detail is analysed.

- Tracing anonymous callers.

- Challenging allegiances to explore opportunities with a view to potentially changing them (eg partners or associates of suspects).

- Offering rewards.

13.2.1 **Offenders as witnesses (SOCPA)**

Witnesses can sometimes be found amongst offenders and defendants. Sections 71 to 75 of the Serious Organised Crime and Police Act 2005 (SOCPA) provide useful legal options for using persons who are offenders to support a prosecution case. These options are: These options are:

- Section 71—granting a conditional immunity from prosecution for assistance.
- Section 72—providing a 'restricted use undertaking' option for information an individual provides for a prosecution or investigation.
- Section 73—powers for a court when sentencing persons who plead guilty to take account of their undertaking to assist an investigation or prosecution.
- Section 74—powers for the person sentenced to be referred back to court for discounted sentence when they assist an investigation or prosecution.
- Section 75—when sentencing under s 74 courts can exclude people from court or impose reporting restrictions.

These sections are often used for offenders who provide evidence against the higher pedigree of serious and organised criminals or terrorism groups. Interviews with 'assisting offenders' is a highly specialised area. Close consultation with nominated high-level Crown Prosecution Service (CPS) personnel, risk assessments, resource- and cost-benefit analysis and detailed planning[1] are required.

13.3 **Offering Rewards**

Consideration of offering a reward to the public for information, either by the police or following a request from a third party, eg a news agency, is used in some situations. This is only likely to happen in the most serious and grave cases, particularly if they remain unresolved.

Every case has to be judged on its own merits, and before embarking on a reward policy the SIO must fully appreciate the pitfalls. An obvious one is the impact this could have on the credibility of the witness if they were to claim the reward. The value of their evidence would have to be balanced against a motive of seeking financial reward, which would be heavily scrutinised and could have an adverse effect on their motives and integrity.

The CPS should be consulted in every case where a reward is considered or offered or indeed claimed, clearly outlining the criteria stipulated for payment and the full circumstances of how the witness came forward. This also applies to any payment made to informants should they later become prosecution witnesses.

All policy decisions made around the use of rewards must be clear and transparent, recognising all the pros and cons of using the tactic and how they are

---

[1] The UK National Crime Agency has a dedicated 'debriefing' unit that can be consulted for advice and guidance when considering using this useful piece of legislation.

managed. It must be proved beyond all reasonable doubt that the highest professional and ethical standards have been applied—for example, clear details being outlined as to what criteria must be met before a reward payment is considered, which is usually for information leading to the arrest and conviction of the offender. Also, details will be required of when a payment will be made: usually not until the conclusion of all court proceedings, including appeals.

Whenever the tactic is used, the motives of the witness claiming the reward are always going to come under close scrutiny, as well as their honesty and credibility. Where such witness claims a reward, this fact **must** be disclosed to the prosecutor, who makes a decision about how it is to be accounted for and disclosed to the court.[2]

KEY POINT

Offering rewards sometimes has the potential for motivating people to provide inaccurate, misleading or false information that may undermine an investigation. The best approach is to proceed with caution when using the tactic and seek corroboration wherever possible.

13.4 Initial Contact and Accounts

Making initial contact with witnesses is not confined to the early stages of an enquiry and might occur at any phase of an investigation, for example during historical or 'cold' cases. Members of the investigation team and any other staff who come into (initial) contact with witnesses must fully appreciate the impact of their actions, attitude, behaviour and approach (communication) style. First impressions count immensely and do influence how a witness perceives they will be treated and dealt with, maybe even unsettling them and their decision to help and cooperate. It may take a long time to win back someone's faith and trust if they have a bad experience at the hands of the first investigator they come into contact with. This point must be stressed to all staff engaged on the enquiry team.

Procedures for interviewing certain categories of witnesses and victims may require the use of special facilities and recording equipment. These interviews, however, cannot always be arranged instantaneously, as trained staff and resources may not be readily available, but delays should not prevent witnesses/

---

[2] See *R v Rowe, Davis and Johnson*, aka 'The M25 three', Times Law Report 25 July 2000. The three defendants successfully appealed against their convictions for murder, causing grievous bodily harm and several robberies on the night of 15–16 December 1988. In the original trial the prosecution case had failed to disclose that a reward had been paid to the main prosecution witness (Duncan) who was also initially treated as a police informant.

victims from providing valuable initial accounts. This enables an assessment of their information and contributes to a decision on what category and status they might be assigned (ie significant, intimidated or vulnerable). Their information may also be needed quickly to help in identifying crucial high-priority lines of enquiry/fast-track actions, such as the arrest of an offender or identification of crime scenes. More detailed and factual accounts can be obtained later with pre-planning.

First accounts given by witnesses need to be recorded accurately and, wherever possible, should be signed. This is often during the initial response phase when people are first spoken to by officers attending the scene or during searches or H-2-H enquiries, in which case potential witnesses should be separated to preserve the integrity of their evidence.

If official documentation is unavailable or impractical to use, then accurate notes or a detailed pocket-notebook entry should be made and signed by the interviewee. This information will be needed by subsequent interviewing teams, prior to conducting the witness interview, and referred to in any subsequent statement or witness account. There will be a requirement to carefully check for inconsistencies or alterations with the initial account. This is particularly important in relation to any description or identification of suspects and vehicles or words spoken and comments made.

If first accounts are recorded by response officers on body-worn video cameras (BWVs), it is important these recordings are properly reviewed **before** making decisions about matters like witness categorisation, lines of enquiry, etc.

KEY POINTS

- Obtaining initial accounts complies with the 'best evidence' rule and golden-hour principle. The longer the gap between incident and interview, the more chance there is for recollections to become contaminated, eg from news reports or discussions with third parties.
- Initial accounts, accurately recorded, can be obtained by using open questions without much prompting or probing (eg 'Tell me…', 'Explain…', or 'Describe…'). These types of questions minimise the risk of the interviewer influencing what the interviewee has to say.
- Discrepancies between initial accounts and more formal witness interviews must be identified, as they can undermine reliability and accuracy.

13.5 **Background Enquiries**

It is beneficial to know what a witness's background is to see if there is anything that could affect their reliability or credibility. This process has come to be known as 'witness-ology' in the same way as 'victim-ology' or 'suspect-ology'. An example might be where a witness has previously made false accusations or allegations, or has numerous convictions for dishonesty. It is best to know this information in advance to determine the likely significance of a person's evidence and before any judicial proceedings that might follow.

If there is any doubt as to credibility or motive, seeking independent corroboration is one solution. Another is to make an objective assessment of the evidence details to determine if the witness is providing special or particular knowledge that only they could have known through an honest and trustworthy observation.

If a witness is a specialist who is required to give expert opinion, it is important to know how they have 'performed' in other judicial cases, ie under cross-examination, and whether any adverse or praiseworthy comments were made by a trial judge or reported in the media or by the case officers. Fortunately, the UK has the benefit of the Specialist Operations Centre (within NCA) that maintains an Expert Adviser's Database containing information about registered 'experts' in a large variety of disciplines. This includes details of any previous cases they have been involved with, and their credibility and reputation as a witness from the viewpoint of investigators who have knowledge of them.

13.6 **Protecting Witnesses**

Some cases have witnesses whose evidence is critical and who are likely to be at substantial risk of harm. If so, a duty of care is owed and most forces, the NCA and some local authorities have in place arrangements for offering support to witnesses, which operate on a sliding scale depending on the perceived level of threat. Witnesses, however, should never be offered any incentive, inducement or guarantee to provide a statement of evidence on promise of special treatment. Support provided must not significantly increase their current living standards.

Witness support measures are highly confidential and cannot be explained in any detail. However, when considering potential candidates for a support scheme, an SIO may wish to consider the following:

- Gravity of their testimony.
- Whether they contributed to their own predicament.
- Background and make-up of their family.
- Threat—whether 'real' or 'perceived'.
- Whether they or their immediate family have a criminal record.
- Level of support required and who it includes (eg extended family).

Expert advice should be sought from specialists on witness protection tactics, at the earliest opportunity. Witness support units usually require a structured assessment and application process, due to resource and financial implications that could potentially, in extreme cases, extend over the lifetime of the witness.

Victims who are also witnesses may need support from an appropriate victim support scheme. Support may also be required for witnesses who are 'secondary victims' because of the traumatic effects of what they have seen.

13.6.1 **Offering protection**

As a general rule, investigators do not openly comment on particular tactics for protection that have been provided for witnesses or concerning any operational element of witness support. To do so would risk compromising sensitive tactics and the very people whom the arrangements have been designed to protect.

However, public statements contained within a communications strategy can reinforce a commitment to protecting witnesses aimed at encouraging people to have confidence in coming forward. It is advisable to seek advice beforehand from an expert such as a Media Liaison Officer (MLO) or Witness Protection Officer who can assist on the most suitable wording. SIOs should aim to send out a positive message of how they and the investigating/prosecuting authorities are jointly committed to supporting witnesses and victims, and, if appropriate, mention some well-known local cases where this has been highly successful.

13.6.2 **Anonymity orders**

Part 3, sections 74 to 97 of the Coroners and Justice Act 2009 (CJA), Chapter 25, which came into effect on 12 November 2009, allows for the application to a court for an 'Investigation Anonymity Order'. This is an order made by a Justice of the Peace (JP) in relation to a specified person prohibiting the disclosure of information:

(a) that identifies the specified person as one who is or was able or willing to assist a specified qualifying criminal investigation; or
(b) that might enable the specified person to be identified as such.

Qualifying offences

An offence is a qualifying offence for these purposes if it relates to either (a) murder, or (b) manslaughter, and the death was caused by one or both of the following:

(a) shot with a firearm;
(b) injured with a knife.

Under the Act it is an offence for a person to disclose information in contravention of an Investigation Anonymity Order and a person guilty of this offence is liable on conviction on indictment to imprisonment for a term not exceeding five years or a fine, or both. A person who discloses information to which an Investigation Anonymity Order relates does not contravene the order if:

(a) disclosure is made to a person who is involved in the specified qualifying criminal investigation or in the prosecution of an offence to which the investigation relates
(b) disclosure is made for the purposes of the investigation or the prosecution of an offence to which the investigation relates
(c) disclosure is in pursuance of a requirement imposed by any enactment or rule of law
(d) disclosure is made in pursuance of an order of a court.

Conditions for making an order

A JP (Justice of the Peace) may make an 'Investigation Anonymity Order' if satisfied that a qualifying offence has been committed and there are reasonable grounds for believing that the following conditions are satisfied:

(a) The person likely to have committed the qualifying offence is a person who was aged at least 11 but under 30 at the time the offence was committed.
(b) The person is likely to have been a member of a group engaged in criminal activities in which it appears that the majority of the persons in the group are aged at least 11 but under 30 at the time the offence was committed.
(c) The person specified in the order has reasonable grounds for fearing intimidation or harm if identified as a person who is or was able or willing to assist the criminal investigation.
(d) The person specified in the order is:
  (i) able to provide information that would assist the criminal investigation as it relates to the qualifying offence; and
  (ii) is more likely than not, as a consequence of the making of the order, to provide such information.

Witness Anonymity Orders are different from Investigation Anonymity Orders, but fall under the same Act. They are an order by a court that requires specific measures in relation to witnesses in criminal proceedings. This is to ensure the identity of the witness is not disclosed during or in connection with court proceedings. The kinds of measures that may be required in relation to a witness include one or more of the following:

(a) The witness's name and other identifying details may be:
  (i) withheld; and/or
  (ii) removed from materials disclosed to any party to the proceedings.
(b) The witness uses a pseudonym.

(c) No questions are asked that might lead to the identification of the witness.

(d) The witness is screened to any specified extent.

(e) The witness's voice is subjected to modulation.

(f) The order will not allow the witness to be screened so that they cannot be seen by:

    (i)   the judge or other members of the court (if any), or

    (ii) the jury (if there is one).

KEY POINTS

- If anonymity measures are used, careful management of information within the enquiry team and management systems such as HOLMES is required to ensure the measures and identities are not compromised.
- A Witness Anonymity Order is required in addition to an Investigation Anonymity Order if it is necessary for the witness to give evidence in court.

13.7 Reluctant Witnesses

A reluctant witness is one who has evidence to offer but is reluctant to do so for a variety of reasons, eg communities where there is a mistrust of the police or where there is fear, hard-to-reach minorities, language and cultural barriers or vulnerable persons. Criminal groups and organised crime gangs (OCGs) can make it highly risky for genuine witnesses to come forward. Alternatively, witnesses may just have a lack of understanding of what is involved in being a witness or be reticent due to witness apathy—a 'not wishing to get involved' attitude.

For those who are in fear of intimidation, an approach needs to be planned and executed that demonstrates an unquestionable intent to safeguard their welfare and eliminate any potential for compromise. This can be achieved by using effective measures and tradecraft, eg similar to those used in CHIS (informant) handling by arranging covert meeting places and not visiting their home addresses. Such measures, once adopted, however, must be recorded within a 'sensitive' policy file to ensure confidentiality and security and maintain the integrity of the process.

Staff with good interpersonal communication skills can be selected to approach and 'handle' reluctant witnesses, and these attributes will make all the difference in securing cooperation. Careful thought and planning, together with research of the individuals concerned, their background, previous dealings with the police, finding someone they have trusted before, etc is beneficial. Trusted third parties, such as community leaders, members of independent advisory groups (IAGs), family, friends and relatives or local authority support units, for example, can sometimes help break down barriers of mistrust or apprehension.

KEY POINT

A record and audit trail of all policies, tactics, approaches and contact with witnesses is essential to avoid any transgression or breach of process accusation. It is optional to use a separate policy file or log for each witness, including a sequential record of events of all dealings and communications between them and the enquiry team.

13.7.1 Summonses and warrants

As an extreme measure, paragraph 4 of Schedule 3 to the Crime and Disorder Act 1998 provides a power to bring reluctant witnesses before a magistrates' court either by summons or warrant, to make a deposition before the court. This should only be considered in exceptional cases where:

1. A person is already charged with the offence in question.
2. The witness has provided information that is of value to the prosecution case but has refused to provide a witness statement.
3. The procedure does not place them at unacceptable risk if the evidence is produced, which cannot be mitigated by special measures (eg anonymity, screens).

13.7.2 Hostile witnesses

Hostile witnesses are those who are believed to have witnessed an offence, part of an offence or events closely connected with it, but who are opposed to assisting the investigation process.[3] This could be due to their lifestyle, criminality, relationship with the alleged offender and/or intention to appear as a defence team witness. Some hostile witnesses simply refuse to cooperate, whilst others may provide false or misinformation intended to support a false account or mislead the police enquiry.

Where a hostile witness consents to be interviewed, it can be recorded in accordance with the significant witness procedure. Where a hostile witness claims not to have any information to assist the investigation, every effort should be made to record this in a witness statement. These 'negative' statements can become useful if the person or their evidence later resurfaces.

13.8 Treating Witnesses as Crime Scenes

Some victims and witnesses have to be treated as crime scenes. For example, if they come into close contact with offenders or evidential items (eg vehicles or

---

[3] Ministry of Justice, *Achieving Best Evidence in Criminal Proceedings: Guidance on Interviewing Victims and Witnesses, and using Special Measures* (Office for Criminal Justice Reform, 2011), para 2.144.

weapons) or there is any potential for the cross-transfer of material such as fibres, DNA, fingerprints or body fluids. This includes occasions where witnesses attempt to detain offenders, or come into close contact with them before or after an offence is committed.

> **KEY POINT**
>
> When a witness is treated as a crime scene any examination or seizure of clothing or possessions needs to done tactfully, in order to maintain their willing support and cooperation.

13.9 **Investigative Interviewing**

Investigative interviewing relates to the process of witness (and suspect) interviews that are professionally undertaken and recorded to realise several benefits. This type of interviewing can:

- direct an investigation (leading to a prosecution of offender(s) or the release of an innocent person)
- support a prosecution case
- increase public confidence in, and credibility of, the investigating team
- prevent the loss of critical material.

SIOs need to consider the (dis)advantages of, and necessity for, recording (DVD or audio) particular interviews with certain categories of witnesses. This is because it safeguards the integrity of the process, allows the witness to recall freely the events without interruption and provides the investigation, and ultimately the judicial system, with a 'best evidence' product. It may also provide strong and compelling evidence in cases where a witness later becomes a suspect. On the negative side, it can prove resource-intensive and time-consuming.

13.9.1 **Interview advisers**

Good use can be made of the cadre of UK nationally accredited interview advisers and they are best involved at the earliest opportunity. An adviser can help determine appropriate strategies and methods to conduct interviews and guide policy decisions on correct categorisation of witness and their interviews. They help take some responsibility away from the SIO by 'managing the process' in a similar way to how, say, a Crime Scene Manager (CSM), would oversee scene examinations. An adviser should also be able to help select appropriate staff for conducting interviews, manage and support them throughout the process. As always, final decisions around policy and tactics always rest with the SIO.

Those selected to conduct interviews with witnesses should be trained to PIP level 2 within the corresponding National Occupational Standards (NOS) competency framework. Consideration should be given to the appropriate competence, background and experience of those chosen, having regard to the nature of the offence under investigation and any individual welfare issues that may arise (eg child death investigations, domestic violence).

KEY POINT

SIOs should satisfy themselves that interviews are being conducted to their own requirements and remain in full control of the process. 'Advisers' are there to do just that—any final decision rests with the SIO.

13.9.2 Witness interview strategies

A witness interview strategy is a high-level overview of the policy, objectives and process in the context of the overall investigation. It is not to be confused with an interview plan, which is more tactical in nature. The strategy is usually discussed and agreed through extensive consultations between the SIO, Interview Adviser and trained interviewers.

A general witness interview strategy should be adequate to cover most witness interviews in any enquiry, the components of which are:

1. Witness categorisation:
   - Vulnerable.
   - Intimidated.
   - Significant.
   - Other (ie none of the above).
2. Management of initial contact:
   - Purpose (eg to obtain initial brief account or to aid categorisation).
   - Process of initial contact (eg under ABE guidelines).
   - Relevant briefing material (eg source of witness information, such as message form).
3. Method and rationale for prioritising interviews:
   - Witnesses to be referred to interview adviser for assessment of their importance (particularly if multiple witnesses).
4. Method for coordinating interviews:
   - Strategies for minimising repeat interviews (eg within small communities or types of witness, such as taxi drivers, sex workers, etc).
5. Resources:
   - Skills of interviewers accessible to enquiry team.
   - Location and means of gaining access to interview suites and portable recording equipment (if required).

Circumstances may arise in which a more specific strategy needs to be developed for an individual witness. Such a strategy tends to be the result of either:

(a) likely nature of their evidence (eg importance to the investigation, inconsistencies with other material, reluctance or hostility); or

(b) specific issues that have an impact on the ability of interviewers to communicate with them (eg young, traumatised, incapacitated, learning disabled, speech and language difficulties).

The components of a specific witness interview strategy are:

1. Witness assessment:
   - Category or categories the witness falls into (significant/key, vulnerable, intimidated, other).
   - Issues likely to have an impact on capacity of the witness to give informed consent to an interview.
   - Likely significance of the witness's account (based on initial information and assessment).
   - Extent to which witness is likely to be cooperative, reluctant or hostile.
   - Any practical considerations (eg medical/psychological condition).
2. Sources of advice:
   - Subject-matter experts.
   - People who know the witness well.
   - CPS in context of 'early special measures discussion'.
3. Information important to the investigation:
   - Matters of general investigative practice, including:
     — comprehensive account from the witness
     — points to prove
     — case law (eg *R v Turnbull and Camello* (1976) 63 Cr App R 132)
     — other people present at time of incident
     — anything said by witness to third party after incident.
   - Case-specific material, including:
     — probable location of any items used in commission of offence (if known by the witness)
     — significant evidential inconsistencies or omissions
     — nature and background of any relationship—witness and suspect
     — anything that might enhance or detract from credibility of witnesses account (eg alcohol or drugs consumed)
     — information regarding likely witness intimidation
     — background information to support a 'bad character' application (subject to the necessary gateway provision with the consent of the trial judge)
     — anything specific to the nature of the incident.

> **KEY POINT**
>
> Some types of incident may highlight specific areas to cover with witnesses. For example, fire investigation experts might wish to establish if a witness saw any flames and if so what colour they were, if any popping or banging noises were heard, what colour and direction the smoke was blowing in, if any doors or windows were seen open or any smoke alarms heard.

13.9.3 **PEACE model**

The PEACE model of interviewing remains the recognised framework for conducting interviews with victims, witnesses and those suspected of offences. It has been around since 1992 and has a proven track record. It provides a structure to stages of the interview process. The acronym stands for:

> **P**—Planning and preparation
> **E**—Engage and explain
> **A**—Account, clarify and challenge
> **C**—Closure
> **E**—Evaluation

13.10 **Witness Categories**

Witnesses are generally divided into one or more of the following groups, which dictates how interviews should be recorded as well as any consequences for how evidence may be given during any future trial process:

1. Significant/key.[4]
2. Vulnerable (YJCE, section 16).
3. Intimidated (YJCE, section 17).
4. Other (Criminal Justice Act 1967, section 9).

13.10.1 **Significant/key witnesses**

Significant witnesses (aka 'SigWits'), sometimes referred to as 'key' witnesses, are the category most likely to be encountered during investigations. It is a function and the responsibility of the SIO to identify and/or confirm those witnesses to be afforded 'SigWit' status. This decision is recorded and incorporated within an overall witness strategy. In some cases, it may also be necessary to explain why a witness has *not* been granted 'SigWit' status to pre-empt questions which may arise later.

---

[4] Ministry of Justice, *Achieving Best Evidence in Criminal Proceedings: Guidance on Interviewing Victims and Witnesses, and Guidance on Using Special Measures* (Office for Criminal Justice Reform, 2011).

KEY POINT—DEFINITION OF SIGNIFICANT WITNESS

Significant witnesses are defined in ABE[5] as those who:

(i) Have or claim to have witnessed, visually or otherwise, an *indictable offence*, part of such an offence or events closely connected with it (including any incriminating comments made by the suspected offender either before or after the offence); and/or

(ii) Have a particular relationship to the victim or have a central position in an investigation into an indictable offence.

There is *no* statutory provision for recorded interviews with significant witnesses to be played as evidence-in-chief; however, this does not prevent defence teams from asking a court for permission to play some or all of the recording in support of their case, eg to challenge the integrity of the process.

There can be a temptation to concentrate on obvious types of witnesses who may fall into this category, such as one who actually sees a crime in the act of being committed. There may be other suitable recipients for this status who are less obvious, such as initial emergency responders to a crime scene, who may observe important events and circumstances. However, the category still needs to be used and applied sensibly. Interviewing a large number of witnesses as 'significant' can be time-consuming and resource-intensive. Having numerous witness products to transcribe and reproduce in documentary format can have a detrimental impact on the enquiry team and hinder the management system from keeping pace with a fast-moving enquiry.

KEY POINT

SigWit interviews can take time to transcribe in order to produce a useful product. One solution is to request the production of investigative interview summaries soon after interviews have concluded to assist in providing sufficient details of what a witness has said.

Significant witness interviews are visually (ie DVD) recorded unless the witness refuses consent. Alternatively, they may be interviewed on audio-recording equipment, also with consent. If both methods of recording are refused, written notes and a statement may be taken, including an explanation that the interviewee has refused visual and audio recording with accompanying reasons.

As the recording cannot be used as evidence-in-chief, evidential material captured needs to be transferred into a format acceptable to the courts, usually in a Criminal Justice Act, section 9 witness statement (Form MG11). This is done by reviewing the recording and compiling a statement to be read and signed by the witness. This should be completed as soon as possible after the

---

[5] Ministry of Justice, *Achieving Best Evidence in Criminal Proceedings: Guidance on Interviewing Victims and Witnesses, and using Special Measures* (Office for Criminal Justice Reform, 2011), para 1.25.

interview to avoid the witness being unduly influenced prior to reading and signing. The signing process does not require recording unless new or changed information is revealed.

The purpose of the SigWit interviewing process is to preserve and protect the *integrity* and *accuracy* of the process, rebutting suggestions that the witness may have been unduly influenced or coerced. They should also allow for an increase in the amount and quality of information gained from a witness. The only occasions when pre-recorded visual evidence can be used as evidence-in-chief is when the witness meets the definition of 'vulnerable' or 'intimidated', and playing the video will enhance the quality of their evidence. However, on some occasions a significant witness may feasibly change status, moving into either of these categories and then become eligible for consideration of special measures, as explained later.

13.10.2 **Vulnerable witnesses**

Vulnerable witnesses are those defined by virtue of their personal characteristics as recommended in *Speaking up for Justice*,[6] plus those defined as vulnerable as a result of their youth.

KEY POINT—DEFINITION OF VULNERABLE WITNESS

Defined by section 16 of the Youth Justice and Criminal Evidence Act 1999[7] (YJCE):

- Child witnesses (under 18 years).[8]
- Suffering from a mental disorder (as defined by the Mental Health Act 1983, as amended by the Mental Health Act 2007).
- Significant impairment of intelligence/social functioning (learning disability).
- Suffering from physical disability.

Courts must take account of the views of the witness in determining whether they fall into this category. In addition, when determining whether the quality of the witness's evidence is likely to be diminished in these circumstances, the court has to consider the likely completeness, coherence and accuracy of that evidence (YJCE, section 16(5)).

---

[6] Home Office, *Speaking up for Justice* (HM Stationery Office, 1998).
[7] As amended by the Coroners and Justice Act 2009.
[8] Section 16 of the YJCA defines a witness as being under the age of 18 years.

Child witnesses (under 18 years by virtue of section 98 of the CJA) are auto-matically 'vulnerable' due to their age. A previous sub-category of 'child wit-nesses in need of special protection' relating to sexual and violence offences has been removed, meaning all witnesses under 18 years of age are on an equal footing regardless of the offence. Section 100 of the CJA amended sections 21 and 22 of the YJCE by making it a rebuttable presumption that a child witness will give their evidence-in-chief by means of a pre-recorded interview and that they will be cross-examined via live television link.

Subject to the permission of the court, a child witness may now 'opt out' of giving their evidence by video recorded interview or by live link or both. If they do so, there is a presumption that the child witness will give their evidence from behind a screen.

13.10.3 Intimidated witnesses

Complaints in cases of sexual assault fall into this category (by virtue of section 17(4) of YJCE), as in these types of cases there is the likelihood a victim will know their offender. Also included here might be those who witness specified gun and knife offences (section 17(5) as inserted by the CJA) and other cases, such as domestic violence, stalking, crimes motivated by race, religion, homophobia and those which are gang-related or involve repeat victims or vulnerable persons. Some families of homicide (or other serious crimes) victims might also fall into this category by virtue of the *Code of Practice for Victims of Crime*.[9]

KEY POINT—DEFINITION OF INTIMIDATED WITNESS

Section 17 of the YJCE defines intimidated witnesses as;

Those whose quality of evidence is likely to be diminished by reason of fear or distress owing to:
- Nature and alleged circumstances of the offence
- Age of the witness.
- Where relevant:
  — Social and cultural background and ethnic origins
  — Domestic and employment circumstances
  — Religious beliefs or political opinions of the witness.
- Behaviour towards the witness by:
  — Accused
  — Members of accused person's family or associates
  — Any other person who is likely to be either an accused person, or a witness in the proceedings.

---

[9] Ministry of Justice, *Code of Practice for Victims of Crime* (HM Stationery Office, 2015).

Section 101 of the CJA gives complainants to sexual offences greater access to visually recorded evidence-in-chief in Crown Courts (not magistrates' courts), but each case must be considered individually and no assumptions made. Some complainants to sexual offences may prefer to give evidence from behind a screen so the defendant cannot see them on the video link; others may prefer to see the alleged offender in open court.

13.10.4 Special measures

The Court of Appeal judgment in the case of *R v R* (2008) EWCA Crim 678 overturned the phased implementation timetable for special measures for vulnerable (YJCE, section 16) and intimidated (YJCE, section 17) witnesses as set out in Part 2 of YJCE, notably visually recorded evidence-in-chief and live TV link.

The effect of the judgment is that *vulnerable* and *intimidated* witnesses are both now eligible for the following special measures in magistrates' (including youth) courts and Crown Courts:

- Use of screens (section 23).
- Live TV link (section 24).
- Giving evidence in private (section 25).
- Removal of wigs and gowns (section 26).
- Use of visually recorded interview as evidence-in-chief (section 27).[10]

Vulnerable witnesses are also eligible for the following special measures:

- Communication through intermediaries (section 29).
- Use of special communication aids (section 30).

The legislation suggests that access to special measures depends on a three-stage test:

1. Whether the witness fits the definition of either vulnerable or intimidated.
2. Whether any of the special measures are likely to improve the quality of the witness's evidence.
3. Which of the available special measures (or combination) are most likely to improve the quality of the witness's evidence.

Even though some witnesses may be eligible for these measures, different witnesses have different needs. It is a matter of judgement and ultimately for the court to decide, based on a consideration of these needs, as well as the circumstances of the alleged offence and the interests of justice as to which special measures may be appropriate in any given case.

---

[10] Section 28 video-recorded cross-examination is in the pilot stage and may be rolled out in due course.

13.10.5 Early special measures discussions

The CPS should be informed of the potential need to make an application for special measures through an 'early special measures discussion'. This used to be called a 'meeting', but it has been recognised that it does not need to happen in person and can be, for instance, over a phone or other communications link. Practical guidance in relation to early special measures discussions is described in CPS guidance.[11]

Early special measures discussions consider how such witness evidence will be presented to the court. It is important these discussions take place either before or as soon after the interview as possible, so that a Criminal Justice Act statement can be prepared while the witness's memory remains fresh if it is decided not to proceed with an application to play the visual recording as their evidence-in-chief. Preparing a statement at a later stage risks exposing the witness to unnecessary anxiety and could be counter-productive, as some of their information may become distorted due to memory fade or contamination as time passes.

13.10.6 Visually recorded interviews as evidence-in-chief

The use of visually recorded interviews as evidence-in-chief (YJCE, section 27) is not routine practice and should be viewed as an exception rather than the rule. The overarching aim is to maximise the quality of the witness evidence, and in some cases this might mean that other special measures, such as live evidence-in-chief from behind a screen via television link, will be of more assistance.

Where an interview is visually recorded with a view to being played as evidence-in-chief, consideration should also be given to the guidance set out in *Advice on the Structure of Visually Recorded Witness Interviews*.[12]

KEY POINT

If eligible, a court must determine whether any of the special measures would be likely to *improve the quality of the witness's evidence*. If so, the court must then decide which of those measures, or combination of them, would be likely to *maximise the quality of the evidence*. In arriving at its decision, the court must take account of the witness's own views and the possibility that the measure might inhibit the evidence being tested effectively.

---

[11] <http://www.cps.gov.uk/publications/docs/best_evidence_in_criminal_proceedings.pdf>.
[12] ACPO, *Advice on the Structure of Visually Recorded Witness Interviews* (National Strategic Steering Group for Investigative Interviewing, 2013).

13.11 **Witness Intermediaries**

An intermediary is a communications specialist who the court approves to communicate to a witness questions that the court, the prosecution and the defence team may ask and to communicate the answers that the witness gives in response. Intermediaries can assist at all stages of the criminal justice process from police investigations and interviews, through pre-trial preparations for court to the trial. They provide communication assistance in the investigation stage.

Checklist—Role of witness intermediaries

- Assist in victim and witness interviews and trials when a witness has limited expressive and/or receptive communication abilities as a result of age or disability.

- Evaluate the abilities and needs of the witness and establish rapport with them.

- Provide advice on how to obtain best evidence from the witness (eg types of questions to avoid, types of questions most likely to elicit an accurate response, duration of the interview, frequency of breaks from questioning).

- Directly assist in the questioning process by asking interviewers to rephrase questions the witness does not understand, or rephrasing questions themselves if necessary.

- Help to communicate a witness's answers.

- Assist in pre-trial preparation of the witness.

There is a witness intermediary team based within the NCA Specialist Operations Centre who can provide support in the use of Registered Intermediaries and offer advice on interview strategies. They can be contacted by email at soc@nca.pnn .police.uk or on 0845 000 5463.

13.12 **Witnesses Who Admit Criminality**

Some witnesses may admit to their own criminality during the course of an interview. This can range from minor drug abuse to helping to move, destroy or store weapons, clothing or vehicles. This may be anticipated in advance from knowledge of the victim, their initial account, lifestyle, background, character and nature of their evidence (ie witness-ology).

Interviewers should be prepared and briefed during the planning phase so they know how to respond should the situation arise. A policy can be prepared, encompassing consultation and agreement with the CPS, outlining what the procedure will be. Depending on the extent of criminality admitted, the CPS will advise on setting a threshold for what is/not in the public interest to pursue and what is so serious it warrants further investigation.

13.13 **Role of Confidantes**

A confidante[13] is a particular type of witness and refers to those in whom an offender has confided. Some witnesses gain information about a crime because offenders tell them what they have done. This is generally to a family member, partner, work colleague or fellow associate or criminal, or to victims' families or associates.

A number of investigative strategies mentioned in this book could include an added requirement to attempt to identify opportunities to uncover 'confidantes'. For example, an intelligence strategy (covert and overt) could cater for the iden-tification of those who are likely to have had an opportunity to witness anything said or done by an offender. This may involve some degree of analytical work to highlight likely candidates by examining lists of suspect's partners, relatives, friends, colleagues or associates. It could also include identifying and profiling those who might be classed as having strong morals and consciences that might make it difficult for them to maintain secrets and loyalties for any length of time.

Another example is in a communications strategy. Appeals for seeking help and information could be designed to reach out to those who may not even know or believe they have information of any value, but could in fact be confi-dantes and hold vital evidence against an offender. This option still applies even when a suspect has been identified and arrested. Those who possess such infor-mation, however, may have very close personal ties with the offender and any approach will have to be planned carefully.

A victim support/family liaison strategy may present a further option. Given that in some crimes the offender and victim are known to each other, it is entirely feasible that their families and associates could be confidantes of the offender. In such a case it is important that staff (eg FLOs) are alert to this possibility and able to recognise opportunities that may be of advantage to the investigation. Information acquired about the victim and their lifestyle and contacts will also facilitate the analysis of potential confidante identification opportunities.

In a suspect interview strategy, interviewers should be aware that suspects may reveal facts and detail about their movements pre- and post-incident and who they came into contact with. Consequently, they may make disclosures that could lead to the identification of confidante-type witnesses. This information may not be volunteered unless the right questions are asked.

Finally, there is the subject of what are known as 'cell confessions', ie offenders who are in custody making admissions to other cell mates. The rule is that these have to be viewed with some degree of scepticism as to the reliability of the

---

[13] Mentioned in Dr Peter Stelfox, (2006) 2(1) *The Journal of Homicide and Major Investigation.*

'witness' and their motives. However, it may be that any information and intelligence gleaned about close associates or movements and lifestyles from suspects and convicted offenders can help identify further confidante-type witness-seeking opportunities.

13.14 Using Interpreters

In some cases it is necessary to use the services of interpreters obtained from the National Register of Public Service Interpreters[14] (NRPSI) to interview witnesses. There are important guidelines and frameworks for working with interpreters. Some useful ones are listed below:

- Identities of interpreters should always be verified (eg on arrival at a police station).
- Interpreters should be separated from other members of the public and anyone connected with the case.
- Interpreters should be supervised at all times when conversing with witnesses.
- Interpreters should only work in the language in which they are fully qualified.
- Whenever possible, witness statements written in another language should be translated into English *at the police station*.
- If ABE interviews have been conducted using interpreters, the wording of any resulting statements must be checked to ensure the interpreter's version is what the witness actually said or meant.

13.15 The Witness Charter

The Witness Charter[15] first came out in April 2009 (revised December 2013) from the Home Office Ministry of Justice and sets out the standards of care that can be expected by a witness to a crime or incident in England and Wales. The Charter applies to all witnesses of a crime and to character witnesses but not expert witnesses. It outlines the standards and sets out the level of service that witnesses should expect to receive at every stage of the criminal justice process, right through to giving evidence at trial and any post-trial support. It is aimed at ensuring every witness receives a level of service that is tailored to their individual needs so that witnesses are more likely to stay involved with helping the case and attending trial to give evidence. This is a document that is essential reading in developing and maintaining adequate knowledge for performing the role of an SIO.

---

[14] See also <http://www.nrpsi.org.uk>, telephone contact number 020 3206 1400.

[15] Ministry of Justice, *The Witness Charter: Standards of care for witnesses in the criminal justice system* (HM Stationery Office, 2013), available at <http://www.gov.uk/moj>.

13.16 **Victim Personal Statements**

A Victim Personal Statement (VPS) is a statement written in the victim's own words. It is different from a witness statement that is a written or recorded account of what happened to the victim. The VPS can be taken at the same time as a witness statement, but can also be taken at a later stage to:

- explain the effect the crime is having (or had) on the victim's life physically, emotionally, financially or in any other way
- express concerns about intimidation from a suspect
- express concern about the suspect being granted bail
- request support from a Victim Support Scheme
- request compensation (completion of form MG19).

The VPS[16] forms part of the case papers, so if the case goes to court, the VPS will be sent to the defence legal team. All victims have the opportunity to make a VPS if they wish and it is very important that they are offered every chance to do so. Bereaved relatives or partners in homicide cases and parents and carers, where the primary victim is a child or vulnerable adult, can also provide a VPS if they so wish. The VPS is basically a person's opportunity to express their feelings and describe the effect of a crime *in their own words*.

References

Ministry of Justice: *The Witness Charter: Standards of care for witnesses in the criminal justice system* (HM Stationery Office, 2013) <http://www.gov.uk/moj>

Ministry of Justice, *Code of Practice for Victims of Crime: Presented to Parliament pursuant to section 33 of the Domestic Violence, Crime and Victims Act 2004* (HM Stationery Office, 2015) <http://www.gov.uk/moj>

Ministry of Justice, *Making a Victim Personal Statement: Victims have a right to explain how a crime has affected them. A guide for all criminal justice practitioners* (HM Stationery Office, 2013)

National Investigative Interviewing Steering Group, *Advice on the Structure of Visually Recorded Witness Interviews*, 2nd edn (ACPO, October 2013)

NPIA, 'Offering Monetary Rewards: A Useful Investigative Tactic when Trawling for Witnesses' (2011) 7(1) *Journal of Homicide and Major Incident Investigation* <https://www.gov.uk/government/uploads/system/uploads/attachment_data/file/183366/witness-charter.pdf>

Stelfox, P, (2006) 2(1) *The Journal of Homicide and Major Investigation*

---

[16] See Ministry of Justice, *Making a Victim Personal Statement: Victims have a right to explain how a crime has affected them. A guide for all criminal justice practitioners* (HM Stationery Office, 2013), available at <https://www.gov.uk/government/publications/victim-personal-statement>.

Homicide Investigation

14.1 **Introduction**

Taking another person's life is the most serious crime one can ever commit. That is why investigating homicide is the supreme challenge for any SIO. Often it is the identification of a homicide that proves equally as challenging and for this reason sudden and unexplained deaths occurring outside of medical settings usually require some form of investigation to confirm whether the death is natural or suspicious. While the majority of deaths actually result from natural causes, the police have a role to ensure that any criminal offences are identified and thoroughly investigated.

The way in which a death is investigated is critically important to a deceased's family and close friends who are mourning a loss and need answers. They depend on a high-quality investigations, which is why the majority of suspicious deaths must come under the control or close supervision of a PIP 3 accredited SIO.

Not all homicides are so easily identifiable, because a deceased person cannot explain or supply information as to how they met their death. It is more challenging to establish causation when the most useful source of information is unavailable for comment. Fortunately information and clues can be picked up from other places to assist in making that all-important decision.

The subject of death investigation and homicide is a complex and risk-oriented business area, both for the individual and their organisation. This chapter is aimed at helping to explain the complexity of roles and processes that are required in comprehensive death and homicide investigations, highlighting essential areas of knowledge and practice that an SIO needs to know.

14.2 **Categories of Death Investigation**

Terms may vary across different agencies and organisations but generally speaking death investigations can be separated into four categories:

1. Deaths that are expected (disease or natural causes, eg old age).
2. Deaths that are sudden, unexpected and unnatural (non-suspicious).
3. Special procedure deaths.
4. Homicide or suspicious and unexplained deaths.

Category (1) deaths are usually accompanied by a death certificate signed by a medical practitioner(s) with very little or no investigation required. Category (2) are those handled by a Coroner and sometimes assisted by the police (eg when the death is accidental) and there may be a requirement for an inquest. Category (3) might attract what are sometimes termed 'special procedure investigations' because they merit a higher level of response and investigation due to their nature. This might include early notification and involvement of a senior detective (Investigating Officer (IO)/Senior Investigating Officer (SIO)) to assume responsibility for supervising and conducting the investigation. This higher level of investigation might include deaths involving:

- persons under 18 years of age
- healthcare settings
- police custody or prisons
- illicit drugs
- outdoor locations and/or in water
- suspected suicides
- fires or fire-related
- work-related
- found human remains, dismemberments, body parts and bones
- vulnerable persons
- persons with prominent public profiles (PPPs)
- Ministry of Defence establishments
- critical incidents
- unusual or disturbing features.

The aim of a category (3) investigation is to better manage the risk by providing more thoroughness, eliminate mistakes and rule in/out any possibility of criminal involvement. These types of deaths are often more difficult to judge and prone to more scepticism and suspicion because of the circumstances in which they occur, the types of individuals involved and the higher degree of risk. Such cases carry a more substantial level of accountability and are likely to attract more public and media interest.

Less experienced investigators who initially respond to and deal with any sudden death, whether they are in the list above or not and for which they have some doubts, should always be encouraged to seek advice from a more senior detective and/or SIO.

Category (4) deaths speak for themselves and require consideration of most of the procedures outlined in this handbook.

14.2.1 **Official categories of murder**

Linking into category (4) deaths are official categories of murder as listed in the *Murder Investigation Manual* (MIM).[1] These are useful to know, though they tend to relate more to command, control and resourcing than decision making. Nonetheless they have been widely adopted and are regularly used in terminology and policy.

---

[1] ACPO, *Murder Investigation Manual* (NCPE, 2006).

Cat. A+	Homicide or other major investigation where public concern and the associated response to media intervention are such that 'normal' staffing levels are inadequate to keep pace with the investigation.
Cat. A	Homicide or other major investigation which is of grave concern or where vulnerable members of the public are at risk; where the identity of the offender/s is/are not apparent, or the investigation and the securing of evidence requires significant resource allocation.
Cat. B	Homicide or other major investigation where the identity of the offender(s) is not apparent, the continued risk to the public is low, and the investigation or securing of evidence can be achieved within normal resourcing arrangements.
Cat. C	Homicide or other major investigation where the identity of the offender(s) is apparent from the outset and the investigation and/or securing of evidence can easily be achieved.

14.3 **Equivocal Deaths**

Equivocal (questionable) deaths are ones that are open to interpretation. These are occasions when it is uncertain what has caused the death of a person, as the circumstances and evidence are unclear or there is missing information. Difficulty can be experienced in making a firm decision based upon initial assessment as to what has happened and what might be the cause and manner of death. As such they are often referred to as 'equivocal deaths'.

Some police forces have a local policy that advises initial responders to make a brief examination of a deceased's body to check for obvious wounds, injuries or recent trauma. Such a visual inspection should only be made of exposed areas of the body such as head, face, neck and forearms, provided it appears safe to do so and protective gloves are worn. Any touching, moving or disturbance of a body must be kept to an absolute minimum and if it can be avoided SHOULD NEVER BE TURNED OVER or subjected to any other movement that might allow body fluids to release (eg out of the nose or mouth) and cause contamination.

Visual inspections, however, are never totally conclusive, but may, in some circumstances, indicate obvious telltale signs. This will not implicate or eliminate homicide, as only a Forensic Pathologist at a post-mortem can do that. Some causes of death, such as strangulation, poisoning, lethal drugs administration or internal bruising and bleeding caused by blunt trauma, for example, are difficult to detect externally even on an examination table. The safer (risk-management) option is to forensically remove the deceased's body to an accredited mortuary and retain the scene until a full forensic post-mortem has been able to provide conclusive answers as to cause of death (COD).

14.3.1 **Gathering and analysing information**

In ascertaining what may have caused a death, information will be needed. The process of seeking and analysing information must be initiated to help determine how and why a person died. Making good use of the interrogative pronouns, 5WH provides a structured approach to obtaining and collating the necessary information. A list of potential questions can be raised relatively quickly and information gaps identified and filled that will help determine why and how a person died.

Checklist—5WH questions

- Who certified death, at what time, where and when?

- What medical treatment has been given, why and who by?

- How was the body found and where (location, position of body, etc)?

- What state was the body found in (any obvious signs of injuries or attack)?

- Where is the body now and who is with it?

- What arrangements have been made for preserving and securing the scene(s)?

- What appears to have happened (likely hypotheses as to cause and manner of death, weapon used, etc)?

- How and why did death occur?

- What clues and information are available (eg witnesses, intelligence)?

- Who is the deceased (ie detailed victimology)?

- Who are their next of kin? (When and how were they told? What were they told and who by? Where are they now? What support have they been given?)

- Who does the deceased live with? (Where are they now? What do they say about the death? What background information can they provide?)

- Who is/are the deceased's spouse, partner, relatives, close friends or associates?

- Who found the body? (What is their relationship to the deceased? What is their background and character? How, why and when did they make the find? What have they said in their initial account?)

- When was the deceased last seen alive, who by, where and under what circumstances?

- Where has death taken place? (What signs are there of the deceased having died elsewhere, eg mud on their clothing, drag or scuff marks, blood trails?)

- When is the death likely to have taken place? (What dated articles are lying around eg mail and newspapers in the house or behind the front door?)

- How long has the person been dead for?

- Why was the body not found sooner?
- What is noticeable at the scene (eg theft, disturbance, forced entry or insecurity, signs of search, missing items, clean-up, blood distribution corresponding to the position of the body)?
- What was the deceased doing leading up to their death?
- What is known about their last movements, moods, problems and behaviour?
- What could be a motive for them having been murdered?
- What evidence suggests anything other than a natural or accidental death?
- What recent activities or events might be linked to their death?
- What other information is available?
- Who has informed the Coroner and what have they been told?
- Who else has been informed or requested?
- What enquiries have been conducted?

KEY POINTS

1. Dealing with uncertain (equivocal) deaths can be challenging and effective decision making will mean the difference between preserving or destroying evidence. Whatever category or terminology is applied, initial responders and crime investigators have an extremely vital role to play. There is only one chance to get it right, which is why the MIM states: **'If in doubt...think murder!'**
2. Some offenders who are associated to a victim and know they will come under scrutiny due to the relationship, **stage** the crime scene to make it appear something else happened, eg a burglary gone wrong. This is to divert attention away from themselves onto alternative suspects and motives. Alternatively, offenders who are strangers to their victim do not need to stage the crime scene as they believe they will not be immediate suspects.)

14.4 **Preservation of Life**

Chapter 5.4 makes reference to the Five Building Blocks Principle, one of which is 'preservation of life'. Initial responders to a sudden death of any description must first check whether there are any signs of life and whenever possible first aid should be administered and medical assistance summoned as an absolute priority. It must be remembered that some people can and do appear dead because their life signs are barely visible, eg in hypothermia cases.

Police officers and other non-qualified responders are not medical experts and must always refer to those who are. Fortunately, in some cases death may have already been certified or be patently obvious due to heavy decomposition, skeletisation, vital body parts missing or when deeply submerged in water. In order to administer first aid, to check for signs of life and to certify death, some movement of or interference with the body of a deceased may be necessary. This may involve attaching monitoring devices, medical equipment or physical movement. These processes can interfere with or contaminate forensic evidence collection opportunities and leave extra marks and traces that need to be accounted for. Defibrillators, for example, leave heavy bruising around the chest area. Therefore, it is important to debrief medical practitioners who have been involved in the initial response and an account obtained of:

- who administered any medical treatment
- what their initial assessments and findings were
- where the body was upon arrival and exact position (face down, on side, etc)
- what treatments, equipment, dressings or drugs were used and why
- what equipment, packaging or dressings they left at the scene
- what actions they took and what, if anything, was found, noticed, moved or removed on or from the body or surroundings in which it was found
- who certified death and precise time this was done
- what notes, details, sketches or photographs were made/taken
- who they saw or spoke to or what they were told or heard
- what they know about the deceased's medical history and doctor's details
- what else was noticed that might be of use to the investigation.

Medical professionals can be asked for their opinion as to what may have caused death based on their medical training, knowledge, experience and assessment. They may have noticed something that, though not conclusive, may help provide an early indication as to what may have been the COD. They should *not* be encouraged, however, to begin examining the body after death is certified, as this may interfere with forensic examination processes required later.

14.4.1 **Certification of death**

Only qualified medical experts can formally declare and certify a person to be clinically dead (aka pronouncing life extinct—PLE). Medical doctors, paramedics and pathologists are the only ones who legally certify that life is extinct. The precise time and date and by whom death is certified is an important piece of information and one that is used as a starting point for establishing 'relevant time', ie significant period during which death might have occurred. The individual who makes the official determination of death must record the reasons of how they have done so and the exact time and date.

The confirmation or pronouncement of death is the first priority before any further steps can be taken, ie forensic examination of the body. Once this has occurred, the treatment and resuscitative efforts cease and jurisdiction passes over to the police for an investigation.

14.4.2 Examination of critical victims

With advancements in medical knowledge and treatments, victims who have suffered severe trauma injuries receive improved levels of treatment. This means there are more cases of victims being treated and kept alive on ventilators and life-support machines despite their injuries initially appearing to be extremely severe and life-threatening. This provides an opportunity to consider whether their injuries can be assessed or samples and photographs taken whilst the victim is still alive.

In some cases, a medical diagnosis may indicate there is little chance of the person surviving and it is suspected criminal acts have been the cause of their physical condition. This is when there may be an option for allowing the victim to be examined by a Forensic Pathologist while still alive, which may prove a delicate tactic for their close family and friends who are likely to be coping with emotional trauma. It would require informed consent from the next of kin but there may be an option for having a police medical expert conduct an external examination pre-death (avoiding using the term 'forensic pathologist'). Any such examination could prove extremely beneficial to the investigation, but would have to be performed very tactfully and not interfere with any treatment.

14.5 Time of Death (TOD)

Also known as 'time since death', this is a contentious scientific area in the pathological sense and in the majority of cases it is preferable to rely upon factual evidence, such as witness testimony or other material such as CCTV if available. However, having an estimated or calculated TOD is a valuable piece of information (and in some cases supporting evidence) which links in with a number of investigative strategies for setting time parameters, eg for alibi enquiries.

Traditional clues can usually be found and utilised, such as the time and date the deceased was last seen alive, dates on unopened (e)mail and newspapers/mail left at their home address, plus information about their movements, appointments, routines, last use of mobile phone, and intelligence. Also, there may be useful observations, such as, if outdoors, changing weather conditions post-mortem, eg rain or snow, where underneath the body is dry.

There can be complicating factors, such as the environment a body has been kept in, inclement weather, indoor heating, air conditioning and the amount of time taken to find the body. These make it more difficult to make accurate assessments that rely upon body temperature. Post-mortem changes such as hypostasis, rigor mortis, and decomposition such as putrefaction or skeletisation are other complications.

A useful list of potential scientific methods for calculating time of (or since) death is as follows:

1. Temperature. Algor mortis (post-mortem cooling) is based upon a steady core body temperature prior to death, presumed to be approximately 37°C. However, any temperature-based method needs to account for the multiple variables that are experienced in crime scenes, such as the effect of different items of clothing and the number of layers worn, the variety of ventilation or artificial heating, activity engaged in prior to death and even the physical position of the body. Submerged bodies and exposure to fires can also alter core body temperatures. One method used is based on loss of body heat following a rectal temperature reading. A common calculation used in this process is based on the work of German scientist C Henssge using a graphical model known as a Henssge Nomogram.[2] A number of issues have now arisen, however, which cast doubt on the reliability of the calculation. As a result, in February 2012 the Home Office Forensic Pathology Specialist Group (FPSG) wrote to all registered Pathologists requiring them to exercise great care when using the calculation to give a time of death. This should now only be treated as a broad estimate stating that:
   (a) time range may be useful in focusing an investigation, but should not be used to establish a range in which the murder was or was not committed; and
   (b) time period established by the model should *not* be used to exclude a suspect from the investigation.[3]
2. Rigor mortis. Muscular rigidity begins immediately but is only observable after three to six hours and can last up to 36 hours, by which time it diminishes. This may also be affected by the temperature of the environment, the degree of muscular activity prior to death and the age of the deceased.
3. Morphological changes. In the absence of blood circulation, red blood cells settle under gravity and livor mortis (hypostasis) develops. The progression of decomposition, however, will depend on factors such as the health of the deceased prior to death, the effects of drugs or medications, the ambient environment (temperature and humidity), extent of animal and insect activity and degree of perimortem trauma.
4. Muscular excitability. This is determined by external electrical stimulation of muscle groups and requires very specialised equipment that is not widely available.
5. Gastric contents emptying (gastroenterology). This method assumes that gastric contents are digested at clear predictable rates. The theory is that if the time of the last meal eaten is known, the extent of gastric (eg stomach) emptying can assist with an estimated time of death. This will depend on the type of food ingested (eg fat content), the physiological and psychological status

---

[2] C Henssge, 'Death Time Estimates in Case Work: The Rectal Temperature Time of Death Nomogram' (1988) 38 *Forensic Science International*, 209–36.

[3] Dr Jeff Adams, 'Time of Death Estimation. Interim Report to the Forensic Science Regulator' by Forensic Pathology Specialist Group (December 2011).

of the deceased (eg degree of stress or fright) and consumption of alcohol or drugs misuse.

6. Ophthalmological changes. This includes analyses of vitreous humour and the chemical constituents of the fluid within the eye (eg changes in potassium concentration).

7. DNA and ultrastructural changes. Assessment of DNA and denaturation could provide a method of time of death estimation, as cells begin to break down with the onset of cellular death. Like other methods, the rate is affected by variables such as ambient temperature, exposure to ultraviolet light and humidity.

8. Entomological methods. The study of insect life cycles may be helpful, as blowflies such as green and bluebottle flies and their larvae (maggots) have a predictable life cycle. Temperature, humidity, manner of death and the presence of drugs within the body may affect the results.

9. Botanical methods. The use of plant growth through the study of palynology and botany assume the seasonal-specific pollen species adherent to articles of clothing or parts of the body, especially within interred remains. Rootlet infiltration of remains can similarly aid with perennial plants through their growth stages.[4]

14.6 **Cause and Manner of Death**

From an investigative perspective the medical cause of death (COD) is the pathological condition which caused the death, ie the reason why a person died. Heart attacks, gunshot wounds and skull fractures are all causes of death. They are the diseases or injuries that alter the victim's physiology and lead to death. This can be differentiated from the *mechanism of death*, which is the actual physiological change or variation in the body's workings that cause a cessation of life (eg brain trauma such as cerebral contusion into the brain or subdural or epidural hematoma which is around the brain). In some cases there might be more than one mechanism of death.

The phrase *manner of death* (MOD) tends to be used as a legal and administrative term. It refers to the root cause or sequence of events that lead to death and is generally divided into five categories:

1. Natural (process or disease).
2. Accidental death (unintentional or inadvertent actions/unforeseeable events).
3. Suicide (intentional deaths caused by the dead person themselves).
4. Murder/homicide (deaths caused by a third party).
5. Unascertained or uncertain (cannot be determined with reasonable certainty).[5]

---

[4] Taken from Dr B Swift, Consultant Home Office Registered Forensic Pathologist in 'Methods of Time Since Death Estimation Within the Early Postmortem Interval' (2010) 6(1) *Journal of Homicide and Major Investigation*, 97–107.

[5] These deaths are when a Coroner cannot accurately determine the appropriate category.

Just as causes of death may involve different mechanisms, they can also have several possible manners. For example, a gunshot wound cannot be a natural death, but it can be a homicide, suicide or accident; or where a person who has heart disease is assaulted in the street and as a consequence suffers a heart attack and dies, the cause of death would be heart attack and the manner homicide (ie unnatural death).

The medical cause of death and pathological interpretation as to manner of death play a role, either in the verdict determined by the Coroner or the outcome of any subsequent criminal proceedings. However, a Forensic Pathologist may not always be able to determine the manner of death. For example, in a case where a cause of death is determined by the Pathologist, eg as a head injury, the manner of death may have to be determined by a Coroner's verdict aided by a police investigation. The conclusion could be that there was a fall without third-party involvement and verdict of misadventure (eg a person who falls down a flight of stairs); or alternatively unlawful killing from being deliberately pushed (from a pathological perspective, it is usually difficult to determine whether someone has fallen or was pushed, therefore this evidence would have to come from elsewhere, eg a witness or CCTV). Therefore sometimes, to establish the manner of death, a combination of a police investigation and pathological findings is required to complete the evidential picture.

14.7 **Forensic Pathology**

The word pathology derives from Greek words for disease and knowledge. In modern usage, pathology means the scientific study of disease. Pathology is a wide-ranging medical specialism and includes microbiologists, haematologists, chemical pathologists and immunologists. There are predominantly two categories of pathologists involved in post-mortem examinations—Histopathologists and Forensic Pathologists.

Doctors usually ask a living patient about the presentation of a disease and their symptoms: this is known as the history. However, the Forensic Pathologist cannot count upon a deceased to provide history of their symptoms and have to rely upon other means and sources to provide the missing information.

Histopathology is concerned with making diagnoses from the examination of human tissue ('*histos*' is the Greek word for tissue). This includes the examination of biopsy material from living patients and the examination of the deceased to establish why they died. Forensic Pathologists have additional training and expertise enabling them to examine traumatic or unnatural deaths and present their findings appropriately to the Criminal Justice System (CJS).

The role of the Forensic Pathologist is contained within the 'Code of Practice and Performance Standards for Forensic Pathology in England, Wales and Northern

Ireland'.[6] These standards do not apply in Scotland; however, separate, but closely related standards apply in that jurisdiction.

Traditionally in the UK, Forensic Pathologists were titled Home Office Pathologists, because they were registered with the Home Office. This term was replaced by consultant Home Office Registered Forensic Pathologist (HORFP). However, some judges, courts and lay persons may still apply the older terminology. There is a relatively small number in this category varying from around 35 to 40 practitioners on the Home Office register at any one time. They are grouped into geographic practice areas and provide a 24/7 service to police and coroners.[7]

HORFPs are concerned with the investigation of suspicious deaths, as opposed to their non-forensic colleagues who may be employed to establish identity and cause of death in non-suspicious cases. Under existing legislation (Coroners and Justice Act 2009) both forensic and non-forensic pathologists are instructed to conduct post-mortem (PM) examinations by one of Her Majesty's Coroners. Although the legal purpose of a PM is to identify the deceased and to determine the cause and surrounding circumstances of death, a forensic PM has an additional purpose, which is the collection of evidence. HORFPs are trained in the collection of forensic medical and physical trace evidence from the deceased and in giving expert opinion in court as to the cause of death.

Amongst all other professionals who assist in the investigation into suspicious death, the Forensic Pathologist has the pivotal role. Close liaison between the Forensic Pathologist and SIO is essential, particularly in the early stages of an investigation. The SIO needs to know how to get information out of the Forensic Pathologist rather than the SIO having to know too much about pathology. It helps, however, if some of the medical terminology and examination processes they use can be understood, even though the Pathologist can always be asked to explain his/her examinations, methods and findings in clear terms. The SIO should never leave the mortuary or crime scene without fully understanding and being able to repeat and explain the Pathologist's opinions and findings.

KEY POINT

A Forensic Pathologist can be asked what they are ruling out as well as what they are ruling in, which may give an indication of what has *not* happened eg a natural death.

---

[6] Published by the Home Office, Forensic Science Regulator, Department of Justice and the Royal College of Pathologists, January 2012.

[7] The Home Office Register of Forensic Pathologists, sometimes referred to as the 'Home Office List' can be downloaded from <https://www.gov.uk/government/publications/home-office-register-of-forensic-pathologists-february-2013>.

Checklist—Role of Forensic Pathologist

- Attend scenes, liaise with SIO, and Crime Scene Investigators (CSIs), forensic providers and other such experts (eg fire investigators).

- Make observations of the body and the context in which it was found.

- Assist with identification.

- Assist with the estimation of TOD.

- Contribute to the formulation of a forensic strategy for evidence recovery from the body, including prior to removal to the mortuary.

- Advise on what samples should be taken.

- Advise on a strategy for safe removal of a body to the mortuary.

- Advise on what samples should be taken from people dying in hospital.

- Carry out full external and internal examination of bodies and coordinate the imaging of any wounds or injuries with a scale by a photographer.

- Advise on what additional tests are required before, during and after the post-mortem, eg x-rays, histology, toxicology, ballistics.

- Provide information to help initiate early lines of enquiry.

- Advise on health and safety issues in relation to the scene of the discovery of the body and the personnel involved in the examination of that scene.

- Identify risks of contamination and possible control measures.

- Advise on what other experts may be required, eg paediatrician for child cases, radiologist and/or ballistics expert for firearms and explosives cases, odontologist for dental examinations.

- Provide full briefing to the SIO post-examination and communicate provisional findings to the Coroner.

- Provide a detailed witness statement to include not only cause of death but also an interpretation of circumstances surrounding the death.

- Attend briefings as and when required and meet with the prosecution team prior to trial to discuss pathological findings.

- Give evidence in court.

- Provide opinions on non-fatal wounds and/or suspicious circumstances.

14.7.1 **Attendance at crime scenes**

After initial contact by the SIO, the Forensic Pathologist usually confirms that the Coroner has been notified and has authorised their involvement. Once authorised, they have the option to attend and assess the crime scene. If they decide to do so, and the SIO is wise to request it, they are in a better position to put their subsequent post-mortem examination into context.

Having the Pathologist attend the scene contributes to the team approach. They have the opportunity to examine the scene and the deceased while in position, clarify and check out information from those present and provide on-the-spot advice where there is doubt as to whether to treat the death as suspicious. Their on-site advice is also very useful when formulating body and evidence forensic recovery tactics. Early interaction between the Pathologist, CSI/CSM, other experts and the SIO forms a solid partnership.

Upon arrival the Pathologist (and any other experts summoned) will require briefing about the circumstances of the case. It is advisable for the SIO to personally make contact with the Pathologist (ie over the phone initially) and explain the circumstances and reasons for requesting their attendance and personally meet them at the scene. The initial call allows for some preliminary discussion about the circumstances of the case and for the Pathologist to make initial suggestions for managing evidential recovery from the body. They may also wish to suggest consulting other experts, for instance an entomologist or anthropologist. This early interaction allows the SIO to calculate and coordinate arrival times and timescales for further required experts and simultaneous attendance and briefing.

> **KEY POINT**
>
> Forensic Pathologists usually like to speak directly to the person in charge, and it is ill-advised to have someone else contact them on behalf of the SIO, particularly if it happens to be an unsociable time of day.

Other important matters may require immediate attention before an approach can be made to a deceased's body, such as searches for offenders or initial scene assessment, and such delays can mean the Pathologist and/or other experts are left waiting around. The Pathologist will have to perform a lengthy post-mortem at some later stage and they will need the necessary resilience, time and energy in order to do so. Provided the fact of death has been medically confirmed and scene preservation arrangements are in place (eg a suitable tent covering the body if out of doors), there may be no great urgency to rush into approaching or removing the body, so the request for a Pathologist may not be so urgent. However, persons in custody awaiting interview or dangerous crime scenes may be issues to consider, as well as an early indication as to likely cause of death if it is not obvious.

Checklist—Pathologist initial briefing

- Details of the SIO/DSIO.

- Details of the CSI and CSM, and any other relevant specialists involved.

- Briefing via 5WH method (case circumstances etc).

- Known health and safety hazards together with contamination issues.

- Details regarding the deceased (identity, medical and social history).

- Reasons why the death is being treated as suspicious.

- What has happened since body discovery (eg any disturbance by members of the public, initial officers attending, relatives or medical staff).

- What relevant material or information will be available and whether they can have access to it (eg CCTV footage or witness statements).

- Details of what is known about any injuries on the victim or weapon used.

- Condition of the body (eg rigor mortis, decomposition, insect activity).

- Any assessments from other experts that have been made.

- What the scope and priorities of the investigation are.

- What time they are required to attend and where (eg scene, rendezvous point (RVP) or police station).

- Where the Major Incident Room (MIR) is located.

- Contact details of all relevant individuals.

- Any other appropriate information they may require.

The SIO should be prepared to re-brief the Pathologist at such time when further information becomes available, eg CCTV recording of an attack. This includes after the post-mortem has been completed, as early information inevitably changes as the investigation progresses and this allows the Pathologist to review their initial findings.

KEY POINTS

- If in any doubt as to cause or manner of death, a Forensic Pathologist should be summoned for their expertise in interpreting circumstances, injuries, marks, medical conditions and crime scenes.
- If still unsure after the Pathologist attends, a scene may be kept secure and sterile until the results of a post-mortem examination are known.

- If criminality is suspected, an SIO has ultimate authority and control of the scene and victim's body. It is their decision if and when to call a Pathologist, though it should always be discussed and agreed with a Coroner beforehand, as it is only they who can authorise post-mortems and movement of a body (local protocols may apply).

14.8 **Initial Tactical Meeting**

Wherever practicable, the SIO should assemble their range of advisers and specialists who have been requested to assist the investigation into a suspicious death for an initial tactical meeting. The ensemble might include a Forensic Pathologist, CSC/CSM, Scene Photographer, forensic experts, fire investigators and any others that have been requested, such as ballistics experts, entomologists, palynologists and anthropologists (who is required will probably not be known until a scene walk through/assessment has been completed). There may be a need to recognise the varying jurisdictional and disciplinary roles and responsibilities that apply to the individuals concerned. The meeting can be staged either: (a) at the RVP near the cordon; or (b) at some other suitable location, such as a police station, incident room or mobile incident trailer or command vehicle. In either case, ideally it should always occur *before* an examination is made of the body.

The SIO should identify specific responsibilities, share appropriate preliminary information and establish the aims and roles of each discipline present at the scene. It should be determined who is/are responsible for the collection of specific types of evidence and the evidence collection priority. All members of the team should identify how they are going to record their exhibit lists and clarity should be provided as to how exhibits should be processed, through liaison with the designated Exhibits Officer.

This is an opportunity to discuss the circumstances and make important decisions and policies on how to enter the scene, approach the body, decide what samples are required from the body while in position and determine how the body will be recovered, protected, removed and transported, as well as what imagery and recording requirements are necessary (eg still photography, digital or high-vantage-point shots). The strategy and tactics should be carefully recorded either in the SIO's policy log or in a stand-alone policy record, once agreed, and then countersigned by all those involved in the decision-making process.

KEY POINTS

1. Initial tactical meetings and briefings allow for a factual information exchange. This includes confirmation of roles and responsibilities, time factors, information known and investigative strategy.
2. A list of all those in attendance should be made and, if at a scene RVP, a record of their times of arrival and departure (which can prove useful if any costs have to be met).

14.9 Conducting a 'Walk Through'

Conducting a 'walk through' or scene assessment[8] provides an opportunity to gain an overview of the overall scene. This is usually the first opportunity to locate and view the body, identify valuable and/or fragile evidence and determine initial investigative procedures for a systematic examination and processing of the scene and body (also a crime scene). It also allows for the reassessment of scene boundaries and to make adjustments where necessary and to view the deceased in position. The SIO should decide who is required to be present when the scene 'walk through' is conducted. The CSI/CSM, photographer and Forensic Pathologist are obvious inclusions.

It is important to maintain an investigative mindset when making a scene assessment, as the location where the deceased is found may not be the actual location where the injury/illness that contributed to the death occurred. It is imperative that the SIO and their team attempt to determine the locations where injury(ies) or illness(es) occurred. Physical evidence at any or all locations may be pertinent in establishing the cause, manner and time/place of death.

Information from witnesses and other sources of intelligence is useful to have prior to and during scene assessments to help put details and surroundings into context. The usefulness of recording information of the body and scene photographically should also not be underestimated. This material creates a permanent record and preserves essential details of the body position, appearance, identity and surroundings. These images also enable the sharing of information with other members of the investigation team.

Scene assessment and walk-through processes should be subject to a debriefing process to help all participating specialists and the SIO share information, thoughts and ideas. This will help determine the evidence examination and recovery plan and clarify roles and responsibilities.

---

[8] Scene assessments are also covered in Chapter 5.

KEY POINTS

- When conducting a scene assessment, evidence of such things as drag or movement marks on the body and ground should be checked, and any other post-injury activity.
- Information from medical staff or initial responders who may have disturbed or moved the body and left items at the scene is essential.

14.10 **Evidence Recovery**

The initial tactical meeting and scene assessment should indicate what, where, when, why and how samples are to be taken, and by whom. This includes any clothing that may have to be removed and the necessary protection of the body's head, hands and other exposed areas as deemed appropriate. Tapings, combings, swabs and scrapings of exposed surfaces may be required in order to prevent loss or contamination of potential evidence when the body is being physically lifted and transported to the mortuary. Bodies can, and do, discharge bodily fluids when disturbed, which can obscure or contaminate trace evidence, particularly from open wounds and orifices. Extreme care must be taken when examining and removing evidence and the body or body part. A proper chain of custody and continuity of exhibits and evidence should be maintained and there should be comprehensive records kept on the preservation, collection and handover of all evidence to ensure the integrity of processes is assured.

The deceased's valuables and property must be safeguarded to ensure correct processes are adhered to and for eventual return to their next of kin. Evidence on or near the body must be safeguarded to ensure its availability for further evaluation. This may include drugs and paraphernalia, and any cash and valuable items, the existence (or non-existence) of which may in itself provide useful information for the investigation.

Detailed photography of the deceased as they are initially found prior to any external examination is very important at this stage. Once a body is moved, this will include photographing the surface beneath the body, using measuring guides where appropriate. These are matters to be discussed with and agreed by the SIO and the other specialists involved, eg CSI and Pathologist.

14.10.1 **External body examination**

At the right stage and time, the process of an external body examination will be required, taking into account the single most important piece of evidence at the scene is the deceased's body. This is why it is important to hold a 'tactical' meeting and even a further one once the initial assessment has concluded as there is only one chance of getting it right. After photography, records should be made to include the:

- position of the body
- physical characteristics
- existence of marks, scars and tattoos
- state of dress/undress
- presence or absence of any items that appear relevant
- presence or lack of blood, bodily fluids, injury/trauma, petechiae, etc
- evidence of any treatment or resuscitative efforts.

Dependent on the initial outcome of the external examination, and providing any of the above list is feasible depending on the circumstances, it may be necessary to make a further evaluation of the need for any further forensic specialists. The body or any other pertinent evidence may be in a fragile state, so none of the above may be possible or advisable.

14.10.2 **Ante-mortem body specimens**

A Code of Practice[9] provides guidance on what material should be considered for recovery at the scene:

   (a) Tapings from exposed body surfaces and uppermost surfaces of clothing (where it is considered likely that trace evidence will be shed on manipulation). If clothing is not to be cut away, the manipulation of the body required to remove clothing may dislodge or contaminate trace evidence; clothing should not be removed until specimens have been taken from head and hands.

   (b) Combings of head hair, beard and moustache hair and pubic hair.

   (c) Plucked hairs from the above sites, each sample being representative of the range of hairs present at those sites.

   (d) Where objective evidence of chronic drug use is relevant to the case, a pencil thickness of head hair, cut as close to the scalp as possible and the cut ends wrapped in foil.

   (e) A swab or swabs from mouth and teeth.

   (f) Taping from the hands where any foreign material is recognised; taping must be taken before fingernail scrapings or cuttings.

   (g) Scrapings from underneath the fingernails of each hand, or fingernail cuttings, using appropriate equipment provided or approved by the CSI or the forensic scientist. Sampling from hair and hands where the death may be related to firearms or explosives must be made using only a 'gunshot residues and explosives sampling kit' approved by the relevant forensic science laboratory and preferably with advice from a forensic scientist.

   (h) Swabs from any moist areas on the body surface where the possibility exists that such moist stains have arisen from a person other than the body. Where there is possibility of sex-related crime, swabs will be taken from

---

[9] Code of Practice and Performance Standards for Forensic Pathology in England, Wales and Northern Ireland, published by the Home Office, the Forensic Regulator, Department of Justice and the Royal College of Pathologists, January 2012.

those areas where semen or saliva may be most likely considered to be present (face, neck, nipples and hands).

(i) A swab or swabs from the perianal skin, taken before a swab or swabs from the anus.

(j) A swab or swabs from vulva and low vagina, taking care to avoid contamination of the latter from the initial swabbing of the former. These swabs must be taken after swabbing the perianal skin and anus (to avoid leakage during the course of the vulval swabbing).

(k) A swab or swabs of injuries that may have resulted from contact with another individual where the skin from that individual may have been shed, eg swabbing of the skin of the neck in postulated manual strangulation.

In each instance, appropriate control swabs must be taken. Multiple swabs from a single area must be numbered in order of their taking.

KEY POINTS

- Forensic trace work on external or exposed surfaces of a body will almost certainly be carried out prior to any pathological examination. This may slow the body recovery process down and create some delay but will form part of the forensic strategy.
- If ligatures or bindings are involved, the golden rule is not to undo or cut any knot. This is to enable a 'knot expert' to be in the best possible position to examine how the binding has been constructed.

14.11 **Removal and Identification**

Once the necessary on-the-spot examinations and samples have been completed, a body (or body part or parts) can be prepared for removal and transportation. Like everything else, this is done only after agreement by the specialists present on the best way to perform the task and will depend on the case circumstances and condition or location of the body. Other considerations may include controlling onlookers, ensuring a safe passageway and maintaining the dignity of the process.

External parts of the body, such as the head, hands and feet are usually covered by plastic bags. Moving a body is often a meticulous and delicate task in order to avoid bodily fluids and other evidence being disturbed, lost or contaminated. Once ready, the body is secured in a sealed and labelled body bag. *The body bag must not be disturbed or opened* until the SIO, CSM and Pathologist are present at the mortuary and it has been agreed to do so (vitally important rule).

The movement of bodies and body parts requires tactful handling, including sometimes concealing the location and exit route to prevent journalists and morbid onlookers viewing or photographing and recording the removal process. Body transportation should be managed skilfully, employing professional personnel (eg undertakers) who have the correct training, skills, equipment and most appropriate vehicles and clothing/uniforms to convey the body to a mortuary, which is also more dignified for victims, their families and relatives.

KEY POINT

If a body is removed prior to, or with/without police supervision, a check must be made to ensure no injuries have been caused while being handled and transported, eg by undertakers removing a body from a limited access location. If witnessed by police officers or other professionals, this information must be transmitted to the SIO.

14.11.1 **Continuity and identification**

When being removed from a crime scene, a body needs to be 'identified' to those transporting and receiving it, eg funeral directors, mortuary staff and the Forensic Pathologist. This duty should be performed before a post-mortem takes place. There has to be continuity of identification from the crime scene to the mortuary with someone accompanying the body to the mortuary in order to make the handover identification. A body is an important exhibit and the integrity of its handling and movement is no less important than any other key item of evidence. Identification procedures should continue when the body bag is first opened and immediately prior to any further examination or autopsy taking place.

Police identification is made through persons who observe a body at the scene, whereas personal identification is performed by a relative or person who knew the deceased where the body is recognisable. In practice, the latter is done at the mortuary, usually in a suitable viewing room once the external examination of the victim has been completed and all necessary external swabs and samples have been obtained. The body can then be cleaned and made as 'presentable' as possible. A post-mortem can be temporarily halted and the viewing and identification completed. This procedure has the following benefits:

- Allows formal identification to be completed without having to wait for the full post-mortem to finish.
- Allows relatives of the victim to have an early opportunity to see and identify their relative, and most are always eager to do so, which should be respected wherever possible.
- Allows the viewing to be made before any further medical interference with the body.
- Provides an opportunity to establish and foster positive relationships with the deceased's family.

This part of the process has to be managed sensitively and tactfully, and the SIO should discuss all options and arrangements with the Family Liaison Officer

(FLO) beforehand. Other considerations may be important, such as the state of the body and the distress it may cause. If the victim is a young child, and even in other cases, the family may want to touch or hold them (some cultural beliefs may also need considering). If so, this will require careful management and supervision with the Pathologist and CSM to ensure there is no compromise of the post-mortem and forensic examination process (this topic is also covered in Chapter 15).

14.11.2 Body identification

The correct and early identification of a deceased is always a top priority. This must be done as quickly as possible so the next of kin can be notified (it is not recommended for them to find out themselves, eg via social media alerts). In most cases, identification is achieved through witnesses or local information, or in some instances using initiative, say, for example, checking personal possessions such as a mobile phone on or around the deceased (provided this will not compromise any forensic procedures that are required). Sometimes, however, the process can become aggravated by mutilation, advanced decomposition, dismemberment or extensive injuries. Known relatives or friends of the deceased may also be difficult to initially contact or trace to attend and confirm identity.

Checklist—Methods of identification

- Witnesses or information (eg through enquiries and appeals).

- Facial identification (visual, photographs, facial reconstruction, facial image analysis or iris recognition).

- Personal possessions (clothing, jewellery, documents, cell phones, digital equipment, keys, vehicles).

- External physical characteristics.

- Fingerprints and DNA.

- Missing person checks locally and through the UK Missing Persons Bureau.

- External and internal physical characteristics (eg tattoos, surgical operations, physical irregularities and modifications).

- Odontology (teeth, gums, contents of oral cavity).

- Dental enamel (to help pinpoint place of birth).

- Osteology (study of the human skeleton—a sub-discipline of anthropology).

- Biological samples (blood, biochemistry, toxicology).

- Radiological imaging (for use in osteology, odontology and facial reconstruction).

- Computed tomography (ie CT scans for two- and three-dimensional imaging).

- Podiatry (using foot analysis for diseases, walking gait, abnormalities, etc).

- Environmental information (specialist examinations to identify likely environment within which a person lived, eg stable isotope fingerprinting to identify geographic region, or pollen, soil and botanical samples).

14.11.3 Senior Identification Manager

A Senior Identification Manager (SIM) is usually appointed by a Gold Commander in cases where there are mass or multiple fatalities, eg in civil disaster-type incidents. A SIM is appointed where there is a need to appoint a specialist officer to positively identify the deceased and oversee the process on behalf of the Coroner or Procurator Fiscal (in Scotland). A SIM is usually a police officer accredited to the same standard as an SIO, ie PIP level 3 (and often an experienced SIO themselves) trained in line with national disaster victim identification (DVI) practices.

Any case where there are a number of deceased persons (eg victims) and/or body parts and dismemberments may benefit from the appointment of a SIM. Some extremely difficult and complex tasks can be assumed by the SIM to improve the professionalism of the approach using (inter)nationally recognised and agreed standards.

However, there doesn't have to be a national disaster to benefit from this role. There are numerous major crime cases in the UK where a SIM has been appointed to assist the SIO. For example, Operation Bridge, where Derrick Bird shot dead 12 people then himself in Cumbria in June 2010; Operation Abnet, the 'Jigsaw murder' of Jeffrey Howe who was dismembered and scattered across five different locations in Leicestershire and Hertfordshire in March 2009; and the 'Crossbow Cannibal' murders committed by Stephen Griffiths in Bradford, where the victim's body was dismembered into 81 pieces and deposited into a local river in 2010.

Checklist—Responsibilities of a SIM

- Victim recovery

- Post-mortem identification procedures

- Casualty bureau functions

- Family liaison

- Ante-mortem evidential harvest

- Ensuring integrity of identification

- Reconciliation (forensic matching)

- Recovery, collection and storage of forensic evidence

- Recovery and storage of personal property belonging to the deceased

- Liaison with the SIO

- Setting the identification criteria in consultation with HM Coroner

- Overseeing setting up a temporary mortuary

- Management of repatriation process

- Maintenance of a policy file

14.12 **Post-Mortem Procedures**

Powers to authorise a post-mortem examination and remove a body to an appropriate location for examination are held by the Coroner (Coroners and Justice Act 2009).

When arranging a post-mortem the SIO must be mindful of some important considerations:

Checklist—Arranging post-mortems

- HM Coroner needs to authorise *beforehand*.

- Coroner needs to know and be kept informed of time/place of post-mortem (in some instances they may wish to attend).

- If a suspect is in custody, their legal team may wish to have a representative present (or subsequent post-mortems if there are multiple offenders).

- Chosen mortuary needs to be placed on alert that a forensic pathological post-mortem is due so they have sufficient time to prepare the examination, viewing rooms and equipment (suitable time and date should be agreed).

- Victim's medical notes and/or hospital records, x-rays, etc, if taken initially to hospital (eg A & E unit), must be obtained and made available for the Pathologist to read and examine before the post-mortem takes place.

- Details of all treatment and drugs prescribed or administered to the deceased and any such items or information recovered from the crime scene or address will be required.

- Details of any infectious diseases, such as HIV or Hepatitis B, must be communicated to anyone who may come into contact with the body, eg mortuary staff.

- Deceased's social history and lifestyle (eg if drug abuser, sexual orientation, reputation, etc) will be useful.

- Exhibits Officer must arrange for all necessary bags, labels, sample buckets, fingernail-cutting, hair-combing and plucking kits to be ready and available (evidence-gathering equipment), though usually the CSI team will have all this equipment also.

14.12.1 Post-mortem attendance

In most cases, the SIO attends a post-mortem in person. This is to observe first-hand any significant findings and partake in discussions as the examination proceeds on all matters that may affect the course of the investigation. In some cases, however, the SIO may wish to delegate the task of attending the post-mortem. This may be due to competing demands and other equally important matters that may take precedence or need attending to, being mindful of the length of time taken for a post-mortem (usually no less than around four hours).

A compromise might be for the SIO to attend at the start and return before completion in order to discuss the findings personally with the Pathologist. The SIO can also be briefed over the phone as the examination progresses. There is no hard and fast rule; suffice it to say, wherever possible the SIO should normally insist on being present throughout this very important process. Many times during post-mortems questions arise and important decisions are required as the examination progresses.

Checklist—Persons required at post-mortems

- SIO (or designated deputy)

- Forensic Pathologist

- Mortuary technician/assistant

- CSM/CSI

- Crime scene imaging staff/photographic experts (still and DVD/digital)

- Other experts as required (ballistics, paediatricians, anthropologists, forensic biologists, toxicologists, palynologists, odontologists, etc)

- Exhibits Officer

If it is requested that medical students be allowed to attend and observe, this requires a judgement call to consider any sensitivities, or potential leaks of information to unauthorised persons and their duty of confidentiality to avoid compromising the investigation. Nevertheless, medical students are the pathologists of the future and need to develop their knowledge and skills.

14.12.2 **Evidence-recovery tactical meeting**

Before commencing an examination, a further tactical meeting (ie in addition to the ante-mortem one at the scene), is required to discuss and agree the forensic evidence recovery plan for the post-mortem. The SIO calls and leads this meeting, which usually takes place at a suitable venue (eg within the mortuary) with all the persons listed at 14.12.1 being present.

The purpose of the meeting is to discuss and re-examine the circumstances of the case and determine and agree what the primary objectives are for the post-mortem, what samples are to be taken and in what order, what photography is required and when (eg before, during and after removal of clothing), and whether any x-rays are required (eg to find bullets, pellets, knife tips). Depending on the type of case, the following are the types of objectives and samples routinely considered.

Checklist—Post-mortem objectives

- Establish or confirm identity of the deceased.

- Assess the size, physique and condition of the deceased.

- Ascertain cause of death (and manner if possible).

- Determine time of death.

- Determine likely survival time of victim after any attack.

- Conduct injury analysis (amount of force used, type of weapon used, precise method details, sexual assault indicators, any incapacitation, direction of blows and position of deceased at time of injury, which wounds were fatal, whether injuries incurred ante- or post-mortem).

- Establish whether any indication of self-defence or if offenders are likely to be injured.

- Establish/confirm place of death (eg look for any evidence of movement of body after death due to drag marks evident on feet/ankles/livor mortis patterning).

- Ascertain lifestyle of victim (eg drug or sexual abuse, health condition).

- Determine if deceased under influence of drink or drugs at time of death.

Checklist—Post-mortem samples

- Further DNA swabs from the body from unexposed areas and/or areas not completed while the body was *in situ* at the crime scene (eg swabs of all biting wounds for saliva traces and any other likely areas for gripping/holding traces).

- Oral, vaginal or penile, and anal swabs, nasal swabs (in special circumstances).

- Fingerprints—which may be essential not just for identification but also elimination from any found at the crime scene.

- Fingernail scrapings and clippings (if victim has long fingernails, photograph as offender may have scratch marks).

- Head and pubic hair (or other bodily hair) combings and cuttings.

- Blood, urine, stomach contents and bile (toxicology/time of death/sperm heads).

- Tissue sections for histology.

- Swabbing of exposed fractures for foreign debris (eg head fractures).

- Internal swabs of areas such as the oesophagus (eg for sperm heads).

- Ocular fluid (toxicology and time of death).

- Liver, lung, brain, fat tissue (in special circumstances).

- Botanical swabs/samples (advice required from palynologist).

14.12.3 Health and safety risk assessments

It is in everyone's interests that for a post-mortem process, health and safety issues are considered and managed effectively even when there is a conflict with the expediency of a criminal investigation. There is a very real danger of risk of infection from deceased persons and any contact, samples or possessions taken must be suitably controlled. A general rule is that all bodies and body parts should be regarded as being potentially infectious.

A risk assessment must be completed at the same time as the post-mortem tactical meeting is conducted and before anyone enters the examination room. The SIO needs to record this in their policy file after consultation with the Pathologist.

The mortuary in which the post-mortem is conducted must have adequate facilities to contain infectious risks, ie ventilation and cleansing equipment. In conjunction with the Coroner, the SIO and Pathologist can request that a more suitable mortuary be utilised.

For health and safety reasons, the SIO should allow only those persons who are absolutely necessary into the examination room. Permitted observers can often be accommodated behind glass screens or in a viewing gallery.

Checklist—Post-mortem risk assessment

- Those in attendance must have been in receipt of up-to-date inoculations for TB, Hepatitis B, polio and tetanus.

- Full protective clothing must be worn, ie full-length gown and mask, face/eye shield, waterproof non-slip boots/overshoes, nitrile gloves.

- Staff who at the time have open wounds/cuts/abrasions or skin complaints must be identified and such matters discussed with the Pathologist.

- Drinking, eating or chewing in the examination room is forbidden.

- Experienced staff should accompany the inexperienced.

- Familiarisation instruction on the layout and facilities of mortuary should be made available.

- Any accidents during the process must be fully investigated and reported.

14.12.4 Preparation and note taking

The SIO should be well prepared before going into the examination room, with suitable writing and note-taking equipment. It is always useful to note what the Pathologist and other experts are saying while the examination is in progress, making drawings/sketches that will assist when back at the incident room (for briefings etc). Useful sketches of injuries or marks can be made and although photographs will be taken, these may not be immediately available. Anatomical body maps can also be used to help indicate the location of significant findings.

14.12.5 Preliminary procedure

A body bag (in effect an exhibit bag) should not be opened or disturbed until everyone is ready and present in the mortuary examination room. Once the bag has been opened, the body should be externally examined once more before any clothing or possessions are removed. Cognisance should be taken of the ante-mortem examination findings and results for which the same persons should be present.

The position and condition of any clothing and personal effects, such as jewellery, may reveal vital clues, particularly if a sexual attack has occurred. Any cuts, tears, holes, rips, etc in clothing will need matching up with corresponding injuries. Evidence of missing buttons, zip fasteners, etc should be checked. A decision should have been made during the tactical meeting as to how any garment should be removed and recovered in order to capitalise on evidence-recovery potential (eg DNA, blood, fibres, etc) and if/what/how much photography is required during the process.

14.12.6 Completion of examination

A further meeting of all those involved should be held once the examination is complete. This is an opportunity to discuss with the Pathologist (and any other experts present) any findings, interpretations and conclusions. Any experts' opinions must always be supported by a plausible rationale (which can and often should be questioned and probed using the ABC principle).

The Pathologist should be in a position to summarise findings and provide an initial verbal report. It may be, however, that some aspects of the examination are still incomplete. Further tests, for example, may be required on samples or parts of the body, eg tests on the brain or toxicology reports from blood, urine or stomach contents may be required, which have to be done separately. Specialist examination of bone fractures may need further analysis. In some instances, a further examination of the body may be necessary to check whether there are any indications of bruising or bite marks that have been enhanced or have surfaced after the passage of time (taking care to distinguish them from artefacts of the removal/post-mortem procedure).

An Exhibits Officer must ensure that all relevant exhibits are accounted for, packaged properly and labelled with correct evidential signatures from the Pathologist and any other expert who handled them. The list of exhibits recorded should be thoroughly checked with the Pathologist as they too should keep a corresponding accurate record of all items and samples taken.

The Pathologist should be kept up to date with evidential developments that may alter their opinions. In some circumstances, they may also wish to revisit the scene before reaching a firm conclusion and ask for any additional information, such as copies of witness statements.

14.13 **National Injuries Database (NID)**

To assist the SIO, Forensic Pathologist and medical practitioner to interpret injuries and marks on victims as well as forensic medical issues, there exists a National Injuries Database. This is located within the NCA and is a free resource provided to support UK serious crime investigation.

The NID has the capability to conduct research on its extensive database to provide support and advice in determining the cause and type of any injury found on a victim as well as forensic medical issues, whether dead or alive. It can also assist with sourcing independent expertise for forensic medical opinions and provide research and expertise in specialist imaging and court presentations.

The work of the unit is mainly victim-focused and it can be used to search for cases to identify possible similarities between a victim's wound or specific injury patterns, with a possible weapon. This is particularly useful for an investigation in cases where the nature of the injuries is unknown and the weapon unidentified. The database currently holds a large number of cases of suspicious deaths, homicides and serious assault cases, including child abuse, sexual offences and self-inflictions. It also has extensive scene, injury and weapon images. The NID can be contacted on 0845 000 5463.

> **KEY POINT**
>
> If any material is passed onto another agency or a second opinion is sought, it is a matter of common courtesy to inform and liaise with the original Pathologist (or other expert concerned). Failure to do so may alienate certain specialists and experts who may have to eventually link up again.

14.14 Types of Death

While it is not possible to go into any great depth or detail about the complex and involved varieties of deaths that occur, this section briefly represents a quick and ready reference guide. These are specialist and complex subjects in their own right and expert advice should always be sought.

14.14.1 Asphyxia and strangulation

'Asphyxia' comes from a Greek word meaning 'lack of pulsation' and in everyday terms means death from an interruption of the process of breathing. Asphyxia may be due to suffocation (blockage of airway), strangulation (external pressure on neck), internal blockage of the airway or interference with the movements of respiration. Asphyxia signs can include:

- petechial haemorrhages in the face, eyes and/or body
- congestion to the face
- cyanosis (blue discoloration) of the face.

To complicate matters, these signs can be mimicked by other events, including heart failure, resuscitation, and hypostasis. Therefore, some circumstantial or supporting evidence is always useful.

Strangulation is traditionally divided into ligature and manual strangulation. Pressure may also be exerted on the neck using a 'bar arm' or 'choke hold' with a forearm. Ligature strangulation may be carried out using a variety of methods, including ropes, cord, wire and improvised items or pieces of clothing (such as a bra). Internally, it can cause fractures to the larynx or hyoid bone, denoting trauma to the neck, and internal bruising or haemorrhaging. Manual strangulation can leave fingernail abrasions and localised fingertip bruises to the muscles in the neck (which may be indicative of attempts at defence or panic removal of the ligature by the victim).

14.14.2 Firearms and gunshot fatalities

There are four factors that affect physical appearance of gunshot wounds on a human body: type of weapon, type of ammunition, range from muzzle to body and any intermediate targets. There are additional considerations for incidents and deaths involving firearms:

- Specialist ballistics expert advice should be considered.
- X-rays will be required to locate bullets/projectiles in a body.
- Swabs should be considered for firearm discharge residue from the body (to help determine how far the victim was away from the firearm).
- Discharge residues on the victim's hands can help determine if they handled the firearm (particularly if suicide suspected).
- Firearms discharge residues should be important forensic preservation/recovery consideration from suspects and their clothing/jewellery/possessions (checks to see if they have any firearms injuries themselves, such as recoil marks on their hands, rival gang or accidental bullet wounds, or adapted clothing to carry and conceal handguns).
- An analysis is required of both entry and exit wounds to help a ballistics expert determine direction of travel of the bullets, the angle the victim was shot from and in what order the shots were fired.
- Recovery and examination of bullets will assist in determining whether there was more than one weapon involved, and possibly what type of weapon was used (eg shotgun or automatic).

Useful firearms definitions:

Spent casing	What is ejected from semi-automatic firearms, or remains in a revolver cylinder after gun is fired
Shot shell	Spent or unspent cartridge fired from a shotgun
Jacket	Covering of a bullet
Cartridge	Live round of ammunition
Bullet	Missile/projectile fired from a firearm
Fragment	Portion of bullet or jacket

NABIS

The National Ballistics Intelligence Service (NABIS) delivers fast-time forensic intelligence as well as tactical and strategic intelligence to tackle all aspects of firearms-related criminality within the UK.

NABIS provides:

- Database (registry) of recovered firearms and ammunition used in crime, or entering police possession through any means. The database provides strategic and tactical intelligence which helps guide law enforcement activity.
- Ballistics comparison capability to link crimes and incidents within 24 to 48 hours in urgent cases.
- Intelligence Cell tasked with developing, understanding and disseminating strategic and tactical intelligence to police forces and law enforcement agencies (LEAs).

- Knowledge and Communications team who develop liaison opportunities between NABIS and its partners, as well as delivering national communications and media strategies.

NABIS works with the police forces of England and Wales as well as partner LEAs such as Police Scotland, British Transport Police (BTP), Ministry of Defence Police (MODP), MI5, National Crime Agency (NCA), UK Border Force (BF) and the Police Service of Northern Ireland (PSNI). It is contactable on 0121 626 7114 and at <https://www.nabis.police.uk>.

14.14.3 Fire deaths

Usually local protocols are in place for investigating fire deaths, which should include arrangements for tripartite investigations between the police, fire service and scientific experts. Aspects of fire deaths and pathology to consider are as follows:

- Post-mortems are often more difficult, as fire damage can cover up injuries or create spurious injuries that mimic assaults.
- Key question is usually whether the deceased was alive or dead when the fire took hold (to give an indication of whether they caused it themselves or were killed by a third party before the fire was started).
- If deceased was alive during the fire, there is often carbon monoxide in the blood, soot in the airways and scorching below the vocal chords. There may be a vital reaction to the burns, but this may be difficult to confirm even under microscopic examination.

The presence of flammable liquids and several seats of fire ignition are good indicators of arson. However, meaningful interpretation of these clues must be left to the experts due to the complexity of fire investigation. The SIO will have to rely upon the Pathologist to try to interpret what injuries are visible, if any, on badly burned bodies.

Deaths resulting from fire are generally caused by the inhalation of noxious gases and fumes. The victim is usually dead prior to the burning of parts of the body flesh. The Pathologist will be tasked with answering the critical question referred to above: whether the victim was alive at the time of the fire.

KEY POINT

Reference is made in Chapter 13 to additional information to seek from witnesses in fire cases (see key point in 13.9.2). When fuel from a filling station is suspected as an ignition source, obtaining control samples from nearby outlets needs to be fast-tracked, as most have frequent new deliveries (ie every 24 hours). The samples can be used for forensic comparison purposes against identical accelerants at the scene and on suspects.

14.14.4 **Bodies in water**

Post-mortems on bodies that have been submerged are more complicated because the body will often be in a poor condition, and the signs of drowning may have disappeared after a few days. Some pointers to consider are:

- Similar to fire deaths, a key fact is whether they were already dead before they entered the water.
- Typical signs of drowning are foam in the airways and over-inflated lungs.
- Spurious post-mortem injuries may be created by boats, fishing equipment, underwater objects, marine life or the deceased's hands dragging on the bottom of the waterway.

The finding of and recovery from water of a human body/body part(s) poses added challenges to ensure forensic evidential material, and how the body/body part will be preserved during a recovery operation. This will require close liaison between a team of experts and the SIO to quickly put together the best option. Time will be critical to avoid further destruction of the body in the water and if at all possible a contingency plan should be prepared in advance if there is a search phase beforehand.

14.14.5 **Body dismemberment**

Dismemberment is a form of mutilation, fragmenting a human body by severing and removing limbs. There are several types of dismemberment, each having different motives. Reference cases from the NCA and NID indicate that the majority of dismemberments occur post-mortem rather than ante-mortem, although in a small number of cases it occurs both post- and ante-mortem. Dismemberment is not to be confused with decapitation (the removal of a person's head) or evisceration (which means disembowelment).

The different types of dismemberment are:

Defensive mutilation	(i) General dismemberment—used to facilitate body removal by disarticulation of the joints to cover up traces of a crime and hinder identification. Most common form encountered.
	(ii) Localised dismemberment—eg removal of head/hands, to try and destroy a person's identity.
Aggressive mutilation	Where aggression is expressed by the perpetrator to the victim after their death or where the cause of death was dismemberment.
Offensive mutilation	Associated with lust, necro-sadistic murders—religious, spiritual or ritualistic, to release sexual pressure, fulfil urges after death or satisfy religious requirements.
Necromaniac mutilation	When a body is dismembered post-mortem and the perpetrator keeps a body part as a trophy (eg genitalia).

The location of what may appear to be dismembered bodies or body parts needs to be considered in the first instance as a crime scene. There will be additional specialists required, not least of all to confirm, if not obvious, that they are human parts rather than animal remains. A Forensic Anthropologist/Anatomist will be required to perform this task, not only to identify the remains as being human, but also to identify the body part. This can extend to seeing what sort of item or tool may have been used to produce the dismemberment, if it was a skilled or unskilled cut, and injury interpretation. The manner of dismemberment might give clues as to the reason for the dismemberment (see above table). Under microscopy, it may also be possible to match a cut or injury to a tool or weapon. Some experts are available who keep an archive of tool marks used to experiment with and produce matches on dismembered body parts (eg saws that leave unique marks on bone).

Dependent on the state of the remains, once confirmed, it will be necessary to identify to whom they belong. In cases of severe decomposition of a head, an expert can be asked to produce a facial reconstruction from the skull (including 2D and 3D manual and computerised reconstruction) using the bone structures as a guide. Isotope analysis of body parts may also be possible for indications of diet, lifestyle, geographic origin and possible geographic movement.

Additional considerations in dismemberment cases include searching for the items used to perform not only the task of cutting and removing limbs etc, but also for concealing the parts and activity (eg wrapping materials, bin liners, cleaning equipment and chemicals, rubber sheets and gloves, and digging tools). Checking for the purchase and acquisition of the necessary items and tools and looking for the place where dismemberment occurred can produce useful lines of enquiry.

When human body parts are found some important questions will arise and the 5WH process of information gathering can be applied, for example:

- Where was it found and when?
- Who found it and how?
- What body part is it?
- Who does it belong to?
- When, how and why was it dismembered?
- Where did the death and dismemberment occur (could be two different activities and locations)?
- Who dismembered it?
- Where are the other body parts?
- How did death occur (was the victim dead or alive during the process)?
- What level of skill was applied?
- What tools were used?
- What other evidence is available (eg sexual assault)?
- Why was the location chosen for leaving it and how did it/they end up there?
- How long has it been there and why wasn't it found sooner?

KEY POINTS

- Some forensic providers provide a service in which images and details of bones and body parts can be emailed to them to provide a quick analysis of the bone or body part to determine origin (ie human or otherwise).
- The NCA NID stores information about dismemberment cases and can provide advice and support with contacts and details of a wide variety of experts.
- The UK Missing Person's Bureau maintains a database of recovered unidentified body parts which can be cross-checked against reported missing persons.
- There is a likelihood that those who dismember bodies are likely to also injure themselves in the process—which may provide useful evidence.

14.14.6 Suicides

The investigative mindset principle of keeping an open mind should always be adopted when dealing with suspected suicide deaths. Investigatively speaking, all deaths should be treated as murder until the facts prove otherwise. Suicides cannot actually be categorised as such until a Coroner has returned an official verdict, until such time they are deemed to be 'apparent' suicides. With suicides, there are three important points to consider.

Checklist—Three suicide considerations

1. Close proximity to the body of the weapon or means of causing death.

2. Injuries or death wounds that appear self-inflicted AND could feasibly and practically have been inflicted by the deceased.

3. Existence of a motive or intent on the part of the deceased to take their own life. Aka the 'Ovenstone criteria'—as cited in I M K Ovenstone 'A Psychiatric Approach to the Diagnosis of Suicide and its Effect upon the Edinburgh Statistics' (1973) (123) *BJP*,15–21.

It must be noted that sometimes weapons can 'go missing' at suicide scenes due to them either being stolen (eg if in a public place) or removed by family or friends (eg to prevent embarrassment).

With wounds, certain factors are obviously not considered as possible indicators of suicide, eg multiple stab wounds in the deceased's body. However, it is sometimes surprising how much a person can injure themselves when intent on suicide. Traditional target areas in a suicide are often called 'sites of election', and include the throat, wrists, chest and abdomen, or the head if with a firearm. Suicidal gunshot wounds usually are close range and there should be evidence of firearms discharge residue around the area of the entry wound, but not in every case on the deceased's hand.

The manner of death can be a good indicator of motive and intent: for instance, putting their head on a railway line or jumping from a building when they have had to pay a special visit to these particular areas. Motive and intent can be established by examining movements, activities and behaviour of a deceased leading up to their death—for example, sourcing a ligature (eg rope) and fixings to hang themselves, purchasing flammable materials to set themselves on fire, visiting buildings or bridges from which to jump to their deaths, telling others of their intent, writing notes, researching suicide websites, history of previous failed attempts, significant changes in behaviour, excessive use of drink or drugs, severe depression and mood swings.

Hanging

These are usually suicidal or accidental, as in autoerotic deaths. Caution should be exercised to ensure they have not been deliberately staged (in which case a telltale sign might be more than one ligature mark/line visible on the neck of the deceased). If the person is obviously dead and there is no need for immediate life-saving methods, nothing should be touched, handled or disturbed until the body and scene have been examined and photographed.

It is surprising how quickly asphyxiation and death occurs when oxygen is cut off from the brain. Usually the body convulses in an effort to relieve the noose and some people try to get their fingers underneath to remove the pressure, causing scratch marks. Involuntary movements during the process of death can mean that areas of the body such as the hands and legs may get bruised if they come into contact with nearby items or surfaces. These marks should not be confused with defensive wounds or an attack from a third party.

If the ligature around the neck must be removed, the knot or tie should not be touched; instead it should be cut in an area that does not disturb the actual knot.

Suicide notes

Suicide notes are indications of suicide, provided they are genuine. That they were actually written by the deceased and voluntarily needs to be confirmed. Any note should be recovered in a manner to preserve forensic evidence, including DNA and fingerprints. Past writings of the deceased should be collected for comparison purposes, and there are specialists who can compare not just handwriting but comparative writing style and grammar.

There is sometimes the possibility that suicide notes (and the means of committing the suicide) may be removed or destroyed prior to police attendance. Investigators should be mindful of family members who can, in some circumstances, experience difficulty in accepting their relative or loved one has committed suicide and remove or destroy evidence. It has also been known for relatives of suicide victims to accuse the police investigation of a cover-up or wrong conclusion and request a formal review in the hope they can change a Coroner's verdict. Diaries, letters, text messages, communications and social media data and similar material can be examined for information that may corroborate details in a suicide note. Any stated or inferred intention of a person to take their own life and sudden and strange precursor activities are important investigative information.

Recovered articles and material can help contribute to compiling a 'psychological autopsy' of the deceased. This is a collaborative procedure involving police and mental health experts in an attempt to determine the state of mind of a person prior to the fatal act.

False reports

Some people commit a murder and try and stage it to appear as a genuine suicide (or other offence, such as an attack by an intruder), then feel duty-bound and compelled to report the death due to their alleged finding of the body and/or relationship to the victim (eg spouse/lover/relative/close friend) to make it appear genuine. What they say and do can provide very useful evidential information for (dis)proving their honesty and truthfulness. This emphasises the importance of obtaining the full contents of any report or emergency call to the emergency services (police, ambulance), which must be carefully scrutinised for precise wording and detail via a transcript/recording (if available) of the exact words used.

Studies have shown that mistakes are often made by offenders in how they report these deaths and how they behave, as indications of guilt can come from their words, language, tonality and general behaviour that can be recognised.[10]

Murder–Suicide

This involves an act in which an individual kills one or more other persons before, or at the same time as, killing oneself. The combination of murder and suicide can take various forms, including:

- Murder encompassing suicide, eg deliberate car crash, suicide bombing.
- Suicide after murder to escape punishment.
- Suicide after murder as form of self-punishment/guilt.[11]
- Suicide pacts (killing another then oneself by agreement).
- Suicide after killing members of own spouse/partner/family/relatives.

14.14.7 Autoerotic asphyxiation

Autoerotic asphyxiation is the term which describes when a person uses some form of self-strangulation and asphyxiation to increase or attain sexual arousal and orgasm. Hypoxyphilia involves a person achieving sexual arousal through oxygen deprivation by means of a noose, ligature, plastic bag, mask or other device or equipment. The activity is usually planned, so that there is sufficient

---

[10] Further details and advice can be obtained from the NCA Crime Operational Support (COS) which has a useful template from the FBI that can be utilised to check for the signs.

[11] Many spree killings have ended in suicide, such as Derek Bird (June 2010) who killed 12 members of the public in Cumbria then turned the gun on himself.

time and planning to allow him/herself the opportunity to escape asphyxiation prior to the loss of consciousness. However, due to equipment failures, errors in the placement of the noose or ligature or other mistakes, accidental deaths sometimes occur as there is strong involvement of risk taking.

These types of deaths can be devastating news for the family and friends of deceased persons. Apart from the grief aspect, they prove hugely embarrassing and it must be borne in mind that, like suicide, those who attend the death scene before the arrival of emergency responders and investigators might wish to remove, cover up or alter things.

Research shows that an autoerotic death scene can reveal key characteristics that provide clues and indications of accidental death, rather than suicide or homicide.

Checklist—Autoerotic death key features

- Absence of suicide note.

- Victim either totally or partially naked and/or genital organs are predominantly exposed.

- If male, dressed partially in women's underclothing.

- Ropes, belts or other bindings arranged so that compression of the neck could have been produced voluntarily.

- Scarf or towel placed around the neck, under the rope to protect against rope burns.

- Body, extremities and/or genitals bound with ropes, chains or leather.

- Pornographic material (especially pictures nearby).

- Evidence of masturbation is apparent (eg semen or vibrators).

- Evidence of repetitive behaviour (eg permanently installed bar, grooves on a rafter or other apparatus).

- Victim is suspended by the neck, with feet on the floor, while sitting in a chair or lying in a bed.

- Act appears to have been performed alone, usually behind locked doors or when privacy was assured.[12]

14.15 Role of HM Coroner

As soon as a death is deemed suspicious and is under investigation, the Coroner who covers the area where a body is found must be notified without delay. This is a key responsibility and task for an SIO.

---

[12] Cited in J L Uva, 'Review: Autoerotic Asphyxiation in the United States' (1995) 40(4) *Journal of Forensic Sciences*, 574–81.

Under section 1 of the Coroners and Justice Act 2009 (chapter 25), the Coroner has a duty to investigate all deaths where there are grounds to suspect any of the following:

(a) death due to a violent or unnatural act;
(b) cause of death is unknown; or
(c) deceased died while in custody or otherwise in state detention.

Under section 5 of the Act, the purpose of the Coroner's investigation into a person's death is to ascertain:

(a) who the deceased was;
(b) how, when, and where the deceased came by his or her death;
(c) details to be registered concerning the death; and
(d) under what circumstances the deceased came to their death.

14.15.1 Coroner's inquests

The Coroners (Inquests) Rules 2013 are contained in Statutory Instrument 2013 No 1616, which came into force on 25 July 2013 and apply to the powers conferred under the Coroners and Justice Act 2009. The rules regulate the practice and procedure relating to inquests, including the management of proceedings, disclosure of documents, witness special measures and provisions relating to inquests before a jury.

The Coroner is required to hold an inquest into the death in all cases where an investigation has been conducted, in accordance with section 6 of the 2009 Act. An inquest must be held under the following circumstances:

(a) the deceased died while in custody or otherwise in state detention and that either:
    (i) death was a violent or unnatural one, or
    (ii) cause of death is unknown;
(b) death resulted from an act or omission of:
    (i) a police officer, or
    (ii) a member of a service police force, in the purported execution of the officer's or member's duty as such; or
(c) death was caused by a 'notifiable' accident, poisoning or disease.

Once an inquest has been held, the Coroner sends a report to the registrar in the district where the death occurred, who will register the circumstances and details of the death. It is the registrar who issues the death certificate. Inquests are held in public and may include a jury. This may involve witnesses being called who are legally obliged to attend and may be penalised if they fail to do so. The Coroner may record the cause of death as:

• natural causes
• accident/misadventure

- industrial disease
- unlawful (ie homicide) or lawful killing
- suicide
- attempted or self-induced abortion
- dependence on drugs or non-dependent abuse of drugs
- open verdict.

The Coroner may also record a 'narrative verdict', which provides more detail than the terms outlined above.

14.15.2 Additional post-mortems and body release

Coroners can authorise the performance of a second post-mortem examination to facilitate the early release of a body to the family. Although the great majority of homicides result in swift arrests, delays can become acute due to the complexity or difficulty of certain types of investigation, or where there are a number of jointly charged defendants. This may cause undue distress to families and relatives. Therefore, the SIO should be keen to seek an early completion of all subsequent post-mortems.

The main objectives and features (as agreed by inter-agency agreements between bodies such as the NPCC, Coroner's Society, Law Society and Home Office) for second post-mortems are:

- reducing delays for release of a body for burial or cremation
- limiting the possibility of miscarriages of justice
- reducing the incidence of multiple post-mortems (on the same body)
- where no one is charged in connection with the death within a month, provision is made for a second, independent post-mortem for use by a defendant in the future.

There is no statutory authority for a person charged in connection with a death to order a post-mortem examination of the deceased. The performance of such an examination, however, has been well recognised by the courts. This examination must only be undertaken on the authority of the Coroner.

The Coroner will not release the body unless all those having a proper interest confirm in writing that they have no objection to the body being released. Before the proposed release of the body, the Coroner will, however, notify his or her intention to do so, in writing, to all those persons who have not yet confirmed that they have no objection to the release of the body.

This should also be a priority for the SIO and FLO in helping the family to cope with their grief, that may be compounded because of cultural and religious beliefs held in certain communities (eg Muslim and Jewish, that burial should occur within 24 hours or as soon as practicable following death).

There may be a natural resistance from some communities in relation to performing a post-mortem examination. This could be based on cultural or religious beliefs that the body should be left intact following death.

14.16 **Human Tissue Act 2004 (HTA)**

This Act introduced a number of provisions that are of relevance to homicide investigation. These include the following:

- Storage of the body of a deceased for the purpose of determining the cause of death must be on premises licensed for that activity by the Human Tissue Authority unless the storage is incidental to transportation.
- Performance of a post-mortem examination may only take place on premises licensed for that activity by the Human Tissue Authority.
- Pathologist undertaking the post-mortem examination must act under the authority of a licence from the Human Tissue Authority authorising post-mortem examinations on those premises.
- Coroners and Justice Act 2009 prevents a Coroner authorising a post-mortem examination if doing so would violate section 16 of the HTA.
- Samples may only be taken for the purpose of establishing or confirming the deceased's identity or determining the cause of death if the post-mortem has been authorised by the Coroner (in non-suspicious cases).

14.16.1 **Taking samples**

Samples of relevant material may be taken for three reasons. The first two, identification of the deceased and determination of the cause of death, are taken for the purposes and under the authority of the Coroner. Thirdly, material required as part of the investigation of crime (ie suspicious death investigations) is taken by the police through powers to seize evidence under section 19 of the Police and Criminal Evidence Act 1984 (PACE) and under common law and is not subject to the HTA restrictions.

All samples taken should be recorded by an Exhibits Officer and given a unique identifier. This record should make clear those samples taken for the Coroner and those taken for the police. Any samples taken at the location where the body was found should be incorporated into this list.

Samples held on the authority of the police do not fall within the consent requirements of the HTA or within the licensing requirements of section 39 of the HTA. However, samples held by the Pathologist on behalf of the police should, as far as practical, comply with the guidance issued by the Human Tissue Authority. It is also advisable for the police to comply with the guidance and it is reasonable to seek a consistent level of approach.

The police investigation into a death can end in a number of different ways. It is therefore a matter for the police to determine, in line with relevant guidance, what must happen to samples seized as evidence (under PACE) and how they should be disposed of. This would be different if the samples had been taken and the death not deemed to be suspicious, as the HTA would stipulate they should be returned to the family without delay and/or disposed of as deemed appropriate.

Given the possibly of a significant period between the post-mortem examination and the end of the enquiry, it may be wise to have made an initial assessment of the need to retain samples soon after the examination. The SIO should also take account of any views expressed to the FLO with regard to this matter.

Section 39 of the Act allows 'relevant material' to be taken, stored and disposed of without consent for criminal justice purposes. It is essential, however, that the family are made aware of what material has been taken and the reasons for its retention. The FLO should ensure relatives of the deceased have indicated a disposal option for 'relevant material' seized by police. There are three choices for the family to make:

- Retention of the material for review, audit, teaching, research and genetic counselling.
- Return of the material to the family of the deceased.
- Disposal of the material by burial, cremation or other lawful disposal by the Pathologist/police in a sensitive manner.

Generally, small tissue samples, slides, blocks and swabs make up the majority of retained tissue; however, in exceptional circumstances it is necessary to retain large body parts, such as the heart or brain. In such cases, the family should be told that an organ or large body part has been taken for additional testing. The family have the option of delaying any funeral or cremation until the body part can be returned. The additional testing should be done as quickly as possible and discussion with the Pathologist should be held to determine timescales and deadlines for completion of testing. This should then be communicated to the family.

If a family proceeds with a funeral before the return of the body part, arrangements for disposal with the family as soon as testing is complete is the best option. The return of the body part is not necessary if it will affect a prosecution case. If limbs or organs are to be disposed of by the police, arrangements should be made to cremate the remains. Any seized tissue should not be kept longer than is necessary. If there is no evidential benefit in retaining tissue, it should be disposed of. At the conclusion of criminal proceedings, the SIO and Exhibits Officer should hold an exhibits review to decide if any 'relevant material' is no longer required and can be disposed of. In some cases, however, it may be necessary to consult with the Crown Prosecution Service (CPS), the Coroner and the convicted person's defence team to ensure any disposal will not affect any appeal/inquest or breach of the Criminal Procedure and Investigations Act 1996 (CPIA).

The future retention of any 'relevant material' taken by police, or subsequently transferred from the Coroner's authority to the police, should be retained in accordance with the minimum periods established by the Code of Practice issued under the authority of section 23 of the CPIA:

- If an investigation results in criminal proceedings being instituted, all material which may be *relevant* must be retained at least until the accused is either acquitted or convicted, or until the prosecutor decides not to proceed with the case.

- Where the accused is convicted, all material which may be *relevant* must be retained at least until:
  - the convicted person is released from custody or is discharged from hospital, in cases where the court imposes a custodial sentence or a hospital order
  - six months from the date of conviction.

14.17 **Conducting Exhumations**

The exhumation of human remains is both intrusive and emotive, but may be the best or only option for an effective investigation. Tactically, it can be used as a means to identify a cause of death, establish or confirm a deceased's identity, conduct a pathological or forensic examination, obtain a forensic sample such as DNA, toxicology or recover artefacts believed buried with a deceased. Whatever the objective or necessity, exhumations can be a traumatic experience for all those affected or involved, and should only be embarked upon after careful consideration and planning.

UK national guidance is available from the NCA that contains best practice and advice in respect of exhuming bodies from graves within established UK burial grounds and cemeteries. It contains guidance on:

- domestic law
- family liaison
- media and communication
- role of the Coroner
- planning and strategy
- finance and resources
- health and safety and risk assessments
- site planning and preparation
- roles and responsibilities
- exhumation processes (and checklists)
- transit and mortuary processes
- re-interment
- operational orders
- key roles and responsibilities (including experts and specialists).

The guidance document is available via the Police Online Knowledge Area (POLKA) website (Major Crime Investigation Forum) and advice and support is via the Specialist Operations Centre on 0845 000 5463.

14.18 **Suspicious Missing Persons and 'No Body' Murders**

A missing person report can be the result of a number of varying reasons, and the majority are non-suspicious. People go missing each and every day for a variety of reasons including voluntarily, lost, under duress, accident, injury or illness. Some people, however, go missing due to becoming victims of crime and, in the most serious cases, homicide. Other serious offences such as human trafficking/slavery and child sexual exploitation can also be the reason.

Any unexplained and suspicious case of a missing person requires an in-depth investigation, in which case the rule of '*If in doubt...think murder*' applies. Suspicious missing person enquiries quickly develop into critical incidents and may involve very serious offences (eg kidnap, torture, sexual abuse or homicide). The initial response and risk assessment (ie high, medium or low) to a report of a missing person, particularly if it involves a child, young or vulnerable person, is critical and should be treated with the greatest urgency as an opportunity to save life AND obtain and secure evidence. This is a vitally important rule because in the first 24/48 hours there is far more chance of saving the life of the missing person and/or mounting a successful investigation if they and any offenders are traced quickly. If the missing person is particularly vulnerable, eg young child, the attention of the media and public will greatly increase. One example is the case of April Jones, aged 5 years, who went missing on 1 October 2012 in Machynlleth, Powys, Wales. This case was very quickly designated a murder enquiry and prompt action from a high-level police response and appointment of an experienced SIO and enquiry team led to the early arrest of a local man named Mark Bridger, aged 46 years. He was later charged and convicted of her abduction and murder, but not before the disappearance had rapidly generated a massive amount of inter/national media coverage.

KEY POINT

The NPCC definition[13] of a missing or absent person is:

Missing 'Anyone whose whereabouts cannot be established and where the circumstances are out of character or the context suggest the person may be the subject of crime or at risk of harm to themselves or another.'

Absent 'A person not at a place where they are expected or required to be and there is no apparent risk.'

A missing person enquiry may reveal evidence that a homicide has occurred, but the victim's body cannot be located. Indications may be obvious, such as an attack site where the victim lived or frequented with trace evidence of their blood. The circumstances in which they have gone missing might also be highly suspicious, such as a wife and mother who leaves behind her husband, children and family and disappears without trace, taking no means of support or communication, and who has recently been the victim of sustained domestic violence (DV). The circumstances would show the disappearance was totally out of

---

[13] ACPO, *Interim Guidance on the Management, Recording and Investigation of Missing Persons* (College of Policing, 2013).

character with no reason or preparation for their absence, and the person, body or remains cannot be found. These types of missing person investigations are often categorised or referred to as 'no body murders'.

In addition to a carefully coordinated and planned search for the suspected missing person's (ie victim's) body, if unsuccessful an SIO may wish to evidence that a person has been murdered by conducting what are termed 'proof of life' (PoL) enquiries. This is actually a contradictory term, as the objective is to prove that a person is deceased. A template has been developed that has been accepted as the national standard and received judicial support for conducting PoL enquiries. The template is a reference document which contains multiple categories and contacts to be considered for checking agencies and departments that might reveal traces of the missing person, such as health authorities, local authorities, utility companies, DVLA, passport office, financial institutions, charities, and judicial services. An SIO can provide witness testimony to a court to show the extent of enquiries and efforts made. Guidance on conducting of PoL enquiries and the template is available from the NCA (0845 000 5463).

14.18.1 **UK Missing Persons Bureau and Missing Children Team**

The UK national and international point of contact for all missing persons and unidentified bodies/cases is the UK Missing Person Bureau located within the NCA-CEOP command. They act as the centre for information exchange and expertise and can assist SIOs through the provision of:

- tactical advice and support on high-risk missing person cases and no-body murders (UK and abroad)
- response and coordination of law enforcement response to high-risk cases
- case analysis using their national database (HERMES) of missing and unidentified persons
- child rescue alert (CRA) system—an investigative tool to alert the public of missing children believed to be in imminent danger
- access to specialist overseas services through Interpol, Europol, SIRENE Bureaux and the NCA's international liaison team
- direct access to the NDNAD, Missing Person's DNA database, National Fingerprint Office and National Dental Index
- central hub for linking police and law enforcement agencies, government departments, NHS trusts, social welfare and non-government organisations
- provision of information for families and friends of missing persons including a range of factsheets that are available.

The UK Missing Persons Bureau and missing children team are available on +44 (0) 845 000 5481 and website: <http://www/missingpersons.police.uk> and <http://www.missingkids.co.uk>.

14.19 **Deaths in Healthcare Settings**

These types of deaths can be referred to the police (eg by a Coroner) if considered suspicious and necessitate an SIO making a mature and objective assessment of the circumstances and evidence. The investigations are, however, not of a routine nature. A decision has to be made on whether to conduct the investigation as per the standard guidelines (ie as per a homicide, the MIM, and many of the processes contained in other chapters of this handbook, once again remembering the maxim of **'If in doubt...think murder'**).

If it appears there may have been corporate failings, eg if the death occurred in the National Health Service (NHS), then liaison should be made with the Chief Executive of the organisation concerned.

One initial consideration must be in terms of safeguarding any vulnerable adults and children, particularly if the death took place in a residential care home (eg whereby all residents may be in need of safeguarding). The Care Act 2014 requires that every local authority must make enquiries or ensure others do so if it believes an adult is, or is at risk of becoming, a victim of abuse and neglect.

Organisational liability under the Corporate Manslaughter and Corporate Homicide Act 2007, and Ill Treatment and Wilful Neglect under sections 20–25 Criminal Justice and Courts Act 2015 and Health & Safety at Work Act 1974 also need to be borne in mind.

In order to reach a decision about likely culpability, the SIO may need to gain the assistance of a Forensic Pathologist, expert adviser(s) from the NCA (0845 000 5463) and specialist CPS case worker (especially when examining 'causation'-type evidence). If there is any evidence of a serious criminal offence (other than, say, a breach of health and safety legislation), then the police should take the lead for the investigation.

In the immediate aftermath of a suspected incident, steps must be taken to secure evidence. This may include physical, scientific and investigative material, although this might be difficult if some time has elapsed before an incident is reported and in some cases, a sensible approach may be required (eg where an operating theatre is concerned).

Checklist—Considerations for deaths in healthcare settings[14]

- Is there is a clear duty of care to the individual concerned?

- Was the death an expected outcome of the individual's illness?

- Was it a result of care and treatment that was necessary and proper?

- Does there appear to have been an unintentional error/mistake?

- Is there a suggestion of intention to kill or commit grievous bodily harm?

---

[14] See also ACPO Homicide Working Group, *An SIO's Guide to Investigating Unexpected Death and Serious Harm in Healthcare Settings* (NPIA, 2015)

- Does it appear an individual is responsible or organisation (eg senior management, policy or systemic failing)?
- Is there any evidence of homicide, manslaughter, unlawful act, gross negligence, ill treatment or wilful neglect?

Although extremely rare, there have been cases across the globe of medical serial killings (eg Michael Swango MD, American serial poisoner of his patients). A famous UK example is Dr Harold Shipman, who injected his patients with large doses of morphine to kill them. These went under the radar even after a police investigation that was heavily criticised in a public enquiry.[15] This type of serial homicide needs to be borne in mind by SIOs who must remain vigilant to the possibility in order to prevent further deaths occurring (**if in doubt...think murder**). Obtaining and examining the correct samples and insisting on a forensic pathological examination and thorough toxicology tests are key decisions. Checking career backgrounds of those suspected might show signs of troubling behaviour or complaints, or unexpected rise in deaths/illnesses in their patients in other locations where they have been operating, including overseas. Some added investigative considerations are:

- interviewing all victims/witnesses and locating any that have moved on
- reviewing all hospital/medical records relating to the suspect and victims (ie to see if their death was linked to medical profiles)
- checking pharmacy records for unusual amounts of drugs being dispensed or anomalies in drug inventories
- arranging forensic post-mortems, exhumations and toxicology tests (must stipulate what drugs or poisons to look for) with reasonable expedition
- checking victim profiles for commonalities
- checking death certificates and Coroner's staff/undertakers/mortuary technicians for anything they may have noticed was unusual (JDLR).[16]

14.20 **Domestic Homicides**

Domestic violence (DV), which includes physical, psychological, sexual, financial and emotional abuse involving partners, ex-partners, other relatives and household members, is a serious threat in the UK. Figures from the 2010 British Crime Survey showed that DV accounted for 14 per cent of all violent incidents; however, DV is often repeated and the level of violence can escalate over time. A domestic attack which results in death is all too common and accounts for the majority of

---

[15] The Shipman Inquiry by Dame Janet Smith DBE, released 14 July 2003, see <http://www.webarchive.nationalarchives.gov.uk>.

[16] This may include notes, drug charts, anaesthetic machines, instruments, syringes, incineration bins, clothing worn by patient and staff, treatment rooms, samples, staff communication devices, and CCTV.

homicide cases in the UK. Often the initial police response will identify the perpetrator and a routine investigation (Cat. 'C' type) will find evidence readily available to support a charge. However, the death is often not a first attack and is likely to have been preceded by varying degrees of DV or abuse. Many people, such as family, friends or neighbours, may well have known about previous attacks, together with various agencies such as the police, social services, probation service, and health service, or there may even be previous prosecutions or injunctions.

The challenge for the SIO is to ensure the ongoing homicide investigation covers this wide range of background information in order to gather the full facts for consideration by a court. A domestic homicide can also trigger a number of other parallel investigations such as a Domestic Homicide Review (DHR), a Serious Case Review (SCR) involving victims under the age of 18 years, an Article 2 Coroner's Investigation (Right to Life under ECHR) or an IPCC investigation covering a 'police-involved death'. These additional implications make what at first appears a simple and straightforward murder case into a quite complex and time-consuming exercise. In addition, the SIO and the Disclosure Officer must have a knowledge and understanding of how this third-party material can be examined and used to progress the investigation in addition to their CPIA responsibilities in relation to disclosure.

14.20.1 Domestic Homicide Reviews

DHRs were established on a statutory basis under section 9 of the Domestic Violence, Crime and Victim's Act 2004, and came into force on 13 April 2011. This placed a statutory requirement on the police to inform the relevant Community Safety Partnership (CSP) whenever a domestic homicide occurs. The chair of the CSP holds the responsibility for establishing whether a homicide is to be subject of a DHR under the above Act, which defines a domestic homicide review:

> Domestic Homicide review means a review of the circumstances in which the death of a person aged 16 or over has, or appears to have, resulted from violence, abuse or neglect by—
>
> (a) A person to whom s/he was related or with whom he was or had been in an intimate personal relationship, OR
> (b) A member of the same household as themselves, held with a view to identifying the lessons to be learnt from the death.

'Intimate personal relationship' includes relationships between adults who are or have been intimate partners or family members, regardless of gender or sexuality.

A member of the same household is defined as:

(a) A person is to be regarded as a 'member' of a particular household, even if he does not live in that household, if he visits it so often and for such periods of time that it is reasonable to regard him as a member of it.
(b) Where a victim lived in different households at different times, the same household as the victim refers to the household in which the victim was living at the time of the act that caused the death.

Note: when victims of domestic homicide are aged between 16 and 18, a Serious Case Review (SCR) should take precedent over a DHR, although a separate DHR could be set up to consider the domestic violence issues. (Serious Case Reviews are covered in Chapter 16.14.)

14.20.2 **Purpose of a DHR**

A DHR is carried out to:

(a) establish what lessons can be learnt from the domestic homicide regarding the way in which local professionals and organisations work individually and together to safeguard victims

(b) identify clearly what those lessons are both within and between agencies, how and within what timescales they will be acted upon, and what is expected to change as a result

(c) apply these lessons to service responses including changes to policies and procedures as appropriate

(d) prevent domestic violence homicide and improve service responses for all domestic violence victims and their children through improved intra- and inter-agency working.

References

ACPO, *Guidance on Disaster Victim Identification* (NPIA, 2011)

ACPO, *Interim Guidance on the Management, Recording and Investigation of Missing Persons* (POLKA, College of Policing, 2013)

ACPO, *Murder Investigation Model* (NPIA, 2006)

NPCC Homicide Working Group, *An SIO's Guide to Investigating Unexpected Death and Serious Harm in Healthcare Settings* (HWG, 2015)

Dogan, K et al, 'Decapitation and Dismemberment of the Corpse: A Matricide Case' (2010) 55(2) *Journal of Forensic Sciences*, 542–4

Journal of Homicide and Major Incident Investigation, vol. 6 Issue 2 Autumn (NPIA, 2010)

NCA, *Exhumation Guide* (Major Crime Investigation, POLKA, College of Policing, 2015)

NPIA, *Suggested Lines of Enquiry for Suspicious Missing Persons Investigations* (NPIA Crime Operational Support, 2007)

Ovenstone, I M K, 'A Psychiatric Approach to the Diagnosis of Suicide and its Effect upon the Edinburgh Statistics' (1973) (123) *BJP*, 15–21

Practical guide to Dismemberment cases (National Injuries Database, NCA, 2014)

Rutty G, *Body Identification: Briefing Guide to Assist in Body Identification* (NPIA National Injuries Database, 2009)

Uva, J L, 'Review: Autoerotic Asphyxiation in the United States' (1995) 40(4) *Journal of Forensic Sciences*, 574–81

15

Infant and Child Deaths

15.1 **Introduction**

Sudden and unexpected deaths in infants and children[1] (SUDI/SUDC) are fortunately quite rare but nonetheless extremely distressing and traumatic events. They deeply affect the parents, carers, families, relatives and local communities. It is hard to imagine anything worse for a family than the sudden death of their child.

Unlike older and more mature people, healthy infants and children are not expected to die. The stark reality is, despite a reduction in infant deaths (eg through education campaigns such as the Department of Health's Back to Sleep Campaign 1991, work of the Lullaby Trust, formerly FSID), statistics show several hundred children in the UK do die before they reach one year of age. The vast majority of these usually occur as a consequence of natural causes, such as disease, physical defect or pure accident. Unfortunately, however, a small percentage are also caused by callous and criminal acts of malicious, intentional and gratuitous violence, maltreatment, neglect, physical abuse or administered noxious substances or drugs. Children and infants can be subjected to deliberately inflicted head injuries, asphyxiation, stab wounds, hypothermia, dehydration, shaking injuries, methadone poisoning, broken/fractured bones, drowning, burns, crushing injuries, ruptured/failed organs (liver, kidney, etc) and abdominal injuries.

Some children, through no fault of their own, are vulnerable not only to poor health, disease and accident, but also callous parents, carers or sexual predators. At a very tender age potential victims are unlikely (and unable) to question or notice inherent dangers; nor are they in a position to object to lethal and deliberately administered noxious substances.

Child death investigations can and do pose particular challenges due to the hidden nature of tangible evidence and telltale signs. Young infants and children's bodies are far tinier and more delicate than adults and therefore indicators of non-accidental injuries are less noticeable. Contact trace evidence in intra-familial child homicides has limited use unless there are specific blood injuries due to regular contact with the suspect(s). Thus, a requirement to accurately diagnose, follow correct procedures and thoroughly investigate all the attendant circumstances of a child death is much more important. At the same time, a difficult distinction has to be made between parents who are suffering from a tragic loss and those who have committed extremely serious and grave crimes.

Child death investigation procedures have consequently become more rigorous and sophisticated, with a legal statutory ('Working Together' report (W/T) 2015, pp 6/7) requirement to involve a variety of experts and specialists, particularly when interpreting injuries. Nonetheless it is not uncommon to encounter conflicting opinion due to the complex and specialist nature of ascertaining a precise cause of death in infants and children. Unfortunately, traditional methods of investigation can be more limited because, unlike adult homicides, the chance of reliance upon passive

---

[1] 'Infant' means under 12 months old, 'Child' is one under 18 years of age (HM Government, *Working Together to Safeguard Children: A guide to inter-agency working to promote the welfare of children* (The Stationery Office, March 2015) (W/T), chapter 5, page 85, para 12).

data, DNA and fingerprint (contact trace) evidence are less likely given the home-based familial nature and likely frequent contact between the suspect(s) and child victim.

Baroness Kennedy in her Report in 2004[2] stated the role of the police was to ensure every child who dies deserves the right to have their sudden and unexplained death fully investigated in order that a cause of death can be identified, and homicide excluded. This helps support grieving parents and relatives by providing answers to the fundamental 5WH questions. It is also enables medical services to understand the cause of death and, if necessary, create intervention plans to prevent future deaths of children.

Surviving siblings also have a 'right to life' under Article 2 of the European Convention on Human Rights (ECHR). In meeting this requirement, an SIO is entrusted with the responsibility of concluding or excluding that a criminal act has taken place and helping to record an accurate cause of death. This chapter is aimed at preparing SIOs for this responsibility and providing (particularly for those on call) a guide for applying the most essential procedures and processes in order to effectively manage and conduct these investigations.

15.2 **Classifying Infant and Child Deaths**

Sudden death enquiries are always challenging, particularly when there is no medical explanation and the circumstances are uncertain or equivocal. This is more so if a young infant or child dies under the care and supervision of parents in the family home. A useful starting point, however, is to clarify the different categories or classifications that may apply to help determine the type of response required and scale of investigation. Most begin as a Category 1 SUDI/C death and can move up (or back down) the scale as the information changes. In order of seriousness, every case falls into one of the following categories.

Category 1	Unsuspicious (but sudden and unexpected,[3] usually natural or accidental with no apparent medical explanation, ie SUDI/C).
Category 2	Suspicious[4] (certain factors raise the likelihood of a criminal act having been committed and warrant a more detailed investigation).
Category 3	Homicide (or other serious criminal offence, see checklist later in this chapter).

---

[2] Baroness H Kennedy, *Sudden Unexpected Death in Infancy: A Multi-Agency Protocol for Care and Investigation* (Royal College of Pathologists and Royal College of Paediatrics and Child Health, 2004).

[3] An 'unexpected' death is defined as: 'the death of an infant or child which was not anticipated as a significant possibility, eg 24 hours before the death; or where there was an unexpected collapse or incident leading to or precipitating the events which led to the death' (W/T 2015, chap 5, p 85).

[4] 'Suspicious' means: 'although there is no direct evidence or grounds to suspect a specific criminal act, there are however factors that raise the possibility a criminal act may have contributed to the death and thereby merit a more detailed investigation of the circumstances of the death' (R Wate and D Marshall, 'Effective Investigation of Intra-familial Child Homicide and Suspicious Death' (2009) 5(2) *Journal of Homicide and Major Incident Investigation*.

By definition, Category 1 cases almost always require a different type of response from those falling within Categories 2 and 3. However, a number of the initial actions will be the same, eg examination of the body, full history from parents/carers, place where the child died examination and multi-agency background checks, as it is not always apparent at the outset which category they fit into. Research conducted in 2004 (Levene, Bacon FSID Archives of Disease in Childhood) suggested that one in ten cot deaths may be as a result of murder or neglect, which means one in ten may be a covert homicide. Equally 90 per cent are from medical or natural causes. Safeguards, therefore, need to be incorporated into this level of investigation to preserve evidence in case the circumstances and classification change. This is vitally important when considering the procedures referred to in other sections of this chapter that are inappropriate for categories 2 and 3. For example, in homicide or suspicious deaths, the classification for the investigation changes from a 'SUDI/SUDC' death to a 'homicide investigation', and the place where death is believed to have occurred (eg a child's bedroom) will be reclassified a 'crime scene'. This triggers standard procedures that are outlined in other chapters of this book due to a criminal act (although in the majority of cases, unless clearly homicide, the body is likely to have been transported to a hospital Accident and Emergency (A&E) unit and not remained in position for forensic examination purposes, as explained later). The SIO will also be making early consideration of making arrests, treating witnesses as 'significant', possibly managing the investigation on a case management system (eg HOLMES), conducting house-to-house (H-2-H) enquiries, witness trawls, etc.

If there is nothing clearly obvious to suggest a suspicious death or homicide has occurred—a *very important judgement call*—the term 'SUDI/C' death is used to describe what is probably a much lesser type of investigative response (though still very thorough, and certainly more comprehensive than the standard police response to a non-suspicious sudden death of, say, an adult). Category 1 types are covered by guidelines outlined in this chapter, while categories 2 and 3 are investigated in accordance with conventional (eg homicide-type) investigative requirements.

Child homicides and suspicious deaths, unfortunately, are not always so obvious or easily recognisable. Consequently it can be more difficult to initially determine what category applies. There may be no obvious signs, such as wounds or fractures. Head and internal injuries, asphyxiation, ruptured blood vessels in lungs, traces of poisoning, abuse and neglect can be very difficult to detect in young children, particularly infants. Therefore child death procedures have been consolidated to ensure all Category 1 SUDI/C investigations meet a higher investigative standard. This is to provide not only adequate safeguards for sensitive parent management and support, but also ensure every effort is made to establish why a child died unexpectedly and rule in or out criminal offences.

There is, however, a requirement to conduct enquiries far more sensitively. One example being the expectation of a more tactful and less obvious use of 'golden hour(s)' tasks; another the need for a greater multi-professional approach to the investigation. SUDI/C procedures ask for a balance to be struck between the requirement for carrying out an effective investigation and the need to acknowledge and cater for the needs of the parents and other children who may be affected. For these reasons, a specialist trained investigator and/or SIO should ideally take the lead on a child death investigation, particularly when it is unclear what category it falls into.

KEY POINTS

1. In all cases of SUDC, whether or not there are any obvious suspicious circumstances, a Lead Investigator[5] should be tasked to immediately take charge of the investigation. It is recommended that the Lead Police Investigator attends the location of the body to liaise with the lead clinician and other medical practitioners (ACPO Homicide Working Group, *A Guide to Investigating Child Deaths* (ACPO HWG, 2014), p 9).
2. Four standard and key questions to ask are: (i) Why did the child die? (ii) What was the cause of death and circumstances? (iii) Were any criminal offences committed? (iv) If so, who was responsible?[6]

Checklist—Category 3-type offences

- **Murder**—contrary to common law.

- **Manslaughter** (including corporate manslaughter, eg deaths in healthcare settings)—contrary to common law.

- **Familial homicide** (causing or allowing a child or vulnerable adult to die or suffer serious physical harm)—section 5 of the Domestic Violence, Crime and Victims Act 2004 (DVCV) (as amended by DVCV (Amendment) Act 2012).

- **Infanticide**—section 1 of the Infanticide Act 1938.

Other related or kindred offences might be:

- **Child destruction**—section 1(1) of the Infant Life (Preservation) Act 1929.

- **Administering/procuring drugs/instruments to procure an abortion or miscarriage**—sections 58, 59 of the Offences Against the Person Act 1861.

- **Exposing a child whereby life is endangered**—section 27 of the Offences Against the Person Act 1861.

---

[5] Reference to Investigating Officer/Lead Police Investigator is understood to mean a member of staff who has attained the national standard in the field of investigating child deaths (ACPO, 2014).
[6] As cited in D Marshall, *Effective Investigation of Child Homicide & Suspicious Deaths* (Oxford University Press, 2012), 35.

- **Concealment of birth**—section 60 of the Offences Against the Person Act 1861.

- **Preventing lawful burial**—concealment of a corpse—disposing of or destroying a dead body.

- **Neglect**—death of infant under three years caused by suffocation while infant in bed with person 16 years or over who is under the influence of drink or prohibited drug—section 1 of the Children and Young Persons Act 1933 (as amended by Serious Crime Act 2015).

- **Wilfully assault, ill-treat, neglect, abandon, expose child under 16 years**—section 1 of the Children and Young Persons Act 1933.

- **Maliciously administering poison etc or noxious thing so as to endanger life**—section 23 of the Offences Against the Person Act 1861.

- **Attempting to choke etc so as to commit an indictable offence**—section 21 of the Offences Against the Person Act 1861.

- **Drunk in charge of child apparently under 7 years**—section 2(1) of the Licensing Act 1902.

- **Child abduction by person connected with the child**—section 1 of the Child Abduction Act 1984 as amended by the Family Law Act 1986 and the Children Act 1989.

- **Grievous bodily harm or wounding with intent**—section 18 of the Offences Against the Person Act 1861.

15.3 **Factors Which May Increase Suspicion**

Whilst every case should be judged on its own merits, in certain cases there may be surrounding facts or circumstances that heighten suspicion. The following are listed as a guide:[7]

1. History of violence in the family to children.
2. Parents or carers who provide an inconsistent account of events surrounding the child's death.
3. Mental health issues within the family.
4. Previous unusual illness, episodes or recent admissions to hospital.
5. Child is older than 12 months (these unexplained deaths are rare and unusual).
6. Intelligence suggests the child has been 'at risk' or precursor incidents suggest this should be the case, eg child or sibling is on a 'child protection' or 'care plan'.
7. Family members of the child are known to social care (services).
8. Parent or carer has a criminal record.

---

[7] See also Mayes et al, (2010) 6(1) *Journal of Homicide and Major Incident Investigation*, pp 77–96.

9. The child has been dead longer than stated.
10. Crusted blood on the face of the type associated with smothering and physical abuse, rather than the 'pinkish' mucus associated with resuscitation.
11. Unusual bruises or petechiae or retinal haemorrhaging, eg in the eyes—symptoms of suffocation or shaking (note: eyes need to be checked quickly as the cornea clouds over after death in a matter of hours preventing any examination of the retina).
12. Presence of foreign bodies in the upper airway.
13. A child has died in the family previously.
14. History of drug, alcohol or domestic violence within the family.
15. Inappropriate delay by the parents in seeking medical help.
16. Position, surroundings and condition give cause for concern.
17. Evidence of high-risk behaviour, eg domestic abuse, drugs/alcohol use.
18. Parent's reaction/demeanour/behaviour.
19. Neglect issues.

15.4 'Working Together'

Success for any type of infant/child death investigation relies upon effective cooperation and liaison between the police, essential experts (paediatricians) and certain other agencies all working together. The death should trigger the coming together of a team of professionals from a number of agencies and is often known as a 'Rapid Response'.

The police have NPCC guidelines and additionally forces may have their own, as may some of the other agencies and bodies that could become involved. In most regions, joint LSCB protocols exist and it is advisable for on-call SIOs to be familiar with them.

All the necessary agencies share responsibility for an investigation to establish the cause of death and a duty of care to the parents and surviving children. An SIO who takes the lead for the criminal investigation will be expected to work alongside highly qualified and experienced professionals, who together must balance the medical, forensic and all other investigative requirements with the welfare of the parents affected and potential risks to other (and future) children.

Between an assembled team of professionals there will be the necessary knowledge, expertise, information and resources to mount a sophisticated joint investigation into why and how a child or young person died. Any sudden and unexplained death must trigger the joining up of such resources, with the SIO ensuring there is trust and confidence amongst the team for a coordinated inter-agency response, particularly in relation to information sharing.

Each agency and individual will have different areas of responsibility. For example, a paediatrician will most likely focus upon issues that have implications for others, such as infectious diseases, in addition to the cause of death. The coroner will focus solely upon the cause and circumstances of the death (ie who, when, where and how) and the social services on safeguarding the welfare of other children in the family. These various agendas are intertwined and viewed as complementary in establishing why a child has died, providing parents and others affected with support, and quickly identifying and investigating any potentially suspicious circumstances.

The W/T 2015, chapter 5, outlines key guidelines. It states the following:

- The designated paediatrician responsible for unexpected deaths in childhood should be consulted where professionals are uncertain about whether the death is unexpected. If in doubt, the processes for unexpected child deaths should be followed until the available evidence enables a different decision to be made.
- As set out the Local Safeguarding Children Boards Regulations 2006, LSCBs are responsible for putting in place procedures for ensuring there is a coordinated response by the authority, their Board partners and other relevant persons to an unexpected death.
- The consultant clinician (in hospital setting) or other professional confirming Fact of Death (FOD) should inform the local designated paediatrician at the same time as the police and coroner. The police should begin an investigation on behalf of the coroner. The paediatrician initiates immediate information sharing between the agencies (eg police, health, local authority and children's social care) to decide what happens next and who does what, when, how, etc.
- A RAPID RESPONSE is required from all agencies that is consistent with the Baroness Kennedy principles and NPCC guidelines.
- Immediate enquiries should commence into the circumstances of the death (in agreement with the Coroner) and liaison with the Pathologist.
- Information collection should begin.
- Support to the bereaved family should be commenced including involving them in meetings as appropriate and keeping them informed/up to date.
- Consent should be sought from the family for the release of their medical notes.
- If the infant/child dies at home or in the community, they should be taken to an A&E department and NOT a mortuary, unless the police deem it inappropriate because of examinations required (ie as crime scene).
- The Lead Police Investigator AND senior healthcare professional should decide whether there should be a visit to the place where the child died, how soon (usually within 24 hours) and who by. This should always be the case in SUDI cases.
- If there is a criminal investigation, the multi-agency team must consult with the Lead Police Investigator and CPS to ensure their enquiries do not prejudice any criminal proceedings.

The diagram below shows the process for rapid response to the unexpected death of an infant or child (cited in W/T 2015, Flow chart 8, p 91).

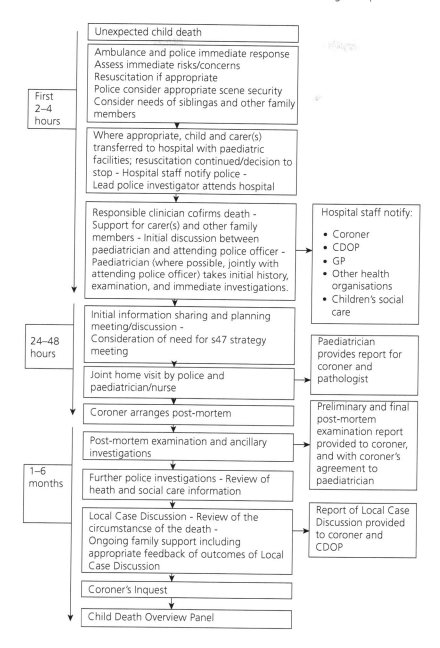

First
2–4
hours

Unexpected child death

Ambulance and police immediate response
Assess immediate risks/concerns
Resuscitation if appropriate
Police consider appropriate scene security
Consider needs of siblingas and other family members

Where appropriate, child and carer(s) transferred to hospital with paediatric facilities; resuscitation continued/decision to stop - Hospital staff notify police - Lead police investigator attends hospital

Responsible clinician cofirms death - Support for carer(s) and other family members - Initial discussion between paediatrician and attending police officer - Paediatrician (where possible, jointly with attending police officer) takes initial history, examination, and immediate investigations.

Hospital staff notify:
- Coroner
- CDOP
- GP
- Other health organisations
- Children's social care

24–48
hours

Initial information sharing and planning meeting/discussion - Consideration of need for s47 strategy meeting

Joint home visit by police and paediatrician/nurse

Paediatrician provides report for coroner and pathologist

Coroner arranges post-mortem

1–6
months

Post-mortem examination and ancillary investigations

Further police investigations - Review of heath and social care information

Local Case Discussion - Review of the circumstancse of the death - Ongoing family support including appropriate feedback of outcomes of Local Case Discussion

Coroner's Inquest

Child Death Overview Panel

Preliminary and final post-mortem examination report provided to coroner, and with coroner's agreement to paediatrician

Report of Local Case Discussion provided to coroner and CDOP

15.5 **Guiding Principles—SUDI/C**

A number of fundamental principles underpin the work of all relevant professionals, especially responding officers and SIOs, when dealing with all three categories of SUDI/C. These are:

- The need to maintain a sympathetic and sensitive approach to the child's family, regardless of the cause of death. Police action has to be carefully balanced between considerations for the bereaved family and recognition that a serious crime may have been committed.
- Retaining an awareness that innocent parents/carers wrongly accused of harming their child are caused unimaginable suffering as a consequence.
- Retaining an open mind as to how and why the child or young person died. A child with seemingly no obvious signs of external or internal injury could still have been the victim of unlawful killing because the signs may be less detectable.
- A coordinated and rapid inter-agency response (as per paragraph 15.4) is required including the police, other specialists and service providers who have particular knowledge and experience of child abuse and development (working together and crucially sharing information).
- Communicating clearly and sensitively with parents/carers (even when they may potentially be suspects).
- Recognising and understanding that all SUDI/C deaths require a thorough and meticulous but compassionate standard of investigation.
- Ensuring there is a proportionate response to the circumstances.
- Preservation of all potential evidence.

15.6 **Hospital Procedures**

Child deaths are likely to be reported directly to the emergency services and routed through an ambulance control centre. Sometimes they even originate directly from A&E units at hospitals. Occasionally a GP will be first on the scene and notify the emergency services. Call handlers are responsible for obtaining as much information from the person reporting the death as possible and organising the rapid despatch of medical care to the scene. In most cases, the police are notified simultaneously and could feasibly arrive before others.

Guidelines in 'Working Together' stipulate that after an initial attempt at resuscitation, a child should be taken directly to an A&E unit (unless obvious and clear signs a homicide has occurred). Taking the child to a hospital rather than a mortuary is to ensure all possible resuscitation options have been considered; it also assists the parents in allowing them to go with the child and receive themselves any necessary initial support from trained hospital staff. It also facilitates initiation of the rapid response procedures, including the early examination of the body by a consultant paediatrician in support of the investigation into the cause of death. Once at the hospital, a lead clinician normally contacts the designated SUDC paediatrician to arrange contacting other agencies, including the police, via standard communication protocols.

A member of nursing staff is usually allocated to deal with and support the family. In some regions some of the rapid response procedures are undertaken by a designated SUDC nurse rather than a paediatrician. They should also begin obtaining initial details from the family and accurately recording them. Hospital staff will be fully briefed by the medical crew who attended and conveyed the child to hospital. The SIO should note that these details are highly valuable sources of information and probably the first account (other than the call to the emergency services) about what took place. If the circumstances develop into something more serious and suspicious, the medical staff may become significant witnesses for the purposes of determining mode of interview.

Once a child has been certified clinically dead, hospital staff will normally facilitate arrangements for the parents to be allowed time with their child. This is usually followed by a more in-depth interview (also known as 'history taking'), normally done at the hospital with the parents, and wherever possible the police should take the lead in this process with a paediatrician involved to interpret all medical and parenting issues. If, however, it is being treated as a non-suspicious death, then it is normally the paediatrician who takes the lead in history taking as it will be more medically focused. This is probably a difficult judgement call to make and will depend on the individual circumstances.

KEY POINTS

It is vital to sit down before approaching the family (ie with the paediatrician) to discuss points including:

- Who will lead introductions?
- Who will be present?
- Who will scribe [sic. ie take notes]?
- Will the child be examined prior to history taking? (This can help inform professional judgement on whether or not the death is suspicious at an early stage.)

D Marshall, 'The Paediatrician's Perspective' in *Effective Investigation of Child Homicide and Suspicious Deaths* (OUP, 2012) p 77.

If the parents are suspected of criminality, the SIO will have to determine whether history taking should take place at all and instead have them treated as 'suspects'. This doesn't necessarily mean they have to be arrested immediately, but it does mean that once that threshold has been crossed, it will be unlikely that the product of any informal history taking could be used in any criminal proceedings.

15.7 Serious Case Reviews (SCRs) and Other Parallel Proceedings

The protection of other siblings is paramount and there may be proceedings being carried out in the Family Court making use of the same witnesses that could be subsequently required in the criminal court. Albeit this may be extremely concerning to an SIO, it can also be a positive situation, with, for example, the medical evidence being rehearsed in a court setting. Limited use of this material can take place with the permission of the Family Court Judge.

In many cases of child homicide, it is likely that the LSCB will commission a Serious Case Review in accordance with chapter 4[8] of 'Working Together', which states that:

> The prime purpose of a Serious Case Review (SCR) is for agencies and individuals to learn lessons to improve the way in which they work both individually and collectively to safeguard and promote the welfare of children. The lessons learned should be disseminated effectively, and the recommendations should be implemented in a timely manner so that the changes required result, wherever possible, in children being protected from suffering or being likely to suffer harm in the future.[9]

15.8 **Initial Police Response**

Most of the procedures outlined in Chapter 5 underpin the initial response, activities and actions when dealing with an incident that may involve a Category 2 or 3-type child death. However, as the majority of unexplained child deaths are not usually the result of criminal acts, ie Category 1, the police response needs to be finely balanced between providing the utmost consideration for the needs of an innocent, grieving family and conducting a thorough investigation into the cause of death. Child deaths come with added sensitivities, complexities and challenges, both from a professional and emotional perspective. These can be emotionally demanding events that require a high degree of composure, experience and tact; therefore using trained child protection/abuse unit investigators is a preferred option, wherever possible. There is also a requirement to look for any factors that may raise suspicion (see earlier) even though everything overtly appears normal. For these reasons, only the most experienced staff, supervisors and senior detectives should be used, whenever possible, in the initial response.

If the initial response requires police attendance at a child's home address, it should, wherever possible, be conducted in a 'low key' and unobtrusive fashion. This is to reduce or minimise any undue attention or distress to the parents and to avoid attracting the early attention of the community, public and media. Plain-clothes officers, particularly detectives in unmarked vehicles, are ideal for using as first response officers if practicable, provided no unreasonable delay is caused as a result (remembering the 'golden hour' principles).

Officers attending should make an initial assessment of not just the scene and circumstances of the child's death, but also the safety and welfare of any other children at the same location. Depending upon the circumstances of the death and the conditions in which other children may be found, it may be necessary to take prompt action to secure their safety and wellbeing (aka 'safeguarding'), a decision ideally taken in consultation with supervisory staff and other agencies.

---

[8] HM Government, *Working Together to Safeguard Children: A guide to inter-agency working to promote the welfare of children* (The Stationery Office, March 2015), chapter 4.

[9] The subject of SCRs is also dealt with in Chapter 16.

> **KEY POINT**
>
> When attending a scene, including hospitals, staff should be careful when speaking to colleagues, or using communication devices such as radios and mobile phones within range of grieving parents, carers or relatives. Overhearing the use of insensitive terms such as 'suspicious death' or 'crime scene' may cause unnecessary distress. Care should also be taken to refer to the deceased child by their name—not 'it' or 'body'.

If the initial police attendance is to a hospital, the first officer(s) liaises with any A&E staff that have examined the child/young person or spoken to parents/carers to establish what is known so far. Careful and accurate note taking of these details is required. They should also ensure that the parents/carers have been informed of the need for police involvement.

It is good practice to give an early explanation for the necessity for police involvement to the parents and the reasons for any action taken. For example, it could be explained that the police are acting on behalf of the Coroner, who requires an investigation is carried out for all sudden and unexplained deaths of any child that occurs with the aim of establishing why the death has occurred. Most parents and carers, however, welcome the opportunity of finding answers to questions such as 'Why did my child die?' which they themselves need in order to move on with their lives.

When dealing with family/carers, there needs to be an early attempt to recover, label and secure any nappies, underwear, clothing or possessions taken from the child by hospital staff that may be important to the investigation (being mindful of cross-contamination). Items seized are treated as potential exhibits and packaged separately and properly to avoid any risk of contamination. They may be later required for forensic examination.

The initial investigation into the circumstances of a child's death includes the obtaining of information and historical details from the parents. This procedure may have already been commenced by medical staff if the body is at hospital (see earlier section under 'hospital procedures'). This process forms an important part of building rapport with the family, parents and relatives, and for the purposes of an investigation is an ideal opportunity for exercising essential tradecraft skills and intuition in order to form an early opinion as to whether there may be any suspicious indicators.

The initial response phase is within the golden hour(s) period, a time when emotions are running high and people at their most vulnerable. Offenders in particular are under the greatest levels of psychological and emotional pressure and can make mistakes or give false and inaccurate accounts and details. This is therefore an opportunity to gauge reactions, observe attitudes, behaviour and demeanour of the parents or carers and look for any suspicious or disturbing signs or comments, or flawed explanations that do not add up or give rise for concern.

As with any other investigation, skilful handling of people (including significant witnesses), information building and accurate record keeping are essential during the initial stages (golden hours).

Checklist—Initial responders—first actions at hospital

- Confirm location of child's body and continuity of movement.

- Make early attempt to locate any nappies, underwear, clothing or possessions taken from the child/young person by hospital staff.

- Obtain and record details of the person/s who removed the items from the body (or later handled them).

- Treat all items as potential exhibits and package/label them separately to avoid any risk of contamination (they may later require forensic examination).

- Seek the consent of the parent/carer (or owner if different) to retain items—there may be sufficient grounds under section 19 of the Police and Criminal Evidence Act 1984 (PACE) if a criminal offence has been committed, or to help establish cause of death.

- Reassure the parents/carers/owner that the items will be returned to them as quickly as possible and in the best possible condition.

- Ask for the duty SIO to be informed and request them to attend as soon as possible.

15.9 Managing the 'Scene' (or 'Place Where Death Occurred')

Even where a child death is being treated as non-suspicious, initial response officers should strive to keep the primary 'scene' (or 'place where death has occurred'—remembering to choose words carefully in front of grieving parents when the cause of death is unknown) as sterile and secure as possible, The whole house and contents could be relevant, eg feeding bottles in the kitchen, heating systems (hot/cold environments), general state of tidiness and cleanliness, toys and food etc, in which case it may be useful to conduct as 'walk through' similar to that described in Chapter 14.9.

Depending on the circumstances (eg it may be possible to securely lock the scene), it might also involve an officer controlling the security of a room until a thorough combined examination can take place. The senior investigator/SIO has responsibility for deciding whether to request the attendance of a Crime Scene Investigator (CSI) and/or photographer (and any other resources as felt necessary), although there is a strong case for CSIs routinely attending all child death scenes with the SIO. The photographing and digital recording of the 'scene' is always to be treated as good practice in every case (even if not initially suspicious), as it a way of ensuring there is permanent record in case the circumstances later develop into something more serious (eg in post-mortem results such as toxicology).

Vitally important is that in cases where there is no immediate suspicion, the preservation process is handled tactfully and sensitively, particularly in a child's home. This may, for example, require an explanation as to why it is a necessary process for the investigation (ie it will significantly help determine why the child died and is standard procedure). Some parents may become highly sceptical of police procedures and require careful management. There is also a need for parents (including carers, relatives and friends) to be dissuaded (and effectively prevented if needs be) from disposing of anything evidential, such as bottles, bedding, nappies, and residue food and drink, that may be useful to the investigation. In extreme cases where parents are obstructive, powers under section 19 of PACE (or even sections 8, 18 and 32 if arrests have to be made) may have to be considered.

It can be common practice for officers to seize bedding and sometimes even the cot or 'Moses basket' in which a child died. Yet it is more beneficial for the bedding etc to be left undisturbed so it can be observed as it is by the SIO and SUDI/C paediatrician/nurse who jointly attend for a home visit and assessment. In natural deaths, bedding can be one of the key items that may hold clues as to how a child died (thickness, position, etc). In many ways there is nothing different between these procedures and standard crime scene procedures about preserving and protecting everything as it is found. One main difference, however, is the requirement to be more sensitive and tactful for the benefit of grieving parents and distressed relatives, especially when in the majority of cases no crime will have been committed.

KEY POINT

There is an urgent requirement for digital recording/photographs of the scene as close to the time of events as possible (and any medical teams who attended are also useful sources of information). The scene is a key piece of information in helping to assess the type of death being dealt with.

15.9.1 Scene assessment and examination

The SIO needs to conduct a thorough and proportionate scene assessment while in a preserved format and arrange for any necessary photographs, visual images, measurements, drawings, etc (always seen as a safer measure for preserving an accurate record, whatever the circumstances). Other experts and advisers such as a CSI or plan drawer may be required to assist the SIO and, if believed suspicious, then the standard procedures need to be applied (eg a Forensic

Pathologist to attend, discuss and formulate a crime scene examination, body recovery strategy, etc).

A confidentiality requirement must be observed so as not to bring undue suspicion upon or attention to the parents or household of the deceased child. Visits to the family home (and elsewhere, if clearly connected to the parents) should be performed as discretely as possible. If a search of the place where a death has occurred (non-suspicious) is conducted, staff should be fully briefed beforehand and the process conducted in a highly sensitive manner. Where items are to be removed from a child's house, it should be explained to the parents why this is standard procedure and how it will help establish why their child died. The SIO should be in a position to justify and explain to the parents/carers the need to remove or seize any item for examination.

Checklist—Scene management

- Check for delays in getting to or finding the child; signs of alteration or staging by parents/carers.

- Searches should include all potential scenes, multiple rooms and vehicles and exterior of any dwelling.

- Check for any rubbish receptacles and laundry for discarded items.

- Obtain photographs, visual imagery and scaled diagrams.

- Take measurements of furniture and seize any relevant furniture items.

- Look for possible weapons or objects that may have been used to cause harm (eg smothering—may be pillow or even child's toy), especially if there are any patterned injuries.

- Give consideration for recovering trace evidence (fingerprints, DNA, blood, hair, fibres, etc) on possible articles, weapons or drugs.

- Check for evidence of soiling, vomit (vomit containing what appears like coffee granules may be blood), illness, colic, messes or spills (and monitors or devices if a special needs child).

- Seize any documentary evidence, eg life insurance policy on child, diaries, medical appointments or birth/health records and midwifery papers.

- Check for evidence of neglect, quality of caretaking (food, warmth, clothing, etc).

- Check for baby bottles and baby food containers.

- Check for evidence of drugs, alcohol abuse, domestic problems, debts (stress inducers).

- Child's clothing, bedding and toys (don't routinely seize bedding without justification).

- Paraphernalia used and discarded by emergency responders.

- Potential toxins and medicines.

- Photographs and DVDs showing child's physical developmental levels.

- Childcare books and magazines.

- Communications data and social media.

- Always apply the 'JDLR' principle (just doesn't look right).

15.10 **Role of the SIO**

The SIO initially liaises with response officers and/or supervision to methodically undertake the briefing/debriefing (see also Chapter 9.4 and 9.5) processes to review what has been done/not done, information known, etc. One of the first considerations should relate to confirming the whereabouts of the child's body, which may have been removed to hospital. A visual check of the body can then be made and identification confirmed. A paediatrician must be contacted (if not already done so) to commence an investigation into why the child died. If the matter is being treated as a homicide or suspicious death, then, as stated, procedures as for any other major investigation should commence and override anything else (eg making early arrests, identifying crime scenes, making significant witness interviews).

However, where circumstances do not point to immediate suspicion, it is statutory guidance (as per the W/T guidelines, see paragraph 15.4) with the SIO working alongside an appropriate paediatrician. If the child's body is at hospital, a joint interview will usually be conducted with the parents or carers (also previously mentioned as 'history taking').

The SIO should arrange to view the body themselves (preferably with the Consultant or SUDI/C Paediatrician at hospital) and record details of any observations. In doing so, they can become personally aware of all visible injuries or marks of concern and the state of the body before any post-mortem takes place, eg hygiene, nutritional state, whether post-mortem staining and rigor mortis is consistent with early accounts given by parents/carers. This information may be needed to brief the Coroner when they are considering the type of post-mortem to hold.

Checklist— 5WH questions

- Were there any suspicious marks or injuries on the child's body?

- What are the parents' explanations as to the circumstances leading up to the death?

- Who was present who may have posed a threat to the child?

- What condition were the parents/carers in (eg drink/drug abuse apparent)?

- What was their behaviour and attitude to the death?

- What evidence is there to suggest neglect (or a SIDS 'cot death'-type case) such as temperature of the scene, condition of accommodation, general hygiene, over/under heating, co-sleeping, heavy tobacco or drug usage and paraphernalia and the non-availability of food/drink?

- What database checks have been conducted and what intelligence is available on the child, parents, siblings, carers, family or regular visitors?

- What other agencies or agents are involved?

- How many times have the police or other agencies been involved with the child or family previously and what for?

- Who was with the child at each stage leading up to the death?

- How many other people (and who) were present in the premises around the time?

- Who was in the child's room/bed?

- What was the sleeping position of the child?

- Where was the child sleeping in relation to the parents/carers and in what?

- Who saw the child last?

- What condition was the child in then?

- When was the child last fed, how (eg breastfed) what with and who by?

- What was the child's behaviour and condition 48 to 72 hours prior to death?

- Who put the child to bed, when and in what position?

- How did the child appear when found (eg blue, stiff)?

- What was the child's sleeping environment like? Who else was sleeping near the child? What was the location or position of the cot relative to other objects in the room?

- What was the health of the child prior to death?

- What previous medical conditions or treatment has the child had (including disabilities or impairments)?

- Were any healthcare professionals involved with the child recently?

- What medicine had the child been taking?

- Was there any bedding over/under the child?

- Was an infant intercom/monitor in place?

- How many other children are in the same household or family?

- What are the social circumstances of the child?

- What other child deaths have the family/extended family experienced?

- Who is the child's and family's GP?

- What, if any, sort of special treatment did the child require after birth?[10]

15.11 **Family Liaison**

Grieving parents may exhibit a variety of reactions, such as overwhelming grief, anger, confusion, hysteria, disbelief or guilt. A key rule is that they should be treated and managed *sympathetically* and *sensitively*, remembering that frustration may be levelled at the police as a manifestation of their distress.

Checklist—Family liaison considerations

- Avoid undue criticism of the parents/carers, either direct or implied.

- Don't refer to the child/infant as 'it'—use their proper name.

- Avoid placing children's bodies into body bags.

- Allow parents to see, touch and hold their loved one, provided it does not interfere with clinical care or any forensic examination and only in the presence of a professional.

- Deal sensitively with religious beliefs and cultural differences while remembering the importance of evidence preservation.

- Allow parents/carers an opportunity to ask questions and have explained to them what is happening at every stage.

- Allow the parents/carers to accompany the deceased infant/ child to hospital.

- Arrange for other children in the household to be looked after.

- Give advice on and consider other support that is available (eg Lullaby Trust have befrienders and useful literature).

---

[10] See also ACPO Homicide Working Group (Child Death Sub-Group), *A Guide to Investigating Child Deaths* (ACPO, 2014).

The police response and activity can prove very distressing to the family, particularly if there are no criminal offences involved. However, the importance and usefulness of a thorough investigation should be emphasised, which is beneficial for them in finding answers to important questions and establishing what caused the death of their child.

KEY POINT

Demonstrating sensitivity and tact in handling child death cases does not prevent a shrewd and tenacious SIO from being 'compassionately sceptical' about the circumstances under investigation. How an SIO presents themselves outwardly may have to betray what they are really thinking and considering inwardly.

15.11.1 Deploying an FLO

Whatever category of child death is being investigated, the SIO may consider it highly appropriate to appoint a Family Liaison Officer (FLO) at the earliest opportunity, although this is not always a routine procedure in Category 1-type SUDC investigations. Certain circumstances may influence this decision, such as a high level of media interest and/or intrusion. There may also be added complications in dealing fairly and equally with estranged natural parents who may have other partners. The SIO may also decide that in order to ensure the family are fully engaged as partners in the investigation process and/or in order to maintain a sensitive, supportive relationship with them, a deployment of an FLO is necessary. If there is, for example, a reliance on tests such as toxicology and specialist examinations of portions of the brain, there may be a protracted amount of time for the parents to await the outcome. This can be a very unsettling, uncertain and stressful time for the parents.

During this period, at the same time as providing support, an FLO can act as the SIO's conduit within the family and home environment, picking up on any vital evidence that may assist the investigation. This is particularly important if there is a greater reliance on circumstantial supportive evidence, especially if a potential offender(s) comes from within or is connected to the child's family (termed 'intra-familial'—see later in this chapter), with family dynamics that can change or intensify.

15.11.2 Allowing holding and touching of the body

It is entirely natural for a parent/carer to want to hold or touch the body of their deceased child/young person and it is known to help with the grieving process. As a general rule, this is normally permitted if the death is not deemed suspicious, provided it is supervised by a professional (eg police officer or hospital staff) who should be present during the process.

In most cases it is unlikely important forensic evidence will be lost by the tactful and sensible use of this activity. It is usually trace evidence being sought if someone else (eg a stranger) other than a person who has legitimate access to the child (eg parent/carer) is suspected of involvement or having caused the death. Individual circumstances dictate whether this is the case. Contact trace evidence in intra-familial homicides, however, has limited use, because parents and family members will have had recent and regular access and legitimate contact with the child.

Any contamination potential can be carefully managed (eg if clothing is required for body fluids or interpretation, then seizing prior to contact with the child would suffice). Any concern about the unlikely possibility of post-mortem injuries being caused during this process can be negated by the ability to easily distinguish between ante- and post-mortem injuries. Thus any external forensic-gathering potential should be balanced against the needs of the grieving family. Though ultimately the decision rests with the SIO, national guidelines favour allowing parental contact, provided appropriate control measures are in place.

A supervised contact session, if and when permitted, is something to be agreed between the SIO, CSI (for advice where possible) and hospital staff. Hospital A&E departments are normally used to dealing with unexpected child deaths and experienced nursing staff should be able to arrange for a child to be protected (eg covered in a blanket) and suitably prepared for the parent/carers to hold. Normally the parents are seated to avoid them dropping the infant, and a member of experienced staff is present to ensure parents comply with any tactful instructions or in case they become overly emotional or unwell during the process.

An SIO must decide on the appropriateness of this course of action, which will depend largely upon the particular circumstances of the case and degree of suspicion falling on the parents. It is beneficial to discuss the process with an experienced CSI beforehand and/or the Forensic Pathologist/Paediatrician. Once permitted, the parents should be closely monitored so they do not mishandle or mistreat the body in any way.

15.11.3 **Requests for mementoes**

Requests for mementoes such as prints of hands and feet, photographs and locks of hair are normally permitted, but in cases where there is a police-led investigation and there are concerns and suspicions, this should not be agreed until after the Paediatric Pathologist has fully examined the body. The police should only refuse the request (and not every family will want them) if there is good reason to believe it would jeopardise a criminal investigation. The responsibility for arranging the taking and delivery of mementoes from the body (which is always potentially a crime scene) always rests with the SIO. If a decision is made to do so, details of the method adopted and agreed terms must be recorded in the SIO's policy log. However, in non-suspicious cases the parents should normally be allowed to leave the hospital with the requested mementoes, as it can be several days before a post-mortem takes place.

15.12 **Post-Mortems**

After life extinct (or 'fact of death') is pronounced, the Coroner has jurisdiction over the infant/child's body examination process. As with adult suspicious death investigations, the SIO liaises with the Coroner to discuss the arrangements for a post-mortem. In child death cases, the post-mortem should always be performed by a Paediatric Pathologist and if deemed suspicious, the SIO can request a Home Office-accredited Forensic Pathologist (who takes the lead) to carry out the autopsy alongside the Paediatric Pathologist.

As in any other death investigation, the SIO should provide a full briefing (and it is advisable to keep a record in case of disputes later) to the Pathologist(s) beforehand, including the showing of any scene recording or photographs (if available) and any information gathered to inform the process. Now that there are prescriptive guidelines for the management of SUDI/C deaths (history taking, joint home visit, inter-agency approach, etc), any additional details should also be provided for the Pathologist before an examination commences. This will include a summary of the child's medical history including relevant background information concerning the family and any concerns raised by other agencies. This is to ensure the Pathologist has as much detail as possible and is intended to be an improvement on previous procedures, which often contained a far less detailed briefing.

Child post-mortems are different to those conducted on adult bodies, if for no other reason than the bodies being examined are much tinier and delicate and important areas cannot be examined or viewed with the naked eye so easily. The range of diseases to be considered can also vary from adults, as the bodies concerned are still in the stages of natural development. Depending on the circumstances, added histological examinations and samples may be required and a wider range of ancillary tests. For example, if 'shaking' or 'suffocation' is suspected, then the brain may need to be examined by a Neuropathologist and the eyes by an ophthalmic expert. These added tests may mean the identification of unlawful and malicious acts can be more difficult and/or take longer to detect. For this reason, the examination involves a Pathologist who has special expertise, such as a Paediatric Pathologist.

It is advisable (as per the Kennedy report) in all cases of infant and young child deaths, prior to the post-mortem examination, for a full skeletal x-ray survey to be performed and interpreted by a Paediatric Radiologist. Skeletal surveys in older children may also be considered on a case-by-case basis. A Paediatric Radiologist can interpret any survey conducted. In cases which may involve head injury, a CT scan should also be considered in consultation with the Pathologist of the head before autopsy commences (note: if a child is alive when brought into hospital with a head injury, a CT or MRI scan are more likely to be performed).

Under the requirements of the Human Tissue Act 2004, a Pathologist is allowed to retain only such tissues as required to ascertain the cause of death. The next of kin (ie parents) must be consulted regarding their wishes about the retention of the tissue for any further research purposes, and the return to them for burial/ cremation or sensitive disposal by other means must be a consideration. It may, however, be in the parents' best interests or for that of others for the Pathologist to retain tissue samples, especially when a definitive conclusion as to cause of death has not been reached. However, this may be a sensitive area and one that has previously caused some degree of controversy. This does not, of course, apply to samples taken for the purposes of a criminal investigation under section 19 PACE (see also Chapter 14.16). There can also be a retention of samples with permission of the Coroner. He/she can authorise retention until an inquest has been concluded.

15.13 **'Intra-Familial' Child Homicides**

This is a term used in certain types of investigation where the offender is a:

- family or extended family member
- person living in the same household
- person visiting the household regularly
- person having care responsibility at the time of the alleged offence, eg teacher, health or youth worker, baby-sitter or child minder
- carer (where the victim is under 18 years)
- carer when the child is in care, eg foster carer or children's home employee.

Section 5 of the DVCV as amended by Domestic Violence Crime and Victim's (Amendment) Act 2012 (DVCVA) 'Causing or allowing a child or vulnerable adult to die or suffer serious physical harm', is a useful piece of legislation introduced to create an offence designed to cater for circumstances where there are two or more parents/carers who may be responsible for the death or serious injury of a child with neither accepting responsibility.[11] Initially, evidence will be gathered in order to prosecute for a primary offence of murder or manslaughter, but where this is not possible then an offence under section 5 can be considered.

An offence under section 5 provides that members of a household who have frequent contact with a child under 16 years or a vulnerable adult will be guilty of an offence if they:

---

[11] Section 6 of DVCVA has special procedures which allow the section 5 offence to be charged with murder or manslaughter and if a case for section 5 is made out, a defence team cannot apply for murder/ manslaughter to be withdrawn until after the defence case during which parents are expected to give evidence or the jury is able to draw an adverse inference from their silence.

- caused the death
- allowed the death, if the following conditions are met:
  — they were aware, or ought to have been, that the victim was at significant risk of serious physical harm (ie grievous bodily harm under the Offences Against the Person Act 1861)
  — they failed to take reasonable steps to prevent that person coming to harm
  — the person died from the unlawful act of a household member in circumstances that the defendant foresaw or ought to have foreseen.

The offence is limited to where the victim has died of an unlawful act, so the 'allowing' element of the offence does not apply to circumstances where there has been an isolated incident with no history of risk to the victim. The offence only applies to members of the same household who had frequent contact with the victim, and could therefore be reasonably expected to be aware of any risk to the victim and to have a duty to protect them from harm. The household member must have failed to take 'reasonable steps' to protect the child. The offence only applies to those aged 16 years and over unless they are the mother or father of the child.

References

ACPO, *Guidance on Investigating Child Abuse and Safeguarding Children*, 2nd edn (NPIA, 2009)

ACPO, *Guidelines: Infant Deaths—Murder Investigation Manual* (Supplement) (NCPE, 2006)

ACPO Homicide Working Group, *A Guide to Investigating Child Deaths* (ACPO HWG, 2014)

ACPO/CPS, 'Liaison and information exchange when criminal proceedings coincide with Chapter 4 Serious Case Reviews or Welsh Child Practice Reviews: A guide for the Police, CPS and LSCB' (May 2014), HWG (child death sub-group)

Department for Children, Schools and Families, *Working Together to Safeguard Children* (The Stationery Office, 2010)

Foundation for the Study of Infant Death, *A Suggested Approach for Police and Coroner's Officers* (FSID, 2005)

Foundation for the Study of Infant Death, *Cot Death Facts and Figures* (FSID, 2008)

Foundation for the Study of Infant Death, *When a Baby Dies Suddenly and Unexpectedly* (FSID, 2007)

Fox, J, 'A Contribution to the Evaluation of Recent Developments in the Investigation of Sudden Unexpected Death in Infancy', Briefing Paper (Department of Sociology, University of Surrey in association with the NPIA, 2008)

Fox, J, 'The Police Response to Infant Deaths' (2005) 1(1) *Journal of Homicide and Major Incident Investigation*

HM Government, *Information Sharing: Further Guidance on Legal Issues* (The Stationery Office, 2009)

HM Government, *Information Sharing: Guidance for Practitioners and Managers* (The Stationery Office, 2008)

HM Government, *Working Together to Safeguard Children: A guide to inter-agency working to promote the welfare of children* (The Stationery Office, March 2015). <http://www.gov.uk/government/publications>

Kennedy, Baroness H, *Sudden Unexpected Death in Infancy: A Multi-Agency Protocol for Care and Investigation* (Royal College of Pathologists and Royal College of Paediatrics and Child Health, 2004), Introduction at 1–16 and The Protocol's Executive Summary at 17–27

Marshall, D, *Effective Investigation of Child Homicide and Suspicious Deaths* (OUP, 2012)

Marshall, D, 'Child Homicides: A Suspect in the Family—Issues for the Family Liaison Strategy' (2008) 4(1) *Journal of Homicide and Major Incident Investigation*

NHS, *A Guide to the Post Mortem Examination Procedure Involving a Baby or Child* (NHS, 2003)

Police Review (18 July 2008), 'New Tricks' (the new section 5 legislation), 18 and 'Defend the Children' (investigating death of a child)

Sidebotham P and Fleming P, *Unexpected Death in Childhood: A Handbook for Practitioners* (Wiley, 2007)

Vaughan, J R and Kautt, P M, 'Infant Death Investigations Following High-Profile Unsafe Rulings: Throwing Out the Baby with the Bath Water?' (2009) 3(1) *Policing*, 89–99

Wate, R, and Marshall, D, 'Effective Investigation of Intra-familial Child Homicide and Suspicious Death' (2009) 5(2) *Journal of Homicide and Major Incident Investigation*

Child Sexual Exploitation

16.1 **Introduction**

Protection of children is one of the most important roles in law enforcement and one of the most serious and organised crime risks in the UK is from child sexual exploitation (CSE, or sexual exploitation of children—SEOC) and child sex offenders (CSOs). The term 'child sexual exploitation' is still relatively new, having been introduced to Wales in 2009;[1] yet an intensity of reporting and high-profile cases has placed this serious and complex problem squarely in the political, media and public spotlight.

Added to this has been the proliferation of historical child sex abuse and contact offences uncovered that were committed by persons with prominent public profiles (PPP). One such example is Operation Yewtree, the Metropolitan Police investigation into child sexual abuse allegations predominantly involving the British TV personality Jimmy Savile (and others).

Operation Hydrant is the UK national policing operation established to manage and coordinate the increasing demand on police forces to respond to, investigate and manage non-recent CSE in institutional settings, or abuse alleged to have been perpetrated by persons of public prominence (operation.hydrant@southyorks. pnn.police.uk or telephone 0114 296 3030).

Public enquiries such as Baroness Jay's report into Rotherham in 2014 and the Oxfordshire Local Safeguarding Children's Board's (LSCB) enquiry in 2015, severely criticised the manner in which offences and offenders were either dealt with, ignored or missed completely. This raised fundamental concerns, particularly for those who were the victims of group- or gang-associated activity or in residential care. Consequently CSE investigations have since been afforded far greater priority and the problem has been designated a UK national threat.

Child sexual exploitation (CSE) is extremely harmful and in some cases life threatening. Not only does it involve serious criminality, but is a violation of human rights that is frequently committed by adults unrelated to their child[2] victims. Inducements, grooming processes or blackmail and extortion can be involved, such as an abundant supply of alcohol, drugs, money and gifts, under which lie hidden motives of sexually abusing the vulnerable recipients or facilitation of such by others.

CSE[3] is a type of abuse which centres around control, power, status and sexual gratification. Exploiters hold the balance of power due to their superior age, gender, status, intellect, physical, cultural or economic advantage. They can manipulate children or young people into believing they're in a loving, consensual relationship by, for example, inviting or taking them to 'parties' where they are given drugs and alcohol then handed around and abused. The abuse can be arranged or committed 'online' (over the internet) and in the 'real world' or sometimes a mixture of both.

---

[1] See Department for Children, Schools and Families (DCSF), *Safeguarding Children and Young People from Sexual Exploitation* (DCSF, 2009).

[2] A child is defined under the Children Act 1989 as being under 18 years of age.

[3] The term 'child sexual exploitation' does not refer to a specific action or a particular criminal offence; it is a general term applied to an array of behaviours and offences ranging from lower non-contact incitement to those at the highest level such as abduction, contact offences or making children pose for indecent images, performing under-age sex acts or multiple rape, physical/mental harm and torture.

Violence, coercion, intimidation and blackmail are common, with victims having little choice but to comply due to their social, economic and/or emotional disadvantage, vulnerability or naivety. Many are incapable of recognising themselves as victims, and may have consented as a coping mechanism for their own personal problems, vulnerability or simply out of fear.

Strong links have been found between CSE and running away from home/care, alcohol and drug abuse and engaging in petty crime. Some children and young people (including vulnerable adults) are even trafficked into or within the UK for the purpose of sexual exploitation and they can also become involved in criminal gangs. CSE remains a hidden crime when victims trust, respect or fear their abusers; not truly understanding they are being abused or just being too scared to formally complain. With online offending, the challenge includes a responsibility for identifying victims from images in order to safeguard and protect them.

A national UK 'pursue' response was developed in 2015 to mitigate the threat posed from online child sexual exploitation (OCSE). A threat analysis from the National Strategic Tasking and Coordinating group (NSTCG) produced a stark analysis of the scale of OCSE occurring at local, regional, national and international levels. This is mainly through the use of various digital web-based platforms for sharing indecent images of children (IIOC) and facilitating the commission of vile child sexual contact offences over the so-called 'darknet'.

This demonstrates how the landscape has changed and there is every likelihood an SIO could find themselves leading a CSE-type investigation. This new chapter has been added with the aim of providing information and practical pointers to raise awareness of the subject and outline useful background details and investigative intricacies for what is now classified as high-priority and grave criminal offending.

No one knows the true scale of CSE in Rotherham over the years. Our conservative estimate is that approximately 1400 children were sexually exploited over the inquiry period from 1997 to 2013...over the first twelve years covered by this inquiry the collective failures of political leadership were blatant, within social care, the scale and seriousness of the problem was underplayed by senior managers. At an operational level, the police gave no priority to CSE, regarding many children with contempt and failing to act on their abuse as a crime.

Alexis Jay, *Independent Inquiry into Child Sexual Exploitation in Rotherham 1997–2013* (2014), p 7.

In May 2012, as a result of Operation Span in Rochdale, nine men were convicted and jailed. The men at the centre of the trial were from Rochdale and Oldham. Offences ranged from rape, trafficking, conspiracy to engage in sexual activity with a child, sexual assault and sexual activity with a child. This case was the first prosecution in Britain of the offence of trafficking within the UK for a sexual offence. Sentences ranged from 19 years to 4 years.

Operation Bullfinch, Oxfordshire: offences were committed between 2004 and 2012. Over 20 young people identified as potential victims. Nine men were charged with offences against six children and convicted on 14 May 2013. Five life sentences were given, with minimum terms ranging from 12 to 20 years.

> The sexual abuse included vaginal, anal and oral rape and also involved the use of a variety of objects such as knives, meat cleavers, baseball bats...sex toys...It was often accompanied by humiliating and degrading conduct such as biting, scratching, acts of urinating, being suffocated, tied up. They were also beaten and burnt. This sexual activity was often carried out by groups of men; sometimes it would go on for days on end.

SCR Oxfordshire Safeguarding Children Board (OSCB) Feb 2015

16.2 Definition of CSE

The police, government, Office of Children's Commissioner and College of Policing[4] all use the same definition, which comes from the UK National Working Group for Sexually Exploited Children and Young People (NWG):

> Sexual exploitation of children and young people under 18 involves exploitative situations, contexts and relationships where young people (or a third person or persons) receive 'something' (eg food, accommodation, drugs, alcohol, cigarettes, affection, gifts, money) as a result of them performing, and/or another or others performing on them sexual activities.
>
> CSE can occur through the use of technology without the child's immediate recognition; for example being persuaded to post sexual images on the internet/mobile phones without immediate payment or gain. In all cases those exploiting the child/young person have power over them by virtue of their age, gender, intellect, physical strength and/or economic or other resources.
>
> Violence, coercion and intimidation are common, involvement in exploitative relationships being characterised in the main by the child or young persons limited availability of choice resulting from their social/economic and/or emotional vulnerability.

(Department for Education 2012)

16.3 Child Protection in England and Wales

Child protection in England is the overall responsibility of the Department for Education, which issues guidance to local authorities. Guidance issued in March

---

[4] The same definition is also cited in the College of Policing APP guidance, College of Policing, *Responding to Child Sexual Exploitation*, APP online (2015) <http//www. app.college.police.uk>.

2013—*Working Together to Safeguard Children*, which not only applies to LSCBs but should also be followed by all practitioners and professionals who come into contact with children and their families in their area. Wales has the All Wales Child Protection Procedures that provide LSCBs with a single set of procedures and a range of protocols.

In many cases there is social services involvement, often prior to police involvement. This may include one or all of the following steps:

1. Referral to local authority children's social care, which can come from the child themselves, teachers, a GP, the police, health visitors, family members or members of the public.
2. Assessment to establish whether the child requires immediate protection and urgent action; or, the child is in 'need' under section 17 of the Children's Act 1989; or there is reasonable cause to suspect that the child is suffering, or likely to suffer, significant harm and whether enquiries must be made under section 47 of the Children Act (see below).
3. If there is a risk to the life of a child or a likelihood of serious immediate harm, local authority social workers, the police or NSPCC must use their statutory child protection powers to act immediately to secure the safety of the child. If the child is identified as being in need, a social worker leads a multi-agency assessment under section 17. Where information gathered during an assessment results in a social worker suspecting a child is suffering or likely to suffer significant harm, the local authority holds a strategy discussion to enable it to decide, with other agencies, whether to initiate enquiries under section 47.

For the purposes of multi-agency assessments, the police assist other agencies to carry out their responsibilities where there are concerns about a child's welfare, whether or not a crime has been committed. If a crime has been committed, the police should be informed by the local authority children's social care.

For the purposes of a strategy discussion, the police discuss the basis for any criminal investigation and any relevant processes that other agencies might need to know about, including the timing and methods of evidence gathering, and lead the criminal investigation where joint enquiries take place. The local authority children's social care has the lead for section 47 enquiries and assessment of the child's welfare.

The priority of any CSE investigation must always be to **safeguard the individual plus any others who might be at risk**. This might include taking a child into police protection or removing them to a place of safety in the first instance and seeking the protection of the courts in the longer term. This involves a multi-disciplinary strategy with partner agencies to discuss the best way to ensure a child's safety and at the same time progress the investigation. The legal options for taking action are under:

1. Section 17 Children Act 1989 (child in need)
2. Section 20 Children Act 1989 (provision of accommodation)

3. Section 46 Children Act 1989 (removal and accommodation of children by police in cases of emergency) and section 44 (court orders for emergency protection).[5]
4. Section 47 Children Act 1989 (child in need of protection)

Section 17 states local authorities have a duty of care to safeguard and promote children's welfare in their area. 'In need' relates to their health needs, including mental health as well as physical, and the promotion of the upbringing of such children by their families. This involves providing a range of services appropriate to those children's needs. This section also requires police to refer these cases to the local authority.

Section 20 is a voluntary agreement between all interested parties where the need to safeguard a child is recognised. It avoids the necessity to go through a court process with the child being placed outside the area to cut all ties and association with offenders, placing them in the care of experienced social workers within a dedicated care home setting.

Section 46 provides a police power to remove a child to suitable accommodation where there is reasonable cause to believe they would otherwise be likely to suffer significant harm (aka police protection). However, the police protection cannot last longer than 72 hours, but an emergency protection order under section 44 can be applied for to a court.

Section 47 if there is a suspicion that a child is suffering, or is likely to suffer significant harm, the local authority and police must make enquiries so they can decide whether they should take any action to protect and promote the welfare of the child. There is usually a locally agreed procedure between the police and the local authority to guide both organisations in deciding how section 47 enquiries should be conducted.

Checklist—Key definitions

1. Children at risk of '*significant harm*'.

A child is defined as being at risk or subject of significant harm where there is ill-treatment or impairment of health or development:

- 'ill-treatment' includes sexual and emotional abuse as well as physical abuse;

- 'health' means physical and mental health;

- 'development' means physical, intellectual, emotional, social or behavioural development;

---

[5] In circumstances where the police have initiated action to safeguard a child, it is their responsibility to inform the local authority and give details of where the child is being accommodated (s 46 Children Act 1989).

- 'significant harm' turns on the question of the harm suffered by a child in respect of his health and development compared with the health and development reasonably expected of a similar child.

(Section 31(10) Children Act 1989).

2. Children 'in need'.

A child is defined as being in need if:

- he/she is unlikely to achieve or maintain, or have the opportunity of achieving, maintaining, a reasonable standard of health or development without the provision for him/her of services by a local authority; or

- his/her health or development is likely to be significantly impaired, or further impaired, without the provision of such services; or

- he/she is disabled.

(Section 17(10) Children Act 1989)

KEY POINTS

1. **Section 11, Children Act 2004** places a duty on a range of organisations and agencies[6] to make arrangements to ensure: (a) their functions are discharged having regard to the need to safeguard and promote the welfare of children; and (b) that any services they contract out to others are provided having regard to that need.
2. The National Decision Model (NDM) provides an effective means to approach and structure decision making when faced with potential CSE cases (see Chapter 3.6.3).

16.4 **Criminal Offences and Legislative Powers**

In law, there is no specific offence or crime of CSE. Offenders are often convicted of associated offences such as rape, abduction or unlawful sexual intercourse with a child[7] (now more commonly referred to as sexual activity with a child—section 9 Sexual Offences Act 2003) and possession/distribution of indecent photographs.

---

[6] These include local authorities and district councils, the police, probation service, NHS bodies, BTP, Youth Offending Teams, governors of prisons, and directors of Secure Training Centres and the NCA (under s 8 of the Crime and Courts Act 2013).

[7] The definition of a child/children/young person is anyone who has not reached their 18th birthday. The fact that a child has reached 16 years of age, is living independently or is in further education, is a member of the armed forces, is in hospital or in custody in the secure estate, does not change his/her status or entitlement to services or protection under the law.

Some general legal considerations may be considered when investigating CSE offences which include:

- Children under the age of 13 years cannot consent to any form of sexual activity—which is classed as statutory rape. There is no defence or mitigation of reasonably believing the child to be 16 or over (as there is if the child is between 13 and 16) under the Sexual Offences Act 2003.
- Sex without consent is rape—plain and simple.
- True consent cannot be given when a person is incapacitated through drink or drugs.
- No person under 16 years can consent to sexual activity.

The Sexual Offences Act 2003 contains a wide range of offences that deal not only with rape (section 1) but others such as sexual assaults of and activity with children under 13 (sections 5–8) and a range of child sex offences (sections 9–15), incitement (section 10) and facilitation (section 14); trafficking within, into and out of the UK for the purposes of sexual exploitation (sections 57–59); grooming as an alternative to abduction (section 15); paying for the sexual services of a child (section 47); causing or inciting, controlling, arranging and facilitating child prostitution or pornography (sections 48–50); trafficking into, within or out of the UK for sexual exploitation (sections 57–59); or committing an act in a country outside the UK which would be a sexual offence in England and Wales (section 72).

The Anti-social Behaviour, Crime and Policing Act 2014 contains the following provisions:

- Section 113 and Schedule 5 amended the Sexual Offences Act 2003 SOPO (Sexual Offences Prevention Order), FTO (Foreign Travel Order) and RoSHO (Risk of Sexual Harm Order) in England and Wales and replaced them with two new orders: the SHPO (Sexual Harm Prevention Order) and SRO (Sexual Risk Order).
- Sections 116–118 allow the police to issue notices to owners or managers of relevant accommodation (eg hotels, guest houses and bed and breakfast-type premises) to disclose information. This applies where the police reasonably believe CSE has been or will be taking place on the premises.

Section 1 of the Protection of Children Act 1978 (PCA) created various offences of taking, making or distributing indecent photographs (or pseudo-photographs) of a child. Section 1(1) subject to sections 1(A) and 1(B) states it is an offence to:

(a) take, or permit to be taken, or to make[8] any indecent photograph or pseudo-photograph of a child; or

---

[8] 'Make' includes downloading images from the internet and storing or printing them out (*R v Bowden* (J) 1999). This concept was expanded in *R v Smith* and *R v Jayson* (2002), which held that deliberately opening an indecent computer email attachment or downloading an indecent image from the internet so it can be viewed on a screen, is 'making' a photograph.

(b) distribute or show such indecent photographs or pseudo-photographs; or
(c) have in his possession such indecent photographs or pseudo-photographs with a view to their being distributed or shown by himself or others; or
(d) publish or cause to be published any advertisement likely to be understood as conveying that the advertiser distributes or shows such indecent photographs or pseudo-photographs or intends to do so.

Section 62(1) of the Coroners and Justice act 2009 also creates an offence of possession of a prohibited image of a child. This legislation effectively 'closed the loophole' in the PCA that doesn't provide for simple possession offences. It also widens the provisions contained within the Protection of Children Act 1978 by expanding the meaning of pornography (ie to include cartoons or drawings) and not just photographs or pseudo-photographs. Section 62(2) states that a prohibited image is one which is:

(a) pornographic; or
(b) focuses solely or principally on child's genitals or anal region (subsection 6) or portrays an indecent act (subsection 7); and
(c) is grossly offensive, disgusting or otherwise of an obscene character.

Section 160 of the Criminal Justice Act 1988 also creates an offence for any person to have in their possession indecent photographs of children (again closing the loophole in the PCA), but section 160(2) states it is a defence if the person can prove they had it for a legitimate reason, had not seen it and did not know or have cause to suspect it was indecent.

Other more general legislative powers that are clearly useful when investigating CSE offences are the Police and Criminal Evidence Act 1984 (PACE) (such as section 8—power to obtain search warrants; sections 17–18 and 32—entry and search without warrant; section 19—power to seize items; section 24—power of arrest; section 50—seize and sift powers; section 78—fairness principle at trial stage); Children Act 1989—warrant may be obtained to search for children who may be in need of emergency protection (section 48); Human Rights Act 1998 (eg article 2 right to life, article 8 right to respect privacy and family life); Regulation of Investigatory Powers Act 2000 (eg acquisition of communications data, surveillance and CHIS); and Criminal Procedure and Investigations Act 1996 (disclosure obligations).

Other related crimes and incidents that could be relevant may include murder, kidnap and abduction, human trafficking, prostitution, physical or indecent assault, anti-social behaviour, theft (eg shoplifting) immigration-related offences, drug and alcohol (under-age drinking), couriering and abuse, frequent missing persons, honour-based violence and forced marriages. It should be noted that some victims may deliberately get themselves arrested for minor offences in order to escape from their exploiters and attract the attention of the authorities.

16.5 **Warning and Assessment Tools**

Early intervention in CSE cases not only helps safeguard victims from further harm but also allows more opportunity for effective evidence-gathering opportunities for the purposes of an investigation. Links to other activities, incidents and criminal acts are frequently involved and the following checklist can be used to help identify children being exploited.[9]

Checklist—CSE warning and vulnerability indicators

- Adults or youths loitering outside or visiting a child's usual place of residence.

- Children who go missing, persistently staying out late, overnight or not returning home on time, or homeless.

- Leaving home/care setting in clothing/appearance unusual for the individual child (inappropriate for age or occasion).

- Unexplainable acquisition of gifts, expensive clothes, cosmetics, money, mobile phones, digital devices, or other accessories and overnight bags/suitcases.

- Possession of contraceptives, lubricating gel, sex toys, pornography, provocative clothing.

- Rapid change in appearance without explanation.

- Truancy/disengagement with/exclusion from mainstream education or considerable change in performance.

- Volatile behaviour exhibiting, expressions of despair, extreme array of mood swings or use of abusive language.

- Disclosure of sexual/physical assault followed by withdrawal of allegation.

- Involvement in petty crime, eg shoplifting and other minor thefts.

- Hanging around fast-food outlets.

- Entering or leaving vehicles driven by unknown male adults.

- Hostility in relationships with parents/carers and other family members.

- Returning after having been missing, appearing well fed and cared for despite having no proper home base.

- Emerging personality disorders such as psychosis, depression, self-harming, suicidal tendencies, drug and alcohol abuse, eating disorder, severe low self-esteem and self-neglect.

---

[9] Some of the list that follows is also cited in College of Policing APP guidance: 'Child Sexual Exploitation > Responding to child sexual exploitation > Risk Factors', <http://www.college.police.uk>.

- Unsupervised/regular/secretive use of internet, social networking, phone apps/chat rooms/sites/sexting.
- Sexually transmitted infections (STIs), numerous sexual partners, pregnancy and terminations.
- Physical injuries, illnesses, frequent visits to medical care.
- Evidence of sexual bullying and/or vulnerability through the internet and/or social networking sites.
- Gang association or residing in a gang-affected neighbourhood.
- Residing in a household where there has been domestic violence or familial child sexual abuse and/or is chaotic or dysfunctional/disrupted upbringing, family conflict.
- Living in a household where there are parental mental health issues or criminality.
- Children in care or experiencing homelessness.
- Children and young people who have been trafficked into the country.
- Children and young people at risk of forced marriage or 'honour-based violence'.
- Having friends or associates who are victims of CSE.
- Victims potentially grooming other victims, leading others astray.
- Recent bereavement or loss.

KEY POINTS

1. Public bodies such as the police and NCA have a duty and responsibility to protect children (who may not always look, appear or behave like 'children') in their day-to-day duties. Although not always easy, officers must try and recognise the signs and look beyond the usual interpretation of 'normal'.
2. Children don't always present as victims, eg 'When I was being groomed...' (one victim said) '...these were the most exciting days of my life...I thought I was in love, romantic care and affection. I certainly didn't look sad' (cited by Dr Alan Billings, Police and Crime Commissioner for South Yorkshire: 'My officers have had to learn that smiles can mask abuse', *Guardian*, 4 August 2015, p 31).

16.6 **Locations of Offending**

There are a range of places where CSE occurs, often linked to the type of 'relationship' that has been developed and the context in which the abuse takes place. Some of these may also be crime scenes.

Checklist—Examples of CSE abuse locations

- Organised parties in a variety of locations eg warehouses/private premises, schools or public places in the neighbourhood such as parks and stairwells (eg when being exploited by peers).

- Vehicles while being transported to meetings/parties, being groomed, trafficked or abducted (the offer of transport may also be the means by which the abuse takes place, eg taxi drivers who exchange lifts for sexual favours).

- Hotels, guesthouses, budget bed and breakfasts and hostels (especially when the abuse activity involves several offenders or so-called 'sex parties').

- Private homes, eg if children have ongoing contact with a group or gang member (source CSE in gangs and groups).

- Public places such as shopping centres, social networks and online gaming sites, arcades, cafes, fast-food outlets, cinemas, alcohol outlets, taxi/bus ranks and any other places where there is little or no adult or parental supervision.

Opportunities may present themselves for identifying victims, offences and offenders at locations such as those listed above. For example, child victims that have to be transported to venues for these offences to occur may provide opportunities for evidence recovery in the mode of transport or along the route. Police stop checks are also another means of identifying offending taking place if children are passengers in vehicles as a consequence of being groomed, trafficked or abducted by CSE offenders.

KEY POINT

Offence locations can provide opportunities for gathering evidence and protecting victims. Vehicle stop checks, for example, can reveal child victim passengers who are being transported, groomed or trafficked for CSE. Officers must remain alert to this possibility.

16.7 **CSE in Gangs**

CSE can be used by criminal gangs to:

- Exert power and control over members.
- Initiate young people into the gang.
- Exchange sexual activity for status or protection.
- Entrap rival gang members by exploiting girls and young women.
- Inflict sexual assault as a weapon in conflict.

Physical abuse inflicted by the use of violence has been found in both groups and gangs CSE with the use of punching, hitting or beating up their victims with the use of physical force to restrain a victim. The use of weapons is also not uncommon where a gang is involved, including the use of firearms, knives, etc to intimidate or coerce a victim into sexual activity. Emotional abuse can also be inflicted on victims with the most prominent involving victims living in a state of anxiety and acute fear of their abusers. Threats are used to ensure compliance, including filming sexual abuse and threatening to post images online. The use of mobile phones, social networking sites and other forms of technology are used as a means of grooming, bullying and pursuing victims.

KEY POINT—DEFINITION OF 'GANGS' AND 'GROUPS'

1. **Gang:** A relatively durable, predominantly street-based social group of children, young people and not infrequently young adults who see themselves and are seen by others as affiliates of a discreet named group who (i) engage in a range of criminal activity and violence; (ii) identify or lay claim to territory; (iii) have some form of identifying structural feature; and (iv) are in conflict with similar groups.
2. **Group:** Two or more people of any age connected through formal or informal associations or networks including but not exclusive to friendship groups.

Source: 'If only someone had listened', Final Report from the inquiry into CSE in gangs and groups 2014 <http://www.childrenscommissioner.gov.uk/content/publications/content_743>

16.8 **Coercion and Grooming**

Victims are often groomed by their exploiters by applying an array of coercive tactics to win them over. Whatever circumstances make a particular victim vulnerable, can be exploited, such as the need to have a sense of belonging or be shown affection and enjoy gifts and luxuries they wouldn't normally have access to.

CSE offenders use a variety of methods and inducements to coerce victims into engaging in sexual activities with them. These can range from gifts such as clothing, jewellery, food and drink, money, and mobile phones, to showing of interest and affection and promises of improved lifestyle opportunities. Other more subtle means used might include fear and intimidation or threats of violence.

Grooming processes usually occur over a period of time. Most victims do not even realise they are being groomed at all. One typical example is where an offender gradually strikes up a relationship with a potential victim and lulls them into thinking they are in a steady relationship together. The taking out, providing treats, money, clothes, affection, false promises, mobile phone, etc is all part of the process aimed at gaining the victim's trust, while all along the real intention is to launch sustained sexual abuse by self and/or others at so-called 'sex parties'.

Coercion and manipulation often feature in abusive situations so that the perception of what is happening is sometimes difficult for the child or young person to comprehend. Offenders may groom and defraud not only the child or young person but also their family, which can mean that a parent or guardian trusts the offender as well as the victim.

KEY POINTS

- A young person who has reached the age of 16 or 17 years, ie the legal age of sexual consent, may still be at risk of CSE. They are still legally defined as children for the purposes of the Children Act 1989 and could still suffer significant harm through sexual exploitation.
- Male victims can also become victims of CSE and face additional barriers to overcome of making formal reports with fears of revealing their sexuality.
- Some victims may not always present as victims of CSE and could be hostile to engagement.
- Grooming equates to a recruitment process—exploitation is the process of the abuse.
- Women have also been known to be perpetrators of grooming for CSE (eg by running a pool of under-age sex workers).

16.9 **Missing Children**

Missing children reports always merit close scrutiny and supervision, particularly when they may be the result of serious criminality (eg abduction, homicide or CSE). There are many cases of CSE that have been linked to children going missing, particularly from foster/care homes and 'frequent' missing children who have been the victims of grooming and sexual exploitation. Response officers and investigators who deal with these reports must be alert to recognising the signs and symptoms of CSE offending as there is a golden opportunity to arrange early safeguarding and gather valuable evidence.

Searches for missing children not only have an objective for locating and protecting the missing individual but also identifying and securing evidential and investigative material. The latter might assist in understanding why the person has gone missing and pursue any necessary investigation; in the longer term it may help disrupt criminal activity and prevent further victims.

In the majority of historical cases child victims have not willingly volunteered information about their abuse because they haven't recognised themselves as victims. The absence of complaints prevented prompt and effective investigations. Therefore supervisors and SIOs who check and formally review child missing person reports and the grading they have been given must ensure that a thorough investigation has been conducted and right decisions have been made and conclusions reached.

Checklist—Missing children

- Any suggestion a reported missing child may be the victim of CSE means the enquiry has to be given a higher priority and response having made good use of the investigative mindset and ABC models (see also Chapter 3).

- Frequent missing children reports should not provide an excuse for a reduced investigative response, such as waiting to see if they return before enquiries are instigated.

- Fast-track actions help locate evidence of CSE, such as checking CCTV, searching possessions and bedrooms for unusual, provocative or soiled clothing, tattoos, jewellery, perfume, cash, expensive items and gifts, contraceptives, lubricating cream, notes about menstrual periods, medical appointment cards, eg for STIs, travel tickets, items with hotel branding, receipts, drug/alcohol abuse, diaries, letters, doodles and drawings, multiple communication devices, SIM cards, sex toys, inappropriate DVDs and pornography; and also physical clues on the missing person themselves such as bruises and abrasions (eg on their knees); early evidence kits (EEKs) could also be considered.

- The level of risk of a child being the victim of CSE increases (not decreases) the more times they go missing.

- A 'return' interview needs to be conducted tactfully to elicit useful information/ evidence and gain their trust.

- Requirement for recognising any possible safeguarding means for that and any other potential victims.

- Photograph and good descriptive details should be obtained in case they go missing again (including tattoos which might also have links to offenders).

There are a range of non-governmental organisations (NGOs) that offer advice and support to young people, parents and practitioners such as Childline (UK's free confidential helpline 0800 1111), NSPCC Child Trafficking Advice and Information Line (CTAIL) on 0800 107 7057 and Missing People who can assist in searching for missing children as well as offering their families advice and support (they are contactable on 116 000 and <http://www.missingpeople.org.uk>). There is also the NCA UK missing children team, which is referred to in Chapter 14.18.1.

16.10 Online Child Sexual Exploitation (OCSE)

Information technology and the worldwide web have provided a multitude of ways and means (such as peer-to-peer sharing, aka P2P) by which offenders can identify, contact and sexually exploit child victims. The internet also offers children the opportunity to create a separate identity in which they can be whoever they wish and take risks they would never countenance offline. It is when these two factors meet that children suffer most from people wishing to cause them harm. That a child's internet presence is inextricably linked to their true identity increases the possibility for exploitation to occur.

CSE occurs online in various forms by:

- Coercing or forcing children to upload onto the internet sexually explicit images of themselves or taking part in live streaming of such images.
- Partaking in sexual conversations online.
- Viewing, posting, downloading, distributing and sharing indecent images of children (IIOC) via various platforms over the worldwide web.
- Using threats to share images of children online (aka 'sextortion').
- Finding and contacting potential victims through social networking sites.
- Posting images of victims with rival gang members.
- Distributing victim details so other offenders can exploit them.

Online offending, once discovered, usually presents good evidence-gathering opportunities for investigations and the planning phases for arrests and searches should incorporate objectives to identify and seize any relevant digital forensic material, equipment and exhibits. However, there are a variety of subtle challenges when investigating CSE online offending.

Checklist—Challenges of investigating OCSE

- Staff resourcing and specialist skills set required (if there are a large number of cases or referrals to investigate).

- Adequate risk assessments to prioritise high-risk victims and offenders (ie identifying offenders who not only possess/share images but have physical access to victims, aka 'contact' offenders—aka 'dual offenders').[10]

- High-volume referrals and caseloads.

- Completing thorough intelligence checks to identify victims and arrange urgent safeguarding and protection needs.

- Attributing ownership of or access to images and equipment under investigation (eg in multi-occupancy premises).

- Hi-tech digital forensic examination of seized equipment, high-volume backlogs, prolonged results timescales and cost.

---

[10] The Kent Internet Risk Assessment Tool (KIRAT) as part of the Fighting International Internet Paedophilia Project (FIIP) was rolled out to all UK police forces in June 2015. It helps identify, from available intelligence, those suspects who are more likely to contact abused children. The tool also assists with the prioritisation and workload management within bulk data indecent image investigations.

- Victim identification from online images.

- Transnational child sex offenders (TCSOs), offences and victims.

- Offenders who are in positions of trust (PoT) or have never come to notice.

- Virtual crime scenes on the internet and in data storage systems.

- Greater use of the 'darknet' using anonymity software.

- Risk management of offenders who possess IIOC (eg higher risk of suicide).

- Live streaming of IIOC through technology (eg 4G mobile networks).

- Images becoming more extreme, sadistic and involving younger children.

- Self-generated indecent imagery (SGII) among children.

16.10.1 **Victim identification**

Victim identification is the term given to the analysis of photographs and films depicting the sexual abuse of children. This is known as child abuse material (CAM). When found there is a responsibility to try and identify locations, offenders and victims. Identifying victims from indecent images of children (IIOC) recovered from online systems in order to protect and safeguard them is one of the primary objectives of an OCSE investigation. The UK Child Abuse Image Database (CAID) has been developed to help identify victims and avoid duplication of effort when searching through and cataloguing identical copied images. Often when digital equipment such as computers are seized there may be thousands or even millions of images on them.

To help compare images, CAID makes use of a unique digital signature assigned to each image known as a hash value—the equivalent of a digital fingerprint. Seized storage systems, such as computer hard drives, can be automatically searched on CAID to see if the resulting signatures match. Other techniques, such as object matching and visual similarity analysis, can also be employed. CAID can then identify known images, classify the content and flag up those never seen before more quickly (aka 'first generation' images), allowing more time to be spent on being victim-centred and safeguarding.

On a much wider global scale and managed by Interpol, the International Child Sexual Exploitation (ICSE) Image database allows law enforcement investigators to share images across the world. Like CAID, it uses sophisticated image comparison software to make connections between victims, abusers and places.

16.11 **Investigative Considerations**

The main difference with a CSE investigation is that due to reasons already outlined (eg reluctance or ignorance), initial information on which to identify suspected offending may have to come from elsewhere other than the victims themselves. This means there has to be a far more proactive and rigorous approach to identify cases that warrant an investigation (and maybe using the information contained in other paragraphs within this chapter, eg Chapter 16.5—'Warning and Assessment Tools'). This is also why information sharing with and amongst other partner agencies is vital in order to identify potential victims and offenders.

The window of opportunity to gather valuable evidence may be quite short with some CSE cases because victims are quite often unhelpful or uncooperative in assisting to preserve and secure evidence, and their consent might become an issue. This is why building a comprehensive intelligence picture and problem profile is so important so that covert proactive tactics can also be considered. In any event investigators need to utilise a full range of powers at their disposal in order to secure the best evidence.

Once an enquiry is mounted, some of the standard and traditional investigative methods covered elsewhere in this handbook can be applied. Some examples follow:

- Passive data: to evidence important movements of persons and vehicles, not only on CCTV but also ANPR for tracking offender vehicle movements and victims. Any victims who have been trafficked from overseas for the purposes of CSE must have had to travel at some point and by some means which may be captured on passive data systems.
- H-2-H enquiries: for example, to evidence parties that have taken place or vehicles and occupants frequenting significant premises or locations.
- Acquisition of (digital) communications data: mobile phone data may provide evidence of contact between offenders not just to and from victims but also between and amongst themselves at relevant times and dates; cell site analysis can be useful for offender and victim locations and movements. It may also help identify those who download, distribute or share IIOC through internet connections and service providers.
- Digital media analysis: through the analysis of media and social networking usage.
- Financial information: providing evidence of gifts purchased, phones purchased and topped up, meals and drinks supplied, clothing and jewellery bought, vehicles hired and refuelled, travel tickets bought, global money transfers made, hotels and accommodation paid for and ATMs used for withdrawals at significant times.
- Search: finding items mentioned in previous bullet point including evidence of social media usage and data storage/transfer devices including memory storage and cloud computing passwords and details (this may mean the search of rooms in residential care homes at relevant times, which may be a tactic that is conducted covertly or overtly). Also confirmation of fixtures, fittings and identities in indecent photographs/videos that identify/confirm the place where offences took place.

- Covert tactics: proactive use of intelligence and innovative covert evidence - gathering methods (eg CHIS, Covert Internet Investigators (CIIs) and surveillance) can provide marvellous investigative opportunities for building a case against offenders and corroborating victim and witness accounts. Offenders and significant locations (eg business premises or hotels) can be targeted as the investigation progresses (note: there are other more sensitive methods that can be considered—but not for mention in this handbook).
- Overt tactics: disruption tactics may be a considered option (eg high-profile activities, use of the media, abduction notices, removal of IIOC from the net).
- Intelligence: early setting of the intelligence requirement is advantageous to ensuring any recorded incidents or events of note (from other agencies as well as the police) are considered as part of the investigation. Trawling for and identifying of linked incidents and activities is an extremely important part of the intelligence requirement as with the identification of those at risk (particularly those who are going missing from their homes or local authority care). This may include checking missing person (aka 'missing from home') reports—past and present.
- Forensic and physical evidence (eg DNA from or physical injuries on victims) and examination of 'virtual' crime scenes.
- Careful planning of victim/witness approaches and interviews (witness management).
- Careful planning of arrests and interviews (suspect management—note that this must incorporate an assessment of whether the suspect has access to children, carefully balancing the needs of safeguarding children and the rights of the suspect and their families).
- Community impact: where offenders and/or victims originate from a particular ethnicity or community group, careful consideration should be given to managing any adverse reaction within the community and from other sources such as the media who may seek to report negatively. This in itself may cause a backlash, and family members of offenders and those released on bail may require some sort of risk control strategy. Utilising MLOs on the day of executive action to manage media reporting is one good option to consider.

KEY POINT

Investigating child sexual offences can be a very distressing and harrowing experience, particularly where the viewing or handling of IIOC is concerned. SIOs must ensure all their staff have access to or receive requisite desensitisation processes, psychological ongoing assessments and welfare support before being involved in these types of enquiries.

CSE investigations can sometimes develop into critical incidents and/or involve partner agencies so it is important there is clear command and control for the investigation. The use of a Gold, Silver and Bronze command structure is usually beneficial, particularly when collaborating with other partner agencies, obtaining resources and dealing strategically with community issues and making decisions about joint media responses. Critical friends such as IAG members may also be invited to become members of a Gold group, particularly when there are certain communities affected by CSE activities.

An SIO/IO should draw up a clear list of objectives and record all their decisions in a policy file, including the priorities and resources available and allocated. There needs to be a careful record made of any other agencies involved and their agreed terms of reference and joint working agreements. These types of investigations have the propensity to expand fairly rapidly and a decision may have to be taken as to who has primacy for who, what, when, where, why and how (5WH).

> The victims almost never cooperated with investigations (again caused by the grooming) and there was a sense that nothing could be done as evidence was therefore weak. The need for disruption, covert surveillance and comprehensive intelligence gathering, despite no formal evidence from victims, was not understood.
>
> (Oxfordshire Safeguarding Children Board, *Serious Case Review into Child Sexual Exploitation in Oxfordshire: from the experiences of Children A, B, C, D, E, and F* (Operation Bullfinch) (OSCB, 26 February 2015) (Operation Bullfinch), para. 1.4)

KEY POINTS

Criminal intent can be adduced through evidence of a child/young person being:

- deliberately given intoxicants or drugs in such quantities as to render them incapable of making an informed decision
- isolated, coerced, intimidated by adults and whose only option is submission
- transported to various unknown or known locations in order to disorientate and/or isolate them and frustrate a criminal investigation.

Checklist—Examples of investigative objectives

- Identify, locate and safeguard any victims or potential victims.

- Identify, locate and arrest any offenders.

- Identify, assess and manage any risks.

- Determine MLOE and use appropriate investigative techniques to gather evidence and mount criminal prosecutions against offenders.

- Disrupt and deter criminals and their gangs from committing CSE-type offences.

425

- Gather intelligence and share what is appropriate with partner agencies.

- Develop an effective communications strategy to maximise investigative opportunities, reassure the public and minimise public/community impact.

16.11.1 **Management of risk**

Whenever there is concern for a child, and at every stage of involvement with that child, decisions will be made which involve identifying, assessing and managing risk. The **management of risk** is an overarching primary consideration and responsibility throughout CSE investigations and has to be put at the forefront of and underpin all decisions made by the SIO in their policy log as an audit trail. There are child victims at stake and the risk of all investigative considerations and decisions, and what effect they might have on identifiable risk factors that must be dynamically monitored and reviewed (see also Chapter 3.11).

The warning and assessment tools (risk indicators) contained within the checklist at paragraph 16.5 are a good means of assessing the risk of a child being vulnerable to, being targeted for or involved in CSE. Some screening tools and frameworks have been developed using similar factors and as a general rule as much information to get a wider picture as possible should be gathered. Officers attending incidents or conducting enquiries where children are present also need to be aware of identifying risk factors in order to determine actions necessary to safeguard children as and where necessary (and discharge duties under s 11 Children Act 2004). If in doubt, advice can always be sought from those practitioners who are better placed to make an effective assessment of any potential risks (eg those in Child Abuse Investigation Units (CAIUs))

The stakes are extremely high with these types of offences. This is because children (some more than others) are particularly vulnerable and the possibility of them coming to harm and unimaginable suffering (physical and psychological) must always remain in the mind of the SIO entrusted with leading these investigations.

16.11.2 **Abduction notices**

'Abduction notices' can be used as a means of preventing and protecting children from the risks of CSE. Potential perpetrators (as identified through missing person information or intelligence) are served with notices that inform that future contact with a specific child will render them liable to arrest and/or prosecution under the Children Act 1989 or the Child Abduction Act 1984.

16.12 **Managing Victims, Witnesses and Suspects**

CSE investigations must always remain victim focused. Historically the police have been criticised for being 'too busy' with investigating the offence/offenders with insufficient emphasis being placed on victims. However, getting young teenage victims to engage with and trust the police/other agencies and investigation/criminal justice process is not always so straightforward due to their chaotic lifestyles and backgrounds. Therefore any approach and victim strategy requires careful planning and forethought. Building trust with each victim is a key element as trauma levels and misguided loyalties can be significant barriers and there may be problems in obtaining accurate accounts through the disorientation and confusion of victims. No two victims of CSE are the same, as the impact of the exploitation upon each individual varies. Each individual must be treated on his/her own merit. Some, for example, might/might not see the police as their rescuer/saviour. Some may have developed coping mechanisms to survive (and be used to openly displaying hostility or aggression) which they may resort to by default when approached by the authorities and behave the same way they do with their abusers. Others may just be too embarrassed or frightened to engage with an investigation process.

A starting point may be to consider a cognitive abilities assessment by a qualified Forensic Clinical Psychologist (FCP) who will be able to provide advice and guidance on how best to conduct an interview. If suitably experienced, they will be able to offer advice on a child's presentation explaining such issues as their reluctance to disclose and the protection of perpetrators they may see as 'boyfriends' rather than abusers. Their expertise can then be used either directly in court as evidence if allowed, and if not allowed, in seeking approval of section 28 measures (Youth Justice and Criminal Evidence Act 1999—Pre-recording of cross-examination and re-examination).

Victims and witnesses will have not only their evidential testimonies to offer, but they are also likely to be in possession of physical evidential material such as mobile phones and other items such as gifts and clothing given to them over the course of the grooming process. They may also be 'crime scenes' themselves and able to provide forensic evidential-gathering opportunities dependent on the nature and circumstances of their exploitation, sexual contact and abuse.

A range of resources are available that can provide support to victims of CSE. In addition to the general measures outlined within Chapter 13, the use of Registered Witness Intermediaries[11] can be extremely valuable. It is important to note that this option needs to be given early consideration at the planning and preparation stage.

In most cases the plan to support and win over the trust and willing cooperation of victims and witnesses is the biggest challenge to overcome. Obtaining the trust and confidence of victims is not an easy process. Tactics such as using highly experienced and trained staff to make the first contact or using a person from an agency who the victim already trusts as conduit can make all the difference to success or otherwise. Making victims aware they are not on their own

---

[11] The Witness Intermediary Service is available through the Specialist Operations Centre at the NCA.

and that lots of others have made similar complaints and provided evidence against their abusers is also key to success.[12]

KEY POINT

A victim's testimony and evidence is likely to come under heavy scrutiny during judicial proceedings and any different versions of events can cast doubt over the reliability of their evidence. Corroboration is always key to ensuring what the victim says is independently supported and verified.

Victims of CSE may have pre-conceived notions about why they should not disclose details about their sexual exploitation. It is worth trying to establish what these might be (either from them directly or via another source) in order to develop a plan to reduce fears they might have. These 'barriers' may include misguided loyalty, not seeing themselves as victims, inability to talk about their abuse, negative views on police and courts system, lack of trust, feeling shamed or embarrassed, bringing shame on their family, and credibility amongst their peers.

Children and young persons who have been the victims of CSE are likely to require a very high level of support and the police are usually responsible primarily for facilitating this, although they cannot be expected to deliver emotional or psycho-logical support which must be provided by other agencies and professionals. A document entitled: *Achieving Best Evidence (ABE) in Criminal Proceedings—Guidance on interviewing victims and witnesses and guidance on using special measures*[13] provides guidelines for conducting interviews with young victims and witnesses and should be followed closely. It provides assistance for those responsible for conducting video recorded interviews with vulnerable and intimidated witnesses as well as those tasked with preparing and supporting witnesses during the criminal justice process. There is also a relevant National Policing Position Statement entitled *Advice on the Structure of Visually Recorded Interviews with Witnesses*.[14] In any event, it is recom-mended good practice that a suitably qualified and experienced specialist interview advisor be brought in to assist with the interview-planning and conducting process.

However, a victim of CSE may not always give their best and fullest account during an initial interview (ie ABE interview or statement). This may be for a variety of reasons, eg they may have been threatened or be fearful of reprisals for themselves or their families. They may not have identified themselves as a victim or they could be fearful the police will not believe their allegations. They may well use the first interview to test the credibility of the police. The key is to be patient with a carefully thought through strategy that will ultimately build up trust and break any link or loyalty to the offender(s). A seemingly contradict-ory account is therefore not a reason in itself to disbelieve subsequent accounts

---

[12] See HMIC, '*Mistakes were made': HMIC's review into allegations and intelligence material concerning Jimmy Saville between 1964 and 2012* (HMIC, 2013).

[13] Ministry of Justice, 2011.

[14] National Strategic Steering Group on Investigative Interviewing, 2013.

by the victim and the contradictory accounts should instead be seen as at least potentially symptomatic of the abuse.

Some victims of CSE may have previous convictions, which on the face of it may cast doubt upon their reliability as a witness of truth. Thorough enquiries need to be made into the circumstances of any offending before coming to any conclusion regarding credibility. The drivers and circumstances of the offending behaviour must be examined carefully as victims sometimes commit 'survival crimes' to look after themselves or to find safety; these may well have been committed as a consequence of being under the influence of the offender.

It is advisable to assess the factors that may work against the credibility of victims of sexual abuse. Such matters may include the offence not being reported, inconsistent accounts, the victim returning to the offender(s), perceived consent, previous untruths from the same victim or the abuse of drugs/alcohol. However, these are factors that are also **indicative** of sexual exploitation and it may be possible to build a case that focuses more on the credibility of the overall allegation rather than focusing primarily on the credibility and/or reliability of the victim.

Specialised support can be provided by a range of national organisations and such support is likely to be essential in ensuring that the child or young person (and where appropriate their parents or guardian) maintains their engagement with the criminal justice system. Examples of these agencies are Rape Crisis England and Wales, the Survivor's Trust, National Society for the Prevention of Cruelty to Children (NSPCC) and Dr Barnardo's victim support. In some areas the Witness Service/Victim Support provides a specialist Young Witness Service and there are others that can be considered as a vital source of support (eg Independent Sexual Violence Advisers—ISVAs).

Support to parents who often feel powerless when confronted with the problem can also be provided through organisations such as PACE (Parents against Child Exploitation).

KEY POINTS

1. 'All services should recognise that once a child is affected by CSE, he or she is likely to require support and therapeutic intervention for an extended period of time. Children should not be offered short term intervention only, and cases should not be closed prematurely.' (Alexis Jay Report, 2104, Recommendation 9)
2. The DPP guidelines on prosecuting cases of CSE issued on 17 October 2013 draws attention to the presentation of CSE victims with paras 48/49 making the following point: 'The Prosecutor should focus on the credibility of the allegation rather than the credibility of the victim.'
3. A new Code of Practice for victims of crime.[15]

---

[15] *Code of Practice for Victims of Crime: Presented to Parliament pursuant to section 33 of the Domestic Violence, Crime and Victims Act 2004*, HM Stationery Office, October 2015) in England and Wales was published in October 2015. Chapter 3 Parts A and B refer to entitlements of victims who are children and young persons. See also Chapter 11.2.

Checklist—Initial considerations—victims and witnesses

- Child victim/witness interviews should be conducted in line with ABE guidelines.

- Begin with initial assessment of interviewee (ie useful background detail).

- Consider a welfare plan (including referral and support planning). Anticipate a wide range of barriers and difficulties, eg some victims may have a range of psychological and physical problems, including STIs (sexually transmitted infections), have been deprived of food or sleep, have been given drugs/alcohol or be in general need of emergency medical treatment.

- Consider a victim and witness needs assessment (see also Chapter 11 as victims needs assessments are mentioned under the *Code of Practice for Victims of Crime*).

- Plan for any language and communication barriers, including literacy or learning disabilities as well as cultural considerations (check if an interpreter is required).

- Determine categorisation and prioritisation (ie vulnerable, intimidated, significant).[16]

- If multiple numbers, consider order in which they are to be approached/interviewed.

- Decide on location for contact (eg home address, foster carers, school, or en route to/from).

- Plan for resources required (eg PIP level 2 specialist interviewers/advisers; registered witness intermediary;[17] NCA tactical specialists from CEOP/HTC/VPT; and the National Vulnerable Witnesses Adviser[18]).

- Facilities and equipment (eg video interview suite or portable equipment).

- What to mention/not mention about the investigation (to victim/witness and parent/carer).

- Arrangements for transport to place of safety.

- Contingencies required (eg prevention of intimidation of self or others, tactics to deal with reluctance/refusal).

- Interview plan and structure (eg witnesses should be 'prepared' as per ABE guidelines, chapter 2, by explaining roles of persons present etc).

---

[16] See also Chapter 13.
[17] Witness intermediaries and the National Vulnerable Witnesses Adviser are available through the NCA Specialists Ops. Centre on 0845 000 5463.
[18] CEOP—Child Exploitation and Online Protection; HTC—Human Trafficking Centre; VPT—Vulnerable Persons Team.

- Identification of fast-track actions resulting from interview.

- Plan for post-interview management of victim/witness (they may need short/medium/long-term support/protection).

- Avoid change of personnel in order to establish and maintain rapport and help the victim to build confidence.

16.12.1 Managing suspects

An investigative strategy for dealing with suspects must be cognisant of the risk that these individuals pose to victims, communities and themselves. They are also likely to be people who are in the habit of frustrating law enforcement tactics by using nicknames and swapping their phones and SIM cards around. They will use addresses and premises that are not easily linked to them and their identification and attribution to victims and evidence is likely to be challenging.

The timing of any executive action (arrests) can be crucial to success. This is because revealing details of the police operation may significantly increase the risk of harm to victims and possibly others. This has to be carefully balanced against the risks posed by not acting expeditiously (risk management once more). This is a decision that needs to be recorded in a policy file (ie to act OR not to act—both need recording whichever is applicable) together with the plan to mitigate risks. Periods of custody for suspects may need to be planned carefully as part of a plan to mitigate risk with PACE custody extension and warrants of further detention being used to good effect.

Offenders who commit sexual offences against children may be/or perceive themselves to be demonised not just by their close friends and family, but the wider general public and media. This may produce an increased risk of them committing suicide or self-harming and is where the production of a risk assessment becomes important. This is a topic discussed in more detail in Chapter 12.7.1 (see Suspect Management).

KEY POINT

CSOs who know they are under investigation are more likely to be at risk of committing suicide. An appropriate suicide risk assessment and management plan must be included in a suspect arrest strategy, particularly to cater for the first 48 hours after police contact.

16.13 **Partnership Working**

The police, NCA Child Exploitation and Online Protection Centre (CEOP), children's services and others in the voluntary sector are expected to work together to tackle CSE and early liaison provides clarity to an investigation. Specific policies and procedures should be put in place that set out the roles and responsibilities of local agencies and professionals and the development of a local team. Information sharing must provide greater opportunities to make connections and raise awareness of the signs and symptoms of CSE across a range of services. Such agencies include sexual health clinics, mental health services, GPs, youth workers, teachers and staff in pupil welfare and support units, school nurses, youth offending teams (YOTs), drop-in or faith centres, hostels and of course frontline police staff. There are also a number of voluntary and charitable organisations that specialise in dealing with victims of CSE such as Barnardo's (BASE—Barnardo's Against Sexual Exploitation) and the Children's Society (Hand in Hand). They will have comprehensive records covering their interaction with victims, meetings in which they are often more candid than when dealing with organisations such as the police and social services who are seen as being authoritative rather than caring.

Any LSCB within each local authority is a key statutory mechanism for agreeing how the relevant organisations in each local area will cooperate to safeguard and promote the welfare of children in that locality, and for ensuring the effectiveness of what they do. Membership of the boards includes the police, local probation trusts, YOTs, NHS trusts, voluntary and community sector organisations as well as others. Anecdotally, SIOs have found the managers of local LSCBs extremely helpful in facilitating work with others, proving to be a more than worthy contact and ally.

Engagement with victims requires the ability to work together and often begins with a sustained approach of building rapport and intensive proactive efforts around outreach to victims. Initial disclosures about exploitation often come from people who a victim trusts and this in turn can be the initial stages of what transforms into a criminal investigation. Information regarding possible warning signs of CSE should be logged as well as any links to gang members in order for a risk assessment to be made and appropriate safeguarding action taken. These processes are aimed at ensuring there is identification of all those who are vulnerable or at risk.

Frontline agencies share a responsibility to develop ways of capturing and recording data relating to cases of CSE. Police forces, for example, need to proactively gather intelligence and develop regular problem profiles of CSE. The agreement of joint agency protocols, for example when responding to and dealing with frequent child missing persons from local authority care homes, will help to avoid missing vital initial investigative fast-track actions.

KEY POINTS

- The aim of partnership working is to get everyone communicating effectively and pulling together to act in the best interests of protecting children and tackling dangerous offenders.
- Where perpetrators use local hotels or hostels in which to commit CSE-type offences, it may be possible to educate hotel staff to notice the telltale signs and set up a system whereby they can and will quickly notify the police of any suspicious activity. This approach was used effectively in South Yorkshire (ie Sheffield), see HMIC, 'Hotel Watch', *South Yorkshire Police's Response to Child Sexual Exploitation* (HMIC, 2013) p 29.

16.13.1 **Working with the CPS**

Early liaison with the CPS is of paramount importance for initial discussions over the investigative strategy. These types of cases are not the usual types of cases that most prosecutors are used to dealing with. They require an extra degree of specialism and knowledge. The CPS has developed a network of solicitors who specialise in CSE and child abuse with a responsibility for establishing general good practice and procedure. The CPS have published guidelines on prosecuting cases of child abuse.[19]

16.13.2 **Third-party material**

It is highly likely many CSE cases will involve and require access to third-party material when building an evidential case. This might include such material as medical notes, social services information, Children's Services material, educational notes, counselling/therapy notes, information or evidence arising in parallel family/civil proceedings, or information kept by voluntary sector organisations.

Partner agencies may have to provide evidence and material for a CSE investigation and prosecution. Corroborative evidence to support a case may have to come from a range of sources such as third parties who can provide evidence about changes of behaviour or victim and offender movements. This may be particularly relevant if a victim is unwilling or reluctant to assist.

Investigators (under CPIA rules) are under a duty to pursue all reasonable lines of enquiry, whether they point towards or away from a suspect. Reasonable lines of enquiry may include queries about the existence of relevant material in the possession of a third party, for example the local authority. This material must be gathered as early as possible as it may contain information that could enhance and strengthen the prosecution case.

If such information is duly gathered and proves to be relevant to the prosecution case, it is worth considering creating a written agreement between the third

---

[19] See CPS, *Guidelines on Prosecuting Cases of Child Sexual Abuse* (CPS, 2013).

party, enquiry team and CPS/Counsel to cover how the information is to be disclosed and when. This can be done prior to trial to prevent any undue delays to proceedings whether it be through PII (public interest immunity) applications or objections to disclosure.

16.13.3 Information sharing

The report entitled *Working Together to Safeguard Children—A guide to inter-agency working to safeguard and promote the welfare of children* (2013) provides guidance on sharing information about children in England (there is similar guidance applicable in Wales). In deciding whether there is a need to share information, police and other professional bodies need to consider their legal obligations, including whether there is a duty of confidentiality. Where such a duty exists, information may be shared provided consent is obtained OR if there is a clear risk of significant harm to a child. The latter is a public interest test and lack of consent to share information can be disregarded where there is a clear concern about a risk of harm to a child or young person.

The Data Protection Act 1998 allows for disclosure without the consent of the data subject in certain conditions, including for the prevention and detection of crime, the apprehension of offenders, and where failure to disclose would be likely to prejudice those objectives in a particular case. 'Data' are defined in section 1 of the Act as, inter alia, 'Information in a form in which it can be processed by equipment operating automatically in response to instructions given for that purpose.'

The Government publication *Working Together to Safeguard Children* (March 2013) reiterated that: (i) a child's needs are paramount and must be put first; (ii) all professionals should share information and discuss any concerns about a child with partner agencies; (iii) initiatives must be based on evidence and available data. This guidance required LSCBs to publish local protocols for assessment and a threshold document specifying the criteria for referral for assessment and the level of early help to be provided. It imposed duties towards safeguarding on a wide range of agencies. LSCBs had to maintain a local learning and improvement framework shared across partner agencies. A national panel of independent experts would advise LSCBs on the initiation and publication of Serious Case Reviews.

16.14 Serious Case Reviews

In certain circumstances, there is a statutory requirement for a Serious Case Review (SCR) or Child Practice Review (CPR) in order to establish what lessons can be learnt and it is important to know the mandatory nature of them. Since the CSE of a child is likely to include elements of abuse or neglect, it follows that where there is a criminal investigation it should be anticipated an LSCB will be legally required to carry out a parallel serious case review (and if death is involved, the rule also applies—see also Chapter 15).

SCRs and criminal proceedings can and often do run simultaneously without jeopardising one another. Both processes are equally important for safeguarding and promoting the welfare of children, which should always remain the primary consideration.

The role and function of an LSCB is set out in law by the Local Safeguarding Children Board Regulations 2006, Statutory Instrument 2006/90. Regulation 5 requires an LSCB to undertake an SCR when certain criteria are present.

Regulation 5(1)(e) undertaking reviews of serious cases and advising the authority and their Board partners on lessons to be learned.

Regulation 5 (2). For the purposes of paragraph (1)(e) a serious case is one where abuse or neglect of a child is known or suspected; and either:

(i) child has died; or

(ii) child has been seriously harmed and there is cause for concern as to the way in which the authority, their Board partners or other relevant persons have worked together to safeguard the child.

Cases which meet one of the above criteria **must always trigger** an SCR (or in Wales a Concise or Extended Child Practice Review—see the Local Safeguarding Children Boards (Wales) Regulations 2006 as amended 2012). The Government does not prescribe detailed methodology for conducting an SCR. There are, however, broad stipulations set out in *Working Together to Safeguard Children* (2013). These include:

- Reviews of serious cases should be led by individuals who are independent of the case and the organisations whose actions are being reviewed.
- Professionals should be involved fully in reviews and invited to contribute their perspectives.
- Families, including surviving children, should be invited to contribute to reviews.
- Final reports of SCRs must be published.

That someone has made a witness statement to investigators, or even that someone has been interviewed as a suspect or is charged with an offence, would not, as a matter of course, preclude an SCR team from seeking to obtain from them any learning which could help protect children at that time or in the future. This may involve a personal interview, an invitation to a practitioner's event, or a request for a contribution to the SCR in writing. However, guidance suggests that if interviews are conducted with those who may be involved as witnesses or defendants in criminal proceedings, the police and CPS should be informed.

There is a general rule that when third parties request information that has been gathered by the investigating team, it will not be usual to disclose material until the criminal proceedings have been completed. This is to ensure the criminal trial process and any continuing enquiries are not prejudiced. The comments of Lord Reid in *Conway v Rimmer* (1968) 1 All ER 874 at p 889 are relevant:

> it would generally be wrong to require disclosure in a civil case of anything which might be material in a pending prosecution, but after a verdict has been given, or it has been decided to take no proceedings, there is not the same need for secrecy.

16.14.1 Disclosure and sharing of material generated by an SCR

The CPIA 1996, accompanying Code of Practice and Attorney General's Guidelines govern the disclosure of information in criminal proceedings of unused material that is relevant to the investigation. This only applies to a *criminal investigation* and an SCR does not fall within that definition. However, the police have a duty to establish whether any 'relevant' material (ie to the criminal investigation) exists. If material relevant to the investigation comes to the notice of the SIO and is obtained from a third party (eg LSCB), it will become unused 'sensitive' material and should be recorded in the usual way and remain under review by a prosecutor to check for relevance to the prosecution or defence case.

[Note: Key guidance is contained within NPCC CPS, 'Liaison and information exchange when criminal proceedings coincide with Chapter 4 Serious Case Reviews or Welsh Child Practice Reviews: A Guide for the Police, CPS and LSCB', HWG (Child Death sub-group) (2014).]

KEY POINTS

- The SIO and/or their nominated representative (eg disclosure officer) should be invited to any meetings held by an independent reviewer.
- Any notes taken at such meetings should be made available to the SIO for relevancy tests to the criminal case.
- A written request can be made by the SIO/CPS to withdraw, or not issue an invitation to a particular witness if believed this might compromise an investigation/prosecution.
- An SCR is not a criminal investigation for the purposes of the CPIA, but there may be material gained via a third party, eg LCSB, that is 'relevant'[20] to a criminal prosecution. The CPS, however, must treat all CSR material gained as 'sensitive' and it should not appear on any schedule provided to defence solicitors.

---

[20] See also ACPO/CPS, 'Liaison and information exchange when criminal proceedings coincide with Chapter 4 Serious Case Reviews or Welsh Child Practice Reviews: A Guide for the Police, Crown Prosecution Service and Local Safeguarding Children Boards', National HWG child death sub-group (May 2014).

16.15 **NCA Child Exploitation and Online Protection**

The NCA Child Exploitation and Online Protection (CEOP) Command works with child protection partners across the UK and overseas to identify the main threats to children and coordinates activity against these threats to bring offenders to account. Their aim is to strive to protect children from harm online and offline, directly through NCA-led operations and in partnership with local and international agencies.

The CEOP Command houses officers specialising in this area of criminality working alongside professionals from the wider child protection community and industry and is a useful resource that has specialist capabilities and advisers for:

- child missing persons
- child protection and safeguarding
- covert internet operations
- online image offending and CSE (grooming)
- victim identification
- transnational child sex offending
- contact child sexual abuse.

Their head office is located at 33 Vauxhall Bridge Rd, London, SW1V 2WG and they are contactable at <http://www.ceop.police.uk> or +44(0)870 000 3344.

References

ACPO, *Child Sexual Exploitation Action Plan* (ACPO, 2012)

ACPO/CPS, 'Liaison and information exchange when criminal proceedings coincide with Chapter 4 Serious Case Reviews or Welsh Child Practice Reviews: A Guide for the Police, Crown Prosecution Service and Local Safeguarding Children Boards', National HWG child death sub-group (May 2014)

Barnardos, *Puppet on a String: The urgent need to cut children free from sexual exploitation* (Barnardos, 2011)

Berelowitz, S et al, *'I thought I was the only one. The only one in the world.' The Office of the Children's Commissioner's inquiry into CSE in gangs and groups: interim report* (Office of the Children's Commissioner, 2012)

Chase, E and Statham, J, 'Commercial and sexual exploitation of children and young people in the UK—a review' (2005) 14(1) *Child Abuse Review*, 4–25

College of Policing, *Responding to Child Sexual Exploitation*, APP online (2015) <http//www. app.college.police.uk>

Child Exploitation and Online Protection Centre (CEOP), *Out of mind, out of sight: Breaking down the barriers to understanding child sexual exploitation* (CEOP, 2011)

Children's Commissioner, *'If only someone had listened': Final Report from the inquiry into CSE in gangs and groups 2014* (OCC, 2013) <http://www.childrens-commissioner.gov.uk/content/publications/content_743>

CPS, *Guidelines on Prosecuting Cases of Child Sexual Abuse* (CPS, 2013) <http://www.cps.gov.uk/legal/a_to_c/child_sexual_abuse>

Department for Children, Schools and Families and Home Office, *Safeguarding children and young people from sexual exploitation: supplementary guidance to working together to safeguard children* (DCSF, 2009)

Department for Education, *Tackling Child Sexual Exploitation: action plan* (Department for Education, 2011)

HMIC, *'Hotel Watch': South Yorkshire Police's Response to Child Sexual Exploitation* (HMIC, 2013)

HMIC, *'Mistakes were made': HMIC's review into allegations and intelligence material concerning Jimmy Saville between 1964 and 2012* (HMIC, 2013) <http://www.hmic.gov.uk>

HM Government, *Working Together to Safeguard Children: A guide to inter-agency working to safeguard and promote the welfare of children* (March 2013)

Jay, A, *Independent Inquiry into Child Sexual Exploitation In Rotherham 1997–2013* (2014)

Ministry of Justice, *Achieving Best Evidence in Criminal Proceedings: Guidance on Interviewing Victims and Witnesses, and using Special Measures* (Ministry of Justice, 2013)

Code of Practice for Victims of Crime: Presented to Parliament pursuant to section 33 of the Domestic Violence, Crime and Victims Act 2004, HM Stationery Office, October 2015, or <http://www.gov.uk/moj>

Ministry of Justice, *Witness Charter* (Ministry of Justice, 2013)

National Policing Position Statement, *Advice on the Structure of Visually Recorded Interviews with Witnesses* (National Strategic Steering Group on Investigative Interviewing, 2013)

Oxfordshire Safeguarding Children Board, *Serious Case Review into Child Sexual Exploitation in Oxfordshire: from the experiences of Children A, B, C, D, E, and F* (Operation Bullfinch) (OSCB, 26 February 2015)

WAG, *Safeguarding Children and Young People from Sexual Exploitation* cited in Dr S Hallett, 'Cascade Research Briefing: Problems and Solution from the perspectives of young people and professionals' (2015) 3 <http://www.nwgnetwork.org/resources>

Index

Printed and bound by CPI Group (UK) Ltd, Croydon, CR0 4YY